Prodigal Daughters

Published for the

Omohundro Institute of

Early American History

and Culture,

Williamsburg, Virginia,

by the University of

North Carolina Press,

Chapel Hill

Prodigal Daughters

SUSANNA ROWSON'S EARLY

AMERICAN WOMEN

Marion Rust

The Omohundro Institute of Early American History and Culture is sponsored jointly by the College of William and Mary and the Colonial Williamsburg Foundation. On November 15, 1996, the Institute adopted the present name in honor of a bequest from Malvern H. Omohundro, Jr.

© 2008 The University of North Carolina Press

Set in Monticello type by Tseng Information Systems, Inc.

Manufactured in the United States of America

Library of Congress Cataloging-in-Publication Data

Rust, Marion.

Prodigal daughters : Susanna Rowson's early American women / Marion Rust.

  p. cm.

Includes bibliographical references and index.

ISBN 978-0-8078-3140-3 (cloth : alk. paper)

ISBN 978-0-8078-5892-9 (pbk. : alk. paper)

1. Rowson, Mrs., 1762–1824—Criticism and interpretation.

2. Women and literature—United States—History—18th century.

3. Women and literature—United States—History—19th century.

I. Omohundro Institute of Early American History & Culture.

II. Title.

PS2736.R3Z86 2008

813'.2—dc22   2007037349

The paper in this book meets the guidelines for permanence and durability of the Committee on Production Guidelines for Book Longevity of the Council on Library Resources.

cloth 12 11 10 09 08 5 4 3 2 1

paper 12 11 10 09 08 5 4 3 2 1

FRONTISPIECE

PLATE 1. *Portrait of Susanna Haswell Rowson. From Rowson,* Charlotte Temple: A Tale of Truth, *ed. Francis W. Halsey (New York, 1905). PS 2736.R3C5, Clifton Waller Barrett Library of American Literature, Special Collections, University of Virginia Library*

For my mother LORAINE MOREY RUST

acknowledgments

. . . .

Standing in a Buffalo warehouse one hot summer evening, I listened to the hard-bitten folk-rock diva Michelle Shocked sing "Prodigal Daughter (Cotton-Eyed Joe)," her classic ballad based on a pre–Civil War slave song. In this powerful lament, a young man who has impregnated a single woman returns home to a triumphant welcome. When his sexual partner "goes home with the oats he's sown," however, she is turned away in shame: she finds "none in the cup because he drank it all up." She gets an abortion from a slave (the "Cotton-Eyed Joe" of the song's title) and survives to sing her lonely song. As a good early Americanist Ph.D. candidate, I had been reading John Locke's *Essay concerning Human Understanding,* Benjamin Franklin's *Autobiography,* and Stanley Elkins's *Age of Federalism* that summer, immersing myself in a form of American Enlightenment mythmaking that emphasized man's capacity to shape his own fate. As Shocked paced the stage, she gave words to my previously vague discontent. In the trope of the pregnant female body, that indelible sign of the shadow that past experience casts over present, I found an answer to Franklin's suggestion that we can correct ourselves at will. Abortion erased a pregnancy, yes, but not without costs of its own; and it did not purchase this daughter forgiveness of the sort her lover obtained. As I stood on a dirty floor in a room smelling of stale beer, this nameless daughter (and the brilliant, troubled woman who sang her plight) powerfully impressed upon me both the limited usefulness of any model of identity premised on self-determination and the double insult done to early American women, who, as beings deeply identified with their biological functions, found the model especially clumsy and ineffectual. *Prodigal Daughters* is the story of their frustration and resilience.

My deep thanks are due to the man who accepted the relevance of this song to my work, even as he insisted that I find eighteenth-century terms in which to describe eighteenth-century ideas. For Jay Fliegelman, Jonathan Edwards provided more purchase than Teodor Adorno. Apparently, there was no idea that hadn't been articulated in the American eighteenth century, and he could direct you to it. As I write this, Jay has just died, and yet I still expect to hear his voice on the phone. With so many of his loving students and colleagues, I say thank you. We miss you.

I am forever grateful to Sharon Block, Alison Booth, Mitchell Breitwieser, Mary Carruth, Mark Edmundson, Jonathan Flatley, Christopher Grasso, Sharon M. Harris, Eric Lott, Deborah McDowell, Carla Mulford, Franny Nudelman, Peter Onuf, Thomas Scanlan, David Shields, Carroll Smith-Rosenberg, Patricia Meyer Spacks, Julia A. Stern, Jennifer Wicke, and Michael Zuckerman for reading versions of this manuscript and offering their support. At Stanford, Terry Castle and George Dekker joined Jay on my dissertation committee, providing sage critique in a tone that communicated unwavering confidence. This project also had the benefit of generous funding from the Mrs. Giles Whiting Foundation, the University of Virginia, and the Lilly Library at Indiana University, Bloomington. At the University of Virginia, Dean Karen Ryan and Chairs Michael Levenson and Gordon Braden provided strategic administrative interventions. As Director of Graduate Studies, Chip Tucker made it possible for me to work with the following stellar graduate research assistants: Camryn Hansen, Brynn Jacqueline Harris, and Sarah Elizabeth Ingle. Administrative staff Cheryll Lewis, Lois Payne, and June Webb were kind and helpful at every turn. I owe the greatest debt to the students who allowed me to direct their dissertations, beginning an exchange that I hope will last for years to come: Wilson Brissett, Mendy C. Gladden, Julie Pal-Agrawal, and Joanne van der Woude. Ben Fagan, Kenneth Parille, Brian Roberts, Melissa White, and Maria Windell also share in my respect and gratitude.

I thank the following institutions for allowing me to make use of their materials: Cecil H. Green Library at Stanford University; Alderman Library at the University of Virginia, with special gratitude to the Electronic Text Center; William T. Young Library at the University of Kentucky; the Lilly Library at Indiana University, Bloomington; the Archives and Library division of the Mississippi Department of Archives and History; the Free Library of Philadelphia; the American Antiquarian Society; the Library of Congress; the Historical Society of Pennsylvania; and the Maine Historical Society. In particular, I thank Edward Gaynor, Margaret Hrabe, Michael Plunkett, Heather Moore Riser, Regina Rush, and the rest of the staff of the Albert and Shirley Small Special Collections Library at UVa. With their warmth, skill, and patience, they made walking into the reading room a highlight of my workday. Reynaldo Anastacio Antonio, Digital and Microphotography Technician in UVa's Printing and Copying Services, found a way to photograph rare and fragile texts to produce most of the illustrations found here. Mary Kelley and Lisa M. Moore generously shared work in progress before its publication. Freelance indexer Cynthia Landeen transformed content into points of access.

Versions of chapters 1, 3, and 4 appeared in the *William and Mary Quarterly, Early American Literature,* and Mary C. Carruth, ed., *Feminist Interventions in Early American Studies* (Tuscaloosa, Ala., 2006). I am grateful to these publications for allowing me to expand the arguments here.

At the Omohundro Institute of Early American History and Culture, Editor of Publications Fredrika J. Teute made this book a reality. Associate Editor Mendy C. Gladden wore her authority lightly while providing invaluable criticism. Senior Manuscript Editor Kathy Burdette caught my errors, improved my prose, and taught me more about writing than I've learned since high school.

The companions I have met since learning who Susanna Rowson was are the best thing about my job. At Stanford, Sarah Luria and Lesley Ginsberg became my friends for life. Over sushi in Charlottesville, Robert Geraci and Franny Nudelman showed me how finishing a book is done. Barbara Smith, Janette Hudson, Sally Kauzlarich, and I hiked and griped to our hearts' content. Lawrie Balfour, Anna Brickhouse, Chad Dobson, Alev Erisir, Grace Hale, Bruce Holsinger, David Holton, John McLaren, John O'Brien, Vicki Olwell, Heather Moore Riser, Elizabeth Thompson, and David Waldner came together in office hallways, on soccer fields, and in kids' gym lobbies to wonder aloud at the work-family ride. Conferences reunited me with delightful colleagues Jennifer Baker, Martin Brückner, Anna Mae Duane, Philip Gould, Sandra Gustafson, Ed Larkin, Robert Levine, Dennis Moore, Susan Scott Parrish, Jeffrey H. Richards, Laura Rigal, Ivy Schweitzer, Frank Shuffelton, Eric Slauter, Elisa Tamarkin, Leonard Tennenhouse, Karen Weyler, and many others. Packmo Tsow, her husband Tenzin Thosam, their daughter Choetsow, Rebecca DesBrisay Jones, Sarah Perkins, and Shari Green made a village of our family with the care they showered upon our children and us, too. Tommy Rust, Deb Levy, Jean Fang, Daniel Salvucci, and Marcia, Joe, Stephanie, Mark, Ben, and Evan Bograd are the best extended family a family could ask for. Behind all these amazing individuals stand the two women who have held my heart for so many years: Mary Bly and Alissa Land. May we grow old together!

No scholar starts with a blank slate. In addition to those named above (and with apologies to others I've inevitably failed to mention), I am grateful to the following brilliant thinkers for inspiring this study: Catherine Allgor, Elizabeth Barnes, Susan Branson, Gillian Brown, Christopher Castiglia, Patricia Crain, Cathy Davidson, Elizabeth Dillon, Christopher Looby, Clare Lyons, Lori Merish, Marianne Noble, and Rosemarie Zagarri.

Finally, I would like to thank the University of Kentucky for its enthusiastic welcome, especially Virginia Blum, Anna Bosch, Thomas Clayton,

Jeffory Clymer, Andy Doolen, Steven Hoch, Pearl James, Peter Kalliney, Alan Nadel, Ellen B. Rosenman, Jené Schoenfeld and Michael Trask.

More than anyone else, my husband, Louis Martin Bograd—a brilliant and generous man—has shared the trials and joys of writing this book with me. Lou has helped chapters cohere and titles ring true. Even more important, he made "co-parent" a meaningful term. I feel grateful every day to have met him. As for Max and Sadie, who would rather read than anything else: I hope someday you take this one off the shelf and have a look. Your faces are on every page.

My father, Ted Rust, listened to me as though I were a grown-up when I was five and played recorder duets with me before I was eight. From him, I learned to converse, as well as the pleasure of working alone at something one loves. My brother, Daniel, flew off the bicycle jump he'd built in front of our house, both wheels high in the sky, to show me that words weren't everything. My mother, Rainy, introduced me to the following: how to make a six-inch blackberry pie; the fine sand of Rose Hill, Ontario, and the ocean-ground gravel of Cronkite, California; cassoulet and potatoes with cauli-flower; mouse houses; Bob Marley after work; swimming slowly; dancing after dinner; reading all night; endurance. Gratitude that deepens with every day. This book is for my dream come true, my mom.

contents

illustrations

Prodigal Daughters

"WHAT THINKS YOUR FATHER
OF THE PRESENT TIMES?"

On January 8, 1808, seventeen days after Thomas Jefferson signed the Embargo Act of 1807, author and pedagogue Susanna Haswell Rowson wrote letters to two former students, Mary Montgomery and Louisa Bliss, and sent them care of Mary's younger sister, Myra. A student at Rowson's Young Ladies' Academy, Myra was just returning to Haverhill, New Hampshire, from Boston, where she had stayed with the Rowson family for a couple of days. As the daughters of General John Montgomery, Mary and Myra were among the more prominent members of a student body drawn largely from Boston's elite. In fact, it was to Mary that Rowson's school owed the privilege of being the first in the area to boast a piano. Louisa brought with her no such bequest—but, as we will see, she held a greater claim on her mentor's attention.[1]

Rowson's letter to Mary epitomizes the commonly acknowledged function of the early American female academy: preparing a young woman to assume the mantle of genteel wife- and motherhood. Writing "my dear M." on the occasion of her upcoming marriage, as Mary prepares to "discard" one name and "adopt" another, Rowson gently cedes the role of instructor: "I could write volumes on this subject, but I should say nothing new; nor anything but what your own good sense will naturally suggest." Her abdication supports the contemporary view that marriage was the fitting culmination of one's scholastic labors. Indeed, since courses of study in early national female academies varied widely in both subject matter and length and since formal matriculation was uncommon, one might say that Mary truly graduated when she married. Rowson's gracious deferral ("Allow me then

1. The general gave the piano to his daughter in 1799, while she was a student at Rowson's Young Ladies' Academy, and it returned to Haverhill when she did. See "An Historical Piano," *Historical Magazine,* II (1867), in Papers of Susanna Rowson, 1770–1879 (hereafter cited as Rowson Papers), MSS 7379, box 2, folder 95, Clifton Waller Barrett Library of American Literature, Special Collections, University of Virginia Library, Charlottesville, Va.; Susanna Rowson to Mary Montgomery, Jan. 8, 1808, ibid., MSS 7379-a, box 1, folder 39; Rowson to Louisa Bliss, ibid., MSS 7379-c, box 1, folder 36.

simply to offer my best wishes") highlights the return of their relationship from instructor and pupil to a structure determined by factors outside the academy, such as class and marital status. As she was on the day before she entered the academy, Mary is now, in many senses, Rowson's superior, and Rowson is astute enough to implicitly acknowledge this.[2]

Not so with her "beloved" Louisa. If Rowson's letter to Mary delineates the externally imposed limits within which female academies could flourish in the late eighteenth century, her letter to Louisa offers a rare glimpse of the intellectual ferment that took place within and its potentially destabilizing effects, as she engages her interlocutor in a discussion of military strategy, commercial policy, the current political administration, and the fate of empire. Just as important, however, this letter demonstrates the author's skill at rendering such ferment tolerable to those with an interest in maintaining the status quo. After a brief review of their mutual acquaintance, Rowson asks Louisa, "What thinks your good father of the present times?" She then elaborates:

> Hard enough no doubt, and so they are, nor is the present storm of the
> political atmosphere half so alarming as the thick cloud which hovers
> in the horizon of domestic peace; for foreign war an united nation may
> be prepared. And what foreign enemy could cope with the unanimous
> power of so mighty a nation as the American states, were their com-
> merce free and their forests converted into towers of defence to protect
> that commerce from insult and invasion, were our citizens all of one
> mind, were our statesmen wise and our lawgivers virtuous. But say the
> opposite party, if the spirit of commerce is so much encouraged, manu-
> factures will languish and the handicrafts be banished [from] the land.
> And indeed in some measure this is true. But a country so young as
> this has never been known to arrive at any high pitch of excellence in
> the arts whether social, or those of a higher class without assistance of
> commerce. Few would be found in a situation able sufficiently to reward

2. A former student writes that the half-dozen women she still knows from her days at Rowson's school "have all made good wives and mothers; have reared large families; some of their sons have become distinguished men, and thus these ladies have fulfilled the destiny which Napoleon considered woman's highest glory." She also gives an idea of the range of ages and levels of study in Rowson's academy. "I was young and not advanced as many there, many of the scholars were from 18 to 20. I was 12 when I went there, and left before I was 14, had been at Bradford Academy previous to going there." See Elias Nason, *A Memoir of Mrs. Susanna Rowson, with Elegant and Illustrative Extracts from Her Writing in Prose and Poetry* (Albany, N.Y., 1870), 200.

the ingenious artificer. Tis therefore our part, I humbly conceive, at present, to profit by the great advantages an extensive commerce affords and by degrees the social arts will rise into estimation, by degrees they will rise into perfection and future ages will in all human probability see new and as yet undiscovered countries receiving the overplus of their manufactures coming to their sea ports as to the chief marts for merchandise, when the now imperial cities on the other side [of] the Atlantic, like Troy Carthage Greece and Rome are sunk into insignificance. May pass but a few centuries more and like Balbec, Palmyra and Jerusalem, their places be only distinguished by a heap of ruins. These reflections my Louisa should perhaps lead us to be indifferent as to present circumstances, since every sublunary scene so rapidly fades from our view, but it has pleased the all wise director of the universe to implant in our minds a patriotic principle which vibrates with delight in beholding promoting or ensuring the prosperity of our native land. For though I am by birth a Briton, my heart clings to dear America and it would be with equal anxiety I should contemplate the misery of either. Power of all might, may the waves of thy ocean ever be the bulwark of revered old England and may the good angels with peace dropping from their pinions hover over beloved America. Defend us from civil discord that not her fertile plains be drenched with the blood of her brave sons, slaughtered by each other. You will be weary my sweet young friend with my serious political letter, but old folks will write and talk of what is nearest the heart and when they once begin they know not when to stop.[3]

This extraordinary passage begins a book about early America's best-selling author and reputed foremother of American sentimental fiction by calling to the fore, and promptly disabusing us of, several assumptions. For those who consider the early Republic's most famous female scribe a political progressive, it reminds us of Rowson's ardent Federalist sympathies and her antagonism to the ascendant Democratic-Republican administration. For those who wish to make her an unlikely token of American exceptionalism, it shows her profoundly conflicted transatlantic loyalties (her anxiety was reasonable given that the "foreign enemy" soon to materialize in the War of 1812 was none other than her native land). For those who consider early American sentimental discourse to preclude explicit engagement with public affairs, this passage starkly delineates the depth of Rowson's concern

3. Rowson to Bliss, Jan. 8, 1808, Rowson Papers, MSS 7379–c, box 1, folder 36.

with matters of state both domestic and international, as she subsumes her fears of Napoleonic invasion, or "foreign war," under the yet greater terrors of civil discord, envisioning American sons "slaughtered by each other." For those who wish to read early American letters as prefiguring a nineteenth-century gendering of public and private spheres, with the feminized domestic realm coming to serve as a haven from the predations of commercial enterprise, she reveals a discomfiting relish for investment and accumulation. Indeed, Rowson's plea for an "extensive commerce"—not three weeks after the Embargo Act forbade all international trade to and from American ports in a doomed attempt to convince England and France of the importance of neutral commerce—is both informed and innovative, as she lambastes those hoping to rely on internal manufactures and extrapolates the virtues of international trade from mere present material comfort to the political and artistic fate of the nation.[4]

4. In the "Dialogue for Three Young Ladies" of 1811, Rowson expands upon her Federalist sympathies, mocking one character as a "strong democrat; / Who would talk of the internal strength of the nation, / Independently great; tho' we've no importation." She also specifically mentions her fear of Napoleonic invasion: "For should [Woglog] his seven league boots keep in motion, / Who knows but he'll stride o'er the great Western Ocean" (Susanna Rowson, *A Present for Young Ladies: Containing Poems, Dialogues, Addresses, Etc., Etc., Etc.* . . . [Boston, 1811], 34, 35).

As an attempt to capture the texture of literate Anglo-American female self-awareness in the 1790s and beyond as it was both recorded and shaped by the decade's most prolific and popular author, this study is rooted in the successes of previous scholarship on gender and textuality in the early Republic. Of particular help in understanding what distinguished the post-Revolutionary practice of gender from its colonial antecedents have been published works by Nancy F. Cott, Jan Lewis, Linda K. Kerber, Mary Beth Norton, Richard L. Bushman, Ruth H. Bloch, Rosemarie Zagarri, and Susan Juster. Early American women's historians Cott and Kerber are careful to point out exceptions to an increasing emphasis on domestic retirement for women after the War of Independence (Cott, *The Bonds of Womanhood: "Woman's Sphere" in New England, 1780–1835* [New Haven, Conn., 1977]; Kerber, *Women of the Republic: Intellect and Ideology in Revolutionary America* [1980; New York, 1986]). Susan Branson, Nancy Isenberg, Philip Gould, Bruce Burgett, Sandra M. Gustafson, David Waldstreicher, and others have explored the nondomestic aspects of early national female ideology and behavior. See Bloch, *Gender and Morality in Anglo-American Culture, 1650–1800* (Berkeley, Calif., 2003); Branson, *These Fiery Frenchified Dames: Women and Political Culture in Early National Philadelphia* (Philadelphia, 2001); Burgett, *Sentimental Bodies: Sex, Gender, and Citizenship in the Early Republic* (Princeton, N.J., 1998); Bushman, *The Refinement of America: Persons, Houses, Cities* (New York, 1992); Gould, *Covenant and Republic: Historical Romance and the Politics of Puritanism* (Cambridge, 1996); Gustafson, *Eloquence Is Power: Oratory and Performance in Early America* (Chapel Hill, N.C.,

Perhaps the most interesting aspect of Rowson's argument, in view of her own literary legacy, is the way it connects the realms of commerce and art in the context of what she elsewhere called her "dear adopted country." In a signature example of her ability to adapt the European forms of her youth to resolve tensions in her current surroundings, Rowson—immersed in the traditions of English literary production to the degree that she had attempted to sell her first novel originally published in the United States by subscription—now welcomes the "assistance of commerce" that she had once looked at askance. The merchant class, she argues, far from threatening the internal "manufacture" of literature and art, can actually found it. Moreover, the merchant class can resolve one of the fundamental tensions of the young Republic: its quest for a distinctive American gentility that both accommodates the "democratic ideals of accessibility" characteristic of republican ideology and maintains that "earlier commitment to rank" of which artistic "ingenuity," in Rowson's parlance, is but one manifestation. As individuals whose wealth derives at least in part from their own labor, merchants can support the arts without casting the foreign taint of luxury and indolence that would have hung over Rowson's earlier aristocratic patrons, such as the duchess of Devonshire or the Prince of Wales. Imagining the founders of "port" and "mart" coming to serve as the nation's first patrons of the arts, Rowson explains no less than her view of the American literary enterprise: transposing the highly trained performance of selfhood once considered the privilege of a leisured aristocracy to a democratic readership of multiple stations. In the process, she also delineates the stakes of her involvement in this enterprise: employing the many dichotomies of her personal history to found a representative Anglo-American female gentility premised on behavior rather than circumstance.[5]

2000); Isenberg, *Sex and Citizenship in Antebellum America* (Chapel Hill, N.C., 1998); Juster, *Disorderly Women: Sexual Politics and Evangelicalism in Revolutionary New England* (Ithaca, N.Y., 1994); Lewis, "The Republican Wife: Virtue and Seduction in the Early Republic," *William and Mary Quarterly,* 3d Ser., XLIV (1987), 689–721; Norton, *Liberty's Daughters: The Revolutionary Experience of American Women, 1750–1800* (1980; Ithaca, N.Y., 1996); Waldstreicher, *In the Midst of Perpetual Fetes: The Making of American Nationalism, 1776–1820* (Chapel Hill, N.C., 1997), 111, 119, 122, 123; Zagarri, "The Rights of Man and Woman in Post-Revolutionary America," *WMQ,* 3d Ser., LV (1998).

5. Susanna Rowson, preface to *Exercises in History, Chronology, and Biography in Question and Answer for the Use of Schools* (Boston, 1822), ii. Rowson published *Trials of the Human Heart,* 4 vols. (Philadelphia, 1795) by subscription. The subscription list contained many notable names, beginning with its patron, Anne Bingham, and

Elias Nason, Rowson's second memoirist, called her life "a beautiful illus-tration of the potency of a large, glowing heart, and a determined will to rise superior to circumstances." As an officer's daughter who nonetheless found herself dependent upon her own labor from the age of fifteen, Rowson not only knew both sides of the Atlantic; she also knew what it was to be a favored Bostonian child of leisure who spent her mornings in conversation with a Revolutionary patriot, to be a teenage British governess support-ing her penniless family in the wake of the Revolution, and to be a young American professional whose skills took her from the socially equivocal role of actress to the authoritative position of school founder and president of a leading voluntary society. She was uniquely equipped, then, to reconcile British and American notions of personal worth and to transform gentility itself, with its dual connotations of class standing and well-mannered socia-bility, from an inherited condition to a practiced art available to any deter-mined and literate Anglo-American woman.[6]

As with the many other resolutions offered women during the 1790s,

including Martha Washington. Perhaps partly because of this increasingly outdated method of publication, as well as its length (four volumes) and diffuse style, it remained Rowson's greatest commercial failure. On democratic sociability, see Catherine Allgor, *Parlor Politics: In Which the Ladies of Washington Help Build a City and a Government* (Charlottesville, Va., 2000), 57, 75.

6. Elias Nason began both his memoir of Rowson and his subscription proposal for the volume with the above description of the author (Nason, subscription proposal, n.d., Rowson Papers, MSS 7379–c, box 1, folder 59). Before the Revolution, the Haswells lived "in comparative affluence," associating with "distinguished individuals," many of them "officers of the Crown." Nason also discusses James Otis's friendship with Susanna Haswell, whom he called "his little scholar" (Nason, *Memoir of Mrs. Susanna Rowson,* 14–15). R. W. G. Vail writes of Rowson's youth in Nantasket "mingling with the best people of the region" (Vail, "Susanna Haswell Rowson, the Author of Char-lotte Temple: A Bibliographical Study," in American Antiquarian Society, *Proceedings,* XLII, part 1 [Worcester, Mass., 1932], 50). On Rowson's early association with aris-tocratic patrons, see Ellen B. Brandt, *Susanna Haswell Rowson, America's First Best-Selling Novelist* (Chicago, 1975), 21–22, 30. Rowson alludes to her experiences as a governess in *Mentoria.* In this novel, Serena Osborne is possessed of a "genteel inde-pendence" (Rowson, *Mentoria; or, The Young Lady's Friend,* 2 vols. [London, 1790], II, 63). Bushman defines the "dilute gentility" that began to spread through the nation in the 1790s as both a material condition ("The line that once divided gentry from the rest of society now dropped to a lower level and separated the middle class from workers and marginal people") and a way of relating oneself to the world ("Gentility heightened self-consciousness, not in any deep philosophical sense, but in the common meaning of becoming aware of how one looked in the eyes of others"). See *Refinement of America,* xiv–xv.

however, this one contained a paradox: for to attain a status that allowed one material comfort, the respect of one's peers, and a measure of public influence, one needed to perform a "deliberate evocation of powerlessness." Both female gender and the traditions of European elitism placed a premium on the disavowal of personal ambition. How was a young woman of the early Republic—who wanted both to know herself and to influence others—to proceed? Very cautiously, Rowson answered, and proceeded to sketch, in novel after song after play, a template. But if her early efforts (most famously that composed in England and repackaged for an American readership, the best seller *Charlotte Temple*) emphasized caution to the exclusion of "active virtue," her later works were more dedicated to elaborating female gentility in the context of the *socius* it informed and was informed by. Indeed, by the end of her career, Rowson's published and unpublished works placed a premium on women's capacity to better their world, both within and without the domestic realm. As we will see, however, such advances were limited (the illiterate, nonwhite, or irredeemably poor need not apply) and came at a cost to the somatic registers of experience: sexual desire, spontaneity, and those forms of happiness that take place out of the public eye.[7]

If the letter to Mary gives us all we might expect from America's first renowned female author and early eminent pedagogue, that to her yet dearer friend speaks to my study here. In essence, I aim to be Rowson's Louisa: one to whom, however covertly, she reveals not only her distaste for what women of the day frequently called their "circumscription" but also her capacities to live beyond corrosive strictures on female deportment and to bring her female readers along with her, all the while maintaining the approbation, and the ear, of resident patriarchs.[8]

7. For more on active virtue, see Chapter 3, below.

8. Allgor, *Parlor Politics,* 33. In Hannah Webster Foster's novel *The Coquette* (Boston, 1797), Eliza Wharton expresses frustration at the prospect of "circumscribing our wishes within the compass of our abilities" (Foster, *The Coquette,* ed. Cathy N. Davidson [New York, 1986], 47). Margaret Bayard Smith wrote of "how hard at times, have I found it, to confine [my soul] within the narrow precincts, to which it is now circumscribed!—to bend it to the humble duties, to occupy it with the little cares, to enchain it to the moderate desires, of woman's destiny." But she also described a symbiotic relationship between domestic constraint and intellectual expansiveness: "No it is—in the little circle which often surrounds our fire side, where, genius, wit, talent, wisdom, display their charms, that my mind is fired with an ambition, is awakened to an activity, that is enimicaeal to the duties of my little sphere—it is in this circle, where mutual esteem and confidence, expands every heart, and gives birth to that aimiable gaiety, good humour and communicativeness unknown in larger circles; that sympathy and tender[n]ess is elicited and that the heart feels its sensibility." Note the shift here from an opposition

What was unique about the ideological climate white female residents of the United States faced in the 1790s? Why should the ability to appeal to multiple audiences evident in Rowson's letters to Mary and Louisa (and, implicitly, her father), be so welcome during this period? The key thing to remember is that, throughout this decade, the range of behaviors available to women expanded even as their attempts to avail themselves of these new opportunities were increasingly stigmatized. This was a conundrum that had plagued women since the dawn of liberalism. Consider the mid-eighteenth-century stigma on female luxury that accompanied colonial women's new opportunities for choice and influence as consumers of an increasing selection of imported British goods. This inverse ratio between material opportunity and ideological imposition grew especially acute after the Revolution. We tend to focus on just one aspect of this crisis, namely the fetishization of motherhood and wifehood as a compensatory surrogate for women's literal disenfranchisement within the political structures of the new nation. But other examples abound. In terms of sexuality, for instance, middle-class white women in Philadelphia—the city Rowson lived in while she wrote much of her most important work of the decade—found themselves burdened with increased expectations of sexual restraint precisely as the city itself experienced nothing less than a sexual revolution. One might also consider the early national outcry against novel reading—an activity in which women played a significant role as authors, characters, and readers—that accompanied the explosion of published novels as the century neared its end.[9]

----

between the "circle" of discussion and that of "duty," to an alliance wherein only "little" circles such as that around a fireside allow profound cognitive and affectual truths to emerge (cited in Fredrika J. Teute, "Roman Matron on the Banks of the Tiber Creek: Margaret Bayard Smith and the Politicization of Spheres in the Nation's Capital," in Donald R. Kennon, ed., *A Republic for the Ages: The United States Capitol and the Political Culture of the Early Republic* [Charlottesville, Va., 1999], 94, 103).

9. On the condemnation of female luxury during a boom in female consumer opportunities midcentury, see T. H. Breen, *The Marketplace of Revolution: How Consumer Politics Shaped American Independence* (New York, 2004), 172–182. Regarding the sexual permissiveness of Philadelphia in the 1790s, see Richard Godbeer, *Sexual Revolution in Early America* (Baltimore, 2002), 300, and Clare A. Lyons, "Mapping an Atlantic Sexual Culture: Homoeroticism in Eighteenth-Century Philadelphia," *WMQ*, 3d Ser., LX (2003), 119–154. On Federalist tolerance for public roles for women, see Waldstreicher, *In the Midst of Perpetual Fetes*, 122, 167, and Rosemarie Zagarri, "Women and Party Conflict in the Early Republic," in Jeffrey L. Pasley, Andrew Robertson, and David Waldstreicher, eds., *Beyond the Founders: New Approaches to the Political*

The instances cited above highlight two important historical truths. First, restrictive behavioral norms tend to develop in response to increased material opportunity. Second, women suffer the effects of ideological strictures disproportionately with men. The first decades after a revolution are almost by definition eras of new opportunity, which in this case included westward migration across the Appalachians, an unprecedented overseas commercial boom as the Napoleonic Wars created opportunities for American merchants, and a dramatic rise in domestic economic prosperity and entrepreneurship. If one considers the transatlantic perspective as well, the 1790s witnessed significant developments in the extent and nature of immigration, the scope of the international slave trade and the resultant organization of slave labor in the southern states, and the sway of imperial powers over widening global territory. With these transformations in mind, one is tempted to interpret the seemingly nondescript young woman who stood at the core of both Rowson's subject matter and readership in almost heroic terms. She holds the globe on her small, sloped shoulders (Plates 2, 3). But her efforts are legible not so much through displays of overt strength as through the compromises and adaptive behaviors by which she transforms shame and condemnation into opportunities for play, humor, and joy.[10]

Let us return to Rowson's letter to Louisa, in order to show just how she constructed one exemplary opportunity for female improvisation in the context of paternalistic oversight. Although the thoughts Rowson shares with Louisa suggest the stakes of my own endeavor here, the literal marks

---

History of the Early American Republic (Chapel Hill, N.C., 2004), 107–128. Herbert Ross Brown was probably the first twentieth-century critic to attend to the outcry against novel-reading in post-Revolutionary America (Brown, *The Sentimental Novel in America, 1789–1860* [Durham, N.C., 1940], 3–9).

10. On the tendency for material opportunity and social stigma to coincide, see Albert O. Hirschman, *Shifting Involvements: Private Interest and Public Action* (Princeton, N.J., 1982), 50. On post-Revolutionary culture's tendency to distribute the weight of ideological opprobrium disproportionately between women and men, see Gillian Brown, *Domestic Individualism: Imagining Self in Nineteenth-Century America* (Berkeley, Calif., 1990), 4–5, and Elizabeth Maddock Dillon, *The Gender of Freedom: Fictions of Liberalism and the Literary Public Sphere* (Stanford, Calif., 2004), 11–12. On post-Revolutionary social and economic transformations, see Steven Watts, "Ministers, Misanthropes, and Mandarins: The Federalists and the Culture of Capitalism, 1790–1820," in Doran Ben-Atar and Barbara B. Oberg, eds., *Federalists Reconsidered* (Charlottesville, Va., 1998), 157–175, esp. 159–160. On changing patterns of slavery in the South, see Allan Kulikoff, *Tobacco and Slaves: The Development of Southern Cultures in the Chesapeake, 1680–1800* (Chapel Hill, N.C., 1986).

PLATE 2. *Portrait of Susanna Rowson. From Rowson,* Mentoria;
or, The Young Lady's Friend, *2 vols. (Philadelphia, 1794), I, frontispiece.
PS 2736.R3, Clifton Waller Barrett Library of American Literature,
Special Collections, University of Virginia Library*

PLATE 3. *"Charlotte Temple." Engraving by C. Tiebout. 1812. Papers of Susanna Rowson, MSS 7379, Clifton Waller Barrett Library of American Literature, Special Collections, University of Virginia Library*

on the fading page inscribe the challenges I face communicating it to you. The significance of this letter is not completely evident from the excerpt above; rather, it requires a description of some markings on the holograph manuscript.

Rowson addresses Louisa directly in the midst of her diatribe: "These reflections my Louisa." This seemingly offhand address is actually the result of an emendation: Rowson has crossed out "my dear Louisa" and added "my Louisa" in superscript earlier in the same sentence. This suggests that she originally had Louisa in mind as her addressee but remembered her invocation of Louisa's father as the motive for such explicit political ruminations and crossed out the spontaneous effusion. On reflection, however, she also regretted omitting Louisa from her address and reinserted her name, only without "dear." (That Louisa was dear to her former mentor is clear from a poem Rowson addressed to her, where she calls her "The friend that to my heart was nearest.") These second and third thoughts, for an author whose manuscripts reveal that she composed with as much haste and as little taste for revision as her detractors have suggested, say a great deal about a fundamental uncertainty at the heart of the Rowson opus: was she writing to please young women or their fathers? Not only this letter but nearly all Rowson's writings proclaim the answer to be "both." But how was one message to satisfy such disparate parties: those who owned and those who could not own; those who voted and those who could not vote; those free to invest and those whose primary capital consisted of their persons? How to acknowledge the dissatisfaction of the latter party without alienating the former, an alienation that, among other things, imperiled the access of the addressee herself?[11]

Consider the three characters involved: Rowson, Louisa Bliss, and Louisa's father. At one level, the author has a common cause with both her interlocutors, one of whom is a woman, one an "old folk." Although Louisa and her father are intended as distinct readers of the letter, each one's access

11. The first stanza of "To Louisa" in manuscript reads:

Oft has my Harp Louisa sung,
When both were gay and both were young.
Oft in my early matron years
When first I knew lifes cares and fears,
Turned still to thee Louisa dearest,
The friend that to my heart was nearest.

"To Louisa," n.d., Rowson Papers, MSS 7379-c, box 1, folder 61.

to it depends on the other. Louisa's father needs Louisa, obviously, because the letter is written to her. Nor could it have been written to him, since it would have been inappropriate for Rowson, a married woman, to express herself so candidly and extensively in a direct address to a man not her husband. If the letter is Louisa's property, she nonetheless may owe a debt to her father for her access to its words. By asking Louisa what her father thinks, Rowson licenses an extended rumination on matters often considered irrelevant, if not damaging, to young women of the early Republic. Louisa, then, in reading the letter to her father, symbolically reads over his shoulder.[12]

At yet another level, she reads from within his head. Rowson, that is, constructs the exchange so that Louisa imagines herself occupying the patriarchal perspective: "What thinks your father of the present times?" In order to reflect on the likely consequences of the administration's domestic and international policy, Louisa becomes capable of influencing it directly for a brief period of time. She is then returned to her own body with the invocation of "old folks" near the end of the disquisition, a phrase that excludes her and reminds everyone concerned that she is, after all, only a daughter.

Such rhetorical gestures are typical of the way Rowson went to complex, if not always fully self-aware, lengths to articulate tentative, tenuous, but momentarily inhabitable readerly spaces within which her female contemporaries could construct themselves as fully empowered subjects. Louisa is free to probe Federalist-themed discontent with the Jefferson administration's embargo policy so long as she does so in both the company and the temporary personhood of her father, and so long as she resumes the modest disavowal of political savvy considered appropriate to her age, sex, and station. Thus are father and daughter rendered happy co-readers.[13]

12. Two early American novels of seduction, William Hill Brown's *Power of Sympathy* (Boston, 1789) and Foster's *Coquette,* discuss the appropriate limits for female participation in political discussion. While including the default perspective that "politics . . . did not belong to ladies," these discussions tended to propose a middle ground more like the one Rowson traverses here, in which women "judiciously, yet modestly, bore a part" as individuals "interested in the welfare and prosperity of our country." Women's novelistic participation in political discussions, however, rarely encompassed commercial and economic matters to the degree Rowson's does above (Foster, *Coquette,* ed. Davidson, 44).

13. By 1811, Rowson's loathing of Napoleon had mellowed enough for her to pen a student dialogue featuring both pro- and anti-Napoleonic voices. Bonaparte is referred to as both a "wonderful hero" and "Woglog the giant" before the young women leave off "political lore" in order to "go a shopping." Since this dialogue was performed at a

These acts of conciliation, to the degree they have been recognized, have not always earned Rowson praise. Fellow British expatriate William Cobbett lambasted her suspect American patriotism as a blatant attempt to curry favor with her new audience, and later critics similarly suggested mercenary motives for everything from the American publication of *Charlotte Temple* to the staging of a patriotic play for her own benefit night. Her perceived opportunism, in fact, might have initiated the charges of hypocrisy that have bedeviled American sentimentalism since its nineteenth-century heyday. And suspicion may be warranted of an author who simply copied verbatim large parts of Jedidiah Morse's *American Geography* (1792) and published it, without giving him full credit, as her own *Abridgment of Universal Geography* in 1805. Nevertheless, by remaining at the level of wry condescension, we do a huge disservice not only to Rowson but, more important, to the culture she informed. If Rowson increasingly knew how to make the best of a bad situation in both her personal life and her narrative productions, her skill helped her contemporary female readers negotiate the paternalistic social and political entity of which Rowson's plight was only one limited instance: the early American Republic.[14]

---

student exhibition, Rowson's willingness to see both sides probably also reflected her tendency to sacrifice political conviction in favor of sensitivity to the divergent views of audience members. See Rowson, "Dialogue: For Three Young Ladies," in Rowson, *A Present for Young Ladies,* 31–37.

14. Vail wrote, "Mrs. Rowson has the distinction of being one of our first professional women writers—professional in that she had to have money and wrote books in order to get it" ("Susanna Haswell Rowson," in American Antiquarian Society, *Proceedings,* XLII, part 1, 60). On sentimental hypocrisy, see Ann Douglas, *The Feminization of American Culture* (New York, 1977); Lori Merish, *Sentimental Materialism: Gender, Commodity Culture, and Nineteenth-Century American Literature* (Durham, N.C., 2000), esp. 3–4; and Robert C. Solomon, *In Defense of Sentimentality* (Oxford, 2004), 4–7. Although Rowson's most famous twentieth-century detractor, Leslie Fiedler, does not explicitly accuse Rowson of opportunism in his savaging of *Charlotte Temple,* he returns obsessively to two aspects of the book that, taken together, suggest callow self-interest on the part of the author. He acknowledges the book's popularity ("the most reprinted of all American books," "more than two hundred editions," "survived among certain readers for a hundred and fifty years") while insisting that it is "adapted to the needs of the American female audience." Rowson is unlikely to have consciously "adapted" her book to an audience she had no idea she would encounter when she wrote the book in England, but the implication that she catered her literary wares to what the market would bear is not unfounded. We ought to question, however, the scorn we direct to such "adaptivity" (Fiedler, *Love and Death in the American Novel,* rev. ed. [1966; New York, 1975], 83, 94).

Philip Fisher has argued that popular culture works because of what it teaches us to forget. If this is true, then the practice of recovering past cultures requires a certain abeyance of our deepest assumptions. Leonard Tennenhouse has taken up this charge in putting forth the unlikely figure of the libertine—to many, a figure for sexual excess and economic unproductivity—as a model for American masculine prerogative in the formation of the new American family. In a similar vein, I suggest that Rowson made sense to literate, female Anglo-American inhabitants of the new Republic for precisely the reasons that she now strikes us as slightly distasteful: her profound relativism and corresponding facility at adaptation. This is a hard truth to grasp because, in keeping with the strictures on novelists, particularly female, of her era, she loved to talk about absolute moral goodness. But it was not what was "good" about Rowson that made her great.[15]

Nor were her compromises always self-serving, as evident in a poem she wrote to her husband in celebration of their twenty-fifth anniversary. This poem has confused critics for centuries, since William Rowson was frequently drunk, often unemployed, unfaithful, and not much of a kindred spirit. Although the most commonly cited evidence for Rowson's disillusionment with her marriage is the epigraph from John Gregory to her autobiographical fiction *Sarah*—"Do not marry a fool"—this caustic witticism can mislead us into thinking that Rowson merely scorned her shiftless mate. Other evidence suggests that her feelings were more complex. An early letter to the couple from Susanna's parents in England takes William's earlier claim that his wife has grown "rather fatter and that sauciness increases with her bulk" as "a fair demonstration . . . that you are both happy." In light of their increasing troubles, William's cited references to his wife's altered appearance and insubordination do raise a red flag; but Susanna's parents also responded to his affectionate tone toward his wife.[16]

In further contrast to the epigraph from Gregory, one untitled, undated, and unpublished verse testifies with particular poignancy to the nature of their relationship:

There's not a sorrow stung this heart,
But what the oft recurring dart,

15. Philip Fisher, *Hard Facts: Setting and Form in the American Novel* (New York, 1985), esp. 4–5; Leonard Tennenhouse, "Libertine America," *Differences: A Journal of Feminist Cultural Studies,* XI (1999–2000), 1–28.

16. William Haswell and Rachel Haswell to William Rowson, Feb. 4, 1801, Rowson Papers, MSS 7379-b, box 1, folders 33–34.

PLATE 4. *Pencil sketch of William Rowson as a young man. C. 1770.*
Papers of Susanna Rowson, MSS 7379, Clifton Waller Barrett Library of
American Literature, Special Collections, University of Virginia Library

PLATE 5. *Left portrait of Susanna Rowson as a young woman. Papers of Susanna Rowson, MSS 7379, Clifton Waller Barrett Library of American Literature, Special Collections, University of Virginia Library*

PLATE 6. *William Rowson. By J. R. Smith. 1819. Papers of Susanna Rowson,*
MSS 7379, Clifton Waller Barrett Library of American Literature, Special Collections,
University of Virginia Library

PLATE 7. *Silhouette of William and Susanna Rowson. Papers of Susanna Rowson, MSS 7379, Clifton Waller Barrett Library of American Literature, Special Collections, University of Virginia Library*

Has still been barbed by thee.
Yet still I cherish every thought
That murders my repose;
The secret sigh, the ready tear,
All, all, that's cruel, all that's dear,
To thee, its being owes!

Clearly, Rowson continued to love her husband enough to be wounded by his inattention.[17]

Rowson's vulnerability to her husband's neglect makes her anniversary composition all the more extraordinary as an expression of her capacity for adaptation to untenable circumstance. To understand the significance of this poem, it's important to realize the context in which it was written. Emendations suggest that this uncharacteristically loving missive was in fact composed on — not merely copied onto — the back of a letter she received from her adopted son (also William), the child of her husband and another woman. Rowson thus composed a poem about her lost beauty ("Twenty five years have stol'n my youth . . . Tho' Time's hard hand has mark'd my brow . . . And tho' the charms of youth are o'er") on a letter from a man her husband conceived out of wedlock.[18]

That Susanna wrote by far her most positive assessment of her marriage onto a missive from the very embodiment of its imperfections speaks volumes about the method by which she dealt with systemic injustices to Anglo-American women. (To understand the systemic aspects of her husband's infidelity, consider the social tolerance of his adultery evinced by her adoption of his son compared to the sorry fictional fates of female sexual transgressors of the period.) One can imagine her reading the letter, being reminded once again of her husband's disloyalty, and harnessing the energy sparked by her discomfiture for the very acts needed to overcome it: turning anger to forgiveness, distrust to commitment. This poem's creation shows the depth of Rowson's ability, or compulsion, to bring her view of any given matter in line with her sense of herself as at least a partial agent in her own destiny — and to see that destiny as a tolerable, if not a preferred, outcome. Careful attention to seeming biographical and textual minutiae can clarify the tools she developed for maintaining a sense of well-being in the face of

17. "There's not a look or word of thine," n.d., Rowson Papers, MSS 7379–b, box 1, folder 9.

18. "To Mr. Rowson on the 25th Anniversary of Our Wedding Day," Oct. 17, 1811, ibid., MSS 7379, box 1, folder 13.

oppression and humiliation, as well as the cost of these coping strategies to her affective capacity.[19]

The losses are not insignificant. In particular, they consist of a turning against the self of energies spawned in response to perceived threats from without. In this poem written on a letter from her husband's illegitimate son, for instance, Rowson begins with many cryptic references to her own "infring'd vow," almost as if she were accusing herself of adultery. Although the broken vow in question turns out not to be fidelity, she chooses another that, we know from her husband's references to her "sauciness," she did not always have much use for: obedience.

> Twenty five years have slipped away,
> Since first I promised to Obey;
> And tho' I've oft infring'd the vow,
> I'm ready to renew it now.
> Renew it to its very letter,
> And think that I should keep it better.

She then expresses confidence that, despite her lost beauty and disobedience, her husband loves her "better than before" and hopes for renewed mutual compassion as they approach death.[20]

Rowson rarely acted on her "promise." She behaved with invincible decorum to her errant spouse. A former student wrote, "If Mrs. Rowson's marriage was not a happy one, no one discovered it by any want of attention on her part," noting that she always stayed up to receive her husband home with "a cheerful welcome, a bright fire and some little delicacy on the table." But it was her economic and social ambitions that determined the family's course, as her acting career took them from Philadelphia to Boston and the success of her school to ever-greener pastures in the surrounding suburbs. This tension between explicit tribute to paternalistic hierarchies demanding female "obedience" and daily departures from behavioral norms she herself set forth informs her works in myriad ways. Most important, it exists as a discrepancy between stated intent and discursive record: between what a text informs its reader is to be his or her experience while reading and what

19. Emendations such as "since then" to "hard hand" and "let us sooth" to "as we sooth" suggest that this version, on a letter dated Aug. 11, 1811, is the original. A later manuscript copy, from Oct. 17, 1811, includes two final lines not present in the original: "Together let us earnest be / To insure a blest eternity" (ibid.; William Rowson, Jr., to William Rowson and Susanna Rowson, Aug. 11, 1811, ibid., box 1, folder 47).

20. Ibid.

that experience feels like page to page. And this tension articulated for early American female readers, in particular, a sensation they were already familiar with as an incompatibility between their proclaimed importance to the survival of the new nation-state and their minimal prescribed role in its formation and elaboration. Others, most importantly Judith Sargent Murray, were more articulate about how the new nation failed its female inhabitants. But no one talked about the effects of this failure, and the need to carry on nonetheless, as thoroughly as its best-loved female author.[21]

Beyond Charlotte Temple

In our day, Susanna Rowson has been translated into Chinese and impersonated at the Medford Public Library in Massachusetts, while her best seller goes on back order in university bookstores at the start of many a semester. In hers, she crossed the Atlantic three times, surviving her own birth (which killed her mother), a shipwreck, Revolutionary imprisonment, a forced and penniless return to England, and a final emigration to the States in 1793. She supported an extended family from the age of fifteen, including her father, his second wife, her alcoholic husband, his son by another woman, and two adopted daughters through her capacities as governess, actress, school founder, and the most prolific and widely read novelist of the United States' first half-century. There, her resourcefulness—in its inventiveness as in its capacity for compromise—struck a sympathetic chord, and she not only published the best-selling novel of the early Republic but also authored popular songs, plays, textbooks, and more. (One measure of the breadth of her popularity: in 1818, characters from her most famous novel appeared in a waxworks show in Columbus, Ohio.) An eventual president of the Boston Fatherless and Widows' Society, she nonetheless represented prostitution sympathetically in print and introduced female protagonists who, far from dying for their sexual indiscretions—as was their fate in most popular literature of the time—married rakes only to get a second chance.[22]

---

21. "Notes regarding Haswell and Rowson Families by Mrs. J. J. Clarke," n.d., Rowson Papers, MSS 7379-c, box 1, folder 55.

22. Shijie Wang, Jiro Akagawa, and Susanna Rowson, *Shao nu zhi wu (Charlotte Temple)* (Shenyang Shi, 1988). The *Medford Transcript,* July 23, 2003, lists actress Jessica Piaia's impersonation of Susanna Rowson and Deborah Sampson. For invaluable book-length biographical studies of Rowson, see Brandt, *Susanna Haswell Rowson;* Dorothy Weil, *In Defense of Women: Susanna Rowson (1762–1824)* (University Park, Pa., 1976); and Patricia L. Parker, *Susanna Rowson* (Boston, 1986). Cathy N. Davidson discusses both Rowson's biography and the plot of the typical American novel of seduction in *Revolution and the Word: The Rise of the Novel in America* (New York,

Why, then, when we think of this author, do we envision a faint-hearted woman's premature death in childbirth? Susanna Haswell Rowson has many autobiographical incarnations, but Charlotte Temple, her most famous protagonist, is not one of them, except in the most distant sense in which an extraordinarily active woman meditates on the forbidden pleasures of passivity. Yet in our need to mourn the retrenchment of political rights and social freedoms for women after the War of Independence, we have made Rowson and Charlotte one, detecting in their composite figure a gloomy early national female culture that loved Charlotte so much it dug her grave. Despite the incontestable post-Revolutionary intensification of gender norms that both exalted women as bearers of a national code of honor and rendered them ever less vital to the public sphere, the fact remains that some women stayed unmarried, worked for wages, participated in print political discourse, traveled widely, had sex out of wedlock, did not bear children, and generally failed to fit the mold of either domestic retirement or moral standard-bearing that can seem ubiquitous in sloppy appropriations of early national feminist historiography. Terms such as "separate spheres" and "republican motherhood" have sensitized scholars to the unique significances of post-Revolutionary womanhood, but perhaps because of their very facility of application, they have allowed us too easy a grasp on early national female selfhood, presuming an "a priori commitment to the publicity of men and the privacy of women." This book encourages us to attend to the activist dimensions of early American gender practice via a thorough investigation of Rowson's multifaceted narrative and wide-ranging life experience.[23]

1986), and "The Life and Times of Charlotte Temple: The Biography of a Book," in Davidson, ed., *Reading in America: Literature and Social History* (Baltimore, 1989), 157–179. Jenny Franchot's brief biography of Rowson appears in Emory Elliott, ed., *American Writers of the Early Republic,* Dictionary of Literary Biography, XXXVII (Detroit, 1985), 256–259. William Charvat documents the waxworks exhibition in *The Profession of Authorship in America, 1800–1870: The Papers of William Charvat,* ed. Matthew J. Bruccoli (Columbus, Ohio, 1968), 20.

23. Lawrence E. Klein, "Gender and the Public/Private Distinction in the Eighteenth Century: Some Questions about Evidence and Analytic Procedure," *Eighteenth-Century Studies,* XXIX (1995–1996), 97–110, esp. 105. Branson objects to "republican womanhood" and "separate spheres" on three grounds: the unexplored potential disparity between these ideological constructs and women's life practices; the presumed implication that "separate spheres" ideology confined women to the domestic realm while preserving their public identities unchanged from the seventeenth century through the eighteenth; and the idea that republican womanhood, which encouraged female education especially in the realm of political affairs, limited women's civic activities (*These Fiery Frenchified Dames,* 2).

Such activism was never untroubled, either for Rowson or her many contemporaries. Deborah Sampson Gannett, a cross-dressing Revolutionary War soldier who went on a lecture tour of the Northeast in a successful attempt to claim a veteran's pension, provides a case in point. Alternating "instruction in Republican Motherhood" with military maneuvers, Gannett offered a public presence that "countered the emergent ideology of gendered spheres that separated society into masculine public and feminine private domains, even as her words reinforced it." Abigail Abbot Bailey's account of her escape from a profoundly abusive marriage in late-eighteenth-century New Hampshire provides another template for early American female activism's deep and illustrative tensions. *The Memoirs of Abigail Abbot Bailey*, first published in 1815, mostly records her husband's innumerable atrocities between 1788 and 1792, including multiple acts of brutality and an incestuous relationship with one of their daughters. Throughout this ordeal, Abigail, an ardent Congregationalist, attempts to reconcile herself to her situation by seeing it as willed by a just and loving God. At the end of the narrative, however, Abigail not only escapes from her husband with her children but divorces him and brings communal sanction down upon him. The faith that once taught resignation now fosters an unshakable determination to alter her condition by any means necessary, including deception, still in the name of obedience to God. What Rowson shares with these women is the capacity to put deference to strategic use in the service of self-interest and social critique.[24]

The poles of republican and liberal sensibility provide another useful frame by which to view the split between Rowson's strategic daring and her fascination with female destruction. Placing their own self-interest beneath that of their brethren, certain of Rowson's heroines enacted republican virtue by offering themselves (often literally) on the altar of service to their fellow man. Such heroines thereby qualified themselves for political

---

24. Gustafson, *Eloquence Is Power,* xvi, xix, 246, 248–249; Ann Taves, ed., *Religion and Domestic Violence in Early New England: The Memoirs of Abigail Abbot Bailey* (Bloomington, Ind., 1989); Brandt, *Susanna Haswell Rowson,* 121. According to *Charlotte's* first American publisher, Mathew Carey, the novel sold at least 50,000 copies in its first eighteen years in the United States. It went through forty-two editions in seventeen cities before 1820 and has the reputation of being the best-selling novel in America until *Uncle Tom's Cabin.* Keep in mind, Thomas Paine's Revolutionary pamphlet *Common Sense* (1776) is reputed to have sold 120,000 copies in the first three months. But what *Charlotte Temple* lacked in speed, it made up for in steadfastness, with editions appearing throughout the nineteenth century. It remained the best-selling fiction of the Republic until the mid-nineteenth century.

agency in the new Republic, despite their exclusion by the polis they championed. In contrast, Rowson tended to serve others through methods that also enhanced her own individual standing.

Although examples of this contrast are strewn throughout her literary record, the most telling instance involves a character played onstage by Rowson herself: Olivia, the Anglo-American ingénue of *Slaves in Algiers* (1794). Attempting to save her father, Olivia offers to sacrifice her sexual agency by marrying her captor—and even her life, since she plans to commit suicide on the eve of the consummation. Rowson, however, helped her own father out of his financial distress through a quite different sort of courtship. In gaining the patronage of such powerful contemporaries as a "reigning queen" of London society, Georgiana Cavendish, duchess of Devonshire, Rowson offered her book, not her body; and far from suffering as a result, she shared in the financial and social benefits of the arrangement. Indeed, Rowson's very immigration to Philadelphia with Thomas Wignell's New Theatre Company was part of an explicit campaign of self-improvement, again aimed at providing for her family, which now included a husband plagued by underemployment. As William Rowson's roles diminished (he was soon demoted to prompter and then replaced), hers increased; when the Chestnut Street Theatre disappointed, she (and many of her company) moved in 1796 to one that offered better terms, the Federal Street Theatre in Boston.[25]

Rowson's fondness for narrating female self-sacrifice as she pursued fame and fortune, then, provides an instantiation of how female submission in this period, far from existing in strict opposition to female empowerment, could be manipulated to achieve social stature and wide public influence. At the same time, the relish Rowson displayed for scenes of female surrender betrays a nostalgic pleasure as well, much the way a very busy person fantasizes about doing nothing. This form of valorization is premised upon the desideratum's limited applicability to present life circumstance and depends on the utter improbability of the wish fulfillment. Thus it can accompany Rowson's other, more strategic deployments of submission for the attainment of power. As such, the depth of her erratic but long-term commitment to womanly self-erasure seems to exceed the commercial, social, and political considerations discussed above. Indeed, it suggests that, for Rowson, female passivity possessed an appeal that was erotic in its intensity. It is the urge to accept the course of one's life as predetermined, as opposed to laboring to exert at least a limited influence over it that Rowsonian narrative marks

25. Parker, *Susanna Rowson*, 9; Brandt, *Susanna Haswell Rowson*, 90–91.

as both profoundly dangerous for women and yet possessed of a lingering attraction. If Charlotte does stand in for her author, she does so as an alter ego.[26]

Given that Charlotte's preternatural capacity for surrender resonated with qualities Rowson chose to minimize in her own life and self-narration, it makes sense that the author would subsequently offer her readers other protagonists more directly drawn from experience. In fact, Rowson's work throughout the 1790s espouses a peculiar blend of cautionary polemic, sly innuendo, and outright reformative challenge when it comes to female agency, sexual and otherwise. Although her most-read book seems to support the perceived national obsession with fictional portrayals of the terrifying prospect of female seduction, her popular songs from the same period celebrate shore-leave flirtation ("America, Commerce, and Freedom" [1794]), male beauty, and the fabulous fickleness of the female heart ("Allegro," "Andante Allegretto," "Allegretto," *The Volunteers* [1795]). Her longest and most autobiographical novel, *Trials of the Human Heart* (1795), features a woman who survives myriad sexual assaults to lead a life of relative content married to her first true love. Meanwhile, although Rowson's surviving letters to her husband only rarely allude to pleasures sexual or otherwise, she conducted spirited, if not downright suggestive, epistolary correspondence with at least one other man and seemed vastly to enjoy her onstage opportunities for flirtatious display. To understand the historical importance of Rowson's widespread appeal, we must engage fully with the author who, while concerning herself with female adversity in all its guises, described a far more variegated sexual and behavioral palate for women than is available through a single work.[27]

26. Useful discussions of Republican and liberal ideology in the early United States range from Gould's *Covenant and Republic* to Gordon S. Wood's *Radicalism of the American Revolution* (New York, 1992), esp. 252, to Elizabeth Dillon's *Gender of Freedom*.

27. Susanna Rowson, *The Volunteers: A Musical Entertainment, as Performed at the New Theatre, Composed by Alex Reinagle* (Philadelphia, 1795), 6, 8, 14, 15. Here is an undated, untitled letter in verse form, sent, apparently along with a bowl of soup, to D. Brown, signed "S. Rowson" and beneath that, "Susan Eliza."

Dear Sir
I have often heard gentlemen say
That a bason of soup on a cold frosty day
Some time 'twixt the hour of eleven and one
To refresh them and cheer up the spirits—

This book takes on *Charlotte Temple* in order to escape it and return to it refreshed. It encourages readers to think of early American gender and literary practices in far more diversified terms than are fashionable. Striking a blow for female adventurism and opportunism, for an insistence on spiritedness against all odds, it casts its lot with creativity, travel, exile, and rebellion over repression, domesticity, and containment.

By engaging literate Anglo-American women in the shared enterprise of reading her work and modeling the forms of intervention contained therein, Rowson benefited some—not all—early national women. Despite her publications' claims to found female self-worth on behavior rather than circumstance and on limited choice rather than pure imposition, she did not reach out to all her potential readers. Rather, the consolidation of power for those she deemed eligible took place at the expense of both nonwhites and others on the margins of the new and expanding middle class. The ostracism of Irish servants, Spanish barbers, Moorish potentates, and even uppity New York farmers' wives from the ranks of the self-improving subjects that both populate her works and constitute their implied reader is neither fleeting nor accidental. Rather, it is central to her efforts to empower those she considered eligible.[28]

So having some made, S. R. ventures to send
This clear frosty morning a bowl to her friend
She wishes it better, but be not offended
If this is forgiven, the next shall be mended
And being forgiven you see it is plain
She is laying a plan friend to trespass again
But tis so with us all, so I pray you excuse it
And as to her soup, why you must not refuse it.

Susanna Rowson to D. Brown, n.d., Rowson Papers, MSS 7379, box 1, folder 37.

28. By the end of the 1790s, as Fredrika J. Teute summarizes, the "Jeffersonian Republican expansion of white male participation in politics" left the rest of the population at a disadvantage. This limit on "social and economic transformation," moreover, was not so much accidental as deeply motivated. The exclusion of women from civic participation had its roots in classical republicanism, which Dillon argues "has little place for women because they are seen as belonging to the realm of necessity . . . and not to the republican realm of freedom and disinterested civic virtue." But its early national permutations were highly specific to the period. Clare A. Lyons suggests that white male Philadelphians tolerated homosexual behavior among men to a much greater degree than their counterparts in European port cities precisely because they aimed to form one cross-class interest group at the expense of women and nonwhites. And Rosemarie Zagarri surmises that republican antagonism to granting women a civic role

In sum, despite her evident fascination with young, educated English and Anglo-American female characters of modest means, Rowson showed a determined reluctance to experience the world from the perspective of a nursemaid, a mechanic, an African sailor, or a French schoolteacher. When she finally did tackle poverty in her last book, it was only to sift the wheat from the chaff, the deserving indigent from the naturally lazy. The North Africans who populate *Reuben and Rachel* (1798), *Slaves in Algiers* (1794), and *Mentoria* (1790) yearn to be dominated by their imperially self-righteous American captives. In *An Abridgment of Universal Geography*, national types exhibit worth to the degree that they correspond with European, English, and, above all, New England standards of womanhood. And when she really wants to let loose with scorn and spite, she chooses a Jewish moneylender. None of this makes Rowsonian narrative unusual among early national, or indeed eighteenth-century British, publications. But neither do such practices suggest a profoundly inclusive definition of the "liberty" she claimed to champion.[29]

Rowson's unwillingness to treat racialized, ethnic, and class-based others with the largesse she extended to her implied readership suggests a crisis of more than authorial proportions. It is evidence, rather, of the difficulties involved in applying that prevailing model of individual self-formation, born of the Enlightenment—wherein pasts exist to be rewritten into futures by a monadic entity in possession of its constituent parts—to subjects defined primarily by some aspect of their bodies. Given that Rowson made Anglo-American women's plight her reason to write, they will receive the most attention here. But every disenfranchised body posed a particular threat to the

---

was strong enough that it engendered a backlash against women's early involvement in the post-Revolutionary political realm. Rowson responded to this programmatic segregation in her work and, in so doing, repeated on behalf of white Anglo-American women the motivated exclusions present in the white male consolidation of interest and power over and against other segments of the population. See Teute, "A 'Republic of Intellect': Conversation and Criticism among the Sexes in 1790s New York," in Philip Barnard et al., eds., *Revising Charles Brockden Brown* (Knoxville, Tenn., 2004), 174; Dillon, *Gender of Freedom*, 144; Lyons, "Mapping an Atlantic Sexual Culture," *WMQ*, 3d Ser., LX (2003), 119–154; Zagarri, "Rights of Man and Woman," *WMQ*, 3d Ser., LV (1998), 203–230.

29. Susanna Rowson, *Reuben and Rachel; or, Tales of Old Times* (Boston, 1798); Rowson, *An Abridgment of Universal Geography, together with Sketches of History Designed for the Use of Schools and Academies in the United States* (Boston, [1805]); Rowson, *Mentoria;* Philip Gould, *Barbaric Traffic: Commerce and Antislavery in the Eighteenth-Century Atlantic World* (Cambridge, Mass., 2003), 102.

ideology of self-governance that underpinned the early national pursuit of happiness or its famous near-synonym in the Declaration of Independence, property. Many historians have shown how one's degree of subordination in the early Republic corresponded to the degree to which one's body was considered to determine one's identity. What Elizabeth Dillon calls "biological determinism" was exhibited, for instance, in the fact that, as Gordon Wood notes, commoners were flogged and had their ears cropped, but not gentlemen. The route to knowledge for the former was assumed to pass through the body, whereas such a punishment would bypass the latter's more abstract sensibilities. The degree of perceived rootedness in one's body, in turn, was seen to correspond to one's inability to perceive, or act for the benefit of, a whole. In keeping with classical republican theory, that is, corporeal need was seen to engender partiality, which made one ineligible for governance because it corrupted judgment and rendered "disinterest" impossible. In accord with the traditions of civic humanism so lovingly perpetuated by the Federalist government, then, the ability to judge impartially in public matters was seen to correspond to freedom from want, leading to the curious identification between the possession of land and the ability to abstract from the body perceived as the source of personal interest. Rowson's project was to qualify white middle-class women for the influence and tolerance accorded those whose own corporeal profile—also white, but male, and with a grasp on its own parcel of earth and/or goods—was seen to free them from bias altogether and hence entitle them to true self-governance at both the individual and national level. In her readers' willingness to attend, they made good on my conviction that she is essential to unraveling the fascinating dichotomies and divergences, struggles and new forms of ease, erratic and extraordinary mood swings that make this period, and the American sentimental novel to which it gave rise, matters of such continual obscurity and persistent fascination.[30]

30. Dillon, *Gender of Freedom,* 11. On Rowsonian narrative's "reinscribing the breach" it would overcome, see Julia A. Stern's discussion of "unresolved maternal mourning" in *Charlotte Temple* (Stern, *The Plight of Feeling: Sympathy and Dissent in the Early American Novel* [Chicago, 1997], 47). "The liberality for which gentlemen were known connoted freedom—freedom from material want . . . and freedom from having to work with one's hands. . . . Mechanics and others who worked with their hands were thought servile and totally absorbed in their narrow occupations and thus unqualified for disinterested public office" (Wood, *Radicalism of the American Revolution,* 29, 33, 107). This simultaneous distinction between and conflation of the individual body and the civil corpus extends back to John Winthrop's famous (and possibly derivative) statement in the sermon "A Model of Christian Charity" that the

The Problem of the Sentimental

Charlotte Temple might have been the first novel published in the United States to make crying a political act, with the droves it attracted to the fictional heroine's real gravestone in New York. As such, Rowson has long been an acknowledged initiator of the massive cultural phenomenon known as American sentimentalism. The popularity of her novels in the United States, after their relatively lackluster reception in England, suggests a continuity between their implied readers and their actual American ones that invites us to view her as, in some sense, the voice of her early national readership. Participants in the early national book market not only consumed Rowson books; they were also consumed by them. The marks they left behind on novels from *Charlotte* to *Mentoria* suggest both a pride in the work they held and an easy familiarity that left them feeling that the text welcomed their own pencil marks. Sally Tucker proudly claimed a copy of *Mentoria* as her own in oversize cursive on the very first page, turning the book and writing bottom to top in order to give herself more room. Gone, then, are the days when every study of Rowson must begin with an apology for the quality of the work. Feminist scholars now acknowledge the richness of her narrative as a scratchy but audible recording of voices otherwise lost for good.

Yet there seems little agreement on what exactly Rowson initiated. In an Americanist context in particular, sentimentalism has been usefully and variously defined in terms that seem incommensurable. In struggling to reconcile idealist and materialist perspectives on the construction of gender, modern scholarship has largely deepened the long-simmering antagonism between those who view sentimental discourse as a function of institutional power dynamics whose subjects operate under the delusion of self-determinism and those who insist upon the subversive potential implicit within its celebration of "human," particularly female, "connection." Joanne Dobson illuminates the idealist theory that finds sentimentalism's source within the individual, labeling it an "imaginative orientation . . . premised on an emotional and philosophical ethos that celebrates human connection, both personal and communal, and acknowledges the shared devastation of affectional loss." Lori Merish, by contrast, provides an equally spirited articulation of a materialist point of view that sees sentimentalism emanating from institutional structures, rendering such "imaginative" processes chimerical at best. She calls it a method of "reinventing political hierarchy as

---

Massachusetts Bay Colony was to function as one body, in which each inhabitant served as a single part.

PLATE 8. *Sally Tucker's signature in her own copy of Rowson's* Mentoria.
From R. W. G. Vail, Susanna Haswell Rowson, the Author of Charlotte Temple:
A Bibliographical Study *(Worcester, Mass., 1933). Ref. Z 8763, XIII, Clifton Waller*
Barrett Library of American Literature, Special Collections, University of Virginia
Library

psychological norms reproduced within the intimate recesses of the desiring
subject" such that "the requirements of a capitalist market society were reproduced within individuals as the very stuff of subjectivity."[31]

31. Joanne Dobson, "Reclaiming Sentimental Literature," *American Literature,*
LXIX (1997), 266; Merish, *Sentimental Materialism,* 3, 4. This dynamic extends
through Ann Douglas's and Jane Tompkins's notorious call and response in *The Femi-*
nization of American Culture (1977; New York, 1988) and *Sensational Designs: The*
Cultural Work of American Fiction, 1790–1860 (New York, 1985), respectively, back to
the contrary views of Helen Waite Papashvily's study *All the Happy Endings: A Study*
of the Domestic Novel in America, the Women Who Wrote It, the Women Who Read It, in
the Nineteenth Century (New York, 1956) and Fiedler's *Love and Death in the Ameri-*
can Novel. Where Douglas emphasized the consumerist, anti-intellectual, and cooptive

In attempting to determine the degree to which American sentimental discourse makes a mockery of human agency or makes it possible, we have emphasized either Charlotte's demise or Rowson's success without acknowledging the mutual indebtedness of both constructs. But whichever extreme one tends to, all seem to agree that sentimentalism, with its twin emphases on subjective affect and social sanction, exists at the crux between institution and individual and works to reconcile a seemingly isolated and usually female subject to a systemic structure that can alternatively support or destroy her. The more sophisticated our grasp of this "tension . . . between relations of sympathy and relations of power" becomes, the more nuanced does our ability to grasp the seemingly oxymoronic means by which agency and submission, autonomy and subjection, choice and mechanism cohere into a single, if unstable, whole.[32]

Key to our increasing ability to grasp the seemingly incommensurate roles of accommodation and subversion is an awareness of the role of pleasure in sentimentalist discourse, both for character and reader. Appropriately, this is often a guilty pleasure, but it nonetheless, as Marianne Noble suggests, is paramount to the manner by which sentimentalism both caters to and finds room within patriarchal discourses of female self-diminution.[33]

---

nature of American sentimentalist discourse, Tompkins found in it a challenge to prevailing gender norms and political complacency.

32. Shirley Samuels, ed., *The Culture of Sentiment: Race, Gender, and Sentimentality in Nineteenth-Century America* (New York, 1992), 6, 8. Two works—Mary Chapman and Glenn Hendler, eds., *Sentimental Men: Masculinity and the Politics of Affect in American Culture* (Berkeley, Calif., 1999), and Hendler, *Public Sentiments: Structures of Feeling in Nineteenth-Century American Literature* (Chapel Hill, N.C., 2001)—explore the importance of sentimentalism to such masculine structures as bachelorhood, fatherhood, the male poetic persona, male temperance, and African American constructions of public masculinity. In addition, another body of modern criticism, notably Julie Ellison's *Cato's Tears and the Making of Anglo-American Emotion* (Chicago, 1999), emphasizes sentimentalism's links to an eighteenth-century culture of male sensibility. The construction of female gender in American sentimental novels featuring female protagonists entails a corollary engagement with male gender, whether perceived as similarly vulnerable (see the fate-tossed and lovely young sailors in Rowson's many poems on seafaring, or the psychic distress experienced by Charlotte's unfortunate seducer, Lieutenant Montraville), set up in opposition to the essential frankness of the female heart (as in the true male villain of *Charlotte Temple,* Lieutenant Belcour), or posited as a salvific, paternal force (like Charlotte's father, who takes in her daughter, or the benevolent stranger who saves Meriel from prostitution in *Trials of the Human Heart*).

33. "Functioning both as a discursive agent for the proliferation of oppressive ideolo-

There could not be a more suitable frame within which to view the published works of Rowson, with her minute attention to the delicious agonies of female self-sacrifice as well as the anxious pleasures of subtle transgression, than that suggested by this critical shift from virtue to pleasure, from novel as unworkable conduct manual to novel as transcript of contorted subjectivity. Indeed, Rowson's published work is increasingly recognized for the narrative complexity that lurks within its aggressively approachable homilies. Moreover, the moments of outspoken radicalism in her plays, novels, lyrics, and textbooks offer us the opportunity to understand how such a shift can continue to acknowledge explicit calls to female autonomy that survive from her opus through that of successors such as Harriet Beecher Stowe (*Uncle Tom's Cabin; or, Life among the Lowly*), Fanny Fern *(Ruth Hall: A Domestic Tale of the Present Time)*, and Rebecca Harding Davis *(Life in the Iron Mills)*, despite wider evidence of "complicitous alignment" that these authors nonetheless exhibit.[34]

But to say that Rowson is recognized as an initiator of sentimental discourse in all its twisted glory is not to say that she has been made party to the revitalized discussion summarized above. In fact, none of the above-quoted works, most of which focus on the mid-nineteenth century, grant her serious attention. Yet she, and the decades she influenced and documented in myriad textual artifacts, is crucial to furthering our understanding of these terms and may offer a way through the thickets that threaten to entangle us even as they challenge us to move beyond a merely oppositional stance between subversion and accommodation. For there is a history to the vexed practice of pleasure in sentimentalist discourse—and that history begins with the twin invocation of didacticism and sensationalism that characterizes the early American novel.

------

gies and as a rhetorical tool for the exploration of female desire," this literature "enabled women to wield power through complicitous alignment with hegemonic ideologies" (Marianne Noble, *The Masochistic Pleasures of Sentimental Literature* [Princeton, N.J., 2000], 4–6, 11). See also Suzanne Clark, *Sentimental Modernism: Women Writers and the Revolution of the Word* (Bloomington, Ind., 1991), 2, 7: "If [the sentimental] calls up literary history, it also calls up the repressed involvement of literature with power—literature as a rhetorical instrument, literature used in the interests of economy and politics, literature as locus of pleasure and transgression. . . . The degradation of sentimental writing . . . has covered over the transgressive content of the sentimental, its connection to a sexual body, and its connection to the representations of consciousness." "Pleasure" may also be conceived of as one aspect of the "bodily response" that Ellison identifies as integral to the nonetheless "social phenomenon" of emotion (*Cato's Tears,* 5).

34. Noble, *Masochistic Pleasures,* 11.

Rowson, like every other novelist of her day, insisted that she wrote to teach. As any conservative critic of her time was happy to note, however, the problem of attributing a normative function to the seduction novel—of which *Charlotte Temple* is considered an archetype—is that the novel's "seducing arguments" introduce the very behavior they seemingly proscribe. The text's "thou shalt not" is followed by a verb, leaving readers with a clearer mental image—some would say a playbook—for how to partake of forbidden pleasures than they had before they thought about what not to do. This is the problem of American letters at least since Jonathan Edwards's "Bad Book Case," where he warned of the lewdness contained within a seventeenth-century midwifery manual and thereby elevated it to the status of pornography—and it continues into readings of the sentimental that attempt to sift its normative and mimetic functions into sedimentary layers. Does the novel teach or merely thrill? If it teaches, does it educate readers to rebel (by imitating the ungodly pleasures of the text) or to conform (by avoiding them)? A third possibility is only beginning to be studied: that the novel of seduction, and the nineteenth-century American sentimental novel that followed from it, might teach precisely by thrilling; that the pleasures of the text might educate without severing the reader from the social fabric. The novel's sensationalist register complicates its didactic function, inviting us to acknowledge the limited applicability of its most prescriptive dicta. But such knowledge may be more "useful," to employ one of Rowson's favorite words, than any simpler formula that, although seemingly more solid, is too brittle to withstand the vagaries of everyday experience. In examining Rowsonian narrative's elaboration of, and potential invitation to, seemingly forbidden behaviors, this book emphasizes the productive interaction, as opposed to mere canceling out, of its proscriptive and descriptive registers. In the words of another critic of the sentimental, Rowsonian narrative manages both to "inscribe authority" and "free up wayward feeling," and it could not do one without the other.[35]

35. Davidson summarizes the early national critical estimation of novels as a "licentious form of literature" in *Revolution and the Word,* 8, 43. The assumption that reading should foster any alteration in behavior during this period is itself a highly contentious one. Critics such as Catherine Kerrison emphasize the similarity of novels to conduct literature in order to suggest that novels were written and read with the explicit aim of giving and getting behavioral advice (Kerrison, "By the Book: Eliza Ambler, Brent Carrington, and Conduct Literature in Late Eighteenth-Century Virginia," *Virginia Magazine of History and Biography,* CV [1997], 27–52). Others, such as Laurel Thatcher Ulrich, emphasize the disparity between the fatal effects of seduction on fictional characters and the acceptance accorded their real-world counterparts (Ulrich, *A*

"And All Truly because I Am an Englishwoman"

Rowson loved Americans, but she never claimed to be one. In fact, she capitalized on her status as a perennial exile, and as we will see ahead, her writing during her time in the United States further complicates American national sentiment with every patriotic huzzah. Her later works thus stand as a testament to modern attempts to liberate early American studies from a tendency toward nationalist isolationism. The corrections have been of two kinds. At the level of the nation itself, scholars have challenged criticism's location of "the cultivation of indigenous production within an enclosed American field," suggesting rather that "the 'national' imaginary depends upon peoples beyond the enclosure it seeks to make immanent." In addition, many have begun to see the domestic realm, often figured as a national microcosm, as not only part of the national public sphere but as crucial to the latter's self-figuration in relation to a global economy, considering "narratives of domesticity and female subjectivity as inseparable from narratives of empire and nation building."[36]

Midwife's Tale: The Life of Martha Ballard, Based on Her Diary, 1785–1812 [New York, 1990], 145–160). For historical analysis of changing patterns of sexuality in America, see John D'Emilio and Estelle B. Freedman, *Intimate Matters: A History of Sexuality in America,* 2d ed. (Chicago, 1997); Godbeer, *Sexual Revolution;* and Clare A. Lyons, *Sex among the Rabble: An Intimate History of Gender and Power in the Age of Revolution, Philadelphia, 1730–1830* (Chapel Hill, N.C., 2006). See also Jonathan Edwards, "The Bad Book Case" (1744), in John E. Smith, Harry S. Stout, and Kenneth P. Minkema, eds., *A Jonathan Edwards Reader* (New Haven, Conn., 1995), 172–178. Richard H. Brodhead describes the interdependence as follows: "We do not grasp the nature of [antebellum domestic fiction's] literary action until we see that these opposed functions are not just mixed but functionally cooperative in these books: that they not only free up wayward feeling *and* inscribe authority in the reader but inscribe authority by way of the feeling they invite" (Brodhead, *Cultures of Letters: Scenes of Reading and Writing in Nineteenth-Century America* [Chicago, 1993], 47). Despite claims of "functional cooperation," however, Brodhead still views feeling as the means to, or "by way of," authority's end, or "inscription." In Chapter 5, I suggest that authority may not possess even this advantage.

36. "You no doubt have seen by the newspapers that the scribblers have made my work a subject to exercise their wits upon, some for, some against, and all truly because I am an Englishwoman, and yet have an unaccountable affection for America and all that appertains thereunto. Why, my dear cousin, do they imagine English people devoid of gratitude or sensibility, I think them bound to forget friendships formed, or benefits because, forsooth, the two nations do not agree in political concerns. Beshrew them, I say for so narrow an idea, for my part I will love and respect virtue wherever I find it, will never forget my friends, tho' we may not perhaps in every thing think exactly alike"

This book builds on these increasingly sophisticated interrogations of the interdependence of domestic ideology with other institutions, from state to marketplace to nation, that both defined themselves against it and drew from it. At the same time, this study emphasizes that, during the period Rowson wrote for an American public, "domesticity and female subjectivity"—which for many possess a metonymic if not a synonymous relationship—were only just beginning to serve as figures for one another in the dominant cultural imaginary. In emphasizing attitudinal and behavioral modes such as deference and self-interest over the implicitly spatial imagery of private and public "spheres," we begin to recover a moment before the ideological triumph of a fetishized domestic feminine realm had taken place.[37]

If Rowson's work as a whole helps us come to terms with post-Revolutionary America's often antagonistic commitments to deferential restraint and self-interested experimentation in the performance of Anglo-American female selfhood, the development of her writings between her return to the United States and her death some thirty years later allows us to witness the shifting nature of the resultant compromises, especially as they affected literate white women at the turn of the nineteenth century. In order to understand this temporal development, we must shift our initial focus from the chronological (Rowson's work as a prefiguring of later sentimental modes) to the geographic (her status as a transatlantic figure). For it is primarily by attending to the transatlantic history of two related phenomena, sociability and sensibility, that we can recognize how early American sentimentalism changed from a narrative mode concerned primarily with individual female rectitude to one that represented female subjects embedded in social contexts. If Rowson's first work to be published in America supports the definition of literary sentimentalism as something that "produc[es] sociability as a value through its absence," her work con-

<hr>

(Susanna Rowson to Anthony Haswell, May 21, 1795, Rowson Papers, MSS 7379-c, box 1, folder 38).

37. Elizabeth Maddock Dillon, "Slaves in Algiers: Race, Republican Genealogies, and the Global Stage," *American Literary History,* XVI (2004), 407–436, esp. 407; Amy Kaplan, "Manifest Domesticity," in Cathy N. Davidson and Jessamyn Hatcher, eds., *No More Separate Spheres!* (Durham, N.C., 2002), 183–208, esp. 186. In the passage excerpted above, Lawrence E. Klein summarizes the tendency toward historical anachronism identified here, which will be further explored in my last chapter: "The a priori commitment to the publicity of men and the privacy of women is an example of the way in which the concerns of analysts of the nineteenth century are imposed on the eighteenth century" (Klein, "Gender and the Public/Private Distinction," *Eighteenth-Century Studies,* XXIX [1995], 105).

ceived after her arrival in the United States makes it ever more possible to support the idea that "to be sentimental was to experience refined emotions through the medium of social exchange."[38]

As sociability became an increasing focus of Rowson's work, her protagonists negotiated ever newer and more productive reconciliations of autonomy and submission. Where Charlotte Temple found and gave solace only in a premature demise, her orphan daughter came into print posthumously to both mother and author to live a long life of civic altruism and influence, sacrificing only her sexuality in the bargain. Between these two poles of Rowson's American publishing career, she employed everything including her personal dress (always immaculate, despite her "ungraceful" figure), the walls of her school (covered with improving mottoes), and myriad forms of publication and performance to demonstrate that conformity can be employed to autonomous ends. Deriving autonomy from submission and, conversely, experiencing autonomy without antagonizing authority unduly, Rowson's life and texts both informed and bespoke a historical and geographical moment in which the competing demands of self-formation and self-regulation not only occurred on personal, social, and political planes but were the very stuff of their as-yet-unspecified linkages. Indeed, one might say that sentimentalism itself, with its tendency to articulate institutional effects through personal affect, constituted one such linkage, making Rowson essential to our understanding of both the most micrological and macrological power structures of the era.

A related way to phrase the interdependence of autonomy and submission during this period is to recognize that, at both extremes of Rowson's literary opus—the isolated Charlotte and the never-alone Lucy—individuality is constructed, not as an alternative to or refuge from social interaction, but as something that is only possible in relation to it. Gillian Russell and Clara Tuite call this "the public and socially oriented production of the individual . . . the individual not as an isolate, but as a socially recognized entity who is required to *perform* his or her individuality within a repertoire of codes and modes of affect." Charlotte's failure to *be* anybody (how many students have complained of her wishy-washy personality?) is thus comprehensible as a result of her isolation.[39]

38. Gillian Russell and Clara Tuite, eds., *Romantic Sociability: Social Networks and Literary Culture in Britain, 1770–1840* (Cambridge, 2002), 6; Teute, "Roman Matron," in Kennon, ed., *Republic for the Ages,* 107.

39. Russell and Tuite, eds., *Romantic Sociability,* 9, citing the work of Niklas Luhmann.

Rowson early demonstrated her capacity to reconcile seemingly intransigent cultural modes in her canny employment of sentimentalism's sensationalist and didactic registers. She developed this ability in her subsequent considerations of how women were to form part of the American nation. These later works were written on American soil, with Rowson in full awareness of her vulnerability as an English expatriate and loyalist's daughter. Given Rowson's ever tenuous position within the social hierarchy she advanced through, it makes sense that her emphasis shifted, as she aged, from fascination with the female subject in isolation to more explicit consideration of her civic roles. It is also fitting that she would turn from novels, typically consumed in much-lamented, much-celebrated isolation, to plays, songs, textbooks, and other, more expressly public forms of entertainment (attending a play, singing in a tavern, reading aloud in a schoolroom).[40]

Finally, to understand how Rowson wrote about women in relation to their communities, it is necessary to understand sentimentalism, here figured as a cultural mode whose dominant moment occurred in the nineteenth-century United States, in relation to sensibility, here associated with the transatlantic eighteenth century. Indeed, it is precisely because Rowson occupies both paradigms, as a transatlantic figure who served to usher in the American sentimental moment, that she is crucial to our understanding of how the transatlantic context of eighteenth-century sensibility informed the American nineteenth century in ways that current scholarly attention to a rather insular, if influential, set of nineteenth-century ur-sentimental novels can obscure.[41]

40. On Rowson's precarious stance between loyalist and patriotic affiliations, see chap. 3 of Julie Pal's "In the Hands of Savages: Representations of Female Barbary Captivity in Anglo-American Narratives, 1722–1818" (Ph.D. diss., University of Virginia, 2005), esp. 127–135. On the public and private valences of novel-reading during this period, see John Mullan, *Sentiment and Sociability: The Language of Feeling in the Eighteenth Century* (New York, 1990), 13–14.

41. Precisely because these words appear together so often, their differentiation remains murky. In his 1823 critique of Rousseau, for instance, Robert Southey considered classes of people to be "sentimental" if they possessed "an ardent and morbid sensibility" (cited in Mark Jefferson, "What Is Wrong with Sentimentality?" *Mind,* XCII [1983], 519–529, esp. 519). Given their relative instability, I choose to focus on the historical and cultural baggage they carry along with them—to define each contextually and by accretion rather than seek a stable and uniform distinction between them. In this, I share Markman Ellis's view:

the terms "sensibility" and "sentimental" denote a complex field of meanings and connotations in the late eighteenth century, overlapping and coinciding to such

In broad strokes, I will suggest two important distinctions here. First, although sensibility has its roots in medical discourse and was conceived initially as a susceptibility of the inarticulate body, sentimentalism refers first and foremost to a discursive mode. One simply cannot be sentimental without an audience, even if that audience is at an unreachable remove (say, the reader of a text in which a forlorn young woman awaits her treacherous lover). Second, although sensibility came to be seen as a quality that pertained primarily to the upper classes, sentimentality, even before it became a term of potential insult, suggested democratic leanings. In order to understand how eighteenth-century British sensibility became nineteenth-century American sentimentalism, one must attend, above all, to how practices once restricted to a narrow social compass expanded to include all those with aspirations to middle-class respectability: the thousands who read *Charlotte Temple* or its sequel in their early American editions or the many who sent their daughters to the burgeoning numbers of female academies.[42]

Eighteenth-century sensibility was, at heart, deeply embedded in the parallel phenomena of sociability and gentility. By exhibiting sensibility, or a refined responsiveness to others, in the conversations that largely comprised sociability, an elite individual legitimized his or her claim to gentility, defined as behavior that demonstrated that one deserved one's wealth and social status—the transformation, if you will, of good fortune to perceived personal worth. If sensibility depended upon and enhanced sociability, then sociability, in turn, depended upon and advanced elite cohesion and distinction from the lower orders. This focus on genteel sociability followed sensibility across the Atlantic as it was practiced among prominent fami-

---

an extent as to offer no obvious distinction. . . . However, though sensibility and sentimental may not be separated, that is not because they share a single unitary meaning, but rather, they amalgamate and mix freely a large number of varied discourses.

Ellis, *The Politics of Sensibility: Race, Gender, and Commerce in the Sentimental Novel* (Cambridge, 1996), 7–8. See also Fred Kaplan, *Sacred Tears: Sentimentality in Victorian Literature* (Princeton, N.J., 1987); and Janet Todd, *Sensibility: An Introduction* (London, 1986).

42. On the medical basis of sensibility, see G. J. Barker-Benfield, *The Culture of Sensibility: Sex and Society in Eighteenth-Century Britain* (Chicago, 1992), xvii and chap. 1, and Mullan, *Sentiment and Sociability,* 16, and chap. 5. Both sentimentalism's inherent discursivity and its implicit egalitarianism are evident in Johann Christoph Friedrich von Schiller's definition of the naïve versus the sentimental. Schiller called his poetry (not himself) "sentimental" in comparison to Goethe's rarer, "naïve" genius. See his *Über naiv und sentimentalische Dichtung* (n.p., 1795).

lies in the salons and clubs of the nation's larger cities. But gentility met particular challenges in post-Revolutionary America, for it contradicted the precept "All men are created equal," even as it supported the structuring of the nation around the necessarily hierarchical project of maintaining and defending private property.[43]

In the preface to her novel *What is Gentility?* prominent early national figure Margaret Bayard Smith responds to these challenges. She states that gentility "is independent of birth, wealth, or condition, but . . . derived from that cultivation of mind which imparts elevation to sentiment and refine-ment to manners in whatever situation of life they may be found." As my choice of another female novelist suggests, the acts of disavowal necessary to render commitment to rank palatable with commitment to egalitarianism were particularly rich in female hands. Self-effacement was already a female virtue. The hostesses and politicians' wives of early national Philadelphia and Washington, D.C., found ways to exert public influence that actually depended on ascribed feminine skills of modesty and sympathy. Soliciting positions for favored relatives and acquaintances or determining who should be included in elite social affairs, where political maneuvering took place un-abated, national politicians' wives and daughters used their very exclusion from official political channels to advance in power and influence. That only elite women such as Bayard Smith herself have been shown to practice these skills, however, demonstrates the degree to which American gentility could have remained the privilege of a leisured few, were it not for the widen-ing reach of American sentimentalism. In fact, Jeffersonian Republicans' broader extension of the franchise to white males eroded even the limited influence this small minority of privileged early national women could ex-tend, as would be demonstrated by the Margaret Eaton affair early in the Jacksonian administration.[44]

43. See Mullan, *Sentiment and Sociability,* 4: "The novels of Samuel Richardson . . . envisage a responsive feminine sensibility as the best embodiment of social instinct." See also Lyons: "By the 1770s men of the elite and upper middle classes may have understood homoeroticism in the framework of acute sensibility. Sensibility stressed the importance of deep authentic emotional feeling and highlighted the importance of emotional expression in primary relationships" ("Mapping an Atlantic Sexual Culture," *WMQ,* 3d Ser., LX [2003], 151). On early national genteel sociability, see David S. Shields, *Civil Tongues and Polite Letters in British America* (Chapel Hill, N.C., 1997); Branson, *These Fiery Frenchified Dames,* chap. 4; Allgor, *Parlor Politics;* Teute, "Re-public of Intellect," in Barnard et al., eds., *Revising Charles Brockden Brown,* 149–181, and "Roman Matron," in Kennon, ed., *Republic for the Ages,* 89–121.

44. Margaret Bayard Smith, *What Is Gentility? A Moral Tale* (Washington, D.C.,

This foreclosure on elite women's political influence by the end of the 1790s might lead us to suspect that genteel sociability disappeared from the post-Revolutionary female arsenal. But Rowson's life and work tell a different story, in which lingering class pretensions gave way to an ever more thorough emphasis on deportment as the one and only correlative of female worth for an ever wider segment of the population. What Bayard Smith articulated in 1828, Rowson anticipated with increasing success in every new publication: a world wherein relentless attention to how one presented oneself not only demonstrated elite status but could actually bring it about. Thus, whereas Rowson's position as a British officer's daughter familiarized her with modes of polite interaction not readily available to the majority of American-born women, her absorption into the labor economy of the new nation allowed her to endorse the empowering possibilities of female sociability after her more socially prominent female contemporaries had found themselves pushed to the sidelines.[45]

In pursuing this course, Rowson remodeled gentility to accommodate contemporary emphases on self-sufficiency, industry, and frugality. She mocked "genteelly" educated misses in *Mentoria,* a novel based on her experiences as a governess in England and France, while providing an alternative standard of deportment in her own Newton, Massachusetts, academy sixteen years later. Not that her curriculum ignored the drawing, music, and dancing familiar to her former charges. In fact, it advertised its music teacher by name and noted that "the drawing will be taught . . . in a new

---

1828), 3; Allgor, *Parlor Politics,* esp. chap. 2 ("Dolley Madison Takes Command"), and chap. 3's discussion of Margaret Bayard Smith ("Washington Women in Public"). Margaret "Peggy" Eaton was a hotel keeper's daughter who married Jackson's proposed secretary of war, John Eaton, despite being scorned by other politicians' wives for her allegedly checkered sexual history. In an administration where female society was no longer integral to Washington politics, however, the techniques that had served these women so well in prior administrations backfired, as their attempts to snub her resulted in the dissolution of Jackson's first cabinet. See Allgor, chap. 5 ("The Fall of Andrew Jackson's Cabinet," 190–238); Andrew Burstein, *The Passions of Andrew Jackson* (New York, 2003), 173–180.

45. Compare, for instance, Bayard Smith and Rowson's responses to the foreclosure on the mixed-sex gatherings of the young that were commonplace in the early 1790s. In 1837, describing the activities of the Friendly Club, where she had met as a young woman for animated discourse with male and female companions, Bayard Smith fabricated betrothals for four participants, so as not to sully the women's reputations. Rowson, on the other hand, emphasized the benefits of homosocial fellowship, both by running a girls' school and by writing novels *(Lucy Temple)* and didactic texts *(A Present for Young Ladies)* that focused on female accomplishments and same-sex sociality.

and superior style, Mrs. Rowson having received instructions lately for that purpose from a professed master of the art." But next to the pencils stood a "Terrestrial Globe," and through it all, Rowson assured her prospective students (and their parents), "Every attention will be paid to their manners, morals and improvement."[46]

Rowson bridged the disparities inherent to American gentility along two primary axes: she was both English (by birth) and American (by residence), and she was both from an elite background and dependent upon her own labor for economic survival. As a British lieutenant's, then captain's, daughter, with a bequest from her paternal grandfather, Rowson hailed from the early Republic's protoaristocracy. As part of a family that lost all its property in the Revolution, however, she did not have the opportunity to remain in the echelon sketched out by historians of elite American female sociability. Although she might have behaved appropriately had she been welcome in the salons of New York and Washington, she was not to have the opportunity. By the same token, her skills, developed under economic duress, outlived those premised on homogeneous and leisured communities. Indeed, not only did Rowson survive the democratization of American genteel sociability, but she taught her readers how to partake of what was left of it. She adapted it to a democratic readership that spanned multiple stations: the Louisas of the world as well as the Montgomery sisters. She was both vernacular and genteel, and she helped her readers reconcile these modes, teaching young women such as Louisa to adapt the pursuit of self-interest and personal satisfaction (say, by a frank discussion of Federalist and Republican party wrangling) to accountability to existing authorities (say, one's father).[47]

46. Rowson, *Mentoria,* II, 86; *Columbian Centinel. Massachusetts Federalist* (Boston), Apr. 15, 1807.

47. In the autobiographical preface to *Trials of the Human Heart,* Rowson explains that "a variety of painful circumstances . . . contributed to deprive me of a decent independence inherited from my paternal grandfather" (xix). According to a former student, Rowson "should have inherited a handsome fortune on her mother's side—but her Grandfather, neglecting to make his will, the male heir in accordance with the English law inherited it. From her Grandfather Haswell she received a small patrimony, which she resigned to liquidate her Father's debts, and became a private Governess in a family with whom she traveled into France." See Mrs. Spoffort to Elias Nason, Aug. 25, 1859, ibid. Clearly, Rowson knew in very personal ways the effects patriarchal property laws could have on individual women. Denied one inheritance by the English tendency to favor the male heir, she sacrificed another, more modest one in order to prop up the male progenitor who could no longer support her. Even when she first went to work, it was to

How did Rowson render this model accessible to her many readers who had never been inside a salon, let alone conversed with the Prince of Wales? She did so not only through her writings and, later, her teachings but also through her literal self-presentation. Contemporaries of Rowson frequently commented on her immaculate dress and deportment. One called her "dignified, staid, formal and matronly. Slow and correct in speech. Of an inelegant and clumsy form; but stylish and tasteful in dress." Another wrote, "She was large or rather stout, far from tall, with a fine intelligent face—with fine expressive grey eyes, her manners always dignified and elegant, indeed she never forgot the lady." Mrs. Rowson might not have been handsome, but she spoke carefully and dressed well. She might not have been happily married, but she maintained a pleasant demeanor to her husband in company. And her students adored her—but, to a one, they remembered the strictness with which she enforced good manners.[48]

Such acts of self-modulation, though minor in the particulars, as a whole were of nothing less than revolutionary import. If self-presentation was a studied art with her, the importance of the endeavor lay in its capacity to approximate self-determination. Behind every monitory or admonitory act lay a deep belief in the enhanced ability to improve one's own station such self-inspection assured those who never let down their guard. And although such constant self-monitoring may not strike us as exactly what we mean by freedom, the opportunity to influence one's own outcome to even a limited degree was no small matter to the women Rowson influenced during her lifetime.

———

support her father's family. Vail noted that Rowson "secured a belated pension for her father" from the Prince of Wales. See Vail, "Susanna Haswell Rowson," in American Antiquarian Society, *Proceedings,* XLII, part 1, 50.

48. In his study of Samuel Richardson, David Hume, and Laurence Sterne, Mullan writes of how "the conception of harmonious sociability was dramatized not only in the books they produced but also in their self-conscious efforts actually to live out models of social being" (Mullan, *Sentiment and Sociability,* 2). See also "Description of Susanna Rowson by Mr. Lord," n.d., Rowson Papers, MSS 7379-c, box 1, folder 57; Mrs. Spofford to Elias Nason, Aug. 25, 1859, ibid., folder 87. A former student provides more details about Susanna Rowson's "personal appearance": "I think her eyes were brown, and her hair almost if not quite black. I remember that she wore dark striped and black silk dresses frequently" ([Nancy?] to ["my dear Sister"], Jan. 23, 1860, ibid., folder 84). A former editor, citing his age (eighty-two), proves less helpful: "I remember Mrs. Rowson perfectly well—but I have entirely forgot all about her" ("Mr. Gilbert [former editor of the *Boston Weekly Magazine*] regarding Susanna Rowson," [Aug. 18], 1859, ibid., folder 77).

An Orphan's Legacy

Rowson's interest in representing women, and engendering readers, capable of triumphing over oppressive circumstance did not emerge fully formed with her first adult step on American soil. In fact, we might see the development of her literary productions throughout the 1790s and early 1800s as a series of experiments in the reconciliation of "the capacity for tender feeling" with the ability to influence others. From Charlotte Temple's suicidal passivity (in 1791) to Lucy Temple's lifesaving decision to enter the teaching profession (in 1824), Rowson's opus continually builds upon the premise that authority may be wrested from post-Revolutionary norms of female citizenship, even as her conservative political affiliations intensified. A revolution in the function of affect accompanies this development: from a potentially disruptive force that alienates Charlotte from all who know her and provides the reader no real means of succor to a disciplinary mode allowing social connections to be formed that create a setting for the exertion of genteel moral influence.[49]

Chapter 1 provides a revisionary reading of the first of these experiments, *Charlotte Temple*. Charlotte, I argue, does not so much fail to resist her impulses as fail to find them. She is almost unable to feel, and when she does, she tends to discount her sensations. Respondents within and without the text, in turn, experience her untimely death only as repetitive and irresolvable longing. In a contemporary setting that increasingly tolerated premarital sexual activity, the novel's American readers recognized that her tale contained a warning beyond its surface call to libidinal restraint, having to do with a crisis of bourgeois female agency that transcended national borders. But *Charlotte* never quite answered the question of how to convert the sense of malaise it generated into any kind of communion or productive action. In different ways, every subsequent major Rowson publication attempted to correct this oversight.

One way to understand Rowson's developing ability to negotiate livable environments for her female protagonists is to think of her fiction as ever more approximating her own self-representation in the United States. From isolation to extensive social networks; from dependence on economic inheritance to laboring economic self-sufficiency; and, most important, from passivity to performative, if not self-formative, abilities—these are the changes Rowson both lived through and wrote into the public record of Anglo-American women's experience in the decades surrounding the turn

49. Solomon, *In Defense of Sentimentality*, 4.

of the nineteenth century. Chapter 2 discusses how, in everything from her physical self-presentation to her letters, her autobiographical prefaces, and her onstage rhetorical flourishes, Rowson performed a canny response to, and anticipation of, the critical establishment's somewhat dubious appraisal of her, fashioning a representative personality that invited greater tolerance both for women and for postwar English immigrants.

Chapter 3 returns to Rowson's fiction to demonstrate how her first novel to be initially published on American soil, the fascinating commercial failure *Trials of the Human Heart,* further extends the range of behavioral opportunities available to its readers by operating as a tonic of sorts to *Charlotte Temple.* Where Charlotte moved only under duress, Meriel Howard cannot sit still. In depicting her endless movement, *Trials of the Human Heart* portrays a heroine who violates nearly every social dictum familiar to young republican women without any lasting ill consequence. And if the conventional rewards her efforts bring her (a handsome, doting husband and a big house) ring slightly hollow after the adventures that precede them, they nevertheless validate the transgressive activities they put an end to, demonstrating the author's dawning insistence on articulating a wider range of subjective poses and social modes for female figures within and without the text.

Chapter 4 adds a new element to the capacity for productive response to female subjection: namely, the ability to work in concert. I address Rowson narratives that propose and/or instantiate an explicitly political public role for women. Where Meriel wandered alone from dastardly father to shiftless mate, the female captives of Rowson's play *Slaves in Algiers; or, A Struggle for Freedom,* one of several texts discussed in this chapter, work together to free themselves from the shackles of patriarchal self-interest that weighed down poor Charlotte. Yet the women's primary weapon remains proffered self-sacrifice, and their right not to act on their offer is assured by a moral, racial, and religious hierarchy that provides Muslim North Africans as the surrogates that allow Anglo-Christian femininity to emerge unscathed. As Rowson's own social fortunes improved, the relationship between the political subject matter of her work (its intervention in contemporary affairs of state) and its gender politics developed in startling ways.

As the founder of Mrs. Rowson's Young Ladies' Academy, Rowson continued to refine a sentimental pedagogy in which the cultivation of affect fostered disciplinary allegiance that provided women opportunities for genteel social connection. Rowson's final novel, the focus of Chapter 5, emerged from this world to redeem Charlotte by explaining the fate of her orphan. In that Lucy (like Rowson) sprang from her mother's loins only to grow up motherless, *Lucy Temple* represents the opportunity to honor Charlotte's misfortune by breaking with the past. Lucy learns to exert authority where her mother only suffered its consequences. Yet Lucy's authority is never cruel: it functions by making people want what is best for them. As she dedicates her days to instructing those about her in the art of charitable intervention, her mother seems from as distant a world as Charlotte's own mother, in her muslin cap, linen gown, and lawn handkerchief, once did from her.[50]

But where the family resemblances might have been slight, that between Lucy and her authorial progenitor is almost uncanny. If *Charlotte Temple* was difficult to fathom as Rowson's creation, *Lucy Temple* shared her circumstances of birth, her career, her dedication to charity, and even a version of her marital infelicity. Both figures subsumed their personal losses into a deep and abiding commitment to an extensive social connection born of their educational and charitable enterprises.

This fate might not have been either author or protagonist's first choice. In fact, both might have set out, like Charlotte, to satisfy a notion of female value and identity based on marital connection—the notion most prevalent in their respective environments. But when this path of least resistance didn't pan out, they devised an alternative subsistence from the materials left lying about. That their constructions bring satisfactions unavailable to those of Rowson's female readers whose own life courses followed more directly from the familial and domestic imperatives denied these two women, is evident from the many lives they touch. Nevertheless, that these constructions are makeshift adaptations to untenable circumstance remains legible in the losses both recount as a failure of intimacy.

As Rowson ended her publications with a return to her most famous literary surname, this, too, is a book of returns: author to childhood locale, daughter to parent *(Charlotte Temple),* lover to first love *(Trials of the Human Heart),* captive to freedom *(Slaves in Algiers),* and schoolgirl to schoolroom *(Lucy Temple).* Encompassing all these, this work explores Rowson's second and final landing on the Eastern Seaboard as it brought many an American daughter from the shores of perceived victimhood to active involvement in the life of the young nation. But in every return, something remains unfinished. Thirteen colonies are now a tenuous nation-state torn between competing partisan interests. The expatriate author, outspoken patriot yet ever the loyalist's offspring, remains poised between two bickering empires. Wayward daughter Charlotte greets her father only to die, depriving him

50. Rowson, *Charlotte Temple,* ed. Davidson, 13.

of a longed-for reunion and offering in her place only a surrogate version of herself as an as-yet-uncorrupted infant. Lifelong itinerant Meriel, at last in possession of both king and castle, cannot resist inviting a distant friend to take up the journey she has put down. The boldest freed captive in Algiers chooses to remain behind in implicit bondage to her father. And young Lucy returns to the classroom as an instructor, longing for an intimacy no longer available to her in the spontaneous exchanges of her students. Betrayed once by her father's abandonment of her mother, Lucy seems destined to exist in a state of unconsummated longing. Even in her seeming near-content, then, persists for the reader a note of caution.

But against what? Chapter 1 poses that question in the form of a contemporary reader's scrawl.

1

WHAT'S WRONG WITH
Charlotte Temple?

Nothing is so liable to drive a woman to a second error as
her being subject to continual reproach for the first.
— *Susanna Rowson,* The Inquisitor; or, Invisible Rambler

At first glance, it seems self-evident what Eliza Netterville meant when she scrawled "Virgins take a warning" across the last page of her 1808 copy of *Charlotte Temple.* She had got the message: if a young lady doesn't wish to end up like Charlotte or her malicious undoer Mademoiselle La Rue, she mustn't have sexual intercourse before she gets married. A seduction novel has made its cardinal point, and a contemporary reader has been forewarned.[1]

The ease with which we reduce this inscription to its most obvious interpretation, however—and with it, the novel itself—should be cause for suspicion. Although there is no doubt that *Charlotte Temple,* along with myriad other popular novels and magazine tales of the period, made much of female chastity, mostly by documenting the fall from grace of an insufficiently cautious young woman destined to abandonment and premature death after giving birth to a bastard child, it is incorrect to assume that readers attended to these tropes for their literal meaning alone or even primarily. First of all,

---

1. *Charlotte: A Tale of Truth* was first published in England in 1791 by Minerva Press. The 1794 American edition was published in Philadelphia. See Susanna Rowson, *The Inquisitor; or, Invisible Rambler* (Philadelphia, 1793), 41; Rowson, *Charlotte: A Tale of Truth,* 2 vols. (London, 1791); *Charlotte: A Tale of Truth,* 2 vols. (Philadelphia, 1794); *Charlotte Temple: A Tale of Truth . . . ,* 3d American ed. (Philadelphia, 1797). Two editions of the novel are currently in print: *Charlotte Temple,* ed. Cathy N. Davidson (New York, 1986); and *Charlotte Temple and Lucy Temple,* ed. Ann Douglas (New York, 1991). A Norton Critical Edition edited by Marion Rust is forthcoming. On the history of *Charlotte Temple's* American reception, see Davidson's "Life and Times of Charlotte Temple: The Biography of a Book," in Davidson, ed., *Reading in America: Literature and Social History* (Baltimore, 1989), 157–179. Following a moderate reception in England, *Charlotte Temple* went through more than two hundred American editions after Mathew Carey first published it.

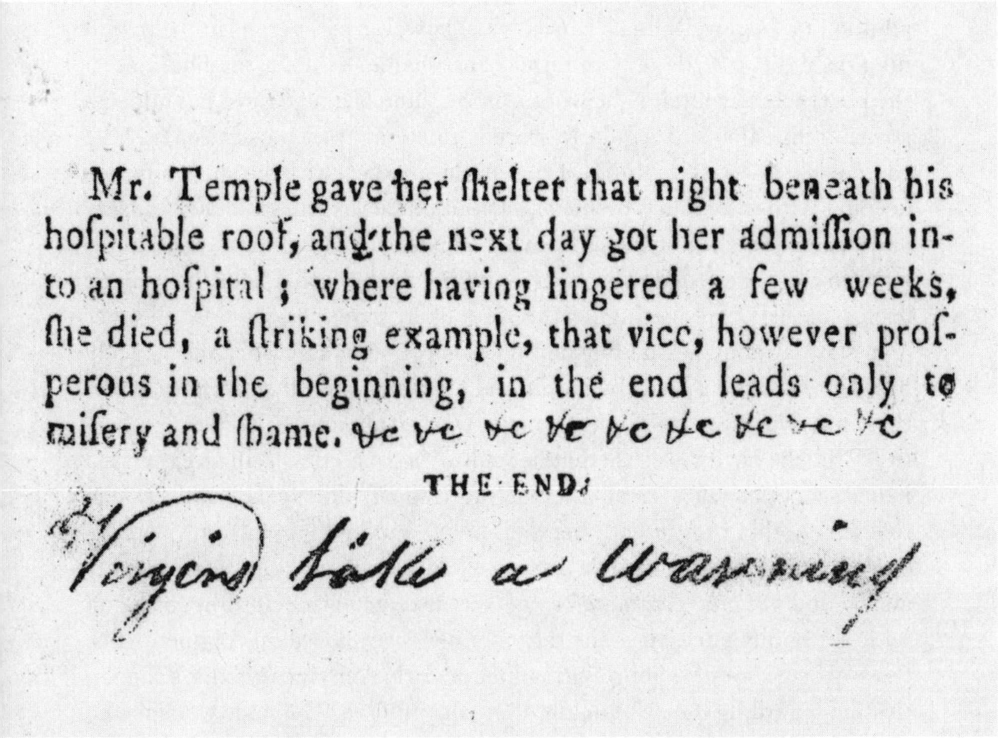

Mr. Temple gave her shelter that night beneath his hospitable roof, and the next day got her admission into an hospital ; where having lingered a few weeks, she died, a striking example, that vice, however prosperous in the beginning, in the end leads only to misery and shame. *ve ve ve ve ve ve ve ve ve*

THE END.

Virgins take a Warning

PLATE 9. *Eliza Netterville's marginalia. From Rowson,* The History of Charlotte Temple: A Tale of Truth *(Philadelphia, 1808). PS2736.R3C5, Clifton Waller Barrett Library of American Literature, Special Collections, University of Virginia Library*

a screed on the importance of female sexual restraint did not speak to the immediate circumstances of a woman like Eliza Netterville, since turn-of-the-century Philadelphia was remarkable for increasing tolerance of unmarried, and in particular premarital, sex. Second, and perhaps more important, Eliza did not consider reading itself to be a matter of mere passive absorption. If we examine her inscription more closely, it becomes clear that she was far more prone to critique than she was to docile indoctrination.[2]

2. On sexual tolerance in early national Philadelphia, see Richard Godbeer, *Sexual Revolution in Early America* (Baltimore, Md., 2002), 257, 300; Clare A. Lyons, "Mapping an Atlantic Sexual Culture: Homoeroticism in Eighteenth-Century Philadelphia," *William and Mary Quarterly,* 3d Ser., LX (2003), 119–154. In addition to *Charlotte Temple,* the most influential seduction novels written by residents of the United States before 1800 were William Hill Brown's *Power of Sympathy* (Boston, 1789) and Hannah Foster's *Coquette* (Boston, 1797), both of which fictionalize the case of the historical

Indeed, another look at the handwriting on the page reveals a disquieting addition to the novel's final clause ("vice, however prosperous in the beginning, in the end leads only to misery and shame"). Along the final line of the page, which contains the words "misery and shame," Eliza has added a string of nine tiny and regularly spaced "etceteras" (see illustration). These could mean at least two things. Eliza might merely have been suggesting, in keeping with the explicit theme of retribution for lost chastity, that "misery and shame" were euphemisms for what female "vice" (nonmarital sex) really leads to—unsanctioned pregnancy—and polite abstractions for the somatic grotesqueries of a lingering death. More likely, however, she describes her own state of mind as she finished the book: bored, sarcastic, and vaguely hostile, to the point that the monitorial lecturing was all starting to sound the same. Was Netterville tired of being warned about her all-precious chastity? Did she have the sense that her culture's concern with it, as expressed in one seduction tale after another, betrayed some other agenda entirely, one that had nothing to do with her well-being and everything to do with its exploitation of her for its own purposes? In fact, this reader was probably angry; and not only *Charlotte Temple* but also the entire cultural obsession with her bodily purity was the target of her rage. Based on comments like these, we need to start appreciating literate early American women's sophistication regarding the print matter they encountered. The same women who enjoyed novels with no more than a nod to the ministers and newspaper pundits who lamented such fare's potential to corrupt the unsuspecting treated the fictional tales themselves with well-deserved skepticism.

Charlotte Temple not only invites this response but also anticipates it by calling into question its own emphasis on histrionic displays of female defilement. In its American republication in particular, *Charlotte Temple* invokes

---

figure Elizabeth Whitman. In *Intricate Relations: Sexual and Economic Desire in American Fiction, 1789–1814* (Iowa City, 2004), Karen Weyler demonstrates the complementarity of Elizabeth Barnes's, Cathy N. Davidson's, and Julia A. Stern's analyses of the major seduction novels of the period. Leonard Tennenhouse surveys seduction stories published in early national magazines, whereas Susan Branson assesses how these magazines treated the topics of gender and female fiction-reading (Barnes, *States of Sympathy: Seduction and Democracy in the American Novel* [New York, 1997]; Davidson, *Revolution and the Word: The Rise of the Novel in America* [1986; New York, 2004]; Stern, *The Plight of Feeling: Sympathy and Dissent in the Early American Novel* [Chicago, 1997]; Tennenhouse, "Libertine America," *Differences: A Journal of Feminist Cultural Studies,* XI, no. 3 [Fall 1999–2000], 1–28; Branson, *These Fiery Frenchified Dames: Women and Political Culture in Early National Philadelphia* [Philadelphia, 2001]).

the well-known architecture of the seduction novel in order to articulate a unique set of concerns for the self-aware female reader. By getting angry at this novel, Netterville was letting it do its job: awakening her to her own dissatisfaction with the limited arena in which her powers of choice and selection were seen to operate. "Virgins take a warning," then, was sarcastic, but it was not only so. The question is, what *was* being warned against, if not premarital sex?

By 1790, American prodigal sons are welcomed back into the fold with new appreciation. A son who disappears and then returns to law-abiding society is considered to possess new, special understanding unavailable to one who has never left. Jay Fliegelman has written about the late-eighteenth-century Anglo-American "adaptation and secularization of the Puritan narrative of the fortunate fall," by which "God had 'allowed' Adam and Eve to fall to permit them eventually to return to an even more intimate relationship with their Father than that they had originally lost." In this post-Revolutionary renaissance of a Puritan standard, the plot remains essentially the same, but shifts in emphasis give it a distinct significance reflecting contemporary sensibilities. One crucial difference in its post-Revolutionary revisitation is an emphasis on the self that in some sense chooses to return, rather than the God that allows the fall.[3]

This early national emphasis on man's individual, as well as political, capacity for self-determination cannot be overestimated for its impact on a culture once schooled in Calvinist doctrines of original sin, sanctification, and justification. John Locke had already countered the notion of inherent depravity with his challenge to the notion of "innate principles" and his observation that "ideas . . . imprint themselves" on the memory of a child, and later an adult, through "sensation" and "reflection." Benjamin Franklin took this challenge a step further in his *Autobiography* (first published in English in 1793) by suggesting that even misbehavior during one's own life can be re-"imprinted." Franklin's approach is best summarized in his use of the term "errata" to refer to moral trespasses. An erratum is a printer's error, especially one noted on a list of corrections inserted in a subsequent print-ing made from unchanged plates. If one considers human fault as a form of erratum, it means we can rectify our mistakes and make up for our failings. As Fliegelman has argued, Franklin's *Autobiography* gives voice to the early national belief that a prodigal son who has corrected himself is more valu-

3. Jay Fliegelman, *Prodigals and Pilgrims: The American Revolution against Patri-archal Authority, 1750–1800* (Cambridge, 1982), 83.

able as a testament to self-improvement than would be one who had never failed.[4]

If Franklin's report of a prodigal son returned exemplifies the young nation's dawning cultural emphasis on man's capacity to learn, and hence to benefit, from his mistakes, it also refers, not to the youth of mankind, but to young men alone. Franklin hardly mentioned women in the *Autobiography,* and elsewhere he used them mostly to illustrate lessons for his implicitly male readers. (See, for instance, "Advice to a Friend on Choosing a Mistress," which explains why an old woman makes a better sexual partner than a young one.) Why are women relatively absent from the *Autobiography?* Likely because pregnancy gives the lie to Franklin's faith in the capacity of the human self to direct its own development. Illicit sexual activity may, for a man, be simply another printer's mistake. A man who impregnates a woman bears no tangible mark of the experience, except possibly venereal disease. But an impregnated woman bears a mark that can be erased only at great physical and emotional cost. Pregnancy is a uniquely tangible sign of past activity; it can't be "corrected" without leaving record of itself. Unsanctioned pregnancy thus threatened the optimism of a newly developing cultural ethos that emphasized man's aptitude for self-direction. Prodigal daughters were correspondingly difficult to reconcile with the ideology of self-determination that was reinforced by welcoming home a prodigal son. Hence the cruel end they inevitably met in the genre dedicated to their story, the early American seduction novel, wherein they purchased their reclamation with their lives.[5]

This point is reinforced by a case in which Franklin, ever the pragmatist, did support single motherhood as a means to augmenting the population in

4. John Locke, *An Essay concerning Human Understanding,* ed. A. D. Woozley ([1690]; Glasgow, 1980), 67, 89, 91; Fliegelman, *Prodigals and Pilgrims,* 111. J. A. Leo Lemay and P. M. Zall usefully index *"Erratum:* as metaphor for fault" in Lemay and Zall, eds., *Benjamin Franklin's Autobiography: Authoritative Texts, Backgrounds, Criticisms,* Norton Critical Edition (New York, 1986), 380.

5. In her analysis of *The Coquette,* Sharon M. Harris discusses an episode from Franklin's *Autobiography* in which he and his friend Collins pretend that Franklin has got a woman pregnant as an excuse to "flee the city." Harris argues that "for young women, Franklin's America offers no such opportunities for escape, nor the possibility of restitution through a rectification of 'errata.'" Through the author's representation of female friendship, however, "Foster suggests . . . that the rectification of 'errata' could become possible for young women" (Harris, "Hannah Webster Foster's *The Coquette:* Critiquing Franklin's America," in Harris, ed., *Redefining the Political Novel: American Women Writers, 1797–1901* [Knoxville, Tenn., 1995], 1–22, esp. 16, 18).

the "Speech of Miss Polly Baker" (1747). Here, he cites abortion and infanticide among the extreme measures to which sexually active single women are forced by the inequitable sanctions imposed upon them as opposed to their male sexual partners. His sympathy does not, however, lead him to question the validity of a model that emphasizes overcoming past error in pursuit of a self that is, above all, the product of its owner's will. Indeed, Miss Polly's speech itself results in her highly improbable marriage to one of her judges. Rather than follow through on the likely consequences for Miss Polly of her transgression, then, Franklin sacrificed veracity to provide her story a happy, if incredible, ending. Miss Polly herself becomes an emblem of clever self-management in a manner that would have been extremely difficult for the real Miss Pollys of the world to carry out.[6]

The implicit threat that pregnancy posed to the "errata" concept may account for the frequency with which the term appeared in the "battle of the sexes" that took place in popular print culture of the late colonial era. Beginning in 1737 with Franklin's reprinting of a British newspaper jest in Poor Richard's *Almanack,* readers were taught to associate errata with female error in particular: "Women are Books, and Men the Readers be, / Who sometimes in those books Erratas see." This joke ends with the suggestion that, since the "errata" are more or less permanent in women's case, it should be the text itself that is changed: "Are Women Books? Says Hodge, then would mine were / An *Almanack,* to change her every Year."[7]

In the mid-1750s, Annis Boudinot Stockton reprised this joke. It had formerly appeared "in a newspaper" as follows:

Woman are books in which we often spy
Some bloted lines and sometimes lines awry
And tho perhaps some strait ones intervene
In all of them erata may be seen.

Stockton, writing as "Emelia," answers this jest by observing that women are not the only ones at fault and suggesting that wise men know "to choose and then to prize their books . . . With them into a world of error thrown /

6. Benjamin Franklin, "Speech of Miss Polly Baker," *General Advertiser,* April 1747, in Franklin, *Autobiography and Other Writings,* ed. Ormond Seavey (New York, 1993), 246–250.

7. Carla Mulford, ed., *Only for the Eye of a Friend: The Poems of Annis Boudinot Stockton* (Charlottesville, Va., 1995), 182–183; *The Papers of Benjamin Franklin,* ed. Leonard W. Labaree (New Haven, Conn., 1960), II, 171.

And our eratas place against their own." With this witticism, Stockton informs her readers that, although women's bodies may highlight their own particular susceptibility to circumstance, men are also at risk of having to come to terms with the fact that they do not always determine their own destinies. No more than women—no more than errata themselves, really, which, as the young Ben Franklin's proposed epitaph suggests, are not always easy to correct in a current edition or a lifetime—are men free of the burdens of experience.[8]

Illicit pregnancy obviously happened only to women; but, as Stockton's riposte makes clear, it stood for a problem that was to a certain degree systemic. For the right, and indeed obligation, to self-determination—which comprised an "article of cultural faith" in the early Republic—was as unwieldy in practice as it was appetizing in the abstract. In placing the subject in a proprietary relationship to his own bodily and subjective experience, the Enlightenment myth of possessive individualism (through which, as John Locke states, "every man has property in himself and thus the right to man-

8. Mulford, ed., *Only for the Eye of a Friend,* 74–75. The epitaph Franklin proposed for himself as a young man, as recorded in Milcah Martha Moore's commonplace book, follows:

The Body of
Ben Franklin, Printer,
Like the Cover of an old Book,
Its Contents worn out,
And stript of its Lettering and gilding,
Lies here Food for the Worms,
Yet the Work shall not be lost,
For it will (as he believ'd) appear once more
In a new and more beautiful Edition,
Corrected and Amended
By the Author.
Was born Jun the 6th. 1706
Died 17

(Catherine La Courreye Blecki and Karin A. Wulf, eds., *Milcah Martha Moore's Book: A Commonplace Book from Revolutionary America* [University Park, Pa., 1997], 219). In the *Autobiography* itself, Franklin also sets limits to human self-direction in reference to errata. Sometimes these suggestions are conscious, as in the comment "This was another of the great Errata of my Life, which I should wish to correct *if I were to live it over again"* (Lemay and Zall, eds., *Franklin's Autobiography,* 34, itals. mine). Other times they seem less so, as when he describes his two initial errata as though each were the first (16, 27). If one forgets prior errata, they are unlikely to be emended.

age himself, his labor, and his property as he wishes") offered opportunities for self-aggrandizement on a formerly unimaginable scale. But in wresting a modern concept of personhood from previously more fluid notions of subjective experience, this model launched, as its Janus-faced other, an infinite regression of self-perceiving entities, with each monad generating yet another to become its perceiver ad infinitum. As such, it was not without its nightmarish aspects, which fell particularly hard on women in a market society and modern liberal state. Even the strongest advocates of a social order based on a self-proprietary model acknowledged these specters in proclaiming their very irrelevance. For instance, Locke abhorred sleeping dreams, which he labeled "extravagant and incoherent." No wonder, since in dreams, the chain of command between perceptual entities gets a little mixed up, and it's difficult to rest easy in the fiction that one is in any sense determining one's outcome.[9]

In the early Republic, literary prodigal daughters served a similar function to dreams in that their "disrepute" reinforced a prevailing worldview, whereas their abundance hinted at its limitations. By explaining away young, single, impregnated, and abandoned women in terms that made their own culpability clear (if also their claim on our compassion), seduction novels could reassure young republican readers that failure to fashion a "self aligned with market relations" did not reflect badly on the system itself but merely on the individual case. Unmarried pregnant women such as the historic Elizabeth Whitman and her numerous explicit and implicit literary incarnations, then, were not offered the welcome their brothers received,

9. Locke, *Essay concerning Human Understanding,* ed. Woozley, 95. The Enlightenment myth of possessive individualism is defined by C. B. MacPherson in his *Political Theory of Possessive Individualism: Hobbes to Locke* (New York, 1988) and refined by Gillian Brown in *Domestic Individualism: Imagining Self in Nineteenth-Century America* (Berkeley, Calif., 1990), 2. See Elizabeth Maddock Dillon's brilliant explication of women's "externalized—but foundational—position" within "the founding fictions of liberalism" in Dillon, *The Gender of Freedom: Fictions of Liberalism and the Literary Public Sphere* (Stanford, Calif., 2004), 11, 17. Mechal Sobel studies dreams to note both the power and inefficacy of ideologies of self-direction that proliferated during this period. As the early American economy "shifted from one based in good part on exchange to widespread market production," she writes, "many individuals buffeted by the economic 'tidal waves' felt personally responsible for their own failures or successes." One consequence of this destructive emphasis on personal responsibility, she notes, was that dreams were held in "growing disrepute." Locke's own scorn for dream life, then, became more widespread in a nation where his faith in private property as the basis for the social contract was also put to the test. See Sobel, *Teach Me Dreams: The Search for Self in the Revolutionary Era* (Princeton, N.J., 2000), 7, 9.

because it was difficult to reconcile their condition with the ideology of self-correctability embodied in the return of a prodigal son. As members of a nation premised on self-determination, women, like men, needed to learn, and learning required experimentation; but the former's experiments were uniquely terrifying, since women did not possess the corollary privilege of having their mistakes expunged from the record. And their stories were so inexplicably popular nonetheless because they spoke to a nation's secret fear that perhaps the model did not quite fit even those it was specifically designed for.[10]

Susanna Rowson narrated early America's most famous prodigal daughter into being. And, like other novelists of the day, she let her heroine die. For this reason, many assessments of Rowson's role in the early Republic conclude that she, too, participated in its brutal silencing of women and other disenfranchised populations. But if Charlotte never returns from her fictional grave, she beckons us to remember her plight nonetheless from the very real stone that marks it in New York's Trinity Churchyard, not far from Ground Zero. Rowson's voluminous contribution to the burgeoning print culture of the early Republic is even more direct in addressing the conflicted status of the nation's literate female inhabitants. In essence, Rowson taught her primarily Anglo-American female readership both the cruel irony of

10. Sobel, *Teach Me Dreams*, 9; Brown, *Domestic Individualism*, 2. *The Power of Sympathy* and *The Coquette* both thematize the Elizabeth Whitman story. Lost chastity was the prevailing, though not the only, sign of female prodigality in the late colonial period. See also, for instance, *The Undutiful Daughter Who . . . Took to All Manner of Evil Course . . . and Continually Scoffing Her Aged Mother* (Philadelphia, 1765), and *The Prodigal Daughter . . . Who because Her Parents Would Not Support Her in All Her Extravagance Bargained with the Devil to Poison Them* (Boston, [1771?]), both cited in Fliegelman, *Prodigals and Pilgrims,* 95. The second, a juvenile poem, was reprinted at least nineteen times between 1742 and 1799. In it, the prodigal daughter, "when she was put into the grave, she came to life again, and related the wonderful things she saw in the other world." The prodigal daughters of the period's novels might also be said to speak from the grave. Anna Mae Duane provides a stunning analysis of how pregnancy simultaneously invokes and interrupts liberal, classical republican, and evangelical post-Revolutionary logics of identity formation. *Charlotte Temple* and *The Coquette* "allot pregnancy a transformative function that ultimately subjugates women's reason to the body's transcendental logic, and positions the fetus as a disciplinary agent that reveals and reshapes the inner world of the mother." In particular, Duane emphasizes the way pregnancy tells a "truth" that belies women's supposed skill at divorcing their visible selves from their core identities. Pregnant women's "unruly interior becomes increasingly visible, and legible, as the body testifies against the mind's supposed agency." See "Pregnancy and the New Birth," MS, 2,4, cited by permission of the author.

their situation, as emblems for an individuality to which they were not in fact party, and how to develop workable selves and workable lives nonetheless.[11]

Charlotte Temple is fond of "lying softly down," and her timing is terrible. She faints into a chaise in Chichester; she crawls into the bed where her seducer, the dashing Lieutenant Montraville, already sleeps; and she takes an afternoon nap that allows his even less scrupulous "brother officer" in the British army, Belcour, to position himself beside her in time for her beloved to discover them together. Given Charlotte's propensity for putting her feet up, it is no wonder that critics have taken the book bearing her name as an unquestionable exemplar of the novel of seduction, a genre wherein the reader "is asked to deplore the very acts which provide his enjoyment." Some see the novel as evidence of "the appalling popularity of the seduction motif" in early American sentimental fiction, whereas others take a gentler view of how the genre "blended the histrionic and pedagogic modes." But whether they favor enjoyment or instruction as the primary narrative impetus behind Charlotte's loss of virginity out of wedlock, most scholars take the centrality of the sex act—and with it, of Charlotte's presumed lust—for granted. A story of "the fatal consequence of Charlotte's . . . illicit sexuality," the novel is said to depict a woman "betrayed by her own naive passions" and thereby provide an "example of virtue fallen through seduction and sexuality."[12]

11. *The Cambridge History of American Literature* asserts that Rowson "extols . . . female subordination" in *Charlotte Temple* (Sacvan Bercovitch, ed., *The Cambridge History of American Literature*, I, *1590–1820* [Cambridge, 1994], 630). *The Columbia History of the American Novel* argues that Rowson "cannot produce a text that itself resists the pieties and homilies of the culture it has been vilifying. . . . In the end *[Charlotte Temple]* winds up promoting the values that cloak forms of (male) oppression" (Emory Elliott, ed., *The Columbia History of the American Novel* [New York, 1991], 19). For discussion of an expanding early national print culture, see Rosalind Remer, *Printers and Men of Capital: Philadelphia Book Publishers in the New Republic* (Philadelphia, 1996); Michael Warner, *The Letters of the Republic: Publication and the Public Sphere in Eighteenth-Century America* (Cambridge, Mass., 1990); and Davidson, *Revolution and the Word.* Rosemarie Zagarri discusses female authors' role in this expansion in "The Postcolonial Culture of Early American Women's Writing," in Dale Bauer and Philip Gould, eds., *The Cambridge Companion to Nineteenth-Century Women's Writing* (Cambridge 2001), 19–37. I examine this topic at greater length in the next chapter.

12. Rowson, *Charlotte Temple,* ed. Davidson, 48, 71, 74, 91; William C. Spengemann, *The Adventurous Muse: The Poetics of American Fiction, 1789–1900* (New Haven, Conn., 1977), 88; Herbert Ross Brown, *The Sentimental Novel in America, 1789–1860*

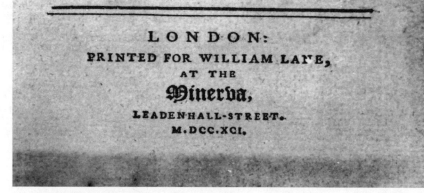

CHARLOTTE.

A TALE OF TRUTH.

IN TWO VOLUMES.

She was her parent's only joy;
They had but one—one darling child.
ROMEO AND JULIET.

Her form was faultlefs, and her mind,
Untainted yet by art,
Was noble, juft, humane, and kind,
And virtue warm'd her heart.
But ah! the cruel fpoiler came——

VOL. I.

LONDON:
PRINTED FOR WILLIAM LANE,
AT THE
Minerva,
LEADENHALL-STREET.
M.DCC.XCI.

PLATE 10. *First British edition of* Charlotte: A Tale of Truth *(London, 1791),*
I, title page. PS 2723.R3C5, Clifton Waller Barrett Library of American Literature,
Special Collections, University of Virginia Library

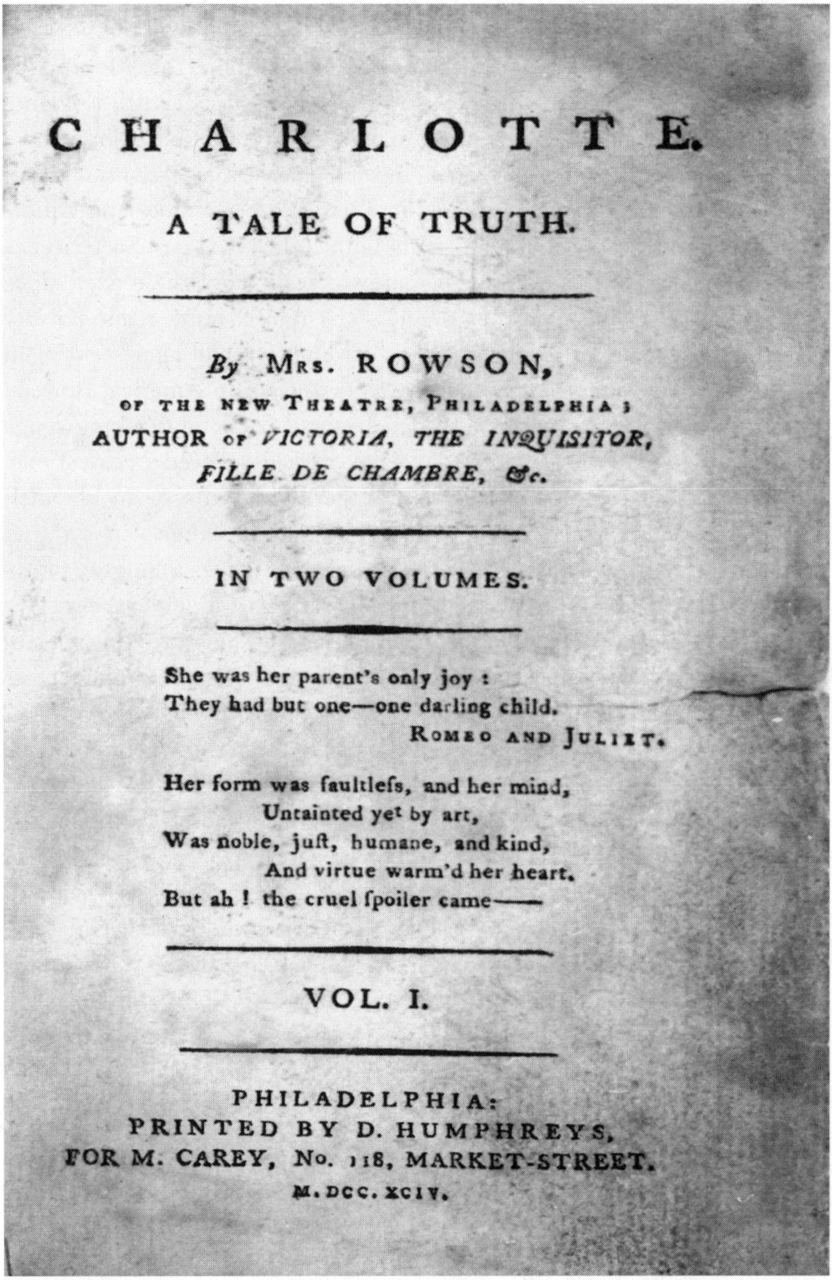

CHARLOTTE.

A TALE OF TRUTH.

By Mrs. ROWSON,

OF THE NEW THEATRE, PHILADELPHIA;
AUTHOR OF *VICTORIA, THE INQUISITOR,*
FILLE DE CHAMBRE, &c.

IN TWO VOLUMES.

She was her parent's only joy :
They had but one—one darling child.
ROMEO AND JULIET.

Her form was faultlefs, and her mind,
Untainted yet by art,
Was noble, juft, humane, and kind,
And virtue warm'd her heart.
But ah ! the cruel fpoiler came——

VOL. I.

PHILADELPHIA:
PRINTED BY D. HUMPHREYS,
FOR M. CAREY, No. 118, MARKET-STREET.
M.DCC.XCIV.

PLATE 11. *First American edition of* Charlotte: A Tale of Truth *(Philadelphia, 1794),*
I, title page. PS 2736.R3C5, Clifton Waller Barrett Library of American Literature,
Special Collections, University of Virginia Library

A closer look, however, calls this emphasis on Charlotte's passion, and its ill effects on her virtue, into question. The novel rarely mentions sex: there is no indication of how the "kindness and attention" that Montraville shows a seasick Charlotte during their voyage from Portsmouth, England, to New York leads, five chapters later, to her "visible situation." Nor is there any discussion of the pregnancy itself beyond Charlotte's description of the "poor unborn" and "innocent infant" in a letter to her mother and a post-humous reference to a "poor girl . . . big with child." Nor can this reticence be attributed merely to a desire to spare the feelings of the reader, since Rowson has no qualms regarding descriptions of pain, hunger, and poverty ("the bleeding body of her brother," a "miserable, small apartment"). In fact, at the same time that the novel was taking off in America, Rowson was in Philadelphia writing stage comedies and patriotic drinking songs in which lust—albeit parodied and racially marked—played a central role. Her musical drama *Slaves in Algiers,* first performed in 1794 in Philadel-phia and Baltimore, makes much of the Algerian dey's "huge scimitar" and includes a scene in which the cross-dressed heroine makes a "mighty pretty boy" in the eyes of her unknowing lover. The sailors drinking to their lasses in "America, Commerce, and Freedom," Rowson's popular drinking song of the same year, show "eager haste" to join the young women running across the beach to meet them over the "full flowing bowl." Even in the novel at hand, desire is given its due as long as it occurs within the sanctified bonds of marriage. Mrs. Temple, Charlotte's mother, is the very picture of marital satisfaction, in continual possession of "the delightful sensation that dilated her heart . . . and heightened the vermillion on her cheeks" in the presence of her husband. The woman who speaks to Charlotte when no one else will and ministers to her in the hours before her family arrives is similarly blessed, as "the most delightful sensations pervaded her heart" at the "encomiums bestowed upon her by a beloved husband." This angel of mercy's name is Mrs. Beauchamp ("beautiful field"), in opposition to Charlotte's female be-trayer, the malicious and cunning boarding-school teacher Mademoiselle La

(Durham, N.C., 1940), 44; John Seelye, "Charles Brockden Brown and Early Ameri-can Fiction," in Emory Elliott, ed., *Columbia Literary History of the United States* (New York, 1988), 168–186, esp. 170; Davidson, "Life and Times of Charlotte Temple," in Davidson, ed., *Reading in America,* 170; Joseph Fichtelberg, "Early American Prose Fiction and the Anxieties of Affluence," in Carla Mulford, ed., *Teaching the Literatures of Early America* (New York, 1999), 206; Maureen Woodard, "Female Captivity and the Deployment of Race in Three Early American Texts," *Papers on Language and Literature,* XXXII (1996), 127.

Rue ("Miss Street," as in, streetwalker). Clearly, Rowson is capable of alluding to erotic attraction—it's just not what she is after in Charlotte's case.[13]

Criticism of *Charlotte Temple* has tended to anticipate concern, like that shown by this study, with the way sexuality relates to female agency. Many scholars have embraced the position problematized here, arguing that the novel is, whether sensational or didactic, really about Charlotte's "insufficiently disciplined 'inclination'"—in other words, that it describes a woman undone by passion. This position, extrapolating from her demise to the fate of the nation at large, tends to read her story as a "warning against the passionate self-interest that threatens all republics." Generally, critics who take this approach consider the novel mostly for its similarities to contemporary works such as *The Coquette* and *The Power of Sympathy,* being one of several novels promoting "a form of 'self-governance' by which [the new model woman] checks both sexual desire and the desire for social eminence." One particular, highly sophisticated reading of this school notes that the above novels all "foreground situations wherein the characters' own emotions or senses lead them astray." "Read along the lines of conventional education, these characters suffer the consequences of their own weaknesses; read in the spirit of seductive subversion, they die from the strength of their passions."[14]

Another body of scholarly work concerns itself more, like this chapter, with what Charlotte lacks than what she possesses and suggests, as Julia Stern states outright, that we stop reading "the novel as a didactic fable warning against the dangers of seduction." These readings focus on omission rather than inclusion (whether of letters or of sexual acts) and on "psychology" rather than "stimulus." For these critics, Charlotte lacks many things, including both voice and "individuation," but most important for this argument, she lacks agency. "Once she softens to Montraville's pathetic

13. Rowson, *Charlotte Temple,* ed. Davidson, 9, 13, 19, 34, 39, 42, 75, 77, 81, 117; Rowson, *Slaves in Algiers; or, A Struggle for Freedom: A Play, Interspersed with Songs, in Three Acts* (Philadelphia, 1794), 59, 79. On early American attitudes toward sexuality within marriage, see John D'Emilio and Estelle B. Freedman, *Intimate Matters: A History of Sexuality in America* (New York, 1988), esp. chap. 2; and Ellen K. Rothman, *Hands and Hearts: A History of Courtship in America* (New York, 1984).

14. Gareth Evans, "Rakes, Coquettes and Republican Patriarchs: Class, Gender and Nation in Early American Sentimental Fiction," *Canadian Review of American Studies,* XXV, no. 3 (Fall 1995), 41–62, esp. 42, 51; Fichtelberg, "Early American Prose Fiction," in Mulford, ed., *Teaching the Literatures of Early America,* 206; Woodard, "Female Captivity," *Papers on Language and Literature,* XXXII (1996), 127; Barnes, *States of Sympathy,* 45.

appeal, she has no will to assert" and "can no longer be spoken of in relation to a rational model of selfhood premised on individual limits and moral agency." Charlotte "is not an agent in her own life," and her "precarious condition" is "exemplary" of the fact that "women . . . lack the ability to act as autonomous subjects." This chapter reveals how this lack functions in the novel in the way that passion does for the aforementioned readings: it serves as both the primary explanation for Charlotte's behavior and as the single quality of her being against which the novel cautions its female readers.[15]

Charlotte is "disappointed" in the only "pleasure" she does expect: the liberal provisions promised by Mademoiselle La Rue at the party to which she is lured early on, where she meets Montraville. Here, Charlotte experiences a rare instance of clear determination: she "heartily wished herself at home again in her own chamber." She then admits to "gratitude" at Montraville's praises of her and, it must be admitted, a certain amount of satisfaction in his "agreeable person and martial appearance." But all her subsequent "blushes" are from shame, not pleasure, and her strongest sensation almost immediately becomes that of not knowing what to do. After Montraville gives her a letter, she turns to her teacher, asking, "What shall I do with it?" With every moment of indecision, La Rue steps in to direct Charlotte's path—"Read it, to be sure"—and it is thus, and not through any overwhelming desire of her own, that Charlotte is impregnated. She meets her lover to tell him she will see him no more, is persuaded by fits and starts to approach his carriage, and ends up literally fainting into it, whereby we are to assume that the fatal deed is done. The less Charlotte credits her own instincts, the more her behavior is described as a form of collapse, in which her future direction is determined by nothing more deliberate than her center of gravity.[16]

15. Stern, *Plight of Feeling*, 41, 52; Eva Cherniavsky, "Charlotte Temple's Remains," in Christoph K. Lohmann, ed., *Discovering Difference: Contemporary Essays in American Culture* (Bloomington, Ind., 1993), 40; Kay Ryals, "America, Romance, and the Fate of the Wandering Woman: The Case of Charlotte Temple," in Susan L. Roberson, ed., *Women, America, and Movement: Narratives of Relocation* (Columbia, Mo., 1998), 90. Omission of sexual acts: see Mona Scheuermann, "The American Novel of Seduction: An Exploration of the Omission of the Sex Act in *The Scarlet Letter*," *Nathaniel Hawthorne Journal* (1978), 106. Omission of letters: see Blythe Forcey, "*Charlotte Temple* and the End of Epistolarity," *American Literature*, LXIII (1991), 237. "Individuation": Ann Douglas, *The Feminization of American Culture* (London, 1996), xxiii.

16. Rowson, *Charlotte Temple*, ed. Davidson, 27, 28, 31; Scheuermann, "American Novel of Seduction," *Nathaniel Hawthorne Journal* (1978), 108.

According to *The Compact Edition of the Oxford English Dictionary,* to seduce is to "induce (a woman) to surrender her chastity." The reader does anticipate Charlotte's defloration from her "blushes" and "sighs" and witnesses its effects in her subsequent condition. The word "passion" is even used a couple of times. But the intercourse itself exists only through its aftereffects, and Charlotte's behavior in this regard is never explained. Not only, that is, do we fail to witness her "surrender," being left to deduce it from subsequent irrefutable evidence, but we never learn just how she is "induced" to do so. In fact, Charlotte does not so much surrender her chastity at all—in the sense of giving up, under duress, something she values—as lose track of it altogether, along with every other aspect of her being. Thus, whereas to be seduced is to put "private and individual needs ahead of others," Charlotte loses her virginity only when she loses the ability to experience need altogether. As the story develops, she becomes increasingly incapable of knowing *what* it is she feels, and she does what she feels she shouldn't, not through an excessive respect for her desires, but rather through an increasing distrust of them. With "her ideas . . . confused," she is soon allowing herself to be "directed" not only by La Rue but also by her "betrayer," Lieutenant Montraville, rather than by her own self-appraisal, according to which she longs to remain loyal to her "forsaken parents." In sum, it is in deadening her sensitivity to her own impulses, and not in giving in to them, that Charlotte loses her virginity and then her life.[17]

Charlotte Temple may be unique among early American sentimental novels in its avoidance of sexually charged language. William Hill Brown's *Power of Sympathy,* for instance, includes the word "seduction" in capital letters on the frontispiece to its 1789 edition. Further evidence that it trades in its fatal vice to a far greater degree than *Charlotte Temple* includes its explicit and footnoted reference to the real-life Elizabeth Whitman scandal. Another popular novel from the 1790s, Hannah Foster's *Coquette,* also invokes Elizabeth Whitman's seduction, abandonment, and death, as first reported in the *Salem Mercury* in 1788. *The Coquette* goes even further than *The Power of Sympathy* in making passion its primary theme. "Sensation" appears twice in its first sentence and "pleasure" twice in its second, giving the astute reader plenty of notice that Eliza Wharton's destruction will be accompanied by sensual indulgence along the way. Eliza thrills in her "con-

17. Rowson, *Charlotte Temple,* ed. Davidson, 28, 47; Michael T. Gilmore, "The Literature of the Revolutionary and Early National Periods," in Bercovitch, ed., *Cambridge History of American Literature,* I, 539–694, esp. 587.

quests" and admits to a pleasant "perturbation" at being so much "the taste of the other sex."[18]

Unlike Eliza, who begins *The Coquette* in constant appreciation of the effect she has on men, Charlotte rarely refers to her own ability to obtain power, or pleasure, from erotically charged social interactions. But she does spend a great deal of time contemplating another aspect of her being: namely, its terrifying absence of self-direction. Given that, just before collapsing into her lover's arms, Charlotte asks of her "torn heart," "How shall I act?" one may explain her habit of prostrating herself as a manifestation of something other than sexual desire. For although fainting and napping certainly share with more licentious behavior the tendency to take place lying down, they also possess another quality that is more important to understanding Charlotte than lust. They both entail the loss of consciousness and, with it, of any capacity for self-direction. Asleep or passed out, Charlotte has virtually no say over how her life unfolds. Awake, she fares almost no better. In this sense, *Charlotte Temple,* despite appearances to the contrary and decades of critical assumption, is *not* really a novel of seduction, in the sense of being a document that provides sexual titillation under cover of pedagogic censure. Instead, far from depicting Charlotte's overweening desire, the novel portrays the fatal consequences of a woman's inability to want anything enough to prompt decisive action. Charlotte falls into compromising positions not so much because she yearns to as because she doesn't, in the words of her evil counsel La Rue, "know [her] own mind two minutes at a time"; and what she loses when she "falls" is not, or at least not importantly, her virginity but her independent agency. Disorientation, rather than passion, leads Charlotte from her British boarding school to her lover's arms and from there to a transatlantic crossing, the outskirts of New York, pregnancy, childbirth among strangers, temporary madness, and death in the redemptive presence of her father.[19]

This reading supports Larzer Ziff's observation that, since Anglo-American women—far from being ostracized for having premarital intercourse—were marrying after conception in record numbers by the late eighteenth century, the novel's extraordinary popular appeal in the new United States could not be explained by its veracity as historical transcript. In fact, *Charlotte Temple* dramatizes a fate that more and more of its readers seemed to be avoiding: a young woman is impregnated by a man who then abandons

18. Brown, *Power of Sympathy;* Hannah Webster Foster, *The Coquette,* ed. Cathy N. Davidson ([1797]; New York, 1986), 8, 12.

19. Rowson, *Charlotte Temple,* ed. Davidson, 44, 47.

her. John D'Emilio and Estelle Freedman provide the historical ground for Ziff's observation, noting that premarital pregnancy rates rose sharply in late-eighteenth-century America to as many as one-third of all brides in parts of New England. This suggests greater leniency toward female sexual desire, since women were able to gain the social sanction accorded by marriage in the face of incontrovertible evidence of having sex out of wedlock.[20]

Given the increasing tolerance of premarital sexual activity during the period the novel was first published in the United States, for *Charlotte Temple's* contemporary urban readers, her struggle to maintain her chastity was probably most important, not as a reflection on her ability to regulate lustful impulse, but rather as a marker of her liminal class status. Popular print media of this period frankly acknowledged the sexuality of women outside the elite. But although women below the middling station, that is, outside the fold of those whom Rowson's work was training, were often depicted in "neutral or even celebratory terms as acknowledging their sexual urges and welcoming opportunities to indulge them," those who wished to claim the status of a lady needed to remember "the emphasis placed upon women's mission as guardians of virtue in the new republic." Attitudes toward sexuality were thus key indicators of social status. As a woman "of modest social background," Charlotte's control over her virginity would determine, for a fascinated young American female reader in a volatile urban setting such as Philadelphia, whether the heroine descended into the city's "naturally lustful and licentious" lower class or qualified as an "exemplar of moral integrity." That she managed to reclaim her virtue, in the guise of her father's forgiveness, even after being seduced, might have comforted those who found the demands of female gentility trying. At the same time, the high cost of her reclamation (imminent death) would remind them of the risks involved in ignoring the developing identification of female social prestige with sexual self-regulation.[21]

20. Larzer Ziff, *Writing in the New Nation: Prose, Print, and Politics in the Early United States* (New Haven, Conn., 1991), 56. Summarizing the work of Joan Hoff Wilson, D'Emilio and Freedman argue that this rise indicates "a breakdown of the traditional familial and community regulation of sexuality," as witnessed in "'a revolt of the young' against familial controls over marriage and sexuality" (*Intimate Matters,* 43). See also Rothman, *Hands and Hearts,* 46; Lee Virginia Chambers-Schiller, *Liberty, a Better Husband: Single Women in America: The Generations of 1780–1840* (New Haven, Conn., 1984), 35.

21. Godbeer, *Sexual Revolution,* 300, 306, 307. On sexuality and gender in late-eighteenth-century Philadelphia, see Branson, *These Fiery Frenchified Dames;* and

The pressure to "assume responsibility for sexual propriety" in a culture dedicated to sexual transgression provides but one example of the myriad difficulties facing a young woman of the early national period hoping to "possess her soul in serenity," to cite Judith Sargent Murray's polemic of a decade earlier. For even as certain valorized traits came to be associated with post-Revolutionary genteel womanhood, women's behavioral options were increasingly limited. Female rights, although not ignored, were conceived of according to Scottish Common Sense notions of societal obligation, whereas men alone, following the alternate trajectory of Lockean natural rights philosophy, possessed liberty, the ability "to choose one's destiny." At the same time, virtue in the previously male-oriented sense of active self-denial for the good of the polis was feminized during the early national period precisely because, as a holdover from classical republicanism, it no longer served a nascent liberal political sphere premised on competition. The savage irony of a notion of female rights that developed after the Revolution only to foster an increased sense of duty to outmoded notions of sexual virtue is made only more severe when one compares it with the ideology of perpetual opportunity facing young men of the period (discussed at the beginning of this chapter).[22]

Clare Lyons, *Sex among the Rabble: An Intimate History of Gender and Power in the Age of Revolution, Philadelphia, 1730–1830* (Chapel Hill, N.C., 2006), which I discuss at greater length in Chapter 4. For an excellent summation of scholarly attitudes toward the history of sexuality in the eighteenth century, see Lynn Hunt and Margaret Jacob, "The Affective Revolution in 1790s Britain," *Eighteenth-Century Studies,* XXXIV (2001), 496–497, which places the work of Lawrence Stone and Michel Foucault in contradistinction. In this chapter, I replicate Foucault's discursive gesture at the opening of *The History of Sexuality,* I, wherein he recounts "the repressive hypothesis" by which "an age of repression" intensified through the nineteenth century, only to turn the story on its head by performing a sort of word count. The more people condemned sexuality, he points out, the more certainly they inscribed it on their world in "a veritable discursive explosion"—the more certainly, that is, they produced it (Foucault, *The History of Sexuality: An Introduction,* trans. Robert Hurley [New York, 1978], 17). Here, I reverse Foucault's gesture by noting how an apparent thematic presence (Charlotte's desire) is in fact more noteworthy as a discursive absence.

22. Godbeer, *Sexual Revolution,* 306; Judith Sargent Murray, "Desultory Thoughts upon the Utility of Encouraging a Degree of Self-Complacency, Especially in Female Bosoms," in Sharon M. Harris, ed., *Selected Writings of Judith Sargent Murray* (New York, 1995), 47, orig. publ. in *The Gentleman and Lady's Town and Country Magazine; or, Repository of Instruction and Entertainment,* VI (1784), 251–253; Rosemarie Zagarri, "The Rights of Man and Woman in Post-Revolutionary America," *WMQ,* LV (1998), 219. See also Ruth Bloch, *Gender and Morality in Anglo-American Culture,*

The terrible consequences attendant upon Charlotte's tendency to fall rather than step into events resonated among female readers with increasingly limited capacity to experience themselves as independent, coherent beings in a post-Revolutionary culture that made them the centerpiece of national identity even as it circumscribed their roles ever more closely. Charlotte thematized their difficulty in reconciling the post-Revolutionary emphasis on bourgeois individualism with equally powerful ideologies of female subservience. Essentially, then, *Charlotte Temple* asks its early American readers how women are to derive an integrated model of the self from the tortured cultural lexicon provided them.

In Charlotte, she shows a woman who seems to fail at this task, only to commit, at the last minute of her life, a single decisive act: the handing of her infant daughter over to her father. This highly charged gesture suggests two contrary impulses. On the one hand, Charlotte vests her female child with a sense of decisiveness unknown to her mother before this moment, as she literally makes her the substance of her first autonomous act. On the other, that act is accompanied by a request to the family patriarch for "protection," as if her daughter were to pick up right where Charlotte left off, leaving her fate to others to determine. "'Protect her,' said she, 'and bless your dying—'" That Charlotte does not finish the sentence that accompanies this gesture further suggests continuity between mother and daughter. The reader is left hanging on the sounds of a wordless infant girl to find out how Charlotte would last have named herself. Will her daughter embody Charlotte's final courage and decisiveness, or the meandering anomie that led to her conception? Not until three decades later would readers of the first American *Charlotte: A Tale of Truth* find out.[23]

1650–1800 (Berkeley, Calif., 2003). For recent appraisals of the tensions between republican ideologies of "property and liberty" and liberal self-interest in the early United States, see Philip Gould, *Covenant and Republic: Historical Romance and the Politics of Puritanism* (Cambridge, 1996), 25; and Nancy Isenberg, *Sex and Citizenship in Antebellum America* (Chapel Hill, N.C., 1998). Both authors delineate how early Americanist republican ideology depended on self-denial. Gould also distinguishes this republican worldview from a potentially encroaching liberalism in which the limitation, as opposed to renunciation, of selfish pleasures loomed large. Summarizing two decades of scholarship, he asks: "Was the nation, in other words, founded on an anticapitalist ideology or on a materialist one?" (*Covenant,* 26) Dillon suggests the interdependence, as opposed to "diametrically opposed" status, of these two ideologies (*Gender of Freedom,* 142–161, esp. 143). For an overview of Common Sense philosophy, see Fliegelman, *Prodigals and Pilgrims,* 23–26.

23. Rowson, *Charlotte Temple,* ed. Davidson, 115; Rowson, *Charlotte: A Tale of Truth* (1794).

Whatever its legacy, Charlotte's final "ability to act," in one scholar's description of late-eighteenth-century female evangelical converts, does suggest some "new knowledge": as La Rue would say, Charlotte does at last know her own mind, and as a result, she experiences agency, the "fortitude to put it in execution." Of what exactly is this new awareness composed? What kind of agency was available to a woman who had previously only seen herself as others saw her, or saw for her? And through what transformative event could she come to experience it? Immediately before awakening to find her father at her side, Charlotte descends into a "phrenzy" that owes much to the evangelical tradition whose privileging of affect as a means to understanding makes it an important precursor to American sentimentalism.[24]

Published female evangelical conversion narratives from the late-eighteenth-century United States reflected women's tendency to apprehend the world in terms of personal attachments, as opposed to men's relationship to an abstract order. For women, the challenge of conversion was to "disengage themselves from over-dependence on friends and family" enough to experience "individuation." Passing through the isolation of spiritual struggle, female converts emerged newly "empowered by recovering their sense of self through the assertion of independence from others." Certainly, Charlotte's progression from misplaced reliance on others to being left "a prey to her own melancholy reflexions," to "the total deprivation of her reason" and to her final awakening makes sense within this frame, except that most of the people Charlotte deemed friends turned out not to have her best interests at heart. Moreover, in that the novel ends with Charlotte dictating

24. Susan Juster, *Disorderly Women: Sexual Politics and Evangelicalism in Revolutionary New England* (Ithaca, N.Y., 1994), 53; Rowson, *Charlotte Temple,* ed. Davidson, 27, 47; Sandra Gustafson, "Jonathan Edwards and the Reconstruction of 'Feminine' Speech," *American Literary History,* VI (1994), 185–212; David S. Reynolds, *Faith in Fiction: The Emergence of Religious Literature in America* (Cambridge, Mass., 1981). In viewing Charlotte's descent into madness through the lens of religious conversion, this chapter expands on a field of inquiry linking American sentimental discourse to evangelism initiated by such scholars of religion and literature as Amanda Porterfield, Sandra Gustafson, Jane Tompkins, and David S. Reynolds. Porterfield argues that, during the first Great Awakening, "religious enthusiasm came to be associated with feminine emotionalism" (*Feminine Spirituality in America: From Sarah Edwards to Martha Graham* [Philadelphia, 1980], 63). Tompkins claims that "sentimental fiction was perhaps the most influential expression of the beliefs that animated the revival movement" (*Sensational Designs: The Cultural Work of American Fiction, 1790–1860* [New York, 1985], 149).

terms to her father, however gently, it supports the idea that evangelical women undergoing religious conversion achieved autonomy by temporarily distancing themselves from those through whom they had formerly experienced life's significance. Torn from her country, her family, her schoolmates, her lover, and penultimately any sense of her own reality (after giving birth, Charlotte "was totally insensible of everything . . . she was not conscious of being a mother, nor took the least notice of her child except to ask whose it was, and why it was not carried to its parents"), Charlotte returns to familiar faces able for the first time to set the terms, albeit not of her own, but of her daughter's future course.[25]

But does the clarity of purpose this act portends, although obtained through isolation, necessarily derive from the forced rending of attachments that has characterized her entire course in the novel? It would seem more likely that the new ability Charlotte demonstrates when she hands over her daughter is how to acknowledge her need for others. Far from showing her to be more distinct from others than she was before her period of "incoherence," Charlotte's final act may, in fact, suggest that connecting with them has become a fundamental aspect of her autonomy. In that case, like Franklin, she has learned from her mistakes. To suggest that Charlotte would have been better off had she acted on any form of preference, even sexual desire, is not only to see sexuality as a figure for agency but also as a fundamental aspect of it. For Charlotte to move from being unable to act on any predilection, including that of a barely registered sexual yearning, to determining her daughter's guardian in the last moments of her life, suggests that the desire she once neither heeded nor subjugated has undergone some form of transmutation in order to serve as the basis for a sophisticated moral agency. There is a tension in the novel, then, between understanding desire as an impediment to autonomy (such that the seduction novel must warn against it in a fledgling republic) and seeing the former as in some sense primary to the latter (as I am suggesting Charlotte's final gesture should be read). The intensity of this struggle to understand the relationship between desire and independent action in the late eighteenth century can be seen in the fourth edition of Samuel Johnson's *Dictionary of the English Language,* published in 1773. Whereas in previous editions Johnson was content to start off by calling will "choice," in the later edition he began quite differently, calling

25. Rowson, *Charlotte Temple,* ed. Davidson, 111. On conversion narratives, see Juster, *Disorderly Women,* 51, 53, 103, 120. Sobel also differentiates male and female experience during this period along a continuum from a communitarian to an individualistic understanding of the self; see *Teach Me Dreams,* chap. 1, esp. 26.

will "that power by which we desire, and purpose; velleity." "Velleity," in turn, is precisely what is left of will in the absence of subsequent action or choice: it is the "quality of merely willing, wishing, or desiring, without any effort or advance towards action or realization." Johnson's insertion of a definition of will that isolated desire from its execution demonstrates that he considered desire to be both will's fundamental impulse and a potential obstacle to its exercise.[26]

This paradox, in turn, points to the difficulty of figuring the self in a liberal polity. As suggested by our brief review of the way women were appointed guardians of features that threatened an ideology of male self-determination, post-Revolutionary America had little use for what Paul Downes has called "the constitutive disjunction of the self." Instead, self-possession was all: as the latter-day French *philosophe* Destutt de Tracy would exult, "individuality . . . is our inalienable property." Learning from one's mistakes was well and good, but the important thing was that one rest assured in the enabling fiction that one did in fact own oneself—that one existed in a fixed and commanding position over one's myriad psychic impulses. Self-formation thus entailed subjugating those aspects of mental experience that did not mesh with a forward-looking, self-promoting, property-obtaining citizenry. And according to this notion, Johnson's later definition of the will, admitting the possibility of ineffectual desire was far less useful than a more resolute model wherein desires that did not result in choices were construed as existing outside the willing self. Authors such as Susanna Rowson and readers such as those that made *Charlotte Temple* a hit were toying with a notion of the self that found little favor in other cultural channels. According to this notion, mistakes need not be expunged but could rather be incorporated into the social fabric, much as Charlotte's daughter becomes part of her grandfather's world after Charlotte herself is gone. Desire did not portend disaster but rather independent action, a quality in short supply as young women learned elsewhere how not to want.[27]

26. Rowson, *Charlotte Temple,* ed. Davidson, 109; *Dictionary of the English Language,* 4th ed., s.v. "will." Johnson granted the novel a role in divesting will of its power, worrying that the desire inspired by fiction could "produce effects almost without the intervention of the will." As Patricia Meyer Spacks glosses the passage, "Johnson's sentence rings with anxiety about the ways that forces other than the will may dominate the mind and the imagination. The violence with which fictional examples operate on the memory corresponds to desire's violence" (Spacks, *Desire and Truth: Functions of Plot in Eighteenth-Century English Novels* [Chicago, 1990], 22).

27. Antoine Louis Claude Destutt de Tracy, *A Treatise on Political Economy,* trans. Thomas Jefferson ([1817]; Detroit, 1973), 41–42, 47.

If one views Charlotte's failure to direct her own life in relation to the behavior of other characters in the novel, one sees these divergent modes of negotiating between impulse and action embodied in distinct characters. Lest there be any doubt that this is a book about making choices, its first words have to do with whether a character prefers to walk or drive. There are two central terms in the novel's discussion of agency, and they are used over and over again in the text: "inclination" and "resolution." Both are considered modes of willing during the period (Johnson's definitions of the verb "to will" include "to be inclined or resolved to have"). Where they differ, not surprisingly, is in their relationship to desire. To be inclined is to be "disposed . . . by . . . desire," whereas to be resolved is to possess "fixed purpose." The latter category, although it does not deny desire outright, is differentiated from the former both by a greater emphasis on taking action and, correspondingly, by an emphasis on controlling impulses to make such action both possible and beneficial. In short, resolution directs will from "velleity" to "choice," from the passions to the understanding, and from proclivity to action, with the latter's implications for self-mastery. As we will see ahead, the struggle between these two terms is evident in Charlotte's own propensities, in the interactions between characters, and in the narrative mode itself, where appeals to the reader's sympathy based on benevolent inclination alternate with calls to disciplined detachment based on steely resolve.[28]

Characters in *Charlotte Temple* tend to respond to these two terms in one of three ways. The most successful individuals, who end the book alive, well, and free from lasting inner torment, generally reconcile both inclination and resolve. Charlotte's father, Mr. Temple, wants Lucy Eldridge for his wife. He discerns that, despite his father's objections and the resultant decline he can expect in his annual income, Lucy will bring him earthly felicity otherwise unattainable, and he pursues her without hesitation. Similarly, much later on, Lucy, now Mrs. Temple, wants to give her daughter a birthday party and goes to some lengths to persuade her reluctant husband to let her do so because the party will make everybody happy (if only everyone, including her daughter, would attend). These are cases where inclinations based on affect (loving the woman, yearning to please the daughter) and resolutions to satisfy inclination (defying the father, persuading the husband) go hand

28. Rowson, *Charlotte Temple,* ed. Davidson, 9; Samuel Johnson, *A Dictionary of the English Language,* ed. Anne McDermott, CD-ROM (Cambridge, 1996); *Webster's Revised Unabridged Dictionary (1913 and 1828),* the Artfl Project, http://machaut.uchicago.edu/websters, accessed Apr. 27, 2007.

in hand. There is no real tension, no danger, and no potential negative consequence to giving in to impulse. Moreover, on the rare occasions where resolution and inclination are in conflict, these individuals are also capable of self-regulation. When, for instance, Mrs. Temple learns of her daughter's perfidy, she insists, "I will wear a smile on my face, though the thorn rankles in my heart," in order to make her father and husband feel better, and she proceeds immediately to "the execution of so laudable a resolution." Having managed to cultivate a passion for duty, these characters embody what one critic considers the novel's mission to "instruct young ladies . . . in being content with one's lot in life," and although such characters lead peaceful lives, they make for extremely boring novels.[29]

Never fear, however, because these exemplars are inevitably accompanied by less benevolent twins, who, although similarly inclined to follow their impulses, arrive at no such happy results for themselves or others. Their deleterious effects derive from two sources: impetuosity and sheer sadism. Like Mr. and Mrs. Temple, Lieutenant Montraville knows what he wants and acts on his wishes, but in his case, the effects on those he meets are disastrous. Thus "generous in his disposition, liberal in his opinions, and good-natured almost to a fault," Montraville is nevertheless "eager and impetuous in the pursuit of a favorite object." And thus "he staid not to reflect on the consequence which might follow the attainment of his wishes," even when he knows Charlotte is too poor to marry. Montraville learns too late the difference between "momentary passion" and lasting love; for him, inclination is all.[30]

Finally, there are those such as La Rue and Belcour, who glory in the suffering of others. Ironically, these are beings capable of intense resolve, happy to put off the satisfaction of a ruinous impulse for greater effect. Thus La Rue can feign indifference whether Charlotte accompanies her on her nocturnal visit to the local regiment and Belcour can (literally) lie in wait for Montraville's arrival rather than accost Charlotte on the spot. Both know how to manipulate momentary impulse in the service of a greater malevolent end. It is significant, however, that Charlotte is finally undone, not by these caricatures, but by Montraville himself, who lifts her into the carriage at Chichester and leaves her alone among skeptical strangers outside New

29. Rowson, *Charlotte Temple,* ed. Davidson, 56–57; Devon White, "Contemporary Criticism of Five Early American Sentimental Novels, 1970–1994: An Annotated Bibliography," *Bulletin of Bibliography,* LII (1995), 293–305, esp. 294 (citing Patricia Parker, "Charlotte Temple: America's First Best Seller," *Studies in Short Fiction,* XIII [1976], 518–520).

30. Rowson, *Charlotte Temple,* ed. Davidson, 38, 83.

York. For pure evil, like pure good, is easy to recognize. It's those with good intentions but no capacity to regulate their outcome—those in whom inclination and resolve are at odds—that the novel trains its readers to detect, both outside and within themselves.

The problem is that even when, like Charlotte, one knows not to act on every impulse, disaster cannot necessarily be averted. Smart enough to doubt her inclinations but not strong enough either to defy or indulge them, Charlotte ends up unable to form a resolution: and it is this fundamental inaction, rather than any particular inclination, that proves her undoing. Ironically, her strongest wish, had she merely obeyed it, was to rejoin her parents. Had she trusted to impulse, as Mr. and Mrs. Temple did before her, she would have been fine. Thus the novel presents contrary, and gendered, models of deportment. For young women such as Charlotte, it seems to suggest a surer grasp on benevolent impulse, a quickness to action that can prevent one from falling into vacuous indecision. For young men such as Montraville, however, the call to action is tempered by another to reflection, since impulse itself in their case seems less altruistic. In what follows, an examination of Charlotte's own indecisiveness, in a book addressed to "the young and thoughtless of the fair sex," will take precedence over Rowson's less-detailed representation of the male subject.[31]

Charlotte has several ways of forestalling choice. First, unable to figure out her own preference, she tends to do things according to whether they will make others think well of her. For this reason, La Rue, ever alert to how best to make others' weaknesses serve her own ends, can mock Charlotte's reticence to run off with Montraville by pointing out that the whole school will laugh at her: "You will bear the odium of having formed the resolution of eloping, and every girl of spirit will laugh at your want of fortitude to put it in execution."[32]

Second, Charlotte possesses a fatal confidence in remediable action. Early in the novel, she observes that, because the wafer on a letter from Montraville is not yet dry, she won't have to break the seal. (In fact, she has unknowingly wet it with her tears.) Hence she might "read it . . . and return it afterwards." Charlotte's misplaced optimism here foreshadows her belated understanding of the finality of lost chastity. In the context of her attempt to decide whether to see the lieutenant again, the fact that she opens a letter from him with the idea that she can make it look as though she hasn't read it serves as a figure for the act to which the letter invites her: namely, her seduction,

31. Ibid., 5.
32. Ibid., 46.

whose ineradicable consequences she also fails to anticipate. In this passage, the act of reading is clearly and, for Rowson, uncharacteristically sexualized, because it both initiates Charlotte's seduction and metaphorically represents it. Although the novel frames this rare act of erotic intimation so as to distinguish between its own narrative workings and those of the illicit missive, it nevertheless provides here a superb instance of how the effort to contain transgressive impulse in pursuit of genteel female self-sufficiency also introduces that which is to be avoided in practice into the realm of imaginative possibility.[33]

Both these habits of mind—her overweening concern for how others will interpret her actions and her unworldly optimism—get Charlotte into trouble. But by far her greatest failing is her faith in her own "stability," as demonstrated in such passages as: "Charlotte had, when she went out to meet Montraville, flattered herself that her resolution was not to be shaken, and that . . . she would never repeat the indiscretion"; or "And in her heart every meeting was resolved to be the last." At one point, she even exults, "How shall I rejoice . . . in this triumph of reason over inclination." Charlotte is good at resolving, or at least planning to resolve, but as Samuel Johnson knew, "resolutions will not execute themselves," and she is incapable of granting any single impetus to action enough sway to direct her once and for all. Charlotte is not in fact impetuous; she does not give in to inclinations once she senses that they might hurt her; but having come to the point of knowing not to do something, she is nonetheless incapable of doing something else, and it is this inability to come to *any* decision that haunts her. At moments of great dramatic import, she is afflicted by a desire to be doing the opposite of whatever she's engaged in, as she explains to her mother: "Even in the moment when . . . I fled from you . . . even then I loved you most."[34]

In a cultural climate where individuality, newly valorized as self-possession, lent heightened importance to the ability to take action consistent with one's intent, for Charlotte not to know what she wants—or not to be able to act accordingly when she does—is for her not to know who she is or, indeed, not to be anyone. Before leaving the novel itself to examine its cultural context more broadly in the following section, we will discuss *Charlotte Temple's* way of bringing the reader to a relationship with the words on the page similar to the relationship that Charlotte experiences with her own fluctuating psychic processes, introducing the reader to a corollary terror

33. Ibid., 32.

34. Ibid., 37–38, 42, 44, 47, 79; Johnson's *Rambler,* no. 193, 1752, cited in *The Compact Edition of the Oxford English Dictionary,* 2d ed., s.v. "resolution."

in the face of potential self-dissolution. To the degree that incompatibilities between "inclination" and "resolve" operate in the book as a mode as well as a topic, with appeals to appetite and stern correctives therefrom occurring simultaneously on the page, the reader becomes an unwilling participant in the processes he or she might hope to have contemplated from a distance.

Characteristic of the late-eighteenth-century American sentimental novel as represented by its best-selling volume is not only its much-denigrated appeal to "convention," its seemingly manipulative and paradoxically quite cold machinery for evoking emotion in spectators both within and outside the text, but also something less purely disciplinary. Many critics deny such a possibility in their assumption that Rowson's narrative persona is seamlessly controlling. Such readings, however, tend to equate a need for control with the achievement thereof. The very ostentation of the Rowsonian narrator's comforting asides might just as easily suggest profound self-doubt. This alternative is supported by an oscillation in the novel's narrative mode, which shifts between monitorial didacticism and an almost ecstatic celebration of submission to benevolent impulse.[35]

Hence the narrative is rent by opposing impulses and seems unable to decide on its own course of action. Instead, it swerves without apparent rhyme or reason between appeals to disciplined detachment and those to sympathetic identification. At the very moment, for instance, that Belcour is abandoning the dying Charlotte—a moment when we might be expected to empathize with her sad state—the description takes place at further and further removes:

> His visits became less frequent; he forgot the solemn charge given him by Montraville . . . and, the burning blush of indignation and shame tinges my cheek while I write it, this disgrace to humanity and manhood at length forgot even the injured Charlotte; and, attracted by the blooming health of a farmer's daughter . . . left the unhappy girl to sink unnoticed to the grave.

35. Forcey, for instance, writes that "Rowson's narrative incursions provide an authoritative unifying voice which gives structure and guidance to the reader," functioning primarily to "inform, improve and enrich the lives of [Rowson's] readers" (Forcey, "*Charlotte Temple* and the End of Epistolarity," *American Literature,* LXIII [1991], 231, 236). See also Donna R. Bontatibus's emphasis on Rowson's pedagogical skills and reformative intent in her *Seduction Novel of the Early Nation: A Call for Socio-political Reform* (East Lansing, Mich., 1999), esp. chap. 1 and conclusion. Stern's analysis of "the absent mother who occupies and directs the narrative frame" explores the alternative possibility that such "guidance" is unworkable (Stern, *Plight of Feeling,* 5).

Why does the narrator feel compelled to mention her own cheek at this moment? By doing so, she inserts another link in the chain separating victim from reader, as we now must witness the narrator watching Belcour watching (or failing to watch) Charlotte. She thereby intensifies the scene's already voyeuristic aspect, creating a spectacle now "dependent not only on the implied spectatorship of the reader/viewer," nor even "on the express spectatorship of internal witnesses" alone, but on a third, explicitly embodied narrative presence. Her comment thus distances us even further from the events at hand and reinforces a sense of remoteness that is at odds with any sympathetic identification with Charlotte. At the same time, however, the narrator provides the reader with an extremely uncharacteristic reference to the narrator's own body. As such, the narrative mimics Charlotte's own blush of shame and encourages the reader to reflect upon what she, too, might have to "blush" for, thereby creating a shared vulnerability with the protagonist. The Rowsonian narrator is thus at her most confessional at the very moment she puts us at the furthest remove from the details of her story. She appeals to our sympathetic and our censorious tendencies simultaneously and thereby leaves us, like Charlotte, like the narrator herself, unable to respond decisively. Instead, we dwell in the same anxious self-doubt that Charlotte herself found so painful.[36]

A similar entanglement occurs at the end of the novel, when the dead Charlotte's father takes in the woman who could be said to have murdered his daughter:

> Greatly as Mr. Temple had reason to detest Mrs. Crayton [nee Mlle. La Rue], he could not behold her in this distress without some emotions of pity. He gave her shelter that night beneath his hospitable roof, and the next day got her admission into an hospital; where having lingered a few weeks, she died, *a striking example, that vice, however prosperous in the beginning, in the end leads only to misery and shame.* FINIS.

Here the reader is treated to one last surrender to benevolent inclination ("he could not") over resolve ("had reason to"), only to be asked to relish it from a distance—to look not on Temple's kindness but on Mrs. Crayton's just desserts. The warmth of forgiveness is elicited, only to be trumped by the far more readily indulged satisfaction at the death of an enemy.[37]

36. Rowson, *Charlotte Temple,* ed. Davidson, 98; Karen Halttunen, "Humanitarianism and the Pornography of Pain in Anglo-American Culture," *American Historical Review,* C (1995), 303–334, esp. 317; Tompkins, *Sensational Designs,* 107.

37. Rowson, *Charlotte Temple,* ed. Davidson, 119–120 (emphasis added).

That American readers welcomed the opportunity to make Charlotte's struggle their own is indicated by the well-known fact that they visited a tombstone with her name on it in New York's Trinity Churchyard. Rowson could ask for no surer emblem of the book's being "consider[ed]," in accordance with her prefatory instructions, "as not merely the effusion of Fancy, but as a reality." It may in fact be the first American novel to take on antebellum sentimentalism's signature task of making narrative engagement result in specific subsequent behaviors, from temperance campaigning to abolitionism. But the behavior depicted here—peering into an empty grave, or at least one necessarily devoid of Charlotte's skeleton—also speaks to the ambivalence that lingers alongside Rowson's call to female action. Through its dissonant appeals to contrary readerly responses, the novel provides an instantiation, as well as an allegory, of the paradoxical nature of female subjectivity during a period in which women were expected to submit to codes denying them both pleasure and agency and yet to conceive of their position as one they chose and from which they derived satisfaction.[38]

Eliza Wharton, the sprightly protagonist of Hannah Foster's *The Coquette* (1797)—the decade's second-best-selling novel, after *Charlotte Temple*— might not share much in the way of personality with her literary predecessor, but she is precisely the kind of woman to have read her story. The coquettish Eliza answers exactly to *Charlotte Temple*'s aforementioned addressee, "the young and thoughtless of the fair sex." She is young, "leaving [her] paternal roof" for the first time as the novel opens. She is thoughtless: as she herself admits, her "bewitching charms" keep her in a constant "state of perturbation." And as a creature both female and alluring, she is doubly "fair": not "so very handsome," she confides, but "very much the taste of the other sex."[39]

Eliza also matches what we know about *Charlotte Temple*'s initial American reception. This was notable first and foremost for its unheard-of dimensions. Mathew Carey, the first American publisher of the book, estimated that more than fifty thousand copies were sold by 1812, by which point at least eighteen editions had been published. *Charlotte Temple*'s readership

38. On visitors to Charlotte's grave, see Francis W. Halsey, ed., *Charlotte Temple: A Tale of Truth* (New York, 1905); Davidson, *Revolution and the Word*, 262; Stern, *Plight of Feeling*, 10–11, 68; Rowson, *Charlotte Temple,* ed. Davidson, preface, 5.

39. Rowson, *Charlotte Temple,* ed. Davidson, 5; Foster, *The Coquette,* 5, 12, 159. For the early publication history of *The Coquette,* see the note heading the "Selected Bibliography" in Oxford University Press's edition of the novel, ed. Cathy N. Davidson (New York, 1986), xxii.

PLATE 12. *Charlotte Temple's gravestone. From Rowson,* Charlotte Temple: A Tale of Truth, *ed. Francis W. Halsey (New York, 1905). PS 2736.R3C5, Clifton Waller Barrett Library of American Literature, Special Collections, University of Virginia Library*

PLATE 13. *"Memorial to Mrs. Rowson." From Rowson,* Charlotte Temple: A Tale of Truth, *ed. Francis W. Halsey (New York, 1905). PS 2736.R3C5, Clifton Waller Barrett Library of American Literature, Special Collections, University of Virginia Library*

during this period was also striking for its economic, social, and geographic diversity. Editions appeared from Alexandria (1802) to Danbury (1803), from octavo to duodecimo, bound in pasteboard, inexpensive cloth, or leather with gilded edges. (When Rowson proposed printing her novel *Trials of the Human Heart* by subscription at the end of the American edition of *The Fille de Chambre* [1794], she named individuals ready to "receive" subscriptions from Charleston and Baltimore to Boston and Vermont.) A range of readers then inscribed these books; people liked to write in their copies of *Charlotte Temple*. Some were still practicing their handwriting: young Timothy Houghton signed his copy five times. Others were capable of eloquent inscription: Ann Pers copied out a four-line verse that also appears on a 1798 gravestone.[40]

Within this diversity, what exactly makes Eliza a typical reader of *Charlotte Temple?* A look at the first United States Census in 1790 is suggestive. First, she is young and of English descent. Anglo-Americans were the largest nationality category of just over two million, and almost half the recorded white males were sixteen and under. Second, she is urban, occupying a novel in which almost all letters circulate between New Haven, Hartford, Boston, and Hampshire. Although the United States "remained a rural country," cities such as Boston and Philadelphia more than doubled in size between 1790 and 1820, and New York almost quadrupled. The print market expanded most rapidly in urban areas, as did fraternity, social, and

40. Bercovitch, ed., *Cambridge History of American Literature,* I, 626; Susanna Rowson, *The Fille de Chambre: A Novel* (Philadelphia, 1794). Nearly forty thousand copies had been sold by 1801 (Bauer and Gould, eds., *Cambridge Companion to Nineteenth-Century American Women's Writing,* 30). Eventually, "hundreds of thousands" would peruse *Charlotte Temple* in more than two hundred editions (Cathy Davidson, "Life and Times of Charlotte Temple," in Davidson, ed., *Reading in America,* 168). In a study published in 1959, William Charvat hazards that "in the Philadelphia area, five towns published twenty-one editions, Philadelphia issuing fourteen of these. New York State published eighteen, fourteen of them in New York City. But of twenty-nine New England editions, only two were issued in Boston (compared to Hartford's thirteen), whereas eight other towns published a total of twenty-seven" (Charvat, *Literary Publishing in America, 1790–1850* [(1959); Amherst, Mass., 1993], 32). Davidson cites "the novel's long history as a bestseller among poor, working-class, middle-class, and even affluent readers" (Davidson, "Life and Times of Charlotte Temple," in Davidson, ed., *Reading in America,* 173). My thanks are due to Palmer Curdts and Kathy Nguyen, undergraduates in ENAM 355, fall 2004, for alerting me to these two examples of inscription from the Albert and Shirley Small Special Collections Library's compilation of more than one hundred editions of the novel (University of Virginia, Charlottesville, Va.).

circulating libraries, making novels such as *Charlotte Temple* available to most readers "of modest to low income" by 1800. Other statistical measures are more ambiguous. Eliza is known for her "extensive reading," and we know that her literacy is of more recent and tenuous vintage than would have been a young man's. In a northern population where the numbers of men and women were roughly equal, however, her familiarity with novels (she not only inhabits one, but knows them well enough not to need the meaning of "a second Lovelace" explained) is typical of her gender: about twice as many of the more than one thousand early American novels Cathy Davidson surveyed had female signatures as male. Moreover, that the villain she mentions derives from a British novel, Samuel Richardson's *Clarissa,* describes an American public that still mostly read imported and pirated English books and chapbooks, even as some printers began to encourage native productions. When Eliza speaks—or rather, as the heroine of an epistolary novel, reads and writes—her voice resonates with the echoes of those who made her and Charlotte's stories integral to a nation undergoing its "first age of mass literacy."[41]

Perhaps the most poignant way in which the character of Eliza refracts the historical circumstances of her and Charlotte's primary readership is in her conflicted relationship to choice, the entity that so beleaguered Charlotte. As a young, unmarried woman, Eliza stands at exactly the point at which she has the most independence and her capacities for selection are

41. See 1790 state level census data, in Inter-university Consortium for Political and Social Research, *Historical Demographic, Economic and Social Data: The United States, 1790–1970* (n.d., n.p.), 1–3; Foster, *The Coquette,* 38, 46, 153–156; Gilmore, "Literature of the Revolutionary and Early National Periods," in Bercovitch, ed., *Cambridge History of American Literature,* I, 20; David S. Heidler and Jeanne T. Heidler, *Daily Life in the Early American Republic, 1790–1820: Creating a New Nation* (Westport, Conn., 2004), "Populations of Major Cities" maps for 1790 and 1820 (pages not numbered); Alan Taylor, *William Cooper's Town: Power and Persuasion on the Frontier of the Early American Republic* (New York, 1995), 407; Victor Neuberg, "Chapbooks in America: Reconstructing the Popular Reading of Early America," in Davidson, ed., *Reading in America,* 81–113, esp. 83–87; Samuel Richardson, *Clarissa; or, The History of a Young Lady* (London, 1748); Davidson, *Revolution and the Word,* 8, 87–89, 188. Between 1773 and 1776, according to Bernard Bailyn, more than one-half of British emigrants to mainland North America were under twenty-five, and more than a quarter between twenty and twenty-four (*The Peopling of British North America: An Introduction* [New York, 1986], 11). By the early 1800s, two-thirds of white Americans were under twenty-four. Estimates of female literacy in the 1790s vary widely, from less than half of all white adult women to almost 90 percent (Jennifer Monaghan, "Literacy Instruction and Gender in Colonial New England," in Davidson, ed., *Reading in America,* 53).

most appreciated; and yet those powers of selection are to be trained upon the event that will rob her of this status. A married woman, or *feme covert,* lost her personal property to her husband upon marriage, and for all intents and purposes her individuality under the law as well. By contrast, an unmarried woman, or *feme sole,* could "make contracts, own and devise property, and head a household. In short, she possessed the same legal capacity as any man." For widows with inherited property, this could be a powerful position indeed. As Eliza makes clear through frequent references to her reduced finances, however, single women often lacked the material resources or the economic opportunities that could give weight to their relatively empowered legal standing. Like widowhood, spinsterhood presented particular opportunities to women. But without the educational and professional resources offered to men in a similar position, unmarried women were also in a certain degree of peril.[42]

Spinsterhood carried less opprobrium within the nineteenth century's consumer-based household economy than it had in a colonial, production-based domestic economy. In New England, more women remained unmarried with every passing decade after the American Revolution, a trend begun later in the South and West. This demographic shift was accompanied by changing attitudes, in which "some Americans . . . questioned whether marriage and motherhood comprised women's only true destiny. . . . Popular culture lauded women who . . . vowed to stay single unless they found a mate equal to themselves in morality, integrity, courage and learning." Indeed, the early American novel can be understood as part of this "cultural reassessment of singlehood" in that it threw the mechanics of courtship in a newly voluntaristic age into high and not necessarily flattering relief.[43]

But if early republican culture offered many women alternative vocations to that of marriage and child-rearing, from teaching to shoe-binding to mill work to caring for aged parents, those vocations rarely offered freedom from economic or familial duress. Most spinsters continued to live at home with parents or siblings and worked only sporadically at occupations that "had

42. Karin Wulf, *Not All Wives: Women of Colonial Philadelphia* (Ithaca, N.Y., 2000), 3. Suzanne Lebsock notes that, in early-nineteenth-century Virginia, "part of the reason that more women were in control of property was that more women were unmarried for significant portions of their lives" (Lebsock, *A Share of Honour: Virginia Women, 1600–1945* (Richmond, Va., 1984), 83. On the feme covert, see Marylynn Salmon, *Women and the Law of Property in Early America* (Chapel Hill, N.C., 1986); D'Emilio and Freedman, *Intimate Matters;* and Davidson, *Revolution and the Word.*

43. Chambers-Schiller, *Liberty, a Better Husband,* 12, 13.

more significance in terms of personal identity and growth than of economic independence or professional life." The easing social stigmatization of spinsterhood, then, did not minimize spinsters' very real vulnerability to poverty and disappointment in a climate that offered limited opportunities for female self-sufficiency relative to male. These fates were generally less dramatic than the horrific ends doled out to Charlotte and Eliza. But they could demean and dehumanize nonetheless. And yet often, as Eliza discovers, there seemed no right path to follow, since the alternative—lifelong contractual union with a person one found unsympathetic—occasioned its own forms of distress, as Rowson knew only too well.[44]

In a sense, then, the fact that Eliza and Charlotte's sexual prodigality literally kills them figures the slower death to which many women of the period were subject. Childbirth out of wedlock, poverty, and unhappy marriage were not necessarily fatal; but neither were they easily made right. And if one considers them consequences of a failed quest for marital bliss akin to Eliza and Charlotte's more dramatic fates, they marked a huge proportion of these novels' early female readership as current or prospective prodigal daughters. Like many of her first readers, then, Eliza lacks the material resources that might free her from the need to seek out a spouse so as to become a feme covert, whose property exists only in her husband's name. Compelled by cultural precedent and economic necessity to transfer her dependence from her parents to a mate, she both needs a husband and anticipates that he will own all she has. Thus, the one significant choice she is given in early adulthood—that of a partner for life—reaffirms, codifies, and makes permanent her "enforced dependence" within her culture.[45]

As we meet Eliza, then, she is most concerned with one aspect of her existence: her choice of whether and whom to marry. In this, she again speaks to a typical concern of a population for whom voluntarism was a newly important aspect of marital union. But if the post-Revolutionary youth of both sexes had more say, relative to their parents, in the choice of a spouse, for women the decision was uniquely fraught. An "erratum" in this regard would cause lasting regret. Most of all, if for men the choice of a spouse was but one decision among many, for women their vast range of capacity seemed narrowed to this one small point. The more they felt compelled to

44. On American female singlehood, see ibid., esp. 4, 31, 43–45.

45. Linda K. Kerber, *Women of the Republic: Intellect and Ideology in Revolutionary America,* 1st ed. (Chapel Hill, N.C., 1980), 139–155; Salmon, *Women and the Law of Property,* xv.

attend to the topic, the more the paucity of their existence relative to that of their brothers suggested itself.[46]

No wonder Eliza is so prone to describing confinement. Her predilection for words such as "circumscribing," "compass," "contracted," "confine," and "cell" reveals more than her fondness for the letter "c." It also provides a discursive map of a cultural terrain that both she and the early national female novel-reader occupied. Thus it comes as no surprise that Eliza puts the following words in her soon-to-depart reverend suitor's mouth:

> Is it not difficult to ascertain what we can pronounce "an elegant sufficiency"? Perhaps you will answer as some others have done, We can attain it by circumscribing our wishes within the compass of our abilities.

This seemingly innocuous moment is of enormous significance. For it provides a rare instance in which an early American female protagonist presumes to view her situation from without. We will see ahead that fiction of the 1790s, although it does not deny social inequity, tends to look for solutions in the individual subject. Self-modification, not social transformation, is the order of the day. As an epistolary novel, composed entirely of missives from one solitary individual to another far distant, *The Coquette* epitomizes these atomistic tendencies of the period. Here, however, Eliza not only hazards a guess at her correspondent Mr. Boyer's point of view but aptly deduces that her version of his words sums up a prevailing bias. Paraphrasing what she thinks her legitimate but "boyer-ing" suitor would say on the basis of what "some others have done," she thus both identifies cultural impositions as such, rather than as aspects of her own mental state, and yet simultaneously describes them as they are experienced from within by their ostensible object.[47]

What exactly does Eliza think she is expected to find "sufficient"? By 1796, "sufficiency" meant simply "adequate provision of food or bodily comfort." As she cites early-eighteenth-century Scottish poet James Thomson's use of the term—"an elegant sufficiency, content, Retirement"—it refers to the property holdings that provide one with the leisure to pursue other forms of development. Eliza's selection of the first item from Thomson's fa-

46. Fliegelman, *Prodigals and Pilgrims,* 123–126; Chambers-Schiller, *Liberty, a Better Husband,* 35–39. Consider, for instance, Fliegelman's comment that "a felicitous marriage served for a woman the function that education did for a man" (126).

47. Foster, *The Coquette,* ed. Davidson, 13, 47.

mous list of the necessaries for happiness suggests that she frankly acknowledges material comfort as the basis for all higher forms of "content." Since her control over this aspect of her life is narrowed in her particular cultural moment down to the choice of whom to wed, that decision must therefore include a careful assessment of the intended's projected net worth.[48]

Eliza's ventriloquized answer, in turn, describes the misery this conflation of sexual, economic, and personal considerations ensures. Thus when she writes of "circumscribing our wishes within the compass of our abilities," she describes not only the project of learning to be content with one's station in life but the more sinister expectation that a young "not so very handsome" woman of modest means should recognize the limited supply of potential spouses she is "able" to draw from. Indeed, this is exactly what Boyer does expect: Eliza, he believes, should love him, modest competency and all, because she should not anticipate more. Eliza's comment prophesies the condescension she will soon experience — after refusing to "circumscribe her wishes" — from disgusted suitors and married friends alike.

It also gives brilliant voice to how the early American obsession with self-determination felt from the point of view of one whose straitened circumstances made control of her destiny rather difficult. In this regard, the crucial word in Eliza's statement is "circumscribe." Errata, remember, can be corrected after the fact; but women such as Eliza were not granted the luxury of emendation. To survive, she needed to shrink her wishes to fit her surroundings, not use her ambition, curiosity, and zest for the unknown to change them, with allowance made for inevitable missteps. Eliza correctly surmises that "some others," including pretty much every other letter-writer in the novel, expect her to hazard only conservative estimates of her potential: to "circumscribe" rather than dream big and hope her "abilities" — a euphemism for "circumstances" if ever there was one — expand accordingly.

Early in a book that will eventually deal her Charlotte's fate, Eliza's response to this view of her prospects is blithe disbelief: "I am not very avaricious; yet I must own that I should like to enjoy it without so much trouble as that would cost me." Directing lighthearted words to a serious situation, Eliza here emphasizes her status as the "coquette" of the book's title, and the red flag raised by her oblivion to her own hazardous state distracts us from the merit and pathos of her previous statement. That Foster sees fit to remind her reader of Eliza's incapacities at just this moment, however,

48. *Oxford English Dictionary,* 2d ed., s.v. "sufficiency"; James Thomson, "Spring," *The Seasons: A Poem* (London, 1730), 86.

may suggest that authorial self-doubt has now entered the field to partially erase a scathing cultural critique. And even though Eliza's tone is inappropriate, her words are still to the point. They show her on the high road to destruction, yes; but they also indicate the cultural climate that made her near-manic denial perhaps the most credible, if not the surest, response to an untenable situation.[49]

If Susanna Rowson and Hannah Webster Foster implicitly addressed, by means of their most famous protagonists, the vexed role that choice played in the construction of a female subject, two contemporaries explicitly articulated the challenges of post-Revolutionary female subject-formation: Mary Wollstonecraft and Judith Sargent Murray. These authors' works circulated through the same houses that contained copies of *Charlotte Temple* and *The Coquette*. As such, they both influenced how the novels were read and re-iterated the anxieties, hopes, and methods of comprehension introduced in the persons of Charlotte and Eliza.

The American publication histories of *Charlotte Temple* and *A Vindication of the Rights of Woman* are closely intertwined. Wollstonecraft's most famous work appeared in London in 1792, one year after Minerva Press published *Charlotte: A Tale of Truth* there. By 1794, *A Vindication* had been published in Philadelphia and Boston. Mathew Carey, Rowson's most important American publisher, was responsible for both the first two American editions of *Charlotte Temple* and two editions of *A Vindication* in 1794 alone. In fact, *A Vindication* was advertised for sale in the first American edition of *Charlotte* and went on to appear in advertisements at the back of early American novels more often than any other philosophical tract. Like *Charlotte, A Vindication* was immediately popular: it was available from some 30 percent of the libraries in America during its first years in print, and the February 28, 1795, issue of the *Providence Gazette* includes both in a list of "new publications." Like *Charlotte,* it was also controversial. Both controversies depended on ad hominem conflations of text and author: in the extended print commentary surrounding each author throughout the 1790s and early 1800s, her works figure far less prominently than do her reputed personal merits.[50]

49. Foster, *The Coquette,* ed. Davidson, 47.

50. *Providence Gazette* data from Marcelle Thiébaux, "Mary Wollstonecraft in Federalist America: 1791–1802," in Donald H. Reiman et al., eds., *The Evidence of the Imagination* (New York, 1978), 201.

Contemporary readers didn't generally discuss Rowson and Wollstone-craft in the same breath, but two of the more colorful writers of the day did find time to reflect on both. William Cobbett and Eliza Southgate could not have been more different from one another: a conservative polemicist famous for his caustic wit and a young, educated woman on her way to an early death, in earnest and respectful epistolary converse with her cousin.

Eliza Southgate had been a student in Rowson's school in the late 1790s. Writing to her older cousin, Moses Porter—himself the product of a col-lege education—Southgate invokes both her teacher and the famous En-glish theorist with measured praise. Her familiar, self-effacing demeanor in these letters cannot hide a spirit of confident self-assurance that allows her gently to mock her teacher and frankly to engage her cousin on topics from marital discord to the mental qualities of the sexes. Indeed, Southgate em-bodies the potential for female self-expression dawning in the early 1790s, as new educational opportunities and the fledgling consumer-based econ-omy freed women of means to fashion themselves in print with unheard-of self-consciousness, eloquence, and pride. Eliza epitomizes the spirit of self-regard that educated, unmarried women in the wake of the Revolution increasingly learned was theirs to cherish and develop. Even she, however, will find it difficult to own her admiration for an author whose ideas she admires but whose reputation she fears might tarnish her own.[51]

The precariousness of eloquent analyses such as Southgate's becomes the more intense when we realize the climate of virulent condemnation that increasingly formed their context. Thus William Cobbett, known to his American readers as Peter Porcupine, savagely humiliated both Rowson and Wollstonecraft in print for their mannish insistence on a place in the public sphere of letters. In 1795, he appended a "Critical Essay" on Rowson to his broader disparagement of the democratic *American Monthly Review.* Five years later, he reprinted British clergyman Richard Polwhele's lengthy

51. Southgate called Rowson "one of the blessings of creation" but claims she left the school with no more than a "few patchwork opinions" (61–62). During the same period that female self-regard found new tolerance, male self-regard became more sus-pect, with seducers, con men, and melancholic depresses exemplifying the excesses of male self-involvement in novels such as *The Coquette, Charlotte Temple,* and Charles Brockden Brown's *Wieland; or, The Transformation* and *Ormond; or, The Secret Wit-ness* (Kent, Ohio, 1982). See Brown, *Wieland; or, The Transformation, and, Memoirs of Carwin the Biloquist,* ed. and intro. Jay Fliegelman (New York, 1991); Eliza Southgate, *A Girl's Life Eighty Years Ago: Selections from the Letters of Eliza Southgate Bowne* (Williamstown, Mass., 1980), 17.

satire of Wollstonecraft, *The Unsex'd Females,* prefacing the poem with an exhortation to American readers to attend to the "disgraceful life" of a "sprightly and profligate woman."[52]

The occasional female author expressed indignation to rival Cobbett's own. The poem "Rights of Woman. [By a Lady]," for instance, published in 1795 in the *Philadelphia Minerva,* describes male tyrants "Who with assuming hands / Inflict the iron bands." In despair at how the American Revolution had betrayed women, this writer exhorted her readers to "the cause maintain." Meant to be sung to the tune "God Save America," the poem insists that women "Endure no more the pain / Of slavery." "Let snarling cynics frown, / Their maxims I disown, / Their ways detest," it concludes in an astonishing instance of untrammeled confessional rage.[53]

More commonly, female Americans responded to Wollstonecraft in terms that mirrored Rowson's own, more measured stance. In particular, these respondents tended to use their comments on the famous British philosopher to articulate their sense of difference from the mother country. Prominent Federalist poet Annis Boudinot Stockton, for instance, initially recorded a sense of widespread enthusiasm for the *Vindication.* This enthusiasm was tempered, however, by a sense that its arguments did not apply as well to the more enlightened American republic as they did in Europe. Stockton wrote her daughter about the two days she had just spent reading Wollstonecraft's treatise, "which I never could procure before, tho it has been much longer in the neighbourhood." She pronounces herself "much pleased with her strength of reasoning, and her sentiment in general." But the United States, Stockton declares, proves Wollstonecraft's claims regarding the degraded state of women in society to be exaggerated. The lesser education of women is "an error daily Correcting—and in this Country, the Empire of reason, is not monopolized by men."[54]

The result, Stockton observes, is that, where in Europe women may be forced to their submissive state, in her country women *choose* their submission.

> From the observation I have been able to make in my own Country, I do not think any of that Slavish obedience exists, that She talks so much

52. Thiébaux, "Wollstonecraft in Federalist America," in Reiman et al., eds., *Evidence of the Imagination,* 212.

53. "Rights of Woman [By a Lady], Tune—'God Save America,'" *Philadelphia Minerva,* Oct. 17, 1795, 4.

54. Mulford, ed., *Only for the Eye of a Friend,* 304, 305.

of—I think the women have their equal right of every thing, Latin and Greek excepted.—and I believe women of the most exalted minds, and the most improved understanding, will be most likely to practice that Conciliating mode of Conduct, which She seems to Condemn, as blind Obedience, and Slavish Submission, to the Caprice of an arbitrary tyrant, which character she seems to apply to men as a sex.—but certainly exercising the virtues of moderation and forbearance—and avoiding desputes as much as possible, can easily be distinguished from Slavish fear—and must certainly tend to strengthen the mind, and give it a degree of fortitude, in accommodating ourselves to our situation, that adds dignity to the human character.

Stockton was not alone in differentiating women's stature in Europe and the United States according to the all-important distinction between forced and self-willed subjugation. In 1796, Elizabeth Sandwith Drinker implied as much when she noted in her journal upon reading "Rights of Woman": "I am not for quite so much independance." Two years later, she rephrased this comparison after reading the author's "Letters Written during a Short Residence in Sweden, Norway and Denmark": "A well informed I was going to say, but rather a highly informed woman—I don't like her, or her principles, 'tho amused by her writings." This later comment more starkly suggests the comparativist terms in which Drinker views her own gender status. As a European, Wollstonecraft is free to stock her mind with lots of knowledge (not least by her northward travels). But quantity, for Drinker, does not equate with quality, and Wollstonecraft's "highly" informed status does not correlate with the wisdom of Drinker's implicitly "well," if not so highly, informed capacities as a reader. For it is Drinker, not Wollstonecraft, who is able to sort through her own store of "observation," distinguishing the merely "amusing" from the instructive in Wollstonecraft's rich but uneven prose.[55]

In asserting this capacity to distinguish between correct and incorrect information, Drinker not only stations herself above the sophisticated European author but also stakes an important claim for her female American peers. Even as she argues against Wollstonecraftian "Independence," she asserts her freedom to read whatever she pleases, despite its questionable ethics. And she does so in terms that locate such freedom within what she considers the narrower compass inhabited by literate American women.

55. Ibid., 305; Elaine Forman Crane, ed., *The Diary of Elizabeth Drinker: The Life Cycle of an Eighteenth-Century Woman* (Boston, 1994), 163.

Thus even within the limited claims for autonomy put forth by readers such as Stockton and Drinker resides a complex but significant capacity for self-assertion. Choosing submission may sound like an oxymoron; but as these commentators make clear through their sophisticated wordplay, it is meaningfully different from forced acquiescence. And if we tend to see these statements as self-comforting euphemisms spoken by those whose choice was perhaps more highly delimited than they were willing to admit, we must also realize through careful attention to the mode as well as the matter of their discourse that choice remained an important aspect of their self-definition: one they were willing to assert through outspoken and informed critique. This expansive mood, moreover, was a particular and short-lived feature of the early-to-mid-1790s. Changing responses to Wollstonecraft demonstrate that by 1800 it was under increasing attack. Rowson's ever more dedicated and outward attempts to articulate the possibilities of autonomous female submission in a variety of genres throughout the decade may be seen as a response to a climate of growing hostility, one she did not anticipate when she penned *Charlotte Temple* or when she republished it in Philadelphia in 1794.[56]

Rowson composed her own response to Wollstonecraft in a poem appropriately titled "Rights of Woman," published in the *Boston Weekly Magazine,* October 30, 1802, and included in her *Miscellaneous Poems* of 1804.[57] In an indication of the growing social conservatism that characterized the early 1800s, Rowson, unlike her predecessor above who published a poem under the same title, made no direct mention of Wollstonecraft. Moreover, the poem quickly makes clear that its title is not meant in homage so much

56. According to Gillian Brown, the willing submission that Stockton and Drinker distinguish from brute subjection as a particularly American quality was indeed typical of their moment, their gender, and their location: "For the early United States," she writes, "women perfectly embodied the permeability of the Lockean individual, whose subjection can be either consensual or nonconsensual" ("The Feminization of Content," introduction to part 2 of Brown, *The Consent of the Governed: The Lockean Legacy in Early American Culture* [Cambridge, Mass., 2001], 109–122, esp. 112–113).

57. According to a much-reprinted excerpt, the poem was recited by a student at Rowson's yearly academy exhibition. Interestingly, the excerpt itself—"the light syllabub, all froth and show, / White, sweet, and harmless, like a modern beau"—has little to do with the rest of the poem. That such a flirtatious passage was excerpted in at least three newspapers within one month suggests that the topic of the female academy appealed to the popular press not least for its sexual overtones. The "syllabub" excerpt appears in the *Balance* (Nov. 23, 1802), the *Commercial Register* (Dec. 20, 1802), and the *United States Oracle, and Portsmouth Advertiser* (Feb. 5, 1803).

as veiled critique. At the same time, this poem's limited doctrine of female rights shares a great deal with the measured appreciation for Wollstonecraft expressed by Stockton and Drinker. Thus, in a gently teasing tone, the poem rhapsodizes about women's innate skill at "domestic matters," "filial duty," and other forms of accomplishment based on paternalistic deference, complete with "tiptoe[ing]" steps and "fathers, brothers to protect us." When challenged by "some discontented fair" that such "rights" are merely "duties," the poet summons the logic of chosen submission employed by Drinker and Stockton to her aid, chiding the young woman for failing to appreciate that "we are free, / Those duties to perform." This poem succinctly demonstrates how Rowson derives the capacity for women to be "good, useful members of society" from their attempts to "merit [fathers' and brothers'] protection." Only thus do women "walk abroad," "show their faces," and lead active lives. Rather than oppose strength to weakness, autonomy to submission, Rowson here derives the former from the latter. This facility positioned her to remain influential long after such poems as the first "Rights of Woman," with its outspoken detestation of male tyranny, had disappeared from the print landscape.[58]

Rowson's polite repudiation of Wollstonecraft was no aberration by 1802. Around 1800, Wollstonecraft's reputation went into a tailspin from which it has yet to recover. *A Vindication* had always been treated with some unease. American magazines, although they offered cautious praise, also divested the work of its more threatening associations by excerpting uncharacteristically innocuous passages. But in 1795, relatively early in the book's American career, it was still perfectly permissible for a woman to call "Wollstonecraft, a friend" in print. Not so five years later, when both actual women and the female rhetorical creations of male journalists were ever less willing to state their views of both author and text. The publication of William Godwin's scandalous *Memoirs* in 1799, combined with a growing tide of anti-Jacobinism and a climate of intolerance aided by the passage of the Alien and Sedition Acts in 1798, no doubt fueled the change of sentiment.

58. In a reprisal of *Slaves in Algiers's* use of the North African coastal region as a foil for western liberty, discussed in Chapter 4, the poem notes that "the poor women of the eastern nation" have the wrong kind of freedom. "Shut from society—hard, hard their case is, / Forbid to walk abroad, or show their faces; / From every care, from thought, and duty free, / Live lives of listless inactivity." See Susanna Rowson, "Rights of Woman," *Boston Weekly Magazine,* Oct. 30, 1802, rpt. in Rowson, *Miscellaneous Poems; by Susanna Rowson, Preceptress of The Ladies' Academy, Newton, Mass.* (Boston, 1804), 98–104.

But the repercussions for female self-expression went far beyond the British philosopher's particular case. As republican print culture came to reject the *Rights of Woman* on the basis of Wollstonecraft's presumed political and sexual profligacy, it demonstrated the consequences of that rejection in the very manner of speech it attributed to its female subjects, who became halting and diffident where once they had spoken out.[59]

This shift appears most concisely in the publications of Charles Brockden Brown. His *Alcuin,* published in 1798, features the bluestocking Mrs. Carter, who corrects her eponymous interlocutor in a lengthy apology for Wollstonecraftian views on women's roles in the professions, marriage, and other social institutions. One year later, Brown's journal, the *Monthly Magazine and American Review,* retracted that support, and in 1800 it published a dramatic dialogue in which two young unmarried women, Lucy and Maria, are shamed out of expressing any positive view of the *Vindication.* Lucy, it turns out, has read the treatise; but she cannot be sure what she thinks of it. She ends up bullied into saying she likes it, only to receive a long explanation of why her answer is incorrect. Witnessing Lucy's discomfiture, Maria decides to pretend she hasn't read the book, even though she considers it to contain "genius." In a backhanded compliment to her own delicacy, she suggests that, by avoiding more than a glance at "so coarse a performance," she has failed to "qualify herself to judge correctly." With this gesture, Maria once again shifts the basis for female worth from knowledge to ignorance: woman is the better for what she does not know. In this, she exemplifies the very state of ornamental femininity and assent to the segregation of mind that Wollstonecraft had decried and Stockton and Drinker had deemed irrelevant to the early Republic.[60]

In light of this development, Eliza Southgate's uncharacteristic reticence

59. In 1792 and 1793, for instance, *Massachusetts Magazine* managed not to include the phrase "rights of woman" (or, indeed, "woman") in the title of either excerpt. See "Rights of Woman [By a Lady]," *Philadelphia Minerva,* Oct. 17, 1795, 4. On the American response to Wollstonecraft as a feature of anti-Jacobinism, see Chandos Michael Brown, "Mary Wollstonecraft; or, The Female Illuminati: The Campaign against Women and 'Modern Philosophy' in the Early Republic," *Journal of the Early Republic,* XV (1995), 391. Evidence for this argument includes the frequent pairing of Thomas Paine and Wollstonecraft. See Thiébaux, "Wollstonecraft in Federalist America," in Reiman et al., eds., *Evidence of the Imagination,* esp. 198, 202–204, 210.

60. Charles Brockden Brown, *Alcuin: A Dialogue* (New York, 1798); "Original Communications," *Monthly Magazine and American Review,* III (1800), 161–163; Thiébaux, "Wollstonecraft in Federalist America," in Reiman et al., eds., *Evidence of the Imagination,* 205–209.

regarding the female philosopher reads, if anything, as a risk in its own right. Thus she "attempts the vindication of her sex" but wants it known that not "every female who vindicates the capacity of the sex is a disciple of Mary Wolstonecraft." Repeating twice the term Wollstonecraft made synonymous with the rights of woman, Southgate is nonetheless loath to praise in print one whose "life is the best comment on her writing." Yes, Southgate gave in to culturewide insistence that Wollstonecraft's life, badly misread, must take the place of anything she wrote. But in attempting her own "female . . . vindication of her sex," she implicitly honors the disgraced philosopher nonetheless.[61]

Lest such reticence be considered in any way uncoerced, it is important to remember just how bad things got for Wollstonecraft in America as the French Revolution turned sour and word spread of the unsanctioned sexual relationships detailed in Godwin's *Memoirs.* As Southgate's letters and Brown's journalistic creations fell into reluctant disavowal of the fact that "women knew Wollstonecraft," both American and British male authors published in the United States spared no exaggeration in describing the monstrous creations that might result from her presumed attempts to do away with gender difference. From Richard Polwhele's "The Unsex'd Females" to journalistic satires of the "manly woman" to Thomas Taylor's account of virgins lusting after "amorous" elephants of "prodigious size," it became clear that Wollstonecraft's "manly women" were possessed of monstrous vaginal and other powers. The viciousness of the attacks on Wollstonecraft throughout the decades spanning the turn of the nineteenth century attests to both the foundational role that hierarchical constructions of gender difference played in early Americans' sense of the world as a manageable place and the shame and animosity that awaited any public attempt to improve women's lives in the early Republic. It also helps explain the shadowy terms in which Rowson made her first such attempt with *Charlotte Temple* and the skill that women from Rowson to Southgate, to Stockton to Drinker developed at staking their claims in roundabout ways that might be overlooked by the potentially antagonistic.[62]

Understanding *A Vindication's* changing fortunes in the early national period is important to our study of Rowson in one more way, which anticipates the topic of the next chapter. For if *A Vindication* was a radical book,

61. Southgate, *A Girl's Life Eighty Years Ago,* 61–62.

62. Brown, "Campaign against Women," *Journal of the Early Republic,* XV (1995), 422; Thiébaux, "Wollstonecraft in Federalist America," in Reiman et al., eds., *Evidence of the Imagination,* 202, 212, 223.

it was also a highly defensive one, shaped to deflect the anger of a potentially hostile audience. Indeed, the eventual accusations of extremism and moral turpitude that dogged *A Vindication* and its author appear all the more tragic in light of the book's own conciliatory and even conservative aspects. Its radicalism is self-evident and can be summed up in one sentence: "It cannot be demonstrated that woman is essentially inferior to man because she has always been subjugated." It's impossible to judge lesser, Wollstonecraft insists, those you have rendered so by denying them educational parity. And *A Vindication* remained fearless in its willingness to raise eyebrows in pursuit of nothing less than a revolution in gender relations, variously referring to men as "sycophants," "sensualists," and "voluptuaries." But Wollstonecraft maintained several key tenets of female circumscription in her blueprints for revolution. Much as *Charlotte* couched its valorization of female will in a shell of languorous, even eroticized, passivity, *A Vindication* famously attributes to women the very qualities it urges them to eschew. And, in proposing that female education leads to the capacity to reason and that informed reason (not innocence, as Jean-Jacques Rousseau and others assumed) leads to female as to male virtue, it justifies its program through a normative understanding of womankind that considers them worthwhile only to the extent that they are good. In a manner that would become familiar to proponents and practitioners of republican motherhood in the United States, women are to be made wise that they may become virtuous, rather than that they may be viewed as something other than a living register of human probity and/or derangement. Both the notion that only the satisfactory performance of particular duties justifies female independence, and the astute (if ultimately failed) anticipation of particular prejudices on the part of her readers to which this notion attests, mark Wollstonecraft as an ally of Rowson's. Their simultaneous appeal to early national female readers in the 1790s, moreover, suggests that such attempts to frame female self-construction within recognizable social limits were particularly welcome during this period.[63]

63. Susan Gubar addresses Wollstonecraft's denigration of her subject:

Wollstonecraft's derogations of the feminine, to be sure, are framed in terms of her breakthrough analysis of the social construction of gender. . . . Her thesis—that a false system of education has "rendered [women] weak and wretched"—emphasizes the powerful impact of culture on subjectivity, the capacity of the psyche to internalize societal norms. Indeed, Wollstonecraft stands at an originatory point in feminist thought precisely because she envisioned a time when the female of the

Despite their compromises, however, many American women took to heart, and perhaps even furthered, the most extreme implication of Wollstonecraft's argument that weak and servile women are made, not born: namely, the possibility that gender itself was not an inherent quality of being but rather a historical artifact. The way they did this, without being called manly women themselves, was by transposing the discussion from the earthly to the spiritual plane and using their actively asserted and often newly refashioned Protestant theology to affirm that, in the words of poets Annis Boudinot Stockton and Susanna Wright, "there is no sex in soul." The chief proponent of this argument was Rowson's only real literary peer: Judith Sargent Murray, a widely published contemporary author of plays, poetry, and essays. Murray was perspicacious enough to anticipate Wollstonecraft's arguments in her early essay, "On the Equality of the Sexes," and brave enough to defend her long after it was fashionable to do so, arguing in 1802 that "her real crime was her able defence of the sex."[64] Moreover,

---

species could shed herself of an enfeebling acculturation of feminization. Yet although (or perhaps because) A Vindication sets out to liberate society from a hated subject constructed to be subservient and called "woman," it illuminates how such animosity can spill over into antipathy of those human beings most constrained by that construction.

In an earlier study, Ralph Wardle discussed Wollstonecraft's emphasis on maternal domesticity:

[she] had always [in A Vindication] to caution her readers that she had no desire to breed a generation of independent and unattached women like herself, but that she sought to develop wiser and more virtuous wives and mothers. Again and again she repeated that education would lead women to a more serious interest in "domestic pursuits" rather than to a longing for distinction in the world; indeed she contended that women would be less likely to crave distinction if they were granted solid intellectual resources.

See Susan Gubar, "Feminist Misogyny: Mary Wollstonecraft and the Paradox of 'It Takes One to Know One,'" *Feminist Studies,* XX (1994), 452–473, esp. 457; Ralph M. Wardle, *Mary Wollstonecraft: A Critical Biography* ([1951]; Lincoln, Neb., 1966), esp. 134-168. "Sycophants" appears in chap. 1 (19); "sensualists" in chap. 2 (35); and "voluptuary" in chap. 4 (88) of the first American edition of Mary Wollstonecraft, *A Vindication of the Rights of Woman* (Philadelphia, 1792).

64. Sheila L. Skemp, *Judith Sargent Murray: A Brief Biography with Documents* (Boston, 1998), 119. Susanna Wright used the phrase at least twice. In "To Eliza Norris—at Fairhill," she wrote, "No Right, has man, his Equal, to controul, / Since, all

Murray's and Wollstonecraft's popularity in the United States proceeded on a parallel track over the course of the 1790s. From being "one of the most influential writers in New England and arguably in the United States" in the early 1790s, Judith Sargent Murray found her "reputation was in decline" by the end of the decade. It is to Murray's role in the early Republic that we now turn.[65]

Murray and Rowson had so much in common that it would have been surprising had they not met. Both were affiliated with the Federal Street Theatre in Boston. Murray had plays performed there in March of 1795 and 1796, whereas the Rowsons engaged with the theater from September 1796 through May 1797. In 1798, Rowson was among the subscribers to *The Gleaner,* a collection of Murray's essays. Murray and Rowson both contributed to the *Boston Weekly Magazine* from its debut in October 1802 through October 1805. (There is some debate over whether Rowson edited this journal, in which case she almost certainly would have corresponded with her contributor.) Unlike Rowson, Murray was born into a stable elite family with deep roots in colonial New England. But both women became ardent Federalists, both suffered financial reversals later in life, and both lived variations on the familial norm of the period. Rowson financially supported her husband and bore no children; Murray engaged in lengthy epistolary exchange with her future husband while married to her first and had two children at the then-advanced ages of thirty-eight and forty. Finally, each raised and

---

agree, There is no Sex in soul" (Carol Berkin and Leslie Horowitz, eds., *Women's Voices, Women's Lives: Documents in Early American History* [Boston, 1998], 191–192, esp. 191). In "On Friendship," she used the same trope to more passionate effect: "As Souls no Sexes have, I claim a Right / To love my Friend with that refin'd Delight / With all that Warmth, with all that pleasing Fire / A most harmonious Being can inspire" (Blecki and Wulf, eds., *Milcah Martha Moore's Book,* 143–145, esp. 144). Stockton's reference is cited later in the text (Mulford, ed., *Only for the Eye of a Friend,* 304–307, esp. 305–306).

65. Murray attributed this decline largely to hostile responses to her Federalist politics, which she believed subjected her to conspiratorial Republican efforts to sabotage sales of her work. (Chapter 4 explores the curious synthesis of Federalist politics and feminist theory in the 1790s.) Beyond "party politics," however, the similar pattern of influence shared by the two most ardent spokespeople for female rights and education during the decade suggests what Jeanne Boydston calls an important "shift in the authorizing discourse of American republicanism, particularly as it affected women." See Boydston, "Making Gender in the Early Republic: Judith Sargent Murray and the Revolution of 1800," in James Horn, Jan Ellen Lewis, and Peter S. Onuf, eds., *The Revolution of 1800: Democracy, Race, and the New Republic* (Charlottesville, Va., 2002), 240–266, esp. 240–241.

educated two young girls from outside her immediate family, demonstrating practical commitment to the tenets of her published writings.[66]

If Wollstonecraft's American reception attests to the climate of female anti-intellectualism that both made the self-abnegatory *Charlotte Temple* a hit and necessitated the covert nature of its call to female agency, Murray helps us understand the appeal of that call to certain of her readers. For it was Murray, more than any other writer of her day, who championed the consideration of self that Charlotte is so tragically lacking. Through essay, drama, and novel, Murray conveyed the principle of female self-approval, which she called variously "self-complacency" "self-estimation," "self-approbation," and "reverence of self." Arguing against the Puritan ideology of chastising children in order to eradicate the original sin of pride, Murray considered parental praise and the resultant estimation of self in young women an essential feature of childhood and adolescence, without which adult "rectitude" was impossible.[67]

The brilliance of Murray's argument here is that she linked a sense of "conscious worth" to the capacity for reasoned judgment, social fellowship, and ethical behavior. Though Murray did not ignore "personal attractions,"

66. Murray published seven poems in the *Boston Weekly Magazine* between Oct. 30, 1802, and Mar. 19, 1803. Rowson was a principal contributor to and possibly the editor of the magazine until it was sold in October 1805. On her potential editorial role, see Ellen Brandt, who supports it, and Dorothy Weil and Patricia Parker, who contest it. Murray contributed one poem to its successor, the *Boston Magazine* (October 1805–April 1806), in December 1805, whereas Rowson was a "frequent contributor." See R. W. G. Vail, *Susanna Haswell Rowson, the Author of Charlotte Temple: A Bibliographical Study* (Worcester, Mass., 1933), 27, 86; Ellen B. Brandt, *Susanna Haswell Rowson, America's First Best-Selling Novelist* (Chicago, 1975), chaps. 4, 6, 9; Sharon M. Harris, introduction, in Harris, ed., *Selected Writings of Judith Sargent Murray*, xxxvii, lx. On the young female relatives who entered the Stevens household in the early 1780s, whose "education was Judith's responsibility," see Karen L. Schiff, "Objects of Speculation: Early Manuscripts on Women and Education by Judith Sargent (Stevens) Murray," *Legacy*, XVII (2000), 213–228, esp. 215–216.

67. Murray, "Desultory Thoughts," in Harris, ed., *Selected Writings of Judith Sargent Murray*, 44. Both *The Traveller Returned* and *The Story of Margaretta* thematize the importance of self-worth in young women. Murray counters prevailing parenting methods as follows: "I would early impress, under proper regulations, a reverence of self; I would endeavour to rear to worth, and a consciousness thereof; I would be solicitous to inspire the glow of virtue, with that elevation of soul, that dignity, which is ever attendant upon self-approbation, arising from the genuine source of innate rectitude. . . . I am, from observation, persuaded, that many have suffered materially all their life long, from a depression of soul, early inculcated, in compliance to a false maxim, which hath supposed pride would thereby be eradicated" (ibid., 48).

her goal was to prevent women from focusing exclusively on the "person," in the eighteenth-century sense of the physical attributes of appearance, so as to involve the intellect in their sense of what made them worthwhile. Self-hood to Murray meant "intellectual existence." Only women who both knew their own mental worth and were capable of appreciating the complex order of their surroundings were able reliably to avoid Charlotte's fate. Arguing that "self-estimation will debasement shun," Murray describes she who does not estimate self in terms that call Charlotte to mind:

> But, lost to conscious worth, to decent pride,
> Compass nor helm there is, our course to guide:
> Nor may we anchor cast, for rudely tost
> In an unfathom'd sea, each motive's lost,
> Wildly amid contending waves we're beat,
> And rocks and quick sands, shoals and depths we meet;
> 'Till, dashe'd in pieces, or, till found'ring, we
> One common wreck of all our prospects see![68]

Whereas *Charlotte Temple* demonstrates the consequences of a lack of "self-estimation," *The Story of Margaretta,* Murray's only novel, tells the same story from the opposite point of view by portraying a character who resists seduction on the basis of the self-worth her adoptive parents, the aptly named Vigilliuses, have instilled in her. *The Story of Margaretta* possesses many of the key elements of *Charlotte Temple,* including a malevolent seducer aptly named Sinisterius Courtland. Margaretta, however, although tempted by Sinisterius, is able to resist his advances because "her self-confidence acts as a barrier against inordinate flattery, the downfall of most young women in early American novels."[69]

Paralleling Margaretta's own independence of mind, the novel eschews the explicit, if convoluted, didacticism characteristic of works such as *The Power of Sympathy* or *Charlotte Temple,* in favor of a looser narrative strategy that leaves a fair amount up to the reader. This approach to reading is thematized in the novel's discussion of how Margaretta should approach the ubiquitous genre. Mrs. Vigillius suggests that, rather than impose a ban on novel read-

68. On the equivalence of selfhood with mental attributes: "You must learn 'to reverence yourself,' that is, your intellectual existence" (Murray, "Desultory Thoughts," in Harris, ed., *Selected Writings of Judith Sargent Murray,* 44–47).

69. Harris, introduction, in Harris, ed., *Selected Writings of Judith Sargent Murray,* xxviii.

ing that is sure to be defied, she and her husband "permit" Margaretta to read them so as to learn to judge for herself. *The Story of Margaretta* allows its reader a similar latitude, not least by means of its own gender-bending authorial self-inscription. Our narrator, Mr. Vigillius, represents himself as a young, married man recently come into a small patrimony. However, by the time this novel, which was initially serialized in the *Massachusetts Magazine,* appeared in book form in *The Gleaner,* most readers would have known that the Gleaner, another male persona, was in fact Judith Sargent Murray, who also occasionally employed the female pseudonym "Constantia." By rendering her own authorial gender ambiguous, Murray attributes a certain humorous irony to the narrator's much-vaunted patriarchal authority as represented by his inheritance and his marriage. Through such devices, *The Story of Margaretta* represents a counternarrative to *Charlotte Temple,* which demonstrated the powerful effects of male privilege only too clearly.[70]

If Murray labored to raise female self-estimation, she did so at some cost to corporeal verisimilitude. According to one critic, Charlotte Temple's pregnancy literally devours her from within and becomes the mechanism by which her redemption is to be attained through the destruction of her body. The act of childbirth in that novel, then, in keeping with its actual status during the period, is both agonizing and deadly. In *Margaretta,* by contrast, it would seem that children emerge as painlessly as do pages from a press. "This very morning, the second day of July, one thousand seven hundred and ninety-four, witnessing the birth of a daughter to Margaretta, hath seemed to complete our family felicity," concludes Mr. Vigillius. In this awkwardly worded final sentence of the novel, temporal specificity is exact. But spatial and bodily representation is far less so. To begin with, the sentence lacks a human agent; its grammatical subject, "witnessing the birth," occurs without anyone there to do it. This act, moreover, completes, not the family itself, which would reference an actual group of bodies, but the abstract entity "family felicity." Margaretta, meanwhile, remains a static by-product of the process, as the cheery morning hour suggests that labor itself cost her no trouble at all.[71]

This juxtaposition of temporal exactitude with the nebulous physicality of the involved parties reminds the reader that, after all, Margaretta exists, not to experience pleasure or pain, but as an aid to the reader's own "fe-

70. Judith Sargent Murray, *The Story of Margaretta* (n.d.), in Harris, ed., *Selected Writings of Judith Sargent Murray,* 153–272, esp. 165.
71. Duane, "Pregnancy and the New Birth"; Murray, *Story of Margaretta,* 272.

licity," itself equated with an abstract "intellectual existence" that made little allowance for daily life. Elsewhere, Murray made this point directly, arguing that "literary improvement" was easily added to women's lives because "our avocations are . . . much less laborious" than men's. One imagines harried bodies attempting to read and stir a pudding at once. Moreover, even those women who attained intellectual parity with men were destined to take on ever more obligations, as Murray herself did when she began editing her husband's writings for publication in response to her family's increasingly desperate financial straits in the late 1790s. After 1805, these were Murray's only forays into print. Female intellectual existence itself, then, could easily be put to the service of daily survival, changing its contours in the process.[72]

Murray's very insensitivity to the female travail that Rowson found so compelling, however, might have made possible her single greatest contribution to female equality: the popularization of the concept of the sexless soul. As one who neither believed the female mind to be inherently deficient nor credited the degree to which bodies can influence mental states, she was uniquely suited for this construct. Armed with the Universalist tenet of universal salvation, a faith she converted to as an adult and that informed both her passionate second marriage and her prolific authorship, Murray was able not only to defend the disgraced Wollstonecraft and preach the merits of female self-regard but also to advise her readers that gender itself—that entity so sacred to the very men, from Rousseau to Benjamin Silliman, who denied women a role as full human beings—did not survive into the afterlife. "On the Equality of the Sexes," March–April 1790, begins with the introductory verse:

> Yet cannot I their sentiments imbibe,
> Who this distinction to the sex ascribe,
> As if a woman's form must needs enrol,
> A weak, a servile, an inferiour soul
> . . .
> Yet haste the era, when the world shall know,
> That such distinctions only dwell below;
> The soul unfetter'd, to no sex confin'd,
> Was for the abodes of cloudless day design'd

72. Harris, introduction, Murray, "On the Equality of the Sexes," and *The Traveller Returned,* all in Harris, ed., *Selected Writings of Judith Sargent Murray,* xl, 10, 118–119.

Anchoring one's claims for gender equality in the hereafter might seem to confer only limited benefits upon the present day. But it soon becomes clear that "soul," as Murray conceived of it, meant much more than the afterlife of the self. Rather, it informed everything from worldview to mood ("depression of soul") to subject position in a decidedly material world ("she who would possess her soul in serenity"). In fact, "soul" for Murray is exactly what we would call "self": not an otherworldly abstraction, but a shaping current of everyday experience.[73]

Murray is thus able to draw power from the spiritual realm of the sexless soul and redirect it toward her current surroundings with exceptional authority and righteous anger: "Yes, ye lordly, ye haughty sex, our souls are by nature *equal* to yours; the same breath of God animates, enlivens, and invigorates us." Here the word "equal" suggests, not sameness, but rather shared worth. And indeed, this soul that supposedly has no sex begins to look positively Amazonian in Murray's subsequent writings. Thus "Observations on Female Abilities" ends by cataloging instances of women who displayed miraculous courage and strength under extraordinary circumstances

73. Murray, "On the Equality of the Sexes," in Harris, ed., *Selected Writings of Judith Sargent Murray*, 3–4. The overlaps between Wollstonecraft's and Murray's arguments are many, and the chronology is shifting, with each anticipating the other on certain matters. Wollstonecraft does refer to the sexless soul in her opening salvo: "To account for, and excuse the tyranny of man, many ingenious arguments have been brought forward to prove, that the two sexes, in the acquirement of virtue, ought to aim at attaining a very different character: or, to speak explicitly, women are not allowed to have sufficient strength of mind to acquire what really deserves the name of virtue. Yet it should seem, allowing them to have souls, that there is but one way appointed by Providence to lead mankind to either virtue or happiness." She also writes, "Yet thus to give a sex to mind was not very consistent with the principles of a man [Rousseau] who argued so warmly, and so well, for the immortality of the soul." See Mary Wollstonecraft, *A Vindication of the Rights of Woman,* Norton Critical Edition, ed. Carol H. Poston (New York, 1988), 19, 42. Benjamin Silliman makes much of this claim in his attack on her: "This female philosopher indignantly rejects the idea of a sex in the soul, pronouncing the sensibility, timidity and tenderness of women, to be merely artificial refinements of character, introduced and fostered by men, to render sensual pleasure more voluptuous." See Silliman, "From *The Letters of Shahcoolen,*" in Wollstonecraft, *A Vindication of the Rights of Woman,* ed. Poston, 237–240, esp. 238. Note here that "female philosopher" is left to speak for itself as a term of denigration, which suggests that his readers would already have understood it as such, associating intellect with unwomanliness. Note also that, despite this introductory shaming, Silliman accurately reprises her argument in the rest of the sentence—he is paying close attention to this so-called promoter of errors.

(running into a burning building to save a child) and who went to similarly incredible lengths when confronted with unspeakable loss (mourning a dead one beyond all measure). "These great expressions of nature," Murray writes, "these heart-rending emotions, which fill us at once with wonder, compassion and terror, always have belonged, and always will belong, only to Women. They possess, in those moments, an inexpressible something, which carries them beyond themselves; and they seem to discover to us *new souls,* above the standard of humanity." The sexless soul, it would seem, is Murray's instrument. But the reappropriated feminine soul is the source of that profound affectual register that will become Rowson's provenance and that of the sentimental novel beyond her.[74]

Given the ambivalence early American women displayed toward the concept of female equality, perhaps it is not surprising that all advocates of the sexless soul did not follow the concept to its most subversive ends. Annis Boudinot Stockton sums up this conscious retraction in her letter to her daughter. "You know it is a favourite tenet with me that there is no sex in Soul—I believe it as firmly as I do my existence." Stockton illustrates her argument in terms that strictly parallel Murray's own claims in "Observations on Female Abilities": "that there are many men, that have been taught, and have *not* obtained any great degree of knowledge in the circle of the Sciences—and that there *have* been women who have excelled in every branch, when they have had an opportunity of instruction, and I have no doubt if those advantages were oftener to occur, we should see more instances." But she backs off, much as Drinker demurred on the "independence" she nonetheless recognized as a worthy option: "but at the same time I do not think that the sexes were made to be independent of each other . . . if our education was the same, our improvement would be the same—*but there is no occasion for exactly the same education.*"[75]

These female American soul searchers, with their endless back-and-forthing between defending the status quo and wanting to alter the social order, speak Rowson's mind in the early 1790s and suggest why she found so many readers stateside. It's not that she was unable to see the efficacy of a more egalitarian society; she just also recognized the fervency with which we hold tight to the familiar, however poorly it may serve our own best interests. Haltingly, however, the female soul that she, her fellow writers, and her readers articulated, with its antagonistic commitments to self-abnegation

74. Murray, "On the Equality of the Sexes," "Observations on Female Abilities," in Harris, ed., *Selected Writings of Judith Sargent Murray,* 8, 43 (emphasis added).
75. Mulford, ed., *Only for the Eye of a Friend,* 306.

and self-approval, to passive acceptance and intellectual assertion, to reasoned moderation and fervent outcry, founds the nineteenth-century sentimental novel and the antebellum domestic counterpublic sphere. Charlotte
is its other, its backward reflection, its Janus face. The rest of this book will
show how Rowson and her readers turned away from Charlotte as the century closed, even as they could never leave her behind.

So what, ultimately, did Charlotte warn virgins against? The importance
of not taking warnings too seriously but instead attending to impulse, that
faint track of self, as something potentially worthy. And Rowson herself was
only too ready to comply. Although cautionary tales continued to pepper her
later novels, poems, plays, and educational tracts, she tended increasingly
to favor modes of articulation based in "complacency" rather than "continual reproach." If Charlotte demonstrated for American readers the consequences of the abdication of female choice, Rowson subsequently turned
from her negative example to consider the successful reconciliation of female
agency with accountability to authority. Rowson would attempt this feat
in a stunning variety of print and performative vehicles. But perhaps the
best indication that she found self-regard an essential precursor to Anglo-
American female agency is the care she took to shape her authorial persona
as a discursive entity that may stand as her most influential creation. Again,
she worked with an acute sense of the pitfalls and prejudices that awaited
her, finely crafting her projected image so as to win over the distrustful and
evade the perennially hostile. The result was a creation that attested both
to the profound "circumscriptions" within which female authorship and the
socially turned female subject it metonymized took place in the early Republic and the ingenuity such limitations inspired. These twin phenomena are
the subject of the following chapter.

2 REPRESENTING ROWSON

The difficulty displaced, the heroic energy diffused in merely living
a life, is an incalculable quantity.
— Adrienne Rich, "Bradstreet and Her Poetry"

It is well established that bourgeois liberalism constructed itself out of the exclusion of women. Their absence from "the quasi-autonomous public of the bourgeois era" constituted that entity rather than merely followed as an effect. Such foundational exclusion, however, did not keep post-Revolutionary women—in particular, literary women—from playing important roles in "civil society," that is, "any and all publics except those dedicated to the organized politics constituted in political parties and elections to local, state, and national office." Indeed, in certain ways, female authors helped address fissures within the early national public sphere itself. Precisely because women of a certain station were deemed caretakers for communitarian virtues (modesty, altruism, self-denial) that were ever less useful in a market capitalist society premised on individual ambition, they were particularly adept at helping readers come to terms with aspects of bourgeois liberalism that didn't go according to plan: when self-interest, for example, didn't lead to universal betterment or when the supposedly self-possessive individual did not, in fact, achieve command over destructive impulse. At the same time, that "Poor woman" who "presume[d] to speak" in print undermined damning analyses of women's capacity for public life merely by entering print culture. Indeed, far from serving as mere embellishments to the fledgling early American publishing industry, female authors paradoxically both fed it with voluminous print matter and allowed it to be perceived in less strictly profit-based terms than were necessarily merited.[1]

1. Joan B. Landes, *Women and the Public Sphere in the Age of the French Revolution* (Ithaca, N.Y., 1988), 6; Mary Kelley, *Learning to Stand and Speak: Women, Education, and Public Life in America's Republic* (Chapel Hill, N.C., 2006), 5; Susanna Rowson, "Rights of Woman," *Boston Weekly Magazine*, Oct. 30, 1802, 2, rpt. in Rowson, *Miscellaneous Poems; by Susanna Rowson, Preceptress of The Ladies' Academy, Newton,*

The particular crisis Susanna Rowson addressed for her readers—not only in her published writings but through her acting, staged dramas, academy exhibitions, poetic orations, teaching, and social leadership—concerned the ill fit between European notions of genteel self-worth and an early national market economy that made gentility accessible to a burgeoning middle class only by transforming it into something almost unrecognizable to its elite origins. Rowson showed how a woman of English blood and birth and a genteel competency, deprived of wealth early on and forced to rely on her own labors to keep body and soul together in the northeastern United States, could not only remain the lady but in fact epitomize a new and more flexible American gentility: one that welcomed participation, including female participation, in the labor economy.

One might well question the value of her accomplishment. To make

---

Mass. (Boston, 1804), 98, 115. Carol Pateman, Gillian Brown, and Elizabeth Dillon have compellingly described how the denial of agency to women within seventeenth- and eighteenth-century political philosophy made possible "the founding fictions of liberalism," from the social contract to possessive individualism to the literary public sphere. Pateman's polemic might be said to initiate this line of inquiry, as it delineates women's foundational, if externalized, relationship to liberal political theory (Pateman, *The Sexual Contract* [Stanford, Calif., 1988]). More recently, Dillon contributes a sustained and passionate analysis of gender and liberalism in early America. Arguing that "since the founding of the U.S. state, women have been overtly excluded from the purview of liberal citizenship," she insists that, "while it is indeed the case that the figure of the woman within liberalism often stands opposed to the autonomous, white male liberal subject . . . this opposition is itself crucial to liberal thought and culture" (Dillon, *The Gender of Freedom: Fictions of Liberalism and the Literary Public Sphere* [Stanford, Calif., 2004], 3, 11). See Brown, *Domestic Individualism: Imagining Self in Nineteenth-Century America* (Berkeley, Calif., 1990), and *The Consent of the Governed: The Lockean Legacy in Early American Culture* (Cambridge, Mass., 2001). Arguing that "fiction had its roots . . . in both the property claims of authors and the sentimental dispossession of women," Catherine Gallagher situates the above "opposition" within the British literary marketplace, addressing both women's active role and their "dispossession" within it. My argument here owes a great deal to her work, in particular her insistence that

> far from disavowing remunerative authorship as unfeminine, [many women writers in the late seventeenth and eighteenth centuries] relentlessly embraced and feminized it. And, far from creating only minor and forgettable variations on an essentially masculine figure, they delineated crucial features of "the author" for the period in general by emphasizing their trials and triumphs in the marketplace.

See Gallagher, *Nobody's Story: The Vanishing Acts of Women Writers in the Marketplace, 1670–1820* (Berkeley, Calif., 1994), xiii, 195.

gentility something many labored to attain rather than the birthright of a chosen few meant to abolish its ease, its commitment to pleasure, its focus on the moment of sociable exchange as opposed to the social capital to be extracted from such a moment, whereas to insist that the increasingly middling masses become genteel was to impose the introjection of authority upon a population for whom the benefits of such internalization were questionable. Not only did a democratized gentility tamp down potential political unrest by suggesting that correct self-management, not social critique, was the key to personal satisfaction, but it did so without providing industrious aspirants to bourgeois status the degree of comfort and leisure that made self-restraint more of a pleasurable performance than a painful sacrifice for the truly wealthy. The cramped kitchens, the stuffy parlors; for what did the inhabitants of such spaces agree not to indulge unruly passions? And although the novel was undoubtedly one of the more pleasurable institutions of the new gentility (hence the suspicion with which it was often viewed), one may be forgiven for imagining a world in which Tabitha Tenney's absurdist picaresque *Female Quixotism* or Phillis Wheatley's soon-forgotten *Poems on Various Subjects* had reached more readers than the salubrious fables of Susanna Rowson, Hannah Webster Foster, and Judith Sargent Murray.[2]

And yet: however the new gentility narrowed horizons for both aspirants to bourgeois status and the increasingly penalized "coarse population" denied such aspiration, it provided literate Anglo-American women an avenue for citizenship that nationality alone did not. It underlay the expansion in female education, the developing emphasis on powerful mothering, even the increasing valorization of unmarried life as a potentially worthy opportunity for self-respecting intellectual inquiry and charitable service. Thus it is no coincidence that Rowson, a loyalist descendant, became a particularly potent emblem of American womanhood to her readers and critics. With her background in elite English society and her willingness to make change

2. Tabitha Gilman Tenney, *Female Quixotism: Exhibited in the Romantic Opinions and Extravagant Adventures of Dorcasina Sheldon,* ed. Jean Nienkamp and Andrea Collins (New York, 1992); Phillis Wheatley, *Poems on Various Subjects, Religious and Moral* (Philadelphia, 1786). On the twin phenomena of public censure of novel-reading and a flourishing indulgence therein, see in particular Richard D. Brown, *Knowledge Is Power: The Diffusion of Information in Early America, 1700–1865* (New York, 1989), esp. 195–196. In *Civil Tongues and Polite Letters in British America* (Chapel Hill, N.C., 1997), David S. Shields delineates the focus on pleasure, play, and enjoyment of the moment characteristic of elite colonial gentility.

a constant in her life, she epitomized American strivings for both cultural legitimacy and unscripted adventure. And she offered just enough of each to make her a household name from Boston to Baltimore.[3]

All the more amazing is that Rowson's early champions saw the activities she embraced in her quest for survival and public recognition as shameful threats to her reputation, which they were only too happy to omit from the historical record. From the anonymous "Candid" to Mathew Carey and John Swanwick in the 1790s to Samuel Lorenzo Knapp in the 1810s and 1820s, Rowson's supporters in print were in a lather to cleanse her reputation of any professional ambition or market savvy. Generally, if one wanted to stand up for Rowson in published writing, one was a progressive-minded supporter of female educational parity, a true believer in the "sexless soul" model of intellectual equality championed by Mary Wollstonecraft, Judith Sargent Murray, and Annis Boudinot Stockton. But whatever Carey and Swanwick wrote about the rights of woman in the abstract, they adopted quite a different tone where their favorite female author was concerned. To keep Rowson from becoming a disgrace in the eyes of their readers, these men dressed her up until she was almost unrecognizable.

That leading advocates for female educational equality should have acted thus suggests that the two modes of expression that constituted a vocabulary for gender discussion in this period were both in constant use by literate early Americans of all stripes. In one, the soul had no sex, and educations and booklists were to be devised accordingly. In another, it most certainly did, and assumed sexual difference grounded deferential and defamatory narrative depictions of women. Understanding what prompted such acknowledged advocates of gender reform as Carey, Swanwick, and

3. Joyce Appleby describes the effects of "commercial growth" and a "more complex economy" on economic and social structures in the 1790s, noting among other things a reappearing "division between rich and poor" (Appleby, *Capitalism and a New Social Order: The Republican Vision of the 1790s* [New York, 1984], 10–11). According to Richard L. Bushman, as the barrier between "polished" and "crude" came to divide, not the elite from the middling and lower orders, but rather the elite and middling orders from the "coarse population," being "on the margins of American culture" became ever more humiliating (Bushman, *The Refinement of America: Persons, Houses, Cities* [New York, 1992], 279). On the relationship between economic development and gender norms, see Nancy Armstrong, *Desire and Domestic Fiction: A Political History of the Novel* (New York, 1987); Gillian Brown, *Domestic Individualism;* Lora Romero, *Home Fronts: Domesticity and Its Critics in the Antebellum United States* (Durham, N.C., 1997); and Lori Merish, *Sentimental Materialism: Gender, Commodity Culture, and Nineteenth-Century American Literature* (Durham, N.C., 2000).

Knapp toward alternately egalitarian and paternalistic representations of womankind greatly helps us see how these contradictory frames of reference delimited (and failed to delimit) the ways in which women such as Rowson and her readers could represent themselves, both introspectively and socially.

In celebrating Mrs. Rowson, why did her early admirers feel compelled to misrepresent her? The answer lies within three areas undergoing rapid transformation in the early national period: gender identity, the quest for a gentility compatible with democratic egalitarianism, and the developing marketplace for books. One important function of early American sentimental fiction was "reinventing capitalist economic and commodity structures as the forms of interiority proper to 'private,' domestic life." In their eagerness to divorce Rowson from circumstantial motivations to textual production, Rowson's critics certainly participated in this process, creating a figure of the female author untouched by the grubberies of the print marketplace and operating purely according to a "proper interiority." Even Rowson's most strident detractor, William Cobbett, reinforced the association between female literary activity and a sanitized market by suggesting that her absorption into the profit-driven publishing industry deprived her of her womanhood, making of her a specter that foreshadowed Wollstonecraft's reputation within the United States after the publication of Godwin's *Memoirs*.[4]

The urge to set female authorship apart from market-based strivings, in turn, reinforced the prevailing assumption that women were to play a regulatory role in liberal capitalist America, consuming according to standards of taste that precluded "indiscriminate enjoyments." Embodying an ethic of restraint and self-sacrifice increasingly associated, as the 1790s progressed, with outdated communitarian ideology, this appraisal of womanhood assuaged anxieties implicit in market capitalist emphases on private property and the "free, autonomous" individual. Moreover, given women's predominance as readers in the early Republic, stressing the distinct status of the female author helped protect against the alarming possibility that reading constituted one venue into, if not an actual aspect of, political enfranchisement. The display of genteel refinement characteristic of early American female authorship as portrayed by these men, then, was possessed of remarkable powers: not only did it ennoble women while simultaneously relieving them of their explicit political potential, but it also allowed the marketplace—and in particular the rapidly expanding publishing industry—to flourish disencumbered of its more threatening and grotesque asso-

4. Merish, *Sentimental Materialism*, 2–3.

ciations. Rowson, as seen by the first to describe her in print, was a crucial figure in this cultural project.[5]

Taking Rowson as its case study, this chapter focuses on four colleagues' representations of her: William Cobbett, Mathew Carey, John Swanwick, and Samuel Knapp. How did Rowson's commentators configure her, and how did the contours of this figure change over the course of her life and her subsequent critical appraisal? How did she herself anticipate, participate in, defy, or defer to this process through her own authorial persona, an equally (but distinctly) biased, ever-changing discursive entity in implicit and explicit dialogue with the images of her put forth by her critics?

The previous chapter introduced two poles along which literate, educated women came to self-knowledge and social fellowship in the 1790s, as they employed the concept of the sexless soul to assert their capacities for meaningful self-direction without being tarnished by the increasingly influential brand of the "manly woman." These two frames of reference may seem to have little in common. In the former, the human subject exists before its gendering, subordinating the categories of "male" and "female" to the business of crafting a self. In the latter, by contrast, gender exerts so deep an influence over personal identity that a woman who attempts to master the skills, engage in the behaviors, and exert the public influence conventionally due to men makes of herself a monster and an outcast.

Yet these concepts are not entirely dissimilar, even though antagonists in the battle for female empowerment developed them. Both envision a breakdown in the distinction between male and female: their differences stem from whether they view this altered state as a welcome clarification (in which the screen of gender difference lifts to reveal a yet greater and universally human potential) or a terrible inversion (in which the two sexes survive intertwined, embattled, mutilated, and horrific). Further testifying to their similarity, both these views found expression in the statements of the same individuals throughout the early national period. We will see ahead that the tension between an essentialist view of womanhood that cast gender difference as innate and the developing current of thought that saw it instead as historical artifact influenced how a wide variety of male intellectuals wrote about the nation's most prominent female author—and how she constituted her own authorial persona in response.

5. Ibid., 86; Dillon, *Gender of Freedom,* 2; Glenn Hendler, *Public Sentiments: Structures of Feeling in Nineteenth-Century American Literature* (Chapel Hill, N.C., 2001), 117.

The struggle to reconcile female entrance into the public sphere with the continued valorization of gender difference occurred on many fronts in the early national period. The rapid increase in female literacy and girls' formal education from the 1790s through the 1820s, for instance, clearly both fostered and resulted from a lessening emphasis on innate differences of intellectual capacity between the sexes. At the same time, a new separatism introduced itself into male and female literacy, as the latter "became conventional by close association with family moral development" at the very moment such development began to be seen as women's work.

The post-Revolutionary spike in female education and literacy rates, moreover, was but one facet of a larger transformation in early national print culture. New print technologies and methods of publication began to augment the number of available books; magazines became far more prevalent; and new systems of distribution, from itinerant peddlers to circulating, social, and subscription libraries, made print matter available to an ever-wider geographic and economic swath of the United States population. Subject matter changed as well, as concern with civic criticism gave way to emphasis on moral reform. With these two shifts, the function of reading changed, as the early Republic experienced a "recasting of the site of critical pressure . . . from that in which political functionaries were made accountable for their actions in public roles to one in which private individuals were presented with fictional representations of ordinary life (for example, those of domestic production and reproduction)." In sum, "a civic ideology of publication" was giving way to "the kind of private imaginary appropriate to nationalism," wherein readers saw themselves less as active members of a corporate body than as the individualized embodiment of the national project.[6]

In all these arenas, competing concepts of the significance of gender and its relation to personal and political agency coexisted uneasily. For instance, through circulating libraries, women gained easier access to their fare of

6. Richard D. Brown, *Knowledge Is Power,* 165. On post-Revolutionary female education and literacy, see Susan Branson, *These Fiery Frenchified Dames: Women and Political Culture in Early National Philadelphia* (Philadelphia, 2001), esp. 21–27; on colonial precedents, see E. Jennifer Monaghan, "Literacy Instruction and Gender in Colonial New England," in Cathy N. Davidson, ed., *Reading in America: Literature and Social History* (Baltimore, 1989), 53–80. On print technology and distribution, see Branson, *These Fiery Frenchified Dames,* 22–23, and Davidson, *Revolution and the Word: The Rise of the Novel in America* (1986; New York, 2004), 27–29. On changing functions of reading, see Grantland Rice, *The Transformation of Authorship in America* (Chicago, 1997), 148; Michael Warner, *The Letters of the Republic: Publication and the Public Sphere in Eighteenth-Century America* (Cambridge, Mass., 1990), 172.

choice—often, novels—only to find themselves the subject of innumerable diatribes against female novelistic license, in which women were posited as more susceptible than men to the dangers of imaginative identification with the villainous or naïve. Similarly, magazines "encouraged women's contributions" and featured an increasing "volume of contributions on the topic of gender roles," only to publish numerous essays arguing against expanded rights for women. And a new emphasis on moral introspection as opposed to civic extroversion possessed special relevance to female readers (in their ascribed roles as gatekeepers of the national conscience) yet discouraged explicit engagement with matters of state that had previously been a standard feature of Anglo-American literacy.[7]

Here, the transformation that most concerns us is in the role of authorship. Authors living in the United States in the 1790s occupied a tenuous first rung on what would, over the next thirty years, become a fledgling profession: a lower rung, in fact, than did printers and publishers, many of whom had begun to make a living at their jobs. Nonexistent or weak copyright laws testified to the fact that authors did not own their work in the sense we now take for granted, and rampant piracy demonstrated the inevitable results of this situation. Women, who often published anonymously, experienced such invisibility disproportionately. Nevertheless, they played a huge role in transforming the industry, as authorship came to be seen as a professional endeavor directed at a popular readership as opposed to a civic duty aimed at a like-minded elite: as Nina Baym points out, "The literary profession, which opened to women early in the nation's history—indeed, it might be more accurate to say that the profession was opened *by* them—supported a very wide range of female endeavor." The dawning of a professionalized print marketplace in the late-eighteenth-century northeastern United States brought forth no less than "a new woman-centered public forum."[8]

Of the innumerable individuals who participated in this new forum—including figures as diverse as Hannah Adams, Abigail Abbot Bailey, Ann Eliza Schuyler Bleecker, Judith Sargent Murray, and Mercy Otis Warren—none has, in recent years, been more identified than Rowson with the transi-

7. Robert B. Winans, "The Growth of a Novel-Reading Public in Late Eighteenth-Century America," *Early American Literature,* IX (1975), 267–275; Branson, *These Fiery Frenchified Dames,* 24–25; Richard D. Brown, *Knowledge Is Power,* 195–196. Indulgence often prevailed over censure, as magazines in the 1780s and 1790s published more fiction than they did denouncements of it.

8. Davidson, *Revolution and the Word,* 35; Nina Baym, *American Women Writers and the Work of History, 1790–1860* (New Brunswick, N.J., 1995), 3; Branson, *These Fiery Frenchified Dames,* 22.

tion from colonial American letters to the publishing enterprise in place by the 1820s. The gift economy of colonial elite civic discourse—where authorship was nonremunerative and most texts (often unpublished letters and manuscripts) circulated within a highly delimited community—gave way by the end of this period to a professionalized commodity marketplace of letters involving a far greater proportion of the nation's inhabitants. And if there is one word associated with Rowson, it is "professional." Scholars have called her "the first American professional writer of fiction," noted her "diligent professionalism," and classed her with Charles Brockden Brown as having "been called America's first professional novelists." As such critics point out, Rowson, along with virtually every other author of the American 1790s, was unable to support herself through novels alone. This was partly because the population was still too sparse and copyright law did not protect her fictions written in England, and partly owing to her own miscalculations as she made the transition from English to American presses. But critics are also unanimous in emphasizing her concerted attempt to profit from her writings: put succinctly, she was a "professional-minded writer" who "wished to exploit the market." Rowson, in other words,

> was ready . . . to conform to American conditions of literary production. . . . This readiness to consult the market and adapt to it her literary stock-in-trade . . . gives Mrs. Rowson standing as an early American writer of true professional temperament . . . [who] did not write for pastime, but from compulsion and for profit.[9]

9. On the colonial gift economy of letters, see Shields, *Civil Tongues,* xxx–xxxi. On Rowson's professionalization, see William Charvat, *The Profession of Authorship in America, 1800–1870: The Papers of William Charvat,* ed. Matthew J. Bruccoli (1968; New York, 1992), 19–24; Davidson, *Revolution and the Word,* 34, and "The Life and Times of Charlotte Temple: The Biography of a Book," in Davidson, ed., *Reading in America,* 160; Mary Kelley, *Private Woman, Public Stage: Literary Domesticity in Nineteenth-Century America* (Chapel Hill, N.C., 2002), 11. Among Rowson's "miscalculations," Charvat includes attempting to publish *Trials of the Human Heart* by subscription and trying to write a historical novel with "no good models to guide her" (Charvat, *Profession of Authorship,* ed. Bruccoli, 21–22). Kelley notes that Rowson was part of a period where "for the first time the American writer could consider the possibility of linking creative effort with vocation" but comments that "neither [Brown nor Rowson] was able to live on earnings from writing." By contrast, Kelley's "pioneer" woman writer is Catharine Maria Sedgwick, who could live "comfortably" on her earnings from publication beginning in the 1820s (Kelley, *Private Woman,* 11, 13). Davidson writes, "Like most novelists in late-eighteenth century England and *every* novelist in America before 1820, Rowson was never able to support herself solely by

PLATE 14. *Catalogue of the Minerva Library. From Dorothy Blakey,* The Minerva Press, 1790–1820 *(London, 1939). The Bodleian Library, University of Oxford*

This wish first expressed itself through her affiliation with Minerva Press in England, where the general practice was to pay anonymous female authors a flat fee per book as publisher William Lane grew rich catering to the wide demand for Gothic and seduction novels in the 1790s. Minerva Press was London's leading printer in the late eighteenth century; it would have been an excellent training ground for Rowson's protoprofessionalism in the United States. Lane treated books like any other commodity, purchasing them in lots where possible, as he probably did with *Mentoria* and *Charlotte,* the first two manuscripts he bought from Rowson. And he understood the importance of creating distribution networks for one's wares, since he

writing novels" ("Life and Times of Charlotte Temple," in Davidson, ed., *Reading in America,* 160).

began his career organizing the circulating libraries that his publications subsequently supplied.

Rowson's choice to work with Lane, after initially publishing with two other successful London printing houses, foreshadowed her equally canny arrangement with Mathew Carey upon arriving in Philadelphia. Like Lane, Carey was superbly skilled at creating distribution networks for his books. In fact, *Charlotte* itself can be seen as a token of the overlapping distribution of reprinted English novels and American productions throughout the northeast in the 1790s. While Rowson happened to be in Philadelphia during the time that *Charlotte* was first printed there, many more of Lane's publications were also imported and stocked in the same circulating libraries and bookpeddlers' wagons that carried the so-called "first best-selling 'American' novel."[10]

When Harriet Venables, a highly sympathetic character in Rowson's partly autobiographical novel, *Trials of the Human Heart,* names her favorite authors, Minerva writers feature largely on the list: Agnes Maria Bennett, Frances Burney, and Sophia Lee. (An early novel by Rowson, *The Inquisitor; or, The Invisible Rambler,* published in 1788, also praises three women authors: Hannah More, Elizabeth Inchbald, and, again, Burney.) *Trials* mentions two Minerva publications by Bennett: *Anna; or, The Welch Heiress* (1785), which Harriet describes herself reading; and *Juvenile Indiscretions* (1786), which appears in a footnote. (Lane also published *Warbeck: A Pathetic Tale* [1786], identified as a French novel translated by Lee, and an 1815 edition of Burney's *Evelina*.) When Harriet exclaims that these authors "would snatch the British novel from oblivion," she not only trumpets

10. In addition to *Charlotte* and *Mentoria,* Lane published *The Fille de Chambre* in 1792, Rowson's last book before leaving England, and a second edition of *Reuben and Rachel* in 1799. *Mentoria* sold for three shillings, *Charlotte* for five. According to Patricia L. Parker, Lane "usually paid . . . between ten and twenty pounds for the copyright and then in the usual practice kept all proceeds himself" (Parker, *Susanna Rowson* [Boston, 1986], 48–49). William Charvat sets the fee at between five and twenty guineas. Rowson's other two English printers were James Lackington and the firm of G. G. J. and J. Robinson (headed by George Robinson, known as "King of the Booksellers") (Charvat, *Profession of Authorship,* ed. Bruccoli, 19). Lackington, Robinson, and Lane are said by Ellen Brandt to constitute "the great London 'triumvirate' of late eighteenth-century printing houses." Brandt provides excellent contextualization for her claim that *Charlotte* is indeed the first best-selling American novel, comparing it to the three novels Frank Luther Mott identified as prior American best sellers, Samuel Richardson's *Pamela* and *Clarissa* and Jonathan Swift's *Gulliver's Travels* (Brandt, *Susanna Haswell Rowson, America's First Best-Selling Novelist* [Chicago, 1975], 33, 53, 60, 63).

Minerva's commercial success but also links the popularization of fiction to aesthetic progress and increased national glory. In transposing Minerva's formula to the United States, where print culture more or less began in the popular mode, Rowson similarly suggested that her own widespread popularity there might serve as an aid, rather than an impediment, to both her and America's cultural standing.[11]

Despite her own frank willingness to accommodate the production of literary commodities to the cultivation of taste, however, several of Rowson's contemporaries were equally committed to the premise that she labored for the good of her soul alone. Not surprisingly, their own reputations had something to do with these efforts. Preserving a notion of innate gender difference as a factor in authorship, they protected their conception of the literary endeavor, its place in the young nation, and their resultant stature as public intellectuals.

To keep Rowson from suffering the fate of a Wollstonecraft, Rowson's first critics did not, as would have a Murray or a Stockton, invoke her fitness as a sexless soul to enter the sphere of symbolic exchange. Rather, they demonstrated that her participation in the public sphere depended upon her womanly capacity to remain above grubby considerations of profit and loss, fame and fortune. In so doing, they worked to preserve a view of authorship as an upper-class, noncompensatory activity, even as the publication practices in which they, and she, participated increasingly took place within "the nomenclature of the market." Ironically, then, in foreclosing on Rowson's capacity to function in professional terms as well as or better than a published male author, they were in fact attempting to preserve a notion of political agency that was undergoing "a very real loss . . . as a tradition of civic authorship was reconfigured by the new demands of a market society." What both they and modern critics who lament this reconfiguration may not fully credit, however, is that, whatever the changing contours of authorial practice, it unequivocally made room in the early national period for a variety of new, and often female, bodies—which found their own ways to exert agency within existing "demands."[12]

11. Susanna Rowson, *Trials of the Human Heart: A Novel,* 4 vols. (Philadelphia, 1795), IV, 74; Rowson, *The Inquisitor; or, The Invisible Rambler,* 3 vols. (Philadelphia, 1793), II, 90; [Agnes Maria] Bennett, *Anna; or, The Welch Heiress* (London, 1785), and *Juvenile Indiscretions* (London, 1786); Frances Burney, *Evelina: A New Edition* ([1778]; London, 1815); [Francois-Thomas-Marie de Baculard d'Arnaud], *Warbeck: A Pathetic Tale,* [trans. Sophia Lee] (London, 1786).

12. Rice, *Transformation of Authorship,* 155–156. Steven Watts summarizes the early national transition from republican to liberal ideology as follows: this struggle of

Thus Rowson's early champions, even more than her sole detractor, demonstrated that, to welcome a female author into the literary public sphere, both she and it must be severely constrained. Their appraisals suggest that the preservation of a gender binary remained crucial, despite their otherwise progressive leanings, because it seemed to offer protection from something more terrifying than even a manly woman: the unchecked self-interest and competitive ethos that underlay the burgeoning market of letters. By insisting that Rowson remain above the market, her advocates only emphasized how pervasive that market was and how deeply they still cherished values such as altruism and paternalistic deference, even if they couldn't quite use

---

"'virtue and commerce' . . . pitted an older ideal of self-sacrifice and civic community against a growing instinct for individual ambition, advancement, and expression. . . . Thus, by the 1790s . . . [a] republican model of politics . . . subtly became a liberal one. . . . In this mercurial atmosphere a market politics was born." Watts notes a correlation between the ascendance of liberalism and the ascription of republican virtues to women: "The old republican tradition of self-sacrificing 'virtue' was becoming feminized and privatized, while an emerging liberal imperative of 'self-interest' appeared increasingly masculinized and publicized." As the genre most closely associated with female culture, the novel was thus increasingly denied a role in political life: "a potential discourse of political perception and power became depoliticized as it was translated into a literary discourse of imaginative, privatized communication." See Watts, *The Romance of Real Life: Charles Brockden Brown and the Origins of American Culture* (Baltimore, Md., 1994), 5, 18, 25, 143. Rice similarly argues for the ascendancy of liberal culture in the 1790s, stating that during this period "a rights-based politics and a liberal jurisprudence attempted to rationalize all cultural activity in terms of private material production." But where Watts associates the novel with disavowed values, Rice points out the novel's long-acknowledged status as liberalism's "literary offspring." Where both critics agree is in the novel's increasing externality to the processes of political formation. Thus Rice suggests that "the twinned tales of virtue and seduction, fidelity and coquetry . . . may remain as symptomatic artifacts" (Rice, *Transformation of Authorship,* 155–156). Although I do not share these critics' view of the political inefficacy of the novel (I think it represents a conflation of attitudes represented in novels with the work of the novels themselves), there is no doubt that women were granted influence over societal values that did not sit well with liberal market society precisely because they were perceived as lacking a constitutive role within that society. That is not to say they in fact lacked one, as Rowson's case exemplifies. Often, as Dillon, Catherine Allgor, Rosemarie Zagarri, and others point out, their ability to enter the liberal public sphere depended precisely upon their association with qualities disavowed within it. For this reason, feminist scholars of late have acknowledged the status of these two formative political concepts, republicanism and liberalism, as "related ideologies" in the 1790s (Dillon, *Gender of Freedom,* 128, 143).

them in their present circumstances. Rowson's supporters made female authors the guardians of a communitarian ethos at the very moment such an ethos no longer particularly served the economic interest—but when it was all the more cherished for that reason.

If the details of this picture have to do with the publishing industry of the 1790s, the overall effect is much broader. As important as any particular set of circumstances that Rowson must transcend was the fact that she must eschew situational motivation altogether so as to cohere into a static figure signifying unchanging truths. Through Rowson, that is, her critics suggested that proper femaleness was the capacity for innateness itself, the pure emblematicity that only those who don't change with historical circumstance can embody. In order for her to function as "an emblematic figure for her male contemporaries, a representation of deserving, dispossessed authorship," Rowson's actual market savvy and relish for self-promotion must be minimized, her self-sacrifice and vulnerability exaggerated. Most of all, her iconic capacity itself must be protected. In this role, moreover, Rowson represented not only the female author but idealized American womanhood itself. Paradoxically, then, critics used Rowson's influential presence in the literary public sphere to inscribe and reify women's supposed absence from the making, as opposed to mere enacting, of history.

Rowson, however, was no passive observer in this project. Perhaps the most profound aspect of her professionalism, in fact, has to do with how she took advantage not only of authorship's changing material conditions in the new Republic but also of its new discursive possibilities. Not least of these was a profound alteration in how and how deeply the author insinuated herself into the reader's mind. The self-conscious representation and distribution of an authorial persona who in some sense transcended anything she wrote, despite the fact that she was created out of exactly those writings, was something new in the post-Revolutionary bourgeois public sphere. This persona could be, and in Rowson's case was, transmitted through prefaces, narrative interjection, stage appearances, and even social deportment. It owed a great deal to changing perceptions of selfhood during the period, from something relatively stable and integrated to a pluralistic, serial entity "composed in, of and for successive performances." Oddly, then, the less stable that selfhood revealed itself to be, the more examination it seemed to merit, and vice versa. And the novel's "exhaustive examination of human character" offered a likely arena for such performances: one that extended beyond the representation of fictional protagonists to the dialogue between a reader and the author that reader devised out of thin air. As such, reading fiction served as a figure for other, seemingly more substantial, forms of interpersonal communication.[13]

Rowson and her printers were extraordinarily skilled at whetting the appetite of her readers to know her better with every self-revelatory declaration. And with every autobiographical allusion, the demand for another only increased. Such references derived in part from "the sound business principle that an author's name is a commodity, and that the public forgets a commodity of which it is not constantly reminded," as evident in the fact that one Rowson production, whether book or performance, often made reference to the author's participation in another. Thus *Charlotte Temple* boasted on its frontispiece that Rowson was "of the New Theatre"; the preface to *Trials of the Human Heart* mentioned another Rowson novel and a play; and the *Miscellaneous Poems* declared her "a preceptress of the Ladies' Academy, in Newton." Rowson also frequently referred to her own sense of vulnerability (as a loyalist's child among patriots or a female author set down among male critics), thus drawing her audience further into her personal world by suggesting they had the power to decide her fate.[14]

In her relentless self-invocation before her reader, was Rowson more manly woman or sexless soul? It might seem axiomatic that as more women entered into print—itself a form of communication in which the proximate physical body gives way to a disembodied presence—the sexless soul prevailed over the manly woman as a basis for conceiving of women in the public sphere. And it could be said that many of the period's most authoritative female authors passed as men for the purposes of narrative authority. Thus Mercy Otis Warren became an acknowledged authority on the male-identified realm of Revolutionary military strategy, whereas Judith Sargent Murray inscribed herself as either or both female and male with the ever-shifting pseudonyms of "Constantia" and "Gleaner." But in many ways, Rowson departed from her female literary contemporaries in this regard, as she continually foregrounded her own female persona: her maternal pres-

13. Jean-Christophe Agnew, *Worlds Apart: The Market and the Theater in Anglo-American Thought, 1550–1750* (New York, 1986); Watts, *Romance of Real Life,* 24–25. On the performative nature of personal identity in early national America, see also Larzer Ziff, *Writing in the New Nation: Prose, Print, and Politics in the Early United States* (New Haven, Conn., 1991), chap. 4; and Jay Fliegelman, *Declaring Independence: Jefferson, Natural Language, and the Culture of Performance* (Stanford, Calif., 1993).

14. William Charvat, *Literary Publishing in America, 1790–1850* (1959; Amherst, Mass., 1993), 57; Susanna Rowson, *Charlotte Temple* (Philadelphia, 1794); Rowson, *Trials of the Human Heart,* I, xiv; Rowson, *Miscellaneous Poems.*

ence in one novel, her sisterly guidance in school performances, her teasing eroticism at the end of her surviving play.

By playing up her gender, Rowson continued to promote herself as a being worthy of attention above and beyond her textual creations. This was attention her contemporary male critics were only too willing to bestow. In their struggle to employ the opposed terminology of sexless and permanently sexed female authorship, however, they created of her a character in near-complete defiance of the very qualities she emphasized as constituting her femininity: resourcefulness, stamina, playfulness, and adaptability to circumstance. While Rowson labored to make female professionalism both evident and acceptable, her first critics worked just as hard to legitimate her presence in the public sphere precisely by denying her accountability to the market.

During the period when Rowson was most discussed in print, female authors were subject to a particular form of scrutiny. Critics tended to use female "productions" to detect a woman's "personal character." This character, in turn, stood in for a national female type, something that both represented the young nation's virtuous womanhood and served as a model for women to emulate in order to become suitably virtuous. Those who failed to render themselves worthy of such emulation served as negative examples, leading to the creation of two primary zones of representation: the superb and the despicable. At one point, poet, playwright, satirist, and political historian Mercy Otis Warren found herself "the most accomplished Lady in America," according to John Adams, owing to what Thomas Jefferson called her "high station in the ranks of genius." During roughly the same period, we have seen, Mary Wollstonecraft's name became synonymous with female turpitude. The *Literary Magazine* achieved both modes simultaneously, comparing two female historians, the American Hannah Adams and the British Catharine McCauley, in the following terms:

> It is a little remarkable, and not a little honourable to our native country, that America has produced a woman, who makes no contemptible figure in the historical field. I allude to Hannah Adams, whose personal character is as much superior, in propriety and dignity, to that of Mrs. McCauley, as her productions are superior in solidity and usefulness.

Despite their antithetical characters, Adams and McCauley share something very important. Both women are "useful" only to the extent that they allow for the predictable measurement of otherwise amorphous qualities, from national identity to gender difference. Hence the repetition of the term "production" (as verb and noun) suggests a certain mechanization that is not accidental. These authors' character both "produces" their literary worth and is itself "produced" by the nation they represent. Indeed, that only America can reliably produce female authors whose "superiority" is evident in their works' greater "solidity" becomes in this passage yet another of the implicit advantages the young republic holds over its rejected mother country. McCauley's implied "contemptible" nature figures here as irregularity: a refusal, or inability, to serve as a stable marker of national identity and gender's place within it.[15]

Rowson interferes in this polarizing tendency in the national press by being represented in both modes simultaneously: as an exemplar of virtuous womanhood and a harpy. Studying her public reputation, one can learn a great deal about how vilification and reverence functioned interdependently in the construction of early American female authorship, despite all attempts to segregate authors according to which of these two attitudes they inspired. Since female authors exemplified a national female persona, this destabilization extends to the expectations held for early Anglo-American women more generally. And since this female persona, we saw above, plays a crucial role in the construction of national identity, the transatlantic Rowson ironically serves to reveal the conflicted and chimerical nature of national identity even as she remains central to its formation.

In England, Rowson's early publications failed to arouse much interest. The relatively sympathetic *Critical Review* of April 1791 summarizes *Charlotte: A Tale of Truth* as "artless and affecting," but since the novel was published anonymously in England, it refers to the author only obliquely. Suggesting that Charlotte "for one error scarcely, perhaps, deserved so

---

15. "A Literary Lady," *Literary Magazine, and American Register (1803–1807)*, III, no. 20 (May 1805), 359. See also Kate Davies, *Catharine Macaulay and Mercy Otis Warren: The Revolutionary Atlantic and the Politics of Gender* (New York, 2005). During the 1780s, the relationship between the Warren and the Adams families deteriorated, culminating in Vice-President Adams's refusal to honor Mercy's request that he aid their troubled son, Winslow. John Adams eventually wrote ten letters fiercely maligning Warren's *History of the Rise, Progress, and Termination of the American Revolution* (Boston, 1805), to which Warren responded with six. See Rosemarie Zagarri, *A Woman's Dilemma: Mercy Otis Warren and the American Revolution* (Wheeling, Ill., 1995), xv–xvi, 125, 150–155; Rebecca Rush, *Kelroy: A Novel,* ed. Dana D. Nelson (New York, 1992), xii–xiii. Hannah Adams's many publications include *A Summary History of New-England* ([Dedham, Mass.,] 1799), which she edited for use as a schoolbook, titled *An Abridgment of the History of New-England* (Boston, 1805).

severe a punishment," the reviewer concludes that "poetic justice is not, we think, properly distributed." Mathew Carey found this review favorable enough to include it as the frontispiece to the second American edition of 1794. Six years later, a five-line entry in David Rivers's *Literary Memoirs of Living Authors of Great Britain* misstates Susanna's first name ("Miss Beverley") and credits her with "the Inquisitor, a novel . . . an octavo volume of pieces, which she was pleased to call POEMS . . . and (we believe) some other pieces."[16]

In the United States, however, Rowson was written about quite a bit, and in terms that were far from uniformly flattering. Rather, demonstrating fascination and discomfort in equal measure, Rowson's first critics attested to the fact that, as a female public figure, she was both a contradiction in terms and a sign of the times, presaging an early-nineteenth-century climate in which "American white women became increasingly restricted by tenets of proper public behavior, just as they grew bolder in their demands on the public sphere." Given her public visibility, it makes sense that critics would have concerned themselves less with what she wrote than with who she must have been to write what she did.[17]

"Mrs. Susanna Rowson," then, was more important to her first American critics than were the words she wrote. Contemporary commentators viewed her published writings primarily as a means to comprehend her "personal character," and they used what they found to justify their attention to material that alone threatened to degrade the critic with its self-proclaimed mediocrity (Rowson rarely began a book without alluding to its ethical virtues and aesthetic deficiencies) and unseemly engagement with matters of the teenage female heart. This critical self-justification by means of an emphasis on authorial profile extends from her day nearly to our own. Thus in 1976, one biographer could claim: "Mrs. Rowson's most successful creation was her persona." As a specimen of "American eighteenth-century personalit[y]," most agree, Rowson might not have been "important"; but she was certainly "interesting."[18]

16. *Critical Review,* April 1791, 468; [David Rivers], *Literary Memoirs of Living Authors of Great Britain, Arranged according to an Alphabetical Catalogue,* 2 vols. (London, 1798), II, 228.

17. Catherine Allgor, *Parlor Politics: In Which the Ladies of Washington Help Build a City and a Government* (Charlottesville, Va., 2000), 112.

18. Dorothy Weil, *In Defense of Women: Susanna Rowson (1762–1824)* (University Park, Pa., 1976), 147; R. W. G. Vail, *Susanna Haswell Rowson, the Author of Charlotte Temple: A Bibliographical Study* (Worcester, Mass., 1933), 4; George O. Seilhamer, *History of the American Theatre: New Foundations* (Philadelphia, 1891), 143.

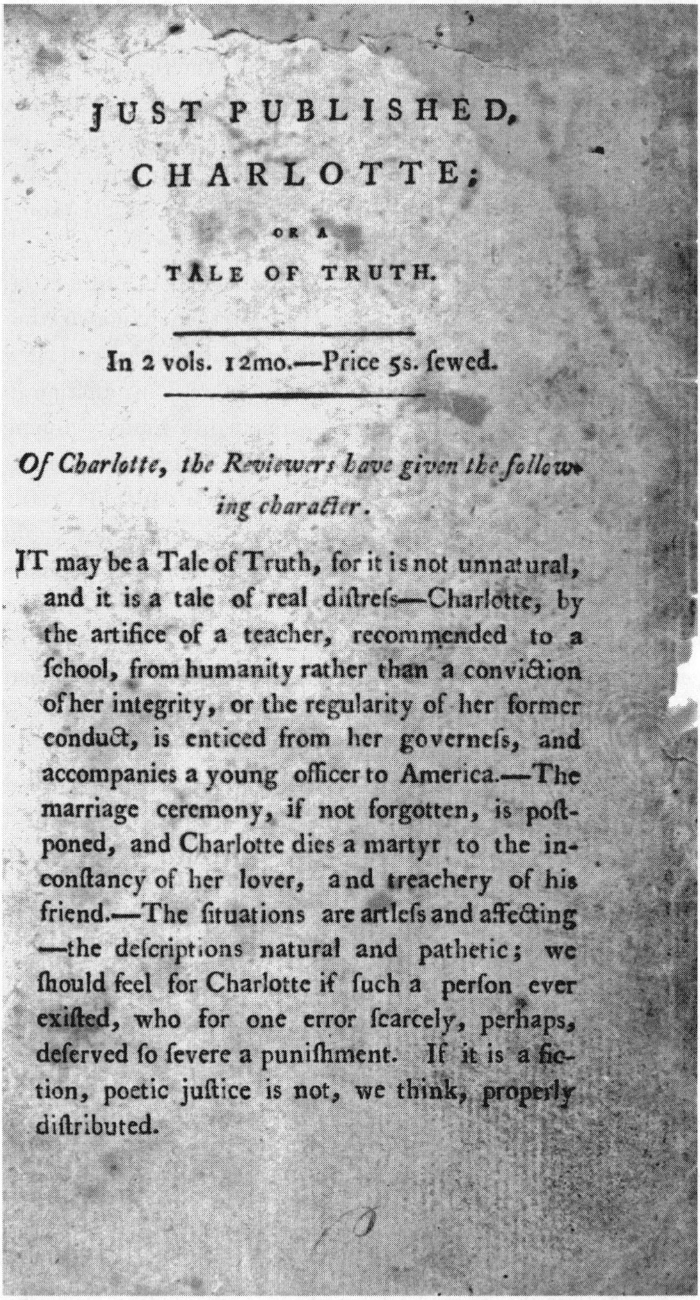

JUST PUBLISHED,

CHARLOTTE;

OR A

TALE OF TRUTH.

In 2 vols. 12mo.—Price 5s. ſewed.

Of Charlotte, the Reviewers have given the following character.

IT may be a Tale of Truth, for it is not unnatural, and it is a tale of real diſtreſs—Charlotte, by the artifice of a teacher, recommended to a ſchool, from humanity rather than a conviction of her integrity, or the regularity of her former conduct, is enticed from her governeſs, and accompanies a young officer to America.—The marriage ceremony, if not forgotten, is poſtponed, and Charlotte dies a martyr to the inconſtancy of her lover, and treachery of his friend.—The ſituations are artleſs and affecting—the deſcriptions natural and pathetic; we ſhould feel for Charlotte if ſuch a perſon ever exiſted, who for one error ſcarcely, perhaps, deſerved ſo ſevere a puniſhment. If it is a fiction, poetic juſtice is not, we think, properly diſtributed.

PLATE 15. *Anonymous review from* Critical Review. *From Rowson,* Charlotte: A Tale of Truth *(Philadelphia, 1794). PS 2736.R3C5, Clifton Waller Barrett Library of American Literature, Special Collections, University of Virginia Library*

This "interest" took widely varying forms. To William Cobbett, her literary productions were worth no more than the sheets they were printed on, which, he claimed, made an "excellent emetic." Given Cobbett's delight in scurrilous invective, his assessment of Rowson comes as no surprise, although his devotion of several pages to her undoing seems out of line with her purported unimportance. But when one considers that Cobbett wrote to diminish, not Rowson alone, but also the American public that tolerated such shameful authorial display on the part of its women, his dedication to her demise makes particular sense. To Cobbett, it mattered little what Rowson wrote (which is just as well, since he seems never to have attended the play whose critique forms the core of his polemic). It was how widely she was read that galled him. Savaging Rowson in order to indict "the whole tribe of female scribblers and politicians" and the culture that consumed their wares, Cobbett reduced female entrance into the public sphere to yet another involuntary, animalistic female function, akin to menstruation or giving birth.[19]

Unfortunately for Cobbett, his rants only helped Rowson's star rise all the faster. George Seilhamer wrote in 1891 that "'Slaves in Algiers' . . . would probably have been forgotten in a few months had it not had the good fortune to fall under the lash of the celebrated William Cobbett." In addition to popularizing her play, Cobbett's attack inspired prominent progressives to come to her defense in print. First, in 1795, Philadelphia poet and statesman John Swanwick adopted the pen name "Citizen Snub" to rush to her aid. Four years later, Mathew Carey published two stinging diatribes against Cobbett in which the plight of female journalists and other literary professionals figured prominently. Finally, in 1811, Rowson's friend Samuel Lorenzo Knapp, an accomplished biographer and the father of her former pupil Caroline Knapp, wrote a "Memoir" of Rowson in which he touted her as an exemplary female author, elaborating on the themes set forth by his two predecessors while developing them in ways pertinent to his own historical moment.[20]

These supporters of Rowson had several things in common. All three

19. William Cobbett, "A Kick for a Bite; or, Review upon Review; with a Critical Essay, on the Works of Mrs. S. Rowson . . . ," *American Monthly Review* (Philadelphia, 1795), in Cobbett, *Peter Porcupine in America: Pamphlets on Republicanism and Revolution,* ed. David A. Wilson (Ithaca, N.Y., 1997), 131, 133.

20. Seilhamer, *History of the American Theatre,* 156. Doreen Alvarez Saar and Mary Anne Schofield confirm that Cobbett's essay "would bring *Slaves in Algiers* to the attention of a wider audience" (Saar and Schofield, *Eighteenth-Century Anglo-American Women Novelists: A Critical Reference Guide* ([New York, 1996], 232).

were active proponents of equal education for women. And in one way or another, all bore some alliance with Mary Wollstonecraft. Knapp was friends with her sister-in-law, also named Mary Wollstonecraft, whom he included among the sketches in his *Female Biography.* Carey published the first American edition of Wollstonecraft's famous polemic, *A Vindication of the Rights of Woman,* in 1792, misspelling her name "Woolstonecraft." And Swanwick asked Cobbett point-blank the central question of the *Vindication:* "Can you prove that a male education would not qualify a woman for all the duties of a man?"[21]

That all three men were eager to test this hypothesis becomes clear from their professional activities. Swanwick himself, as a "Philadelphia radical and pioneer of female education," was a patron of the nation's most eminent school for women, the Young Ladies' Academy of Philadelphia. He was also a regular on the female academy lecture circuit and the author of "Thoughts on Education, Addressed to the Visitors of the Young Ladies' Academy in Philadelphia, October 31, 1787." Carey listed Wollstonecraft's *Vindication* at the back of his first edition of *Charlotte* (1794), in an advertisement that supported the *Vindication's* own call to minimize the distinction between male and female education by allowing the novel's female readers to delve uncensored through Carey's wide-ranging supply of titles, from the *Essay on Old Maids* to *Bell's Surgery.* In a similar vein, Knapp, a leading chronicler of his day (along with Daniel Webster, he was the official eulogist for John Adams and Thomas Jefferson in 1826), published a popular *Female Biography* (1833, reprinted at least five times by 1846) in which "equal educational rights for women" featured as a "major national goal."[22]

What happened, then, when these men made Rowson their cause?

21. On Wollstonecraft's views regarding female education, see chap. 2, "The Prevailing Opinion of a Sexual Character Discussed." Concluding that "it cannot be demonstrated that woman is essentially inferior to man because she has always been subjugated," Wollstonecraft notes, "Many are the causes that . . . contribute to enslave women by cramping their understandings" and exhorts her readers to "Teach [women], in common with man, to submit to necessity, instead of giving, to render them more pleasing, a sex to morals" (Mary Wollstonecraft, *A Vindication of the Rights of Woman: With Strictures on Political and Moral Subjects* [Boston, 1792], iii–viii, 31, 51, 52). See also her prefatory letter to M. Talleyrand-Perigord and chaps. 3, 4, and 12.

22. Cobbett, *Peter Porcupine in America,* ed. Wilson, 120; Ben Harris McClary, *Samuel Lorenzo Knapp and Early American Biography* (Worcester, Mass., 1985), 53; Roland Baumann, "John Swanwick: Spokesman for 'Merchant-Republicanism' in Philadelphia, 1790–1798," *Pennsylvania Magazine of History and Biography,* XCVII (1973), 140–141.

Neither the critic nor the object of his attention was easily recognizable. Indeed, they approached their common nemesis, Cobbett, within the confines they sketched for appropriate female authorial deportment. Casting himself in the role of knight-errant to Rowson's damsel in distress, Swanwick premised his continued support of Rowson on her refusal to return Cobbett's salvo in print herself. Any such retort would be unladylike, he claimed, and would thereby unfit her for his continued services. Carey, in his address to Cobbett, spelled the latter's off-color jokes backward, in hopes that "the ladies . . . cannot . . . decypher" them. And Knapp, although distinguishing Rowson's work from "the numerous volumes of sentimental nonsense, which issued from the Minerva press," failed to note that Minerva had in fact published her most famous novel.[23]

Rowson's earliest champions, then, as surely as her adversary, found themselves drawn to write about her in terms premised upon her own silencing. The nonutterances were of three kinds: for Carey, "ladies" must not read forbidden words; for Swanwick, Rowson must not pen them; and for Knapp, items she had penned that did not fit with his agenda were to be expunged from the record. That leading advocates for female educational equality should have employed such terminology is important because it shows that the two frames of gender relations described above—one emphasizing the capacity for gender neutrality in the public sphere, the other the chaos that ensued when women assumed the authority of men—did not separate into distinct fields of utterance. Rather, they competed and cohered within particular individuals' written and oral expression throughout the print spectrum of late-eighteenth-century America.

From a man who favored the pseudonym "Peter Porcupine," which William Cobbett tried out for the first time in his attack on Rowson, it would be naïve

23. Carey introduces two of Cobbett's jokes in the following manner, spelling the sexually suggestive parts backward: "The following quotations are unfit for female eyes to see, or female ears to hear. I therefore print them in hieroglyphics, which the ladies, if any deign to read these pages, cannot, I hope, decypher" (Mathew Carey, *A Plumb Pudding for the Humane, Chaste, Valiant, Enlightened Peter Porcupine*). Knapp wrote: "It appears that the prejudice existing among parents against any thing which was called a novel, was much stronger at that time than at present; and it must be acknowledged that the numerous volumes of sentimental nonsense, which issued from the Minerva press, furnished but too sufficient ground for such a prejudice" ([Samuel Knapp], "Memoir," in Susanna Rowson, *Charlotte's Daughter: or, The Three Orphans. A Sequel to Charlotte Temple. To Which Is Prefixed, a Memoir of the Author* [Boston, 1828], 7). *Charlotte: A Tale of Truth* was first published in 1791 in London by William Lane.

to expect less than excoriation. Indeed, "A Kick for a Bite; or, Review upon Review; with a Critical Essay, on the Works of Mrs. S. Rowson" lives up to its pseudonymous antagonism. But if the first critic to engage Rowson at any length was her fiercest, he was also in many ways the most like her. A British immigrant to the United States in the early 1790s, he held political views that were, if anything, even more erratic than hers. Indeed, although Cobbett scoffed at Rowson's undeniable political adaptability, attributing her newfound patriotism upon her second emigration to the United States to the exceptional quality of the local air, he possessed even more contradictory views over the span of his lifetime than she.[24]

As "the leading advocate of English government reform" upon his return to England in 1800, Cobbett would come to be known for a set of beliefs unrecognizable to his prior incarnation as Peter Porcupine, "attacking the iniquitous poor laws, sinecures and placemen, the rotten-borough system . . . and the compulsory tithes for the support of the clergy." Cobbett's role in the British parliamentary reform movement would eventually gain him lasting fame for his proto-Marxian "respect for physical labour" and his awareness of class privilege as the consolidation of the means of production in the hands of a wealthy elite. Returning to the United States from 1817 to 1819, he gave voice to these radical convictions in *A Grammar of the English Language, in a Series of Letters,* meant for working-class students, as evidenced by its full title: *Intended for the Use of Schools and of Young Persons in General; but, More Especially for the Use of Soldiers, Sailors, Apprentices, and Plough-Boys.* His later causes included manhood suffrage and the reduction of the working day to ten hours.[25]

What is less often remembered about Cobbett is that he came to this position from one just as notable for its conservatism (a position whose traces remained in his lifelong prejudices against blacks, Jews, and "unbelievers," as well as women). This is the role he occupied during his first and most lengthy stay in the United States, when he wrote his critique of Rowson. During his first residence in Philadelphia, from 1792 to 1800, between pam-

24. Cobbett's "Kick for a Bite," first published in the *American Monthly Review* in 1795, was written in reply to an earlier essay in that journal attacking his "Bone to Gnaw for the Democrats." Regarding Rowson's patriotism, Cobbett wrote: "There are (and I am sorry to say it), some people, who doubt of her sincerity, and who pretend that her sudden conversion to republicanism, ought to make us look upon all her praises as ironical. But these uncandid people do not, or rather will not, recollect, what the miraculous air of America is capable of" (*Peter Porcupine in America,* ed. Wilson, 133).

25. Pierce W. Gaines, *William Cobbett and the United States, 1792–1835* (Worcester, Mass., 1971), xvii.

phlets decrying the "hell of democracy" in the United States, France, and England, Cobbett wrote public attacks on, among others, Joseph Priestley, Thomas Paine, and, later, Benjamin Rush, whom he accused of killing George Washington through neglect and who won a libel suit against him. Perhaps the single best indicator of the extent of Cobbett's volte-face is that, after reviling Paine as a "Judas" who "has done all the mischief he can in the world, and whether his carcass is at last to be suffered to rot on the earth, or to be dried in the air, is of very little consequence," Cobbett ended up exhuming Paine's bones and keeping them until his own death.[26]

Nothing better embodied the United States' hellishness to the young Cobbett than its gender politics. During the 1790s, he became a prominent spokesman for the anti-Wollstonecraftian views described above, whereby women who attempted to encroach on male privileges within the literary public sphere made of themselves only monstrous fools of grotesque sexual ambivalence. The United States, where "that *genius* is not worth a curse, that is not masculine, feminine and neuter, all at once," was full of such monstrosities, Rowson preeminent among them. Thus Rowson is "the personification of *genius*" precisely for the way she can shift a pronoun: "First it is *her,* then an *it,* and by-and-by it acts like a *man.*" He may as well be speaking here of the author herself, who, in becoming a manly woman, loses her humanity altogether.[27]

Given that Cobbett despised manly women, he was also not above mocking womanly men. To Swanwick's question whether "a male education would not qualify a *woman* for *all* the *duties of a man,*" Cobbett retorted that it might, but he hoped it wouldn't: "I want the ladies to continue women, and not turn men." And he followed by challenging Swanwick's own manhood, using his pen name, Snub, which he emended to "Scrub," to compare the latter's sexual adequacy to that of an "old washerwoman." Elsewhere, Cobbett further mocked Swanwick's gender ambivalence. Swanwick was known for his "suave discourses in the ladies' academies"; Cobbett had a slightly less flattering opinion of the old man's lectures:

Being upon this subject, it is hardly fair to omit mentioning a great and mighty democrat, who is universally allowed to be a perfect platonist both in politics and love, and yet has the unconscionable ambition to set

26. Cobbett, *Peter Porcupine in America,* ed. Wilson, 2–3; Gaines, *William Cobbett and the United States,* xiii; Raymond Williams, *Cobbett* (New York, 1983), 7–9, 13, 20, 21, 79.

27. Cobbett, *Peter Porcupine in America,* ed. Wilson, 22, 130.

up for a man of *gallantry*. He has taken it into his head to run dangling from one Boarding School to another, in order to acquire by the art of speechifying, a reputation for which nature seems to have disqualified him. My imagination cannot form to itself any thing more perfectly comic than to see a diminutive superannuated bachelor, cocked up on a stool, and spouting out compliments to an assembly of young Misses. Ah! Dear Plato! take my word for it, if your reputation had been no higher among the Democrats than among the ladies, your name would have never found a place on their list.[28]

In the meantime, Rowson, "our American Sappho," was his favorite example of the masculinized female. Generally, Cobbett didn't bother to write about "the fair." His misogyny was such that it influenced almost everything he wrote, from off-color references to female sexuality (even a joke or two about oral sex at women's expense) to his well-known depiction of women giving birth on the floor of the House of Representatives. But although he enjoyed insulting men by calling them women, he did not consider females per se worthy opponents. Thus his attack on Rowson provides an unusual glimpse into what someone who found women beneath public notice thought of one he couldn't help noticing.[29]

Cobbett was famous for conducting character assassinations on those with whose written work he disagreed. Carey wrote that, when reading Cobbett, "men imbibe the lamentable and delusive idea, that all who differ from them in opinion are villains"; and indeed, Cobbett tended to support his accusations of political misprision with references to "personal infidelity" on the part of the concerned party. Rousseau is accused of "incorrigible vice," Paine's second marriage is lambasted, and "the politics are seen to follow from such characteristics." Rowson was no exception. Even before reading what Cobbett has to say about "Mrs. S. Rowson," one suspects that his general tone will be dismissive; for the section on her is tacked on as a seeming afterthought. In this appendage, Cobbett castigates the sinking

28. Cobbett, preface, "A Bone to Gnaw, Part II," and "A Bone to Gnaw, for the Democrats," in Cobbett, *Peter Porcupine in America,* ed. Wilson, 113, 135–136; Baumann, "John Swanwick," *PMHB,* XCVII (1973), 140.

29. Cobbett, *Peter Porcupine in America,* ed. Wilson, 128, 131. "In my opinion, it is not that which cometh out of the lips that defileth the woman, but that which she receives within them" (cited in Carey, *Plumb Pudding,* 46). Cobbett also wrote, "When a woman has swallowed six glasses of good Madeira, she is fit for *anything*" (Carey, *The Porcupiniad: A Hudibrastic Poem in Four Cantos: Addressed to William Cobbett* [Philadelphia, 1799], canto I, verse 25, footnote).

standards of publication in post-Revolutionary America while mockingly praising Rowson's work as representative of the general emasculation of print culture. Throughout, he derives character traits from textual minutiae and casts literary deficiency as gender confusion.[30]

If, for Cobbett, the specter of the dehumanized female author is the most important thing to emerge from Rowson's writings, the works themselves are correspondingly reduced to the status of mere commodities. As such, they suggest the gloomiest implications of the following shift: "Whereas authorship and books had for centuries been defined in political terms as public 'actions,' they were, in the last years of the eighteenth century, increasingly considered in economic terms autonomously as private 'things,' or property." In fact, Cobbett claims to ingest rather than read her publications:

> The inestimable works that she has showered (not to say *poured,* you know) upon us, mend not only our hearts, but, if properly administered, our constitutions also: at least, I can speak for myself. They are my *Materia Medica,* in a literal sense. A liquorish page from the *Fille de Chambre* serves me by way of a philtre, the *Inquisitor* is my opium, and I have ever found the *Slaves in Algiers* a most excellent emetic. As to *Mentoria* and *Charlotte,* it is hardly necessary to say what use they are put to in the chamber of a valetudinarian.

A valetudinarian is an invalid obsessed with his own real and imagined illnesses. With her readers cast as hypochondriacs and her books as love potions and stimulants to purging, Rowson has been suitably chastised for her presumptuous entrance into the literary marketplace.[31]

By limiting his appreciation of Rowson's works to their "literal sense," Cobbett certainly played into the association of women with a prelinguistic physicality that justified their exclusion from full citizenship. But if his mockery depended upon this commonplace of liberal ideology, its end lay elsewhere, in the indictment of those who made her a success. In the United States, Cobbett implied, the value of a work referred only to what the publisher got for it, and the desire to profit had completely taken over the wish to enlighten as the impetus to publication. Given his estimation of American culture, then, Cobbett did Rowson no favors by nominating her to the

---

30. Carey, *Porcupiniad,* canto I, verse 18; Williams, *Cobbett,* 8, 9.

31. Rice, *Transformation of Authorship,* 155; Cobbett, *Peter Porcupine in America,* ed. Wilson, 133.

position of poet laureate. Suggesting that she be placed on salary, he described the presumably desiccating effect of a profit-driven marketplace on aesthetic practice, again by reference to the persona of the female author. Cobbett invoked Rowson's outspoken presence in the public realm and her semicomic claims to female superiority to suggest both a sluttishness and a monstrously inappropriate masculinity on the part of professionally active American women—a form of cultural degradation that her readers mistook for national progress.

If Rowson the author epitomized the manly woman as a figure for American democracy, it was only by casting her as a reader that Cobbett commented on female gender itself. Suggesting the intensity of his hostility, this rhetorical move makes it clear that he was writing to, as well as about, Rowson and that he meant for her to be wounded by his barbs. Chastising its editors for omitting "to take notice of the voluminous productions of the celebrated *Mrs. Rowson*" and insinuating women's insatiable demand for sexual satisfaction, the essay notes:

> Sins of omission are ever inexpiable when a lady is in the case; the fair
> do generally, in the long run, pardon sins of commission, but those of
> omission they never do. . . . You had here the fairest opportunity in the
> world of ingratiating yourself with the whole tribe of female scribblers
> and politicians; this opportunity you have neglected.[32]

Women, it would seem, read only to seek out their own image. Not to mention them is to commit, then, the unpardonable "sin . . . of omission." This inability to view the world except in its narrow capacity as a suitable or unsuitable mirror for the self implicitly renders the female reader of poor service as an author. Cobbett thus mocked the claims of "female scribblers" to authority even as he satirized their supposed superiority of taste, their position as the ultimate consumer whom every man must please. In this sense, he prefigured Rowson's champions, who, driven by their rage against Cobbett to take to the page to sing her praises, made startlingly similar assumptions about the range of the female mind.

Whereas Cobbett gained attention for deriding the state of American print culture in the 1790s, Mathew Carey might well have served as its poster child. Far from fearing the increasing tendency to see books as salable commodities rather than mental activities alchemically embodied, Carey seemed

32. Cobbett, *Peter Porcupine in America,* ed. Wilson, 128.

driven by the premise that the more books people bought, rented, and borrowed, the more widely informed a populace would result. As the primary force behind the creation of "a publishing scene to which everything that had gone before would be only a prelude," Carey's "success as a bookseller, his efforts to organize the trade and to improve the distribution of books, were as notable as what he published." Knowing the local Philadelphia market couldn't support him, he sent fifty agents as far as Halifax and Georgia. He developed wholesale publishing by supplying his and other publishers' works to more than one hundred dealers. He was the first to use Greek type in America. He earned at least sixty thousand dollars on two books alone, Guthrie's *Geography* and Goldsmith's *Animated Nature*. And, although he made savvy use of British materials (*Charlotte Temple* being a case in point), he encouraged native authors by selling their works at a discount.[33]

Carey's success, like Rowson's, depended on stamina, vigor, creativity, and resilience; but perhaps most of all, what the two shared was a willingness to consult the market in crafting works for an American readership. For Carey, as for Rowson, this led to charges of opportunism. Regarding Carey's 1794 publication of John Bunyan's *Divine Emblems,* for instance, one bibliographer exclaimed, "How Carey, a Catholic, could print a work so directly opposed to his religion surpasses understanding." Such catholicity is less astonishing, however, when one considers the more than seventy other works Carey published that same year (including *Charlotte Temple*). These included an American captivity narrative *(The Affecting History of the Dreadful Distresses of Frederic Manheim's Family. To Which Are Added, the Sufferings of John Corbly's Family),* Scottish philosophy (James Beattie, *Elements of Moral Science*), and British light opera (Isaac Bickerstaffe's *Lionel and Clarissa; or, The School for Fathers*).[34]

What might seem opportunism in one context, moreover, reads as informed tolerance in another. Thus Carey, America's leading publisher of the

33. Charvat, *Profession of Authorship,* ed. Bruccoli, 18; John Tebbel, *A History of Book Publishing in the United States,* I, *The Creation of an Industry, 1630–1865* (New York, 1972), 106, 109; William Clarkin, *Mathew Carey: A Bibliography of His Publications, 1785–1824* (New York, 1984); Earl Bradsher, *Mathew Carey: Editor, Author, and Publisher* (New York, 1912); Rosalind Remer, *Printers and Men of Capital: Philadelphia Book Publishers in the New Republic* (Philadelphia, 1996); William Guthrie, *A New Geographical, Historical, and Commercial Grammar; and Present State of the Several Kingdoms of the World* (1770; Philadelphia, 1809); Oliver Goldsmith, *An History of the Earth and Animated Nature* (Philadelphia, 1795).

34. Clarkin, *Mathew Carey,* 21; John Bunyan, *Divine Emblems; or, Temporal Things Spiritualized. Fitted for the Use of Boys and Girls* (Philadelphia, 1796).

Bible, had no compunction admitting his childhood love of less ennobling fare.

> I had been a great, indeed a voracious reader before I was bound apprentice—and had clandestinely subscribed to a circulating library, contrary to the wishes, and indeed without the knowledge, of my parents, who were opposed to the kind of books which, alone, I was desirous of reading. I used to be dissatisfied that I could not exchange books oftener than once a day. I used to sit up till twelve and one o'clock, reading novels and romances. Yet now, when attending a bookstore, as I did for two years, where there was scarcely any business done, and where, of course, I had leisure to read four-fifths of my time, I did not read as much in a month as I was wont to do in a week. Strange perversity of our nature! which leads us to pursue with avidity whatever is forbidden or attainable only with difficulty, and to neglect the self-same things when courting our acceptance![35]

Carey's capacity to appreciate the many different kinds of pleasure, both licit and illicit, that reading could bring befitted the first American publisher of *Charlotte Temple*. And he continued to respect the "novels and romances" that he had once hidden from his parents. He frankly admitted to Rowson his estimation for her best seller, which he wrote her was "by far the most popular and in my opinion the most useful novel ever published in this country and probably not inferior to any published in England."[36]

Carey respected novels, and he also respected their authors, even when they were women. Lest one think Carey is merely flattering a primary source of revenue in commending Rowson, it's helpful to see that he makes no bones in the same letter about two less successful ventures: "[*Mentoria*] never was very popular. The sales of the Trials of the heart have been slow." All in all, he seemed to enjoy a forthright relationship with one of his most successful authors; and he had no recalcitrance about discussing the financial aspects of publishing with her, even as he felt no need to include her in his distribution of profits. Carey's outlook is testament to this transitional

---

35. Carey accomplished his aim to "dominate the nation's Bible business" by publishing both an ornate King James Bible in 1800 and inexpensive duodecimo school Bibles until 1820. See Remer, *Printers and Men of Capital*, 172 n. 45; Mathew Carey, *Autobiography* (New York, 1942), 3 (first published serially in the *New-England Magazine*, July 1833–Dec. 1834). Letters VI–IX discuss his fight with Cobbett.

36. Letter cited in Bradsher, *Mathew Carey*, 50.

period in American publishing, when to be professional, we have seen, was more a matter of attitude and activity than actual remuneration. Clearly, Carey welcomed Rowson into this circle of literary endeavor, though he was in no hurry to raise authors to the rung publishers first occupied in the early national period as self-sufficient earners in the print market.[37]

Carey extended this view of women's fitness for the publishing industry to his assessment of women as readers—and, more important, buyers—of his books. On the final pages of the first American edition of *Charlotte: A Tale of Truth,* he included three documents: "Books, etc. for Sale by *Mathew Carey*"; "Just Published, by *Mathew Carey,* the First Volume of a New System of *Modern Geography*"; and a list of works presumably tailored to women, "Books, Published by M. Carey." The last included *Short Account of Algiers, Short Account of the Malignant Fever,* Mary Wollstonecraft's afore-mentioned *Vindication of the Rights of Woman* (this title appears on two lists), and Susanna Rowson's *Inquisitor.* This textual apparatus indicates a rather open-minded approach to female reading in the new Republic on the part of the nation's leading publisher, just as it suggests that women alone did not read *Charlotte Temple.* Even the list tailored to a female readership includes a range of volumes from adventure narrative to feminist theory, and Carey saw fit to include his entire book list as well, suggesting that there wasn't much he considered off-limits to the female mind—or pocket-book.[38]

Nor was he oblivious to women's particular economic difficulties. In 1829, he waged a campaign to raise the weekly salaries of seamstresses employed by the government. His pamphlet detailing this campaign, "Wages of Female Labour," reveals his keen sense of the conditions under which many women lived—poverty, single parenthood, illness, and hunger—and of the resources they marshaled to survive these challenges. "Wages" even contained arithmetic proving that no government-employed seamstress could "pay room rent, and purchase fuel, and the provisions and clothing necessary to support human nature" on her earnings. Clearly, Carey understood the economic challenges many women faced as wage laborers who nevertheless remained powerless in a labor economy that did not recognize the existence of the women it employed. Far from banishing women from the public sphere, he worked hard to improve their standing within it.[39]

37. Ibid.

38. Susanna Rowson, *Charlotte: A Tale of Truth,* 2 vols. (Philadelphia, 1794), 84, 91.

39. Mathew Carey, *Wages of Female Labour* (Philadelphia, 1829).

Carey's documented respect for and sympathy with female laborers within and without the world of letters makes his treatment of women in a bitter print exchange with William Cobbett all the more mysterious. Although Carey does not mention Rowson by name in either of his attacks on Cobbett, he considered her "one of his major discoveries" during the five years that preceded his published retorts to Cobbett. Indeed, Carey's "partiality to Rowson may have been the hidden reason behind William Cobbett's otherwise unprovoked attack on the author in 1795." He had published four editions of *Charlotte Temple* between 1794 and 1801 and a second American edition of Rowson's *Inquisitor* (1794), served as an agent for *Trials of the Human Heart* (1795), and kept a healthy stock of Rowson's books for sale in his bookstore. "Probably the most important and influential of Rowson's new literary patrons," he knew her well, and his references to women driven by necessity into the tumultuous realm of professional letters suggest that she was very much on his mind when he charged Cobbett with slander against the fair sex. Carey expressed his fury in two documents phrased as reluctant acts of self-defense: *The Porcupiniad: A Hudibrastic Poem in Four Cantos: Addressed to William Cobbett* and *A Plumb Pudding for Peter Porcupine* (both Philadelphia, 1799).[40]

The proximity of "lovely woman" and "the dead" in the following passage from *The Porcupiniad* should not lead us to assume he equated the two:

Not e'en the dead vile Cobbett spares,
His malice lovely woman shares.

But it would not be going too far to suggest that an uncharacteristic pallor shades the women found in these tracts. Whereas the advertisements in Carey's editions of *Charlotte Temple* indicate a respect for female literacy on a par with male, here he lambastes Cobbett for including material "unfit for female eyes to see, or female ears to hear." And whereas his pamphlet on "Female Labour" attests to women's capacity for economic independence by detailing the obstacles placed in their way, his attacks on Cobbett represent women as dependent beings in need of patriarchal protection. Regarding Cobbett's reference to "the temple of Cloacina," *The Porcupiniad* exclaims: "What a train of ideas this elegant paragraph must excite in the mind of a lady! And how refined must be the taste of those heads of families, who allowed their wives and daughters to peruse a paper containing such pro-

40. Brandt, *Susanna Haswell Rowson,* 108.

ductions!" Something in Cobbett's behavior catalyzed a remarkable shift in Carey's estimation of the female mind, as he reverted to a patriarchal stance toward beings he had once thought fit for Wollstonecraft and would soon rally in support of organized labor.[41]

The surest indication that women suffered a loss in becoming a means to attacking Cobbett occurs in the following passages. First, *The Porcupiniad* makes the point in iambic tetrameter:

Her sex to woman nought avails.
With coarse abuse he still assails
Maids, wives, and widows. None escape
This demon cloth'd in human shape.
E'en by the painted Cherokee,
Or savages of O-why-hee,
The sex would more respected be.

In *A Plumb Pudding,* Carey restates the point in prose:

Here, the blackguard's vocabulary is exhausted to collect terms of re-proach to heap upon editors, printers, and publishers. And, "O shame! "where is thy blush!" even when the editorship of a Gazette devolves, by the death of a husband, on a helpless widow, beings who call them-selves men, and who feel proud of the privileges of the name, forgetful of that respect for the sex, which the untutored Indian in some degree feels, assail, with coarse and obscene abuse, women, incapable of de-fence!

41. Carey, *Porcupiniad,* canto III, verse 30, and canto II, verse 9; Carey, *Plumb Pud-ding,* 46. Cobbett mentioned Carey by name in his *Life and Adventures of Peter Porcu-pine, with a Full and Fair Account of All His Authoring Transactions; Being a Sure and Infallible Guide for All Enterprising Young Men Who Wish to Make a Fortune by Writing Pamphlets* (Philadelphia, 1796). First he took Carey to task for condescending to him in rejecting his *Observations on the Emigration of Dr. Joseph Priestley* (Cobbett, *Peter Porcupine in America,* ed. Wilson, 173). (Apparently, Carey had called him "my lad" during the visit and shown no great civility.) Later in the same pamphlet, he named Carey as representative of the "cruel race" of booksellers (176). After Cobbett's return to the United States in 1816, this time as a patriot, he "admitted to his former antago-nists that he had been mistaken" and made up with Carey (Wilson, introduction to *Peter Porcupine in America,* 45). The Temple of Cloacina is part of the Roman Forum. The cloacina is the sewer that ran through the Forum. The goddess Cloacina was often identified with Venus.

The "widow" of the verse is now a particular sort of widow, a newspaper editor's wife who takes over his professional duties upon his death. And yet despite the evident skill and aplomb that would make her a likely object for such "devolution," in the context of Carey's attack on Cobbett, she must nevertheless be "helpless" and "incapable of defence." A helpless newspaper editor is something of a contradiction in terms. And Carey well knew Rowson's own canny persistence as an author and actress. So why describe her class of female literary professionals in such ill-fitting terms?[42]

In answer, one might consider the Native American in comparison with whom Cobbett suffers. Given Carey's resort to such stock phrases as "painted Cherokee" and "untutored Indian," it is fair to suggest that the plight of the depleted Native American population was not what concerned him in these essays. Instead, he summons the mythology of the "Vanishing American" primarily to take advantage of its Rousseauean claims for the innate virtue of natural man by contrasting Indian civility with Cobbett's "tutored" barbarity. Similarly, he made womanly weakness the means to an end that had little to do with women themselves. The more fragile the "maids, wives, and widows" who appear in these diatribes, the more brutish Cobbett seems for attacking them. The catch is that, although establishing female dependence was not Carey's aim, it nonetheless followed as one outcome of his argument.

If Rowson remained an informing presence behind Carey's attack on Cobbett, she played a more direct role in inspiring another prominent intellectual to come to her defense against Cobbett's vitriol. Born in 1740, John Swanwick was elected in 1795 as a Democratic representative in Congress from Pennsylvania and served until his death in 1798. A Philadelphia merchant and frequent speaker at local academies, he also published a volume of poetry, *Poems on Several Occasions,* in 1797. In "A Word of Comfort to Mrs. Rowson," Swanwick, like Carey, defended Rowson in terms that ironically reinforced the substance of Cobbett's attack. Like Cobbett, he directed his readers' attention away from textual analysis toward the figure of the authoress and subscribed to a hierarchical and gendered ordering of public

42. Carey, *Porcupiniad,* canto III, verse 31; Carey, *Plumb Pudding,* 35–36. On the interdependence of praiseful words and treacherous deeds toward Native Americans in the early nineteenth century, see "The Curse of Metamora," chap. 8 of Jill Lepore's *Name of War: King Philip's War and the Origins of American Identity* (New York, 1998), 191–226. As mentioned in Chapter 1, above, Rowson herself might have served as editor of the *Boston Weekly Magazine.*

and private spheres whose threatened violation he took as his primary cause. Arguing that "man's deference to women is commensurate with his refinement," Swanwick faulted Cobbett for dragging Rowson from the "polite circles" of "literary refinement" into rough-and-tumble political debate. He derided him for refusing to take his own properly masculine place in the public sphere, being instead abnormally "secluded from an intercourse with the world." And he insisted, as the sole condition of his continued interposition on her part, that Rowson remain silent on the matter: "It will redound to her credit if she connives at the insult; because were she to condescend to expostulate with you, it would inspire you with a fallacious sense of your own importance, and if she resolves to indulge her audience with another epilogue at her next benefit, I would particularly advise her not to mention your name. Let her attend to this injunction, *lest her friendly Snub, who intends to be present, may assume the tone of censure,* instead of commendation and applause."[43]

Invoking a cultural ethos of male deference and female "refinement," Rowson's defender effectively barred her from full participation in the early national realm of letters even as he championed her earlier appearances. He then, like both Cobbett and Carey, used her to suggest that the publishing world must similarly refine itself, eschewing combative stances and an emphasis on profit in order to assume that mantle of "literary refinement" that alone would fit it for the now-defanged female playwright, actress, or editor. In essence, Swanwick harkened back to a model of elite, privately circulated belles lettres as a refuge for a female author who he feared would be polluted by association with popular print. As we know, however, Rowson's first American publication was one of the very texts that formed the scaffolding of early national print culture, circulating through untold households in innumerable editions. And as we might expect, she had no more intention of obeying such orders from her champions than from her detractors. Instead,

43. John Swanwick, "A Word of Comfort to Mrs. Rowson," in Swanwick, *A Rub from Snub; or, A Cursory Analytical Epistle: Addressed to Peter Porcupine* . . . (Philadelphia, 1795), 73, 76, 79 (emphasis added); Swanwick, *Poems on Several Occasions* . . . (Philadelphia, 1797). Almost all the poems in this book are titled in honor of various women, especially friends' wives and daughters. See, for instance, "To Mrs. Brodeau, on Female Excellence," "To Mrs. Brodeau, on Her Family," and "On a Very Accomplished Young Lady of Philadelphia, Inscribed to a Miss A. Brodeau" (Swanwick, *Poems,* 44, 63, 76). See also Charles Lanman, *Biographical Annals of the Civil Government of the United States, during Its First Century: From Original and Official Sources* (Washington, D.C., 1876); *Biographical Directory of the American Congress, 1774–1961* (Washington, D.C., 1961).

she defied Swanwick to respond to Cobbett in the preface to her next novel, in terms at least as ad hominem and sexually suggestive as his own.

One should note that both Porcupine and Snub responded not only to the subject of Rowson's work but also to her perceived sentimental excesses: "In a labyrinth of sweets," Cobbett noted, "it is almost impossible not to lose one's way." Swanwick faulted Cobbett for making too much of Rowson's grammatical missteps and rhetorical flourishes, but his defense seems as premised on separating her from her word choice as Cobbett's is on collapsing the two. Noting, in regard to *Slaves in Algiers,* that "the most frivolous and fallacious mode of judging of a commedian's sentiments, is from the language dictated to his characters," Swanwick evinced his discomfort with the author's depictions of cross-dressing sex play and strong drink, neglecting to mention that Rowson appeared onstage in the epilogue as none other than herself, still in a highly flirtatious mood. In both Cobbett's and Swanwick's cases, the danger Rowson posed to the new nation involved more than her insistence on representing women as participants in the public sphere; it also had to do with the way her discourse mirrored this potential unrest in its very rhythms.[44]

Rowson's last great contemporary champion worked to contain these disturbing elements. On the basis of Rowson's publications, Samuel L. Knapp put forth a theory of the female novelist as especially suited to the craft of fiction precisely because she lacked the ability to fancify. The instrumentality that Cobbett found suspect, and Carey and Swanwick elided, Knapp saw as safeguarding her works from the dangerous tendencies that inflicted other novels created by more imaginative pens. In this, he departed from the majority of scholars, from Rowson's day to our own, who struggle to justify their attention to her work in light of its perceived mediocrity. For Knapp, what was best about Rowson was precisely that, to his mind, she was no better than ordinary; for this reason alone, she could do no great wrong.[45]

Samuel Knapp's "Memoir" of Rowson appeared in the *Boston Gazette* in 1811 and was included as a preface to the first edition of Rowson's posthumously published novel, *Charlotte's Daughter,* in 1828. By 1811, Rowson, now the august founder and director of a highly successful academy for

44. Cobbett, *Peter Porcupine in America,* ed. Wilson, 130; Swanwick, *Rub from Snub,* 74; Amelia Howe Kritzer, ed., *Plays by Early American Women, 1775–1850* (Ann Arbor, Mich., 1995), 94.

45. More than a century later, Henri Petter takes a similar approach, selecting Rowson as "an average writer of the age" at the outset (Petter, *The Early American Novel* [Columbus, Ohio, 1971], 22).

young women, occupied quite a different position in the public eye than she had as a newly arrived young actress, playwright, and novelist. Her nemesis, Cobbett, had gone back to England. Meanwhile, despite increasing hostilities with Britain, Rowson's diverse services to her adoptive home put her patriotism beyond question, and her greater age made her less vulnerable to being sexualized in print (as either prostitute or damsel in distress, depending on whether one favored Cobbett or Swanwick). Novels, the literary genre with which she was most identified by virtue of her best seller and several other solid successes, were becoming less suspect, a development to which Knapp's "Memoir" both contributed and testified. What's more, Rowson publicly eschewed them now in favor of more strictly pedagogical fare. (This public stance was at least mildly disingenuous, given that she wrote and began efforts to publish *Charlotte's Daughter* during her tenure at the academy.) By 1811, what Rowson needed in her increasing ill health was less a defender than a memorialist; and this she found in her friend and former student's father.[46]

As replete with lavish praise as Cobbett's "Kick" with sarcastic barb, the "Memoir" goes further than any preceding Rowson critique to legitimate Rowson's presence in the public sphere. As such, rather than aim to keep her work above the fray of 1790s print culture, as had Swanwick, Knapp fashioned her as an exemplary participant within a more established publishing scene. In so doing, he not only made a place for women squarely within, as opposed to at the margins of, the novelistic enterprise, but he legitimated the genre itself. Just as Cobbett derided Rowson in order to mock the nation that loved her, Knapp celebrated her as a means (to his mind) to a yet greater end: the defense of novels as the last refuge of instructive entertainment.[47]

And yet it would be wrong to assume that, because Knapp was comfortable with Rowson's fame, he subscribed to a nongendered view of published authorship. Rowson was no sexless soul to Knapp. Rather, he used her gender to feminize the novelistic enterprise itself. This alone suggests a significant shift from Cobbett's heyday in the 1790s, when to insert women into traditionally male public spaces was to render them laughable and corrupt. Now it would seem that women, far from tainting the public sphere,

46. Wilson, introduction to Cobbett, *Peter Porcupine in America,* ed. Wilson, 34. Cobbett's *Porcupine's Gazette* experienced a heyday in 1798 during the peak of anti-French sentiment caused by the XYZ Affair, but sales had declined as the Federalists lost power. By the end of 1800, the *Gazette* had folded, and Cobbett had returned to England. He would return to the United States a changed man.

47. "The third decade of the nineteenth century . . . constituted the first stage in the serious publishing of American novels" (Kelley, *Private Woman, Public Stage,* 11-12).

could actually civilize it. Their role as repositories for inconvenient civic-republican virtues now paradoxically befitted them for certain kinds of participation in the male-identified polis. And the novel was becoming one such recognized arena. This is not to say that novels had not always been to some degree coded female, but merely that, as such, they had not been acknowledged as playing a constitutive role in civic discourse. As Rowson's changing public profile (and posthumous novel) demonstrates, this was soon to change.

Crucial to the novel's developing disciplinary apparatus was a professed fealty to the everyday event over the wildly improbable invention. To Knapp, the job of the novelist was to promote a "pure and elevated morality," and the best way to do this, he thought (not surprisingly for a biographer or a reader of Samuel Johnson), was to draw from "life" rather than "fancy." Thus, in keeping with his lifelong goal of documenting the "demi-great" among his contemporaries—those minor and characteristically American figures who succeed more by dint of "individual exertion" than genius—Knapp is drawn to Rowson precisely because, as a fitting member of her sex, she does not reach too high. "It is no trifling merit," he wrote, "that she should have drawn her characters and incidents directly from the life, when it was the prevailing fashion of writers of fiction to riot exclusively in the regions of fancy." Instead, she records "the innocent foibles and amiable weaknesses of woman." That Rowson's own life and work should have to be so miscast in the name of celebrating novels' mimetic fidelity provides a wonderful example of the poor correlation between prescriptive gender ideology and the day-to-day realities of women's lives during this period. It also demonstrates that, even as antipathy to female participation in the public sphere diminished, a widely known woman still underwent significant mutations in being fitted out for popular public consumption. "The same incompatibility between women's real lives and what was prescribed for them by moralists" persisted, even as their presence in the literary public sphere expanded.[48]

The most telling example of Knapp's reluctance to acknowledge the grittier details of Rowson's personal history occurs in the discussion of her marriage. The "Memoir" cheerfully recollects:

> She was now to enter upon a new sphere of duty, and a new field for the exercise of her affections as well as her talents; for in the same year in which her first work was published, Miss Haswell united her fate with

48. Knapp cited in McClary, *Samuel Lorenzo Knapp,* 58; [Knapp], "Memoir," in Rowson, *Charlotte's Daughter,* 5, 8, 17; Richard D. Brown, *Knowledge Is Power,* 161.

the man of her choice, and became the wife of Mr. William Rowson. In the happiness occasioned by this event, she did not forget the duty which she had imposed on herself as the friend and instructor to the young of her own sex. Her systematic arrangement and strict economy of time, enabled her still to continue the work of composition.[49]

In fact, Mrs. Rowson had no opportunity to forget her "duty," and her strict arrangement of time was born of necessity, for she had to support both herself and her husband through her novel-writing and a host of less reputable activities Knapp sees fit to omit (such as acting and composing lyrics to popular drinking songs, presumably sung by both sexes). Susanna used all her "talents" to survive a "choice" that, once made, was in her eyes irrevocable, and her "happiness" was no doubt of a correspondingly complex nature. Knapp's portrait of a marriage, although lovely, would have seemed a joke to the young Mrs. Rowson.

Knapp might have had a discernible motive in presenting Miss Haswell in attitudes of wifely submission. This had to do with his impetus for writing the sketch itself, namely keeping the novel safe for genteel society. Friend or not, Knapp would not have chosen to include Rowson in his collective *Female Biography* unless he found her exemplary both as a novelist and as a woman. Moreover, given that he valued her craft to precisely the degree it recorded her own typically feminine experience, for him the other two were one and the same.[50]

For Rowson to be a good novelist, then—"good" being doubly significant here, since for Knapp a worthy artist promotes the virtuous—she would need to be a good wife and daughter and to be capable of transmuting this requisite goodness from life to the page and back. This she did admirably, "enforc[ing], by example, the filial piety which she had already recommended by precept and story." Thus despite the fact that "she cannot be pronounced a consummate artist," her "personal character" ensures the worth of her fiction. Rowson is doubly exemplary: her life epitomizes virtues promoted in her work, and her work, as a life transcript, epitomizes the proper format for the novelistic genre.[51] In his zeal to legitimate the genre of the novel and to keep its authorial ranks open to women, then, Knapp rendered her life experience, as the direct template for her literary transcripts, an enforcement of precept rather than something that might respond to

49. [Knapp], "Memoir," in Rowson, *Charlotte's Daughter*, 6.
50. Ibid.
51. Ibid., 6, 11, 12, 17.

events and thereby alter precept. Knapp granted Rowson everything she could have hoped for in the way of dignity and influence; but he denied her the capacity to learn.[52]

In order to solidify Rowson's claim upon critical attention of the sort that could legitimate her participation in the literary marketplace, her early supporters, from Swanwick to Knapp, insisted upon her decoupling from market-based strivings. And they all, in one way or another, rendered her life experience a static predictor of her literary craft rather than a responsive process in which experience worked upon the self to alter it—and thereby to alter not only the substance of its authorial inscriptions but the very dynamic between author and text. This tendency, as shared by the commentators discussed above, helped secure women's paradoxical foundation of and exclusion from the bourgeois public sphere. To enter the market of letters, Rowson had to swear her impermeability to it, her timeless capacity for innate as opposed to situational motivation—her fitness as emblem. What is saddest about this practice is not the particulars of how Rowson was misrepresented but rather that she should have been rendered static in any form—that she should have been denied the capacity for humanity in order to assert her suitability as icon.

Modern scholars have furthered this understanding of Rowson as the incarnation of a particular ideal. While maintaining early commentators' emphasis on demeanor, however, late-twentieth-century critics have tended to foreground the very ambition that earlier scholars disguised as selfless persistence:

> A woman of considerable energy, she espoused strong moral principles and expressed her opinions on personal freedom and a woman's world with a vigor that seems to mark her determined march through life.

Compare this to "Candid"'s statement in the *Maryland Journal* of September 1795.

> I do not pretend to bring this lady forward as a first rate actress, but she is always perfect, and attentive to the business of the scene; and there is a degree of ingratitude in depreciating her merit, *for she has often come forward in parts of consequence, when illness has prevented Mrs. Shaw*

52. Ibid., 5, 12.

*from preparing . . . and she has persisted in performing her theatrical
duty, when . . . she herself* [was] *labouring under severe indisposition.*

Candid anticipates the modern emphasis on Rowson's "considerable energy,"
but he attributes her behavior to "duty" rather than determination.[53]

More recent biographers continue to emphasize Rowson's drive and ambition. Writing of Rowson's "remarkable productivity," one study calls her
"eager" and possessed of "diligence," "enthusiasm," "vigor," and "ambition" as she "busily plied her pen." Another begins, "Mrs. Susanna Haswell
Rowson enters breathless." And another notes that Rowson's "retirement
from the stage in 1797 . . . *did not herald the onset of idleness.*" These and
other feminist biographers deserve our lasting gratitude for the dedication
and thoroughness of their recuperation of Rowson's life and works from
decades of condescension. But by suggesting that we identify the author
with one aspect of her narrative self-inscription rather than question what
might lead her to present herself in such terms, they have limited the significance of the otherwise accurate observation that "Mrs. Rowson, like Jane
Austen in *Persuasion,* recommends keeping busy as the antidote to the woes
of life."[54]

What did Rowson stand to gain from the way her first critics saw her, and
where did she reveal this vision's inaccuracy? We now attend to Rowson's
life-writing in its capacity as complement to and deflection of the essential-
izing profiles in which her earliest, and to a certain degree even her later,
biographers would see her.

Nothing in Rowson's work suggests that she would have been offended by
her early respondents' tendency to privilege the author over her text. In fact,
upon her second emigration to the United States in 1793, she was not above
exploiting her slightly forbidden appeal to American audiences—as both
an English exile and a formidably prolific female public presence—and, as
we have seen, she interjected her authorial persona into much of what she
wrote for performance or publication. In the epilogue to her most popular
drama, for instance, she strode onstage to ask her audience, "How d'ye like

53. Walter J. Meserve, *An Emerging Entertainment: The Drama of the American
People to 1828* (Bloomington, Ind., 1977), 115; Vail, *Susanna Haswell Rowson,* 9–10
(emphasis added).

54. Parker, *Susanna Rowson,* 9, 12, 13, 15, 18, 23, 26; Cheryl Turner, *Living by the
Pen: Women Writers in the Eighteenth Century* (New York, 1992), 81 (emphasis added);
Weil, *In Defense of Women,* 110.

my play?" In novels, she included footnotes to indicate which of the events portrayed were drawn from experience *(Rebecca);* or she attached prefaces detailing her personal history *(Trials of the Human Heart, Sarah, Rebecca);* or she created an outspoken narrator linked to the author through a preface that established a shared outlook and personal style *(Charlotte Temple).*[55]

In fashioning herself for her readers, Rowson emphasized the particulars of her life experience, contextualizing her actions within "a variety of painful circumstances," including familial separation, financial need, geographic dislocation, marital disaffection, and longing for a lost mother. She thus stressed the externally motivated quality of her behavior—including her writing—representing it as a series of responses that varied according to the demands of the occasion. Of course, as we have seen, her contemporary critics preferred to read her actions as those of an inborn native spirit that remained timeless and iconic. This ideal stood in direct counterpoint to post-Revolutionary female authorial practice, even as it exerted a powerful hold on readers' expectations. By examining Rowson's own life-writing in the context of what people first wrote about her, we can begin to understand how a literate woman of the early Republic might carve out a coherent existence from the often contradictory demands of pressing material circumstance and oppressive ideology.[56]

Rowson was certainly capable of playing along with her critics by reminiscing about "leisure hours" she never had in which her writing took place like the pleasant hobby it never was. But she complicated these reveries, both to flaunt her participation in a literary marketplace others would have her reflect kindly upon from a distance and to offer a counterdefinition of female gentility itself. Where her early champions invested her with refinement as something immutable, she insisted upon its fragility. Where they suggested it adhered to her as closely as her own skin, she detailed the labors involved in its maintenance. Where they associated it with a humorless and pristine demeanor, she resorted to irreverence. Where they divorced it from labor, she continually reminded her readers that industry was the secret to happiness, success, and security. Even as her early supporters emphasized the sincerity of her oft-expressed patriotic sympathies and her fitness as a representative female writer for the new nation, they associated female authorship with a gentility more proper to the lands from which they had sprung, whereas she, the most recent arrival of any of them on west-Atlantic

---

55. Susanna Rowson, *Slaves in Algiers; or, A Struggle for Freedom* . . . (Philadelphia, 1794), 94.

56. Rowson, preface to *Trials of the Human Heart,* I, xix.

shores, updated the norm to make it more appropriate to a nation character-ized by a "large bulge in the center of the social pyramid."[57]

The following pages explore how Rowson's self-presentation uses the messy circumstantial detail that enlivened her novels, her personal narrative, and her life experience to resist being reduced to the uniform abstractions that others would have her embody. This investigation owes a great deal to the concept of "representative personality," that is, "personal exemplifica-tion of an underlying commonality." In this study, representative personality calls attention to the conflicting tendencies between Rowson and her first critics as well as within her own self-presentation. For to the extent that an authorial persona is a consistent, communicable entity, it must possess some regularity, something abstractable into a representation. In its dual senses as "by proxy" and "by portrait," representation reached a watershed mo-ment in the late eighteenth century, which featured revolutions in pursuit of representative government and the push for an aesthetic capable of rep-resenting the concerns of a rising middle class. At the same time, however, personality, another concept beholden to the late eighteenth century, is itself inextricably lodged in the particular, the distinct, the ungeneralizable. It refers to the freaks and foibles that make people discrete (from one another as well as from their own past and future selves) and that at the same time lend a particular profile to each human existence.[58]

Becoming a representative personality, then, was never a mean feat. But when that personality was female, the effort was particularly fraught. On the one hand, women, like other disenfranchised groups, were seen to possess an especially intimate relationship with the material world, the very stuff of experience. On the other, this dubious privilege challenged their perceived authority to articulate their experience in language. Precluded from engag-ing in activities that depended on the ability to abstract from the particular to the general, such as voting, holding office, or many forms of publication, women were among those judged incapable of disinterested reason by virtue of some aspect of their physical being. What happens, then, when we ex-plore the phenomenon of representative personality from the point of view

57. Susanna Rowson to D. Brown, n.d., in Papers of Susanna Rowson, 1770–1879, MSS 7379, box 1, folder 37, Clifton Waller Barrett Library of American Literature, Special Collections, University of Virginia Library, Charlottesville, Va; Appleby, *Capi-talism and a New Social Order*, 11.

58. Mitchell Robert Breitwieser, *Cotton Mather and Benjamin Franklin: The Price of Representative Personality* (Cambridge, 1984), 2. Jay Fliegelman notes "the emergence of personality as a concept" during the period in which Thomas Jefferson wrote and read aloud the Declaration of Independence (Fliegelman, *Declaring Independence*, 4).

of one who, because her female body was "seen to constrain and encumber" her, was "understood to lack the constitutive agency that would enable [her] to participate in liberal subjectivity"? And as for the rare female author who managed to negotiate such turmoil to emerge into the public eye relatively unscathed—what did she have to offer the public that a more suitably qualified male author lacked?[59]

Rowson suggested one advantage to female representative personality when she offered her public "not myself indeed, but what is nearly the same thing, the offspring of my imagination." As a woman, she was able to identify herself with the text in a way that Franklin never attempted in, say, his autobiographical letter to his son. For Rowson, the text, as literary "offspring," emerges from the very body of the author. And, to considerable effect, she exploited the greater material residue presumed to adhere to female-authorized words. In contrast to her female contemporaries, such as Murray and Wollstonecraft, Rowson actually uses the fact that she is "encumbered" by a female body to derive unprecedented cultural authority: as maternal surrogate, as scornful object of desire, and as dutiful daughter who nonetheless, precisely because she is not eligible for enfranchisement in either of two warring nations, feels free to develop her own political values drawing from her American and British affiliations simultaneously.[60]

Susanna Rowson has many autobiographical incarnations, beginning with her first novel, *Victoria*, which is dedicated to Rowson's patroness the duchess of Devonshire. In it, the duchess makes a cameo appearance as "the ornament of the British nation" and the benefactress of the protagonist, Lucinda Harlow. Then comes *The Inquisitor; or, The Invisible Rambler*, where we meet a "young creature" at the printing office trying to sell her first novel. Third is Helen Askham—a.k.a. "Mentoria," of the novel *Mentoria; or, The Young Lady's Friend*—like Rowson, a governess whose father was a loyalist naval officer.[61]

With the American publication of *Rebecca; or, The Fille de Chambre*, Rowson foregrounds the autobiographical aspect of the novel, perhaps in order to capitalize on the public interest that, as a successful actress,

59. Dillon, *Gender of Freedom*, 11.

60. Rowson, preface to *Trials of the Human Heart*, I, xii.

61. Susanna Rowson, *Victoria: A Novel*, 2 vols. (London, 1786), I, 126. The character Miss Philimore further honors the duchess: "During breakfast, it came into my mind that there was a woman, the ornament of the British nation, whose breast was the residence of every social virtue; in short, ladies, I thought to apply to Her Grace of D——."

lyricist, and author of a best seller, she is now likely to arouse in her own right. (*Rebecca* was to become Rowson's second biggest seller in the United States during her lifetime.) The novel contains a lengthy section paralleling Susanna's childhood experiences in Revolutionary New England. In it, Rebecca joins a teenage girl named Sophia Abthorpe and her parents, Colonel and Mrs. Abthorpe, on their journey to America. The adventures of this family—their care for a dying British soldier, their imprisonment during the Revolution, the kindness of certain American friends—make the Abthorpes direct counterparts to Rowson's own birth family, with Sophia standing in for Rowson herself (and with Rowson heavily footnoting to establish the correlation). Brandt calls this section of *Rebecca* "as . . . engrossing a piece of writing as Susanna Rowson ever achieved," owing in part to its lively and detailed chronicle of the family's hardships.[62]

That the author receives rare unmitigated praise for this particular section is significant. Writing that calls attention to her own straitened circumstances during the Revolution reminds us how much the Rowsonian protagonist's identity was continually re-forming itself in response to its environment rather than serving as a fixed emblem of "pure and elevated morality." By calling attention to Sophia's, and by implication Rowson's own, youthful geographic, economic, and familial challenges, the author does not throw off the mantle of representative womanhood altogether; but she grants it the flexibility to respond. For Rowson, female virtue follows from experience; it does not reside, any more than depravity does, within the untested female body.

If Rowson's life experience founds *Rebecca,* it informs her next two novels with autobiographical overtones in even more profound (if less explicit) ways. In these works, Rowson is neither as forthcoming regarding the parallels to her life nor as faithful to detail in describing shipwrecks, burning lighthouses, and prisoner exchanges. Nevertheless, *Trials of the Human Heart* partakes of her life deeply in its relentless exposure of the difficulties faced by a young woman deprived of familial connections and financial security. Subsequently, *Sarah,* a novel "written in despondency over her marriage," contains cryptic allusions to physical abuse and emotional neglect. It also lays out the reasons a woman suffering these ills might choose to stay married, ranging from unwillingness to break a promise to the callous treatment that awaits her at the hands of the larger community should she depart.[63] Rowson never specified whether fidelity to life experi-

62. Brandt, *Susanna Haswell Rowson,* 115.
63. Ibid., 89; Parker, *Susanna Rowson,* 89.

ence or artistic license best accounts for these aspects of the novel, beyond her oft-cited epigraph "Do not marry a fool." But she wrote a preface to the book version of *Sarah* (appearing ten years after its serial publication) that, in spelling out the depth of the author's disillusionment, suggests a reflection of her life. Clearly, the further Rowson progressed in her marriage, the more willing she became to share its travails as both a caution to others and a potential source of relief.

Thus what Rowson denied to gossips in the way of revealing her marital hardships, she more than made up for in her prefaces to *Trials of the Human Heart, Sarah,* and *Rebecca.* Taken together, these documents provide a shockingly informative alternative account to that established by her contemporary commentators. They suggest that, for Rowson, as for the critics, the authorial persona rivals the protagonist as a vehicle for enlightenment of the novel-reader. But the nature of the enlightenment in each case is radically different. In her personal narrative, Rowson steers the reader away from any comfortable fiction of the feminine, particularly one that puts gender in the service of some greater agenda, whether that be discrediting American commercialism (Cobbett) or defending it by holding out a sphere untouched by the complexities of mercantile capitalist development (Carey, Swanwick, Knapp). She emphasizes diversity of experience, implication in worldly structures, and the capacity to learn from one's past, so as to prevent any static perception of womanhood. Rowson uses her own "private history" to fix herself upon readers' minds as a presence akin to her protagonists— one to be emulated precisely for her imperfections, themselves the inevitable result of life in a messy world.[64]

In order to understand the significance of Rowson's self-presentation, one must first come to terms with her sense of the role that literary characters played in the lives of their readers. Rowson delineates this understanding in the preface to *Trials of the Human Heart,* taking her cue straight from Dr. Johnson. Characters, she agrees, should not be "above probability" if they are to succeed in the novel's chief function, moral education; "for what

64. This analysis follows the order in which the prefaces themselves were written, which differs from the publication sequence of the novels: first *Trials of the Human Heart* (1795), then *Sarah; or, The Exemplary Wife,* published in book form with preface in 1813 after appearing in weekly installments in the *Boston Weekly* in 1803–1804; then the 1814 introduction to the second American edition of *Rebecca* (first published London, 1792; Philadelphia, 1794). Taken in this order, the prefaces themselves form a kind of linked narrative, in which their protagonist, Susanna Rowson, moves from youthful optimism through despair to resilient, if guarded, hope.

we cannot credit, we shall never imitate." Instead, they should display "the highest and purest that humanity can reach." Rowson then claims that her novel is written on this plan, in particular through its depiction of a "Heroine, though not wholly free from error . . . not altogether unworthy [of] imitation."[65]

Instead of dedicating the rest of her lengthy preface to elaborating this plan, however, Rowson then begins to describe her own recent travails in the publishing world before turning to an exculpatory account of her early life history, meant to verify the patriotism Cobbett maligns. What becomes clear through this account is that Rowson is "endeavour[ing] to form" not only her heroine around Johnson's ideal but her own literary persona as well. Rowson will "not envy the honours which wit and learning obtain . . . if I may be so happy as to awaken in the bosoms of my youthful readers . . . a spirited emulation." As it turns out, however, Rowson is to be emulated, like Johnson's protagonists, on the basis of her faults. In this preface, then, Rowson includes enough references to personal confusion to unfit her for the role that, in various ways, Cobbett, Carey, Swanwick, and Knapp all prepare for her. She is neither immune to principle, as Cobbett would have it, nor a perfect incarnation thereof, as her defenders would have it. Instead, she is a survivor, doing the best she can with what she has been offered.[66]

Those used to the dismissals of her rhetorical skill handed out by all four literary lions above will be struck, no doubt, by her biting insinuations of sexual inadequacy in her most strident detractor. Cobbett, she implies, is prone to premature ejaculation, a "noisome reptile" that, "swelling with envy, should the smallest part of public favour, be conferred on another, spits out its malignant poison." Given this debility, he is correspondingly afflicted by flaccidity, having recently "crawled over the volumes, which I have had the temerity to submit to the public eye. I say *crawled over* them, because I am certain it has never penetrated beyond the title-page of any." If Cobbett misses his mark, however, he nevertheless provides Rowson with a perfect excuse for indulging her public with "a slight sketch of my private history." Not above using the rhetoric of imperiled chastity so extravagantly bandied about by Carey when it serves her, Rowson claims "the blush of offended delicacy" in order to justify launching into a personal narrative that, she hopes, will set the record straight.[67]

65. Rowson, preface to *Trials of the Human Heart,* I, xii, xiii, citing Johnson.
66. Ibid., xx.
67. Ibid., xiii–xv.

In this account, two sources of instability resurface, both lending a touch of Johnsonian believability to a life presented as a model worthy of readerly imitation. The first is national citizenship; the second, class status. Both of these categories provide opportunities for Rowson to negotiate between uniform abstract principle and untidy circumstantial detail. In aiming to be emulable, Rowson attempts a degree of consistency; she means to stand for something, to be a *representative* woman.

But in providing instances of divided loyalty, disappointment, and doubt, she simultaneously insists on the primacy of what she calls "existance" over "principle." In this, she might be said to embody rather the "representative *woman*," since to be female in the early Republic, we have seen, is to account for exactly those aspects of experience that don't lend themselves to linguistic abstraction. For Cobbett, the female body's unseemly secretions of blood, milk, and babies made it the perfect image of America's incapacity for self-governance. For Carey and Swanwick, by contrast, the penetrable female body was particularly vulnerable to the predations of the post-Revolutionary publishing industry, whereas for Knapp, women's incapacity for invention qualified them to safeguard the liberal public sphere. In all four cases, women were severed from a productive connection with the word in order to preserve their symbolic capacities inviolate. Rowson, however, renders the discomforts of existence in all their glory, leaving the reader to settle for a less orderly vision of a nonetheless more accurately realized authorial figure.[68]

Rowson highlights this tension in her return to the notion of "principle" throughout the preface to *Trials,* each time setting it in apparent opposition to some other term (such as "existence" or "humanity") with which it ends up intimately allied. We are advised that this will be a life of principle, of loyalty to abstract formulations, in Rowson's early account of her father's persistent loyalism in the face of overwhelming American opposition: "No one who considers the nature of an oath, voluntarily taken . . . will blame him for a strict adherence to principles." Strangely, however, her father's loyalty to principle turns out to express not so much a reverence for abstract ideation (commitment to the good, however figured) as a desire to live consistently with past experience. These so-called principles are more a matter of habit than ratiocination; they "were interwoven as it were with his existence," her father having "served thirty years under the British government." Therefore, he espouses anti-Revolutionary principles, not out of any reverence for their inherent correctness, but merely to remain on the side he has always

68. Cobbett, *Peter Porcupine in America,* ed. Wilson, 131.

been on. Familiarity, for him (at least according to his daughter), is a surer guide than investigation.[69]

The next time Rowson employs the word "principle," it is again opposed to another term, "humanity." Rowson is now describing the American response to her father's loyalty to the British cause: "For while their political principles obliged them to afflict, the humanity, the Christian like benevolence of their souls, incited them to wipe the tears of sorrow from the eyes of my parents, to mitigate their sufferings, and render those afflictions in some measure supportable." Afflicting on the one hand while trying to comfort on the other sounds less like "benevolence" than sadism to the casual observer. Indeed, there is a deeply masochistic strain to Rowson's ardent love for America, as we will see in a future chapter. But what makes the experience of incarceration and deportment by Revolutionary soldiers particularly useful to Rowson is that it brings together the realms of principle and humanity, as well as those of abstract thought (which women are deemed incapable of within liberal discourse) and the compassionate physical nurture that better befits their bodily encumbrance. The tendency to figure sensibility through its somatic elaborations occurs repeatedly here, as the soldiers "wipe the tears of sorrow from the eyes of my parents," "mitigate sufferings," and "render afflictions supportable."[70]

Rowson's own political principles will similarly appear in a scene rich with emotional pathos. But where the soldiers' pity conflicts with their beliefs, Rowson's makes the two symbiotic, in a manner unique to representative womanhood. Rowson begins disingenuously, claiming herself "too young . . . to have formed any political principles of my own" during the period she describes above. She employs this apparent lack, however, precisely to allow her own principles to develop in contradistinction to her father's reliance on habitude. Just as Rowson, in this book's opening pages, created a space for her friend Louisa to reflect on current events by imagining herself in the place of her father, here the author both plays up her respect for her father's political views, which, she writes, she "may naturally be supposed to have adopted," and quietly comes up with a radically new perspective on the relationship between the warring nations.[71]

This perspective is, in a word, neutrality. Rowson phrases her dawning awareness as that felt by "a person . . . who having a tender lover, and an affectionate brother who are equally dear to her heart, and by whom she is

69. Rowson, preface to *Trials of the Human Heart,* I, xvi.
70. Ibid., xvii.
71. Ibid., xix.

equally beloved, sees them engaged in a quarrel with, and fighting against each other, when, let whichsoever party conquer, she cannot be supposed insensible to the fate of the vanquished." Her first political principle, that is, is righteous doubt: the validity of choosing not to choose.[72]

As important as the sophistication of this concept are the familial terms in which it is phrased. According to Susanna, her father didn't think much at all about what he believed: he just did what had, to his mind, always been done. In articulating her own reluctance to choose sides, by contrast, Rowson demonstrated that she had not inherited his faith in inheritance, his respect for precedent, any more than she had his lost sinecure. Unlike him, she is driven to come up with a point of view that satisfies her own notions of what is true and right. But by representing this view in allegorical terms that call to mind a young woman's transition from birth family ("brother") to marital union ("lover"), Rowson shrewdly placates those for whom a woman's authority derives, not from her capacity for reason, but rather from her deferential relationships to men. She thus introduces a crucial political principle—neutrality—into circulation and cloaks it in a feminized rhetoric that makes it less threatening. Here we witness the entrance of the representative woman, called to integrate precept (the capacity to "represent") and affect (the capacity to be a "woman," whose authority is bestowed by others in exchange for services such as nurture and compassion) in a manner not yet demonstrated by her male compatriots. Rowson derives pacifism from the very implication in birth, love, and death—in matters of the heart, not the mind—that others have claimed bar her sex from political enfranchisement.

Rowson's phrasing of political neutrality as the sensation felt by an (implicitly female) observer to a duel between lover and brother is also suggestive of the role her uncertain class status will play in her self-portrait and in her national identity. Her reference to a consummately genteel form of engagement is not accidental, any more than her pretense that she wrote her previous books during "many a leisure hour." (Rowson had few such hours, and many more pressing concerns than being "amused" and "beguiled" by the fruits of her pen.) Almost any female author of the period attempting to reach an audience without offending it needed to assume the stance of the lady of leisure in order to avoid being besmirched with the taint of ambition, greed, or worse. But Rowson employs the trope to greater effect than merely soothing her readership into soporific acceptance of her entitlement to "appl[y] myself to my pen." For her gentility is soon to encounter several

72. Ibid.

rude shocks.[73] As such, she revisits the question explored in our Introduction (and articulated elsewhere by many scholars): how does one determine gentility in a society presumably dedicated to the principle of equality? This is an important issue for early national Americans, and Rowson makes herself of consummate interest to them by becoming a test case for it.

Initially, Rowson emphasizes her genteel British heritage. Her father, she states, was an officer, granting her a correspondingly elevated station among her new companions: "blest with a genteel competency, and placed by his rank and education in that sphere of life, where the polite and friendly attentions of the most respectable characters courted our acceptance." So far, Rowson has merely reassured her readers that they are not wrong to look to her regarding matters of taste and deportment; reading her works will improve, not corrupt or degrade, their manners. More important, she has reinforced the notion that inherited status distinctions are a worthy principle of measurement; in venerating her, they do no wrong. A safe pose, certainly, but not one to inspire the kind of unabashed attachment that the author of the nation's first best seller might seem to merit.[74]

Rowson is soon, however, to come much closer to the experience of many of her readers than her beginnings suggest. For maximum rhetorical effect, she stages this transformation as a second arrival, a new beginning of sorts. Upon her return to England, "a variety of painful circumstances, unnecessary here to recount, contributed to deprive me of a decent independence inherited from my paternal grandfather, and at length to bring me back to America, *in a very different situation, I must confess, from that in which I left it.*" This time Rowson arrives, not as an Englishwoman, but as a prototype of the young immigrant, without much in the way of resources and with an uncertain future ahead. This robs her of some of her authority, but it grants her something more important: likeness. Rowson is now more worthy of imitation precisely because she is less inviolate. In fact (and politely elided in the "unnecessary here to recount" reference), her financial troubles began in Revolutionary America with the confiscation of her father's property. He never received his navy commission upon his return to England, and the family never regained its former "genteel competency." But the young nation's culpability in this regard is more than offset by the opportunity it extends Rowson to transform herself from a stagnant member of an inherited status group into a living, breathing, thinking, developing individual. Like the Revolutionaries who afflicted and comforted Rowson's family in equal

73. Ibid., xv.
74. Ibid., xvi–xvii.

measure, America robs her of her gentility (person confined, property confiscated, prisoners exchanged) and then holds out the promise of its return—and it is this promise that excites Rowson. Thus she arrives in triumph even in the midst of distress, her "heart, still glowing with the same affectionate sensations, and exulting in [the nation's] evident improvement." Now that "the arts are encouraged, manufactures increase, and this happy land bids fair to be in the course of a few years the most flourishing nation in the universe," it can certainly find a place for the likes of her. Standing before "America and its inhabitants" to give an account of her life, she demonstrates that she has attained such a place.[75]

No wonder she offers "ardent prayers for a continuation of their prosperity"; "theirs" is now, though she need not speak it, "ours." In a fascinating turn of events, the gentility that once allowed Rowson to claim a place before the reader's eye is now attested to by that very place. And no wonder she phrases her accidental return as a teleology fulfilled (her only comfort on leaving the first time "was indulging in the delightful hope, of being at some future period permitted again to revisit"). For although it might seem unlikely that one should wish oneself back in a place that stole one's money, put one under house arrest, and kicked one out in a prisoner exchange as part of a military "cartel" between warring nations, it is only here that Rowson claims to be able to use the instability of her "circumstances" (and the consequent variability of her responses) as a feature of, rather than an immovable impediment to, self-realization. In her account of gentility reclaimed as of national identity forestalled (she continues to speak of "their" prosperity in reference to American citizens throughout the preface), Rowson phrases America as a land in which idea and existence can come into fruitful interplay, particularly in the creation of a female author for whom self-representation will never be a matter of Franklinian self-possession. Even her wish to have American "influence extended throughout every nation under heaven" seems slightly less chilling when one reads it not only as a program for imperial domination but as the effusion of a young author carried away by optimism that her present success might be enjoyed far and wide, by her and women like her all over the globe.[76]

Sadly, such optimism proved unwarranted. In fact, no amount of dexterity in devising principles capable of both accounting for and altering circumstance would save Rowson from the one aspect of her life over which she seemed to feel she had no influence and no choice but to endure: her

75. Ibid., xix (emphasis added).
76. Ibid., xviii.

marriage. This is the topic of her preface to the novel *Sarah; or, The Exemplary Wife* (1813), and it revisits the themes of *Trials* only to cast them in far darker terms. Again, Rowson resorts to the standard of the virtuous novel, namely that one must avoid "unnatural appearance" or else one's "example will lose its effect." But where Rowson used this tenet as a means to describe her resilience in the face of material deprivation in *Trials,* here she drags it out only to explain her heroine's unhappy end. Triumphing over geographic dislocation and lost inheritance is one thing, she suggests, but escaping an unhappy marital union is quite another.[77]

It should come as no surprise that the realm of principle has ventured here from the political to the scriptural. If Rowson is to maintain any faith in justice in the face of irresolvably depressing circumstance, it's going to have to be according to God's law. Thus her protagonist forestalls her reward from the here and now to a better, if less certain, place: no "faultless monster," she nevertheless "endeavours to make his laws the rule of her actions, and trusts in his promises for her reward." In the last paragraphs, Rowson depicts a loveless marriage in terms that leave little doubt that she knows of what she speaks: "For surely no life can be pictured so completely wretched as where two persons, knowing from experience the turpitude of each other's heart, are obliged to wear out the last remnant of existence together, in mutual jealousy, hatred and recrimination."[78]

As the bearer of such knowledge, however, Rowson can claim "emulation" of only the most limited sort. To those capable of staying out of such a mess, she warns, "Beware . . . how you select a partner for life." For those already in her situation, she might at least help them manage: "When once the choice is made and fixed beyond revocation, remember patience, forbearance, and in many cases perfect silence, is the only way to secure domestic peace." Revealing the depth of her despair, Rowson then extends this uncharacteristic invitation to passive endurance to the female sex in general: "Why, in truth, there is seldom any [marriage] so perfectly felicitous, but that instances may occur where patience, forbearance, and silence, may be practiced with good effect." In this ultimate call for wider-spread emulation, Rowson shows how low she has sunk—for in the service of representative personality, she has here deprived herself of all that originally gave her claim to the title.[79]

One year after the publication of *Sarah* in book form, complete with its

77. Susanna Rowson, preface to *Sarah; or, The Exemplary Wife* (Boston, 1813), i.
78. Ibid., iii, iv.
79. Ibid., iv.

pessimistic preface, Rowson again wrote a new preface for a previously published novel, *Rebecca*. Without *Sarah* to intervene between her current undertaking and the preface to *Trials,* this one might seem merely a somewhat more matter-of-fact recapitulation of the issues set forth in *Trials.* Once again, she reminds her reader of leisure hours once enjoyed and now long past. Once again, these hours are a fiction, as she sets them "twenty-two years ago," which would be 1792, during which time Rowson and her new husband were on their way to Edinburgh to begin their careers on the stage. And once again, she reiterates the "vicissitudes of fortune" experienced "on both sides of the Atlantic" during her youth.[80]

But if the preface to *Trials* set forth these vicissitudes in order to render its authorial protagonist suitable fodder for emulation, in *Rebecca* the didactic agenda trumpeted in both previous autobiographical accounts has receded. It receives token acknowledgment in the last paragraph, where Rowson trusts that "the character of my heroine, Rebecca, is such as every young woman may . . . imitate with advantage." This time, however, Rowson is beyond advertising the advantages flawed moral beauties hold over perfection or of using such proclamations to justify her inclusion of autobiographical travails. Instead, she seems to relive her youthful experiences in order to triumph over the silent despondency of *Sarah*'s preface, which receives no mention here. In revisiting "scenes in her father's family" from 1769 to 1778, she does indeed catalog an impressive collection of "vicissitudes": her abuse at the hands of an unfeeling employer whose family she enters as governess, "the distress at sea, the subsequent shipwreck; the burning Boston lighthouse, the death of the poor marine, the imprisonment of the family, the friendship experienced by them in the most distressed circumstances, the removal farther into the country, and exchange to Halifax." But however much suffering these instances occasioned at the time, she now finds them evidence of the reclamatory power of present recollection over past circumstance. "Dear to memory are the scenes of our early days," she writes, "though in them the cup of existence was often mingled with the tear of affliction or bitter regrets."[81]

Unspoken here is the wish that the present circumstance alluded to in *Sarah* might also one day be rendered malleable by the mind and thereby freed of its power to hurt. One might take this to include the hope that in fact her marriage might become a memory—that is, that it might no longer exist. Or one could merely infer her wish that its sufferings might abate

80. Rowson, preface to *Rebecca; or, The Fille de Chambre* (Boston, 1814), iii, iv.
81. Ibid., iv, vi.

enough for her to treat past irritations in the kind light shed upon them, for instance, by her wedding anniversary poem. Either way, Rowson seems far less concerned than previously with how her prose will affect its readers. Rather, she is caught in an almost private moment, wielding her pen to regain her equanimity through the renewed recall of familiar events.[82]

In a sense, this is Rowson at her least representative. Despite the abundance of correlations between authorial and protagonistic personae, Rowson has loosened the reins, allowing her protagonist to play the role of She Who Shall Be Emulated while her authoress roams freely and alone, largely unnoticed by her readers as she puts the narrative to purposes unspecified in its pages. If early pundits miscast what exactly Rowson aimed to represent, they certainly never noticed those moments in which she forwent the honor altogether. And yet for this reader, these rare moments of retreat speak to a commonality more lasting than any proclamations of feminine authorial bravado.

Two worlds have been described in recent criticism: a flourishing realm of eighteenth-century belles lettres in which manuscripts circulated privately (if widely) without authorial concern for financial recompense and a newly developing professional marketplace consisting primarily of journalism and novels for rent or purchase. Writing is two different things in these realms: a process or a product, an event or a commodity. Too often, scholars describe these worlds as if they didn't intersect. But by the 1790s, they did, particularly in the increasing number of novels, histories, poems, and essays by and about women. For the more pervasive female participation in a developing market economy of letters became, the more the work of the nation's first female authors was seen to derive from models of literary exchange characteristic of colonial belles lettres, most especially "an economy of gift rather than a market." Indeed, women ironically had to assume the mantle of writing for leisure in order to be accepted for publication within the market economy. Hence the proliferation of works "By a Lady," with that term's dual indication of womanhood and social stature. The acts of self-obfuscation and self-assumption this dilemma imposed on female authors indicates that the new female-centered literary public sphere recognized by scholars from Branson to Baym was both vigorous and massively unstable, continually dependent upon its own disavowal for its very survival.[83]

82. Ibid.

83. Branson, *These Fiery Frenchified Dames,* 24. Carla Mulford writes, "Literary historians have taken the rise of print culture during this period as signaling the mo-

Perhaps because of Rowson's roots in a British gentry affiliated with older models of authorship, however, even many who had trouble recognizing professionally active early American women for what they were found her worthy of comment. In fact, Rowson was part of both a gift and a market economy of letters from her earliest days as an author in England who published with Minerva and was sponsored by a duchess. Rowson's public persona provides us a rare opportunity to look into the void, as it were, between elite and popular, private and public, republican and liberal, British and American realms as they have been constituted in recent criticism. For if Rowson was ideally situated in many ways to serve as an emissary between these twinned worlds, her achievements generally depended on her ability to exploit the overlaps and inconsistencies between them. A canny self-promoter whose success resided largely in her ability to appear as if she promoted the general good at her own expense, she adapted her genteel heritage to her participation in the labor economy, all the while representing herself as the trusted intimate of the solitary misled daughter who, in the aggregate, formed more than half a nation. Faking an increasingly dubious elitism to appeal to a popular audience, then throwing herself into peer exchange with her American readers even as she cherished her British otherness, Rowson reveals the contestation and mutuality of these opposed realms despite a critical tradition that often fails to put them into dialogue. Thus, even as the novel helped make "moral" refer to individual interiority as opposed to civic entirety, even as it reconstituted reading as an act of private consumption, the splitting of private and public realms these associations signify should not mislead us into considering the rupture complete.

If the status of literary discourse as a truly new kind of female-centered public depended partly on the increasing ratio of women to men who both wrote and featured in its pages, the sheer volume of texts that characterized this forum possesses its own special relevance. For if women wrote, read, and featured as subject matter in novels and magazines in unprecedented numbers, they did so because these works contained something of value to

------

ment when authors began to be read and to achieve some prominence and popularity. By studying printed materials alone, scholars have assumed that only printed works indicate an author's popularity and success as a writer. But this is a false assumption, one that denies the importance of the oral and manuscript cultural transmission of the eighteenth-century elite. It is an assumption, too, that has enabled the continued dismissal of much that was important to women of the eighteenth century" (Mulford, ed., *Only for the Eye of a Friend: The Poems of Annis Boudinot Stockton* [Charlottesville, Va., 1995], 7–8). Rebecca Rush and Tabitha Tenney both employed the ubiquitous "By a Lady," as did countless others still unknown to us.

them. With all our attention to how early American sentimentalism tells the story of the birth of a nation, the motives of those who constituted this revolution have remained shrouded: and these, I have suggested, largely concerned the attainment of something previously kept under lock and key to all but a chosen few. That something, in turn, was paradoxically the very thing that such numbers could not sustain without changing it irretrievably: an illusion of intimate, leisured sociability. Thus by the 1790s, "on the consumption side of the literary transaction, an individual's subscription to a polite magazine or purchase of a novel served as a marker of one's imaginative commitment to gentility, cosmopolitanism, and the pursuit of pleasure." And "magazines did for a wider audience what salons did for only a few groups of elites: create intimate, private spaces where critical discussions took place." Indeed, this "marker," this "doing for" was the single greatest motivation behind the largest transformation the American publishing industry had yet seen and a key element in the entrance of women into public discourse.[84]

84. Shields, *Civil Tongues,* 316; Branson, *These Fiery Frenchified Dames,* 24.

3

FEEL WRITE

In the last chapter, we saw Rowson skillfully managing her authorial self-inscription to shape readers' responses to her published writings as well as the author they created from those writings. Her efforts derived, not from mere vanity, but from the well-placed sense that her reputation as a professionally active woman would influence the tolerance accorded Anglo-American female ambition within the late-eighteenth-century public sphere. Rowson's strategic self-referentiality, however, also betrays a sense of vulnerability, as in the following passage from the preface to her *Mentoria; or, The Young Lady's Friend:*

> Shall I tell the reader my design in publishing these volumes? I will;
> It was an anxious desire to see all my dear country-women as truly amiable as they are universally acknowledged beautiful. . . . Whether I have executed this design well or ill, must be hereafter determined, not only by those partial friends whose kind encouragement prompted me to submit these pages to the inspection of the public; but, a well-a-day for me, I must also be judged by some sage critic, who, "with spectacle on nose, and pouch by's side," with lengthened visage and contemptuous smile, sits down to review the literary productions of a *woman.* He turns over a few pages, and then
>
> > Catching the Author at some that or therefore,
> > At once condemns her without why or wherefore.
>
> Then, alas! What may not be my fate? Whose education, as a female, was necessarily circumscribed, whose little knowledge has been simply gleaned from pure nature, and who, on a subject of such importance, write as I feel, with enthusiasm.

Here, Rowson alludes to her well-known antagonist William Cobbett, who did spy out grammatical infelicities in her work and use them to deride it in its entirety. But her larger point extends beyond the crankiness of any particular commentator. Rather, the "sage critic" stands opposed to the "partial friends" above and reveals Rowson's uncertain position between two contested modes of reading. Her "friends" represent an older, European-influenced reading community engaged in the free exchange of holograph and print texts. The critic, however, here figured as a public inspector, belongs to a newer, broader, and more anonymous literary marketplace in which texts were bought and sold, consumed privately rather than in company (think of Mathew Carey sneaking home to read his library books, away from the watchful eye of his parents), and most of all reached far beyond the circle of authorial acquaintance to readers of multiple stations and localities.[1]

In that Rowson's friends are here said to have encouraged her "to submit" to such a public, they become complicit in her fate at the hands of its representative. Perhaps they did not anticipate her rough handling, insensitive to the advantages they possessed: an author's acquaintance met both the person and her works. But the book itself was all the sage critic had to work with. Hence the simultaneous appeal and frustration of the prefaces that buffered most late-eighteenth-century fiction, including virtually every Rowson publication. In *The Female Spectator* (upon which *Mentoria* was modeled), Eliza Haywood justified prefaces as offering her the opportunity "to get as well acquainted as I can with an Author, before I run the risque of losing my Time in perusing his Work." But no amount of prefatory matter, such as the introduction containing this very sentiment, gave the reader anything but more print characters with which to "acquaint" him- or herself.[2]

The problem with Rowson's sage critic is that he denied his own complicity in this regard. Rather than acknowledge his "*woman* . . . Author" as a result of his reading, he placed his invention ahead of her text. Knowing what he would find based on her ascribed gender identity, he sought out markers that confirmed his expectations and, presumably, ignored those that contradicted them. He then comfortably concluded that the text not only contained meanings consistent with what he expected "of a woman" but was in fact a mechanical "production" of those very expectations. The

1. Susanna Rowson, preface to *Mentoria; or, The Young Lady's Friend,* 2 vols. (London, 1790), I, iii–iv.

2. Eliza Haywood, *Selections from "The Female Spectator,"* ed. Patricia Meyer Spacks (New York, 1999), 7.

same conditions (another woman, another pen) would have led to roughly the same results. To write as a woman is to write only as a woman: who one is and what one makes are of a piece.

Rowson's response to this state of affairs provides a clue to her method of forestalling such prejudgment beyond the self-inscription explored in the last chapter. Put simply, the passage above claims the female sentimentalist's privilege. To her "little knowledge" and her "necessarily circumscribed" education—euphemisms, if not outright surrogates, for the condescension that led more conventionally schooled male readers to misread her work—the author opposes the capacity to "write as I feel, with enthusiasm." Like colonial enthusiasts from Anne Hutchinson to Hannah Dustan, Rowson cites a higher law than the trained cognition of the formally elect. In place of the latter's authorized truths, she institutes a direct relation to the source of authority: in this case, not God, but the human heart. In anticipation of Harriet Beecher Stowe's incendiary call to "feel right," Rowson prepares the ground by "writ[ing] as I feel."[3]

Let critics condescend: "partial friends," too, may be formed from reading experiences. For if the critic prejudges and hence denies himself the opportunity to respond to an author he renders speechless, "my dear countrywomen" possess the ability to be more "amiable." Unlike the (also potentially imaginary) friends who set her on this course, even the most sympathetic readers will lack the advantage of prior acquaintance mentioned above. They will be unlikely to have met Rowson, seen her onstage, enrolled a daughter in her academy, or heard from someone who has. But if they remain open to what the text has to offer, they will not only construct a sympathetic authorial figure from it; they also will render themselves affectionate respondents. The reading experience will thus partake of the qualities of sociable exchange foreclosed upon by the desiccated print culture market and its representative, the lonely, chair-ridden critic. Projected by this same market on an unprecedentedly massive scale, this sympathetic affect can then serve as the basis for a utopian vision of widespread amity and just distribution of communal resources, a vision Rowson began to articulate in her final novel.

3. This phrase comes from a famous passage in Harriet Beecher Stowe's *Uncle Tom's Cabin:* "But, what can any individual do? Of that, every individual can judge. There is one thing that every individual can do,—they can see to it that *they feel right.* An atmosphere of sympathetic influence encircles every human being; and the man or woman who *feels* strongly, healthily and justly, on the great interests of humanity, is a constant benefactor to the human race" (Stowe, *Uncle Tom's Cabin; or, Life among the Lowly,* ed. Elizabeth Ammons [(n.d.); New York, 1994], 385).

Thus do exclamation points and run-on sentences, the sources of Cobbett's scorn and Swanwick's embarrassment, become the basis for a benevolent sociability. In what follows, we will see that, although Rowson reinforces the idea that bourgeois individualism matched an emphasis on (male) self-expression with one on (female) self-regulation, she continually insists upon semantic overflow as the necessary result of even the most strident attempts at "circumscription," whether self-imposed or externally initiated. Sentimental communion is signified not only by the meaning of words but by their sheer rush and mass, their apparent disregard for stylistic modesty as they leap past the "that or therefore." It is no coincidence, then, that the reactionary Cobbett phrases his loathing for Rowson as a response to her poor syntax or that the prudish Swanwick makes excuses for her mistakes; discursive abundance in the face of normative restraint will be the American sentimentalist's trump card. Rushed sequences of events, haphazard meetings of long-lost acquaintances, extravagant declamation, and, yes, unremitting pathos will be the means by which Rowsonian sentimentalism ensures that, in becoming "amiable" to even the grouchiest patriarch, her early readers maintained a capacity for excess that escaped, even as it opposed, "condemnation."[4]

This chapter links sentimentalism's development in the antebellum United States to the condition of early national American women. As long as the fashion for sympathetic tears evoked by the spectacle of abjection remained cordoned off in the terminology of European and especially British sensibility—a male-originated, medically derived, and elite-identified method for valorizing affective response in a scientistic era—its value might be debated, but it was never truly derogated. Indeed, in her "Ode to Sensibility," Rowson herself championed the virtues of a good Common Sense school of compassion that "drop'st the silent tear / At other's grief" and "guid'st the generous liberal hand, / To give relief." But once the discourse of sensibility began its democratization and feminization in popular print vehicles—first in the hands of British institutions such as the Minerva Press and ever more rapidly in American magazines, books, and performances of the 1790s—its popularity was rivaled by the loathing it inspired. This denigration both

4. According to Steven Watts, early sentimental novels both partook of the early Republic's "exuberant individualism" and responded to the fact "that individual sensation could corrupt as well as educate" by "popularizing a bourgeois discourse of genteel self-restraint." Early American republican "culture simultaneously asserted the freedom of self-control over one's own destiny and demanded the restraint of self-control over one's passions" (Watts, *The Romance of Real Life: Charles Brockden Brown and the Origins of American Culture* [Baltimore, 1994], 8, 18, 22).

fostered and expressed a generalized hostility to female sexual, political, and social self-expression in Federalist America and beyond. However much we debate the significance of sentimental excess, therefore, we cannot question its value without realizing that we are simultaneously questioning the value of the historical practice of womanhood. This is not to say that all women behaved, spoke, or wrote sentimentally between the American Revolution and the Industrial Revolution, merely that their productions could not be made meaningful to their peers apart from the discourse of sentimentality.[5]

It is the purpose of this chapter, then, to discern sentimental aspects of 1790s print culture that both ground later formations and depart from them in very important ways—ways that may lead us to question some of our most cherished convictions regarding sentimentalism as a whole. For however ingeniously literate women continued to retort to "the contemptuous smile," we did in fact lose something as the nineteenth century progressed. It is time to identify, if not regain, what was lost.[6]

5. Susanna Rowson, *Miscellaneous Poems; by Susanna Rowson, Preceptress of the Ladies' Academy, Newton, Mass* (Boston, 1804), 29. Jay Fliegelman addresses the role of Scottish Common Sense philosophy in early American sentimental aesthetics in *Prodigals and Pilgrims: The American Revolution against Patriarchal Authority, 1750– 1800* (New York, 1982), as does Elizabeth Dillon in "Sentimental Aesthetics," *American Literature,* LXXIV (2004), 495–523.

6. Clare A. Lyons, *Sex among the Rabble: An Intimate History of Gender and Power in the Age of Revolution, Philadelphia, 1730–1830* (Chapel Hill, N.C., 2006), 290. Mendy Claire Gladden poignantly reminds us how pervasive anachronism is within the study of the past. Early American novels, she writes, "present unrealized visions of the American future": from the perspective of that which has been realized, however, we have difficulty discerning these previously conceived alternatives, even in texts that present them to us outright (Gladden, "Property and the Pursuit of Happiness: Lost Futures and Post-Revolutionary Literary Homes" [Ph.D. diss., University of Virginia, 2004]). Twentieth-century critiques of antebellum sentimentalism highlight three key and related features of ascribed nineteenth-century female identity: fetishized domesticity, economic unproductivity, and absent libido. On sentimental domesticity, see Gillian Brown, *Domestic Individualism: Imagining Self in Nineteenth-Century America* (Berkeley, Calif., 1990); Lora Romero, *Home Fronts: Domesticity and Its Critics in the Antebellum United States* (Durham, N.C., 1997); Shirley Samuels, ed., *The Culture of Sentiment: Race, Gender, and Sentimentality in Nineteenth-Century America* (New York, 1992); Nancy Armstrong, *Desire and Domestic Fiction: A Political History of the Novel* (New York, 1987). Regarding the economic implications of a "separate spheres" ideology often associated with sentimentalism, see Ann Douglas, *The Feminization of American Culture* (New York, 1977); and Lori Merish, *Sentimental Materialism: Gender, Commodity Culture, and Nineteenth-Century American Literature* (Durham, N.C., 2000). On early national foreshadowings of the desexualized "Cult of True Woman-

The House That Is No Home

The following passage exemplifies the tendency to figure early national women in opposition to public life:

> If women generally subordinated themselves and their private interests to the greater good of the world that men made, sensible men honored female self-suppression by accepting that their public virtue should parallel the gentle persuasions of domestic life and maternal sympathy and generosity. . . . Delicate women, modest, graceful, and well dressed when subject to the public gaze, were meant to act with companionable efficiency to preserve harmony in the home; sensitive and uncorruptible men were meant to act virtuously and generously to public advantage.

In this analysis, an emphasis on women at home is accompanied by a parallel accentuation on new modes of affect fostered within this realm, creating a synthesis now commonly referred to under the rubric of "sentimental domesticity." By calling attention both to the material conditions of middle-class female existence and to the rhetorical means by which these conditions were transformed into moral imperatives, sentimental domesticity has served scholars with a faithfulness demonstrated in its ubiquity in the investigation of gender, race, class, and nationalism in the early Republic and beyond. It pervades the study of the early American sentimental novel to the degree that "sentimental novel" and "domestic novel" are often used as interchangeable terms to describe works depicting a feminized domestic realm as both refuge from the competitive labor market and a site where women's ethicizing influence can exert itself through maternal nurture and measured consumption.[7]

---

hood" identified by Barbara Welter in 1966 in reference to the years 1820–1860, see Marianne Noble, *The Masochistic Pleasures of Sentimental Literature* (Princeton, N.J., 2000). Challenges to using these modes to explain eighteenth-century womanhood include Susan Branson, *These Fiery Frenchified Dames: Women and Political Culture in Early National Philadelphia* (Philadelphia, 2001), esp. 2–5; and Cathy N. Davidson and Jessamyn Hatcher, eds., *No More Separate Spheres!* (Durham, N.C., 2002). Julie Ellison discusses works by three early national authors—Sarah Wentworth Morton, Ann Eliza Bleecker, and Philip Freneau—that "are organized by sensibility that apprehends the continent, or even the hemisphere, through tropes of mobility rather than settlement" (Ellison, *Cato's Tears and the Making of Anglo-American Emotion* [Chicago, 1999], 123, and chap. 5).

7. Andrew Burstein, *Sentimental Democracy: The Evolution of America's Romantic*

Cathy N. Davidson was among the first to observe that "the circumscription of the female character within the domestic sphere constitutes a defining feature of sentimental fiction." Richard L. Bushman went on to figure sentimental domesticity as a function of shifting class as well as gender roles in the new Republic, noting that sentimental fiction "engaged the central problem of the period: how to adapt genteel values to middle-class life." These "efforts at adaptation can be summed up in the word 'domestication.'" Explorations of the literary use of the "intimate" ideological space of the home to, in the words of Lauren Berlant, "bind persons to the nation" have noted what Elizabeth Barnes calls "a surprising conflation of the personal and the political body" in "a sentimental politics designed to make familial feeling the precondition for inclusion in the public community." Julia A. Stern focuses on the enlightening aspects of this conflation, whereby "translating restrictive conceptions of political enfranchisement into the intimate grammar of domestic life . . . early American fiction registers the elaborate cost of the Framers' vision." Studies like these have lifted the fog of degradation that once rendered American sentimentalism as a "blight" and a "universal calamity, "the unmistakably feminine treble which dominated the opening chorus of American fiction."[8]

Given the tendency to read American sentimentalism through the lens of domestic ideology, however, it is strange that Rowson should have been claimed as the nation's first prominent sentimentalist. She rarely described her own habitation with anything like the comfortable hominess she attrib-

---

Self-Image (New York, 1999), 21; Shirley Samuels, *Romances of the Republic: Women, the Family, and Violence in the Literature of the Early American Nation* (New York, 1996), 17.

8. Cathy N. Davidson, *Revolution and the Word: The Rise of the Novel in America* (New York, 1986), 179; Richard L. Bushman, *The Refinement of America: Persons, Houses, Cities* (New York, 1992), 281; Lauren Berlant, "Poor Eliza," *American Literature*, LXX (1998), 635–668, esp. 636; Elizabeth Barnes, *States of Sympathy: Seduction and Democracy in the American Novel* (New York, 1997), 1, 3; Julia A. Stern, *The Plight of Feeling: Sympathy and Dissent in the Early American Novel* (Chicago, 1997), 2; Leslie Fiedler, *Love and Death in the American Novel,* rev. ed. (New York, 1975), 75. "The virile bass notes of Hugh Henry Brackenridge's *Modern Chivalry* served only to bring into shrill relief the unmistakably feminine treble which dominated the opening chorus of American fiction" (Herbert Ross Brown, *The Sentimental Novel in America, 1789–1860* [Durham, N.C., 1940], 100). Further examples of how the domesticity thesis has been used in the study of early American literature include Amelia Howe Kritzer's "Playing with Republican Motherhood: Self-Representation in Plays by Susanna Haswell Rowson and Judith Sargent Murray," *Early American Literature,* XXXI (1996), 150–166; and Samuels's *Romances of the Republic.*

uted to her sage critic above, who sat down to read with a pouch and a pipe at the ready. The homes described in her fiction rarely belong to the female protagonist, who inhabits them with all the ease of a guest on a rollaway bed. In fact, Rowson devoted the entire novel on which this chapter is centered, *Trials of the Human Heart,* to extended meditation on the discomforts of a series of dwellings that the heroine, Meriel Howard, cannot peacefully inhabit. As for the maternal instinct said to invest such domiciles with their reclamatory influence, Meriel's short-lived daughter is born in a footnote, which states simply, "Between this and the preceding letter, several are omitted, as they contained only the common events of life." A second infant is stillborn and never mentioned again.[9]

Rowson's preface to this novel suggests that she knew of what she spoke in describing Meriel's domestic alienation:

> As a person of sensibility, whom business or necessity, forces into the house of an entire stranger, (especially if that stranger is his superior in genius, education or rank,) experiences a sensation undescribably painful, in being necessi[t]ated to announce himself, and explain the intent of his visit: so I feel myself inexpressibly embarrassed and timid, whilst performing the unavoidable task of writing a Preface. It is addressing myself to, and calling up the attention of a multiplicity of strangers; it is introducing not myself indeed, but what is nearly the same thing, the offspring of my imagination, to their notice, and conscious as I am, that it will be perused by those, who are infinitely my superiors, this awkward timidity encreases, to an almost unconquerable degree.[10]

Rowson's introductory analogy is telling in the parallel it establishes between her role as an author and her heroine's many dark adventures on the road from one unaccommodating dwelling to another. According to Rowson, writing for publication is like being forced into someone else's house. This passage twists the house into something strange and threatening, attributes a coercive aspect to the inhabitation thereof, and associates the act of writing with this deformed domesticity. It turns Rowson into a hermaphrodite, man enough to deserve the pronoun "his" ("his superior"), woman enough to bear "offspring." Collapsing the standard rhetoric of the period in which the "needle" is substituted for the "pen" as the tool that befits the hand of

9. Susanna Rowson, *Trials of the Human Heart: A Novel,* 4 vols. (Philadelphia, 1795), III, 61, 129.

10. Ibid., preface, xi.

a woman (a move she explicitly thematized in her heroine's own abortive attempts to support herself as both writer and milliner), Rowson here takes the tropic equivalent of a needle (her feminine "offspring") and binds it to the world of the pen ("of my imagination"). She thus suggests the degree to which writing for publication makes it impossible to inhabit comfortably the realms scholars have cordoned off with the rhetoric of sentimental domesticity and, in fact, transforms those realms irrevocably. As a woman writing, Rowson cannot remain even figuratively at home any more than she can escape the realm of the domestic altogether—she is permanently in the house of a stranger. And if *Trials of the Human Heart* is any indication, any woman who hoped to experience the degree of agency that Rowson found requisite for happiness in the United States of the 1790s would have similarly found herself in a strange house, among strangers, sooner or later—even if that house were her own.[11]

Although Rowson's sense of domestic anomie is important, the passage cited above suggests another concern that the novel will develop, having to do not only with where the author finds herself but what she describes herself doing. In "addressing myself to, and calling up the attention of a multiplicity of Strangers," she evokes Meriel's own persistent, if (as Meriel repeatedly claims) reluctant, attempts to interest strangers in her fate so as to gain relief for herself and her family. Generally, these attempts are limited to begging; but there is one point at which Meriel considers exchanging sex for money. Like her author, she submits uneasily to being "perused" by people more powerful than she. In the presence of her first (and last) sexual client, Meriel finds her "feelings . . . beyond description, poignant." Nevertheless, both author and protagonist soldier on, continuing to solicit strangers in a variety of capacities as they both struggle to make a living.[12]

Passages such as these make good on the novel's early claim that it will introduce an unfamiliar form of female virtue to the world it depicts. Meriel's mother, it is said, possesses merely "passive virtues"; but "Meriel's will prove active ones." Deciding what exactly "active virtue" consists of for a young, white, unmarried woman is the novel's mission and drives its otherwise almost plotless meanderings. Meriel is not rewarded with the husband she first meets early in the book until she has "proved" her skill

11. Ibid., xi–xii. For a brilliant play on the needle/pen theme, see Anne Bradstreet's "Prologue" (1678): "I am obnoxious to each carping tongue / Who says my hand a needle better fits" (Jeannine Hensley, ed., *The Works of Anne Bradstreet* [Cambridge, Mass., 1967], 16).

12. Rowson, *Trials of the Human Heart,* II, 33.

at this quintessentially masculine, ancient republican value. As such, she must reconcile "the passion for pursuing the public good" to her status as a genteel woman for whom virtue, we have seen, is coded private even when it undeniably takes place within the public realm. It is not enough that she prove her capacity to herself; onlookers must also be convinced, a heroic task indeed when it seems that almost everyone she meets finds an opportunity to slander her. According to Joseph Fichtelberg, *Trials* "sought both to capture the occasion of slander and to convey its internal mechanisms, by depicting how Meriel's story is appropriated and distorted by others." Despite her unlucky beginnings, however, Meriel persists not only in wanting to do good but in wanting to do so on a grand scale, and she does not rest until she has brought those around her to see things her way.[13]

To understand active female virtue in this book, it is helpful to begin with its seeming opposite, active female vice, succinctly contained in the figure of the prostitute. Prostitution's perceived viciousness in this period depended not merely, nor even primarily, on its sexual aspects so much as its requirement that women place themselves in public view—literally, that they become "streetwalkers." Note that, whereas a "publicus," or public man, is a citizen, a "publica," or public woman, is a prostitute—a linguistic oddity indicating that simply joining the terms "public" and "woman" is to epitomize female vice, with unlicensed sexual practice as both figure and by-product of such a union. Of course, a published female author is just such another "public woman." Thus Rowson's intimations of sexual vulnerability and exposure in the above passage, in the service of plying her authorial trade, are no accident. Prostitution remains the profession that the novel's author and protagonist define themselves both through and against, as Meriel finds herself continually accused of sexual profligacy in the pursuit of social betterment. From the day she is tricked into bringing a strange man home to meet her mother, through her first unwitting approach to her eventual madam, until the last of many times a householder accosts her and then tells his wife she was a willing participant, Meriel is far less likely to be seen as a hero of classic proportions than as a woman whose behavior is inherently vicious.[14]

13. Ibid., I, 14, 33; J. G. A. Pocock, *The Machiavellian Moment: Florentine Political Thought and the Atlantic Republican Tradition* (Princeton, N.J., 1975), 472, 524 ("the republican principle that virtue is active"); Joseph Fichtelberg, "Uncivil Tongues: Slander and Honour in Susanna Rowson's *Trials of the Human Heart*," *Eighteenth-Century Fiction*, XVIII (2006), 425–451, esp. 426. Fichtelberg explores the novel's representation of slander as an authorial comment upon Cobbett's attack on her.

14. Jay Fliegelman thanks John Barrell for insight regarding the Latin meanings

By 1800, the American public would have been familiar with the equation of female authorship with prostitution, in part through the first American edition of George Walker's *Vagabond,* in which a prostitute named Mary is identified as Mary Wollstonecraft in footnotes. As Walker's attack on Wollstonecraft or Cobbett's on Rowson exemplifies, any English or American public figure of the late 1790s risked her sexual reputation merely by exposing herself in print. In repeatedly undergoing libelous attempts to label her a prostitute as well as admitting that she did at one point fit the description, Meriel both reclaims the dignity of prostitutes and displays the tenacity that authorial proponents of active virtue such as Rowson herself must demonstrate in order to withstand defamation by the very strangers whose attention they solicited.[15]

Trials of the Human Heart: *An Overview*

Trials of the Human Heart appeared by subscription to commercial and critical blahs in 1795, shortly after the wildly successful American publication of *Charlotte Temple* and in the midst of Rowson's moderately well received stint as an actress and playwright with Thomas Wignell's New Theatre Company in Philadelphia. As "probably Rowson's least popular work," it anticipates another fascinating commercial failure, Fanny Burney's *The Wanderer; or, Female Difficulties* (1814), in its sandwiching of the extraordinary peregrinations of an iconoclastically self-reliant heroine—one who tries her hand at everything from millinery to authorship to prostitution in pursuit of survival—between the conventional bookends of a promising marriage.[16]

Trials is not frequently read, perhaps because it is neither short, like *Charlotte Temple,* nor easy to follow. For both these reasons, and because the

---

of "publicus" and "publica" in Fliegelman, *Declaring Independence: Jefferson, Natural Language, and the Culture of Performance* (Stanford, Calif., 1993), 130, 228 n. 30.

15. A representative footnote follows: "Memoirs of Mrs. Woolstonecraft Godwin. A Democratic Review says, my treatment of Mrs. Godwin, in these volumes, *is brutal.* If repeating verbatim her own sentiments be brutality, then am I guilty. But if they mean that such sentiments brutalize a woman, I cannot help that" (George Walker, *The Vagabond: A Novel* [Boston, 1800], 116 [see also 83], Early American Imprints, 1st Ser., 38973). See also Mary Wollstonecraft, *Maria; or, The Wrongs of Woman* ([1799]; New York, 1975); Rowson, *Trials of the Human Heart,* III, 129. Lyndall Gordon describes a "scandalous link between prostitution and women's advance—disseminated in the late 1790s and renewed by Victorians" (Gordon, *Vindication: A Life of Mary Wollstonecraft* [New York, 2005], 389).

16. Ellen B. Brandt, *Susanna Haswell Rowson, America's First Best-Selling Novelist* (Chicago, 1975), 122.

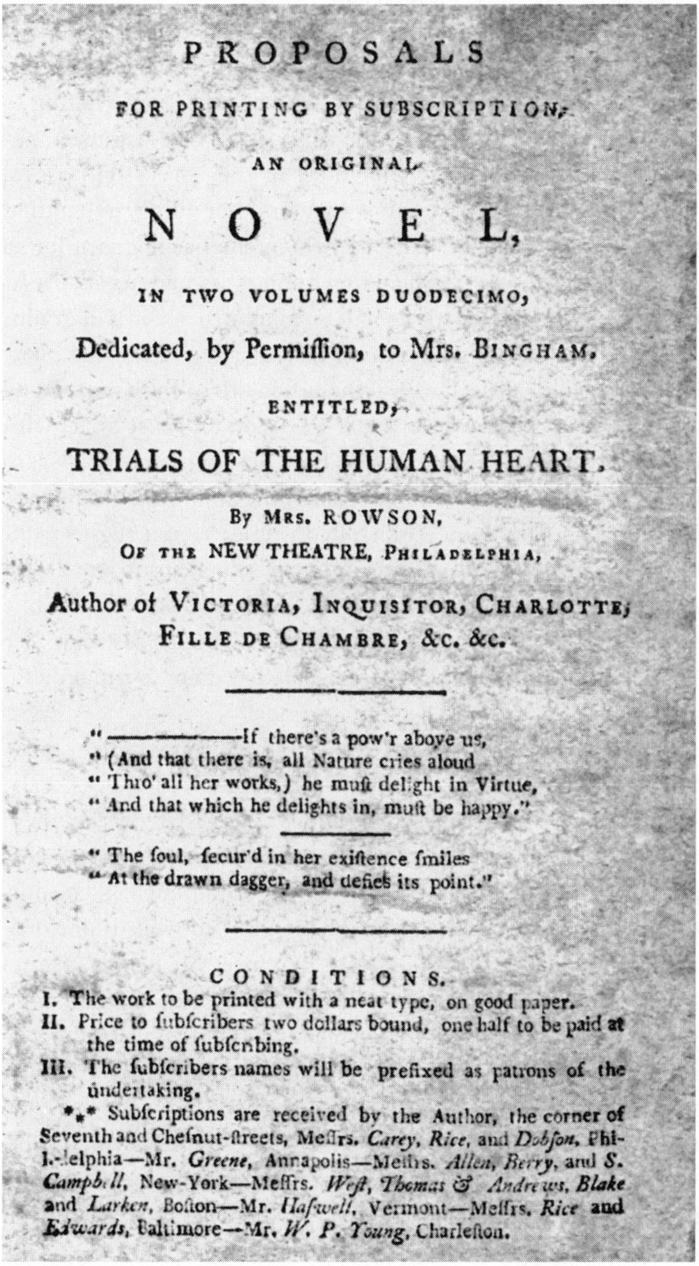

PROPOSALS

FOR PRINTING BY SUBSCRIPTION,

AN ORIGINAL

N O V E L,

IN TWO VOLUMES DUODECIMO,

Dedicated, by Permiffion, to Mrs. BINGHAM,

ENTITLED,

TRIALS OF THE HUMAN HEART.

By MRS. ROWSON,

OF THE NEW THEATRE, PHILADELPHIA,

Author of VICTORIA, INQUISITOR, CHARLOTTE,
FILLE DE CHAMBRE, &c. &c.

" —————If there's a pow'r above us,
" (And that there is, all Nature cries aloud
" Thro' all her works,) he muft delight in Virtue,
" And that which he delights in, muft be happy."

" The foul, fecur'd in her exiftence fmiles
" At the drawn dagger, and defies its point."

CONDITIONS.

I. The work to be printed with a neat type, on good paper.
II. Price to fubfcribers two dollars bound, one half to be paid at
   the time of fubfcribing.
III. The fubfcribers names will be prefixed as patrons of the
    undertaking.
  ₊ Subfcriptions are received by the Author, the corner of
Seventh and Chefnut-ftreets, Meffrs. Carey, Rice, and Dobfon, Phi-
l.-lelphia—Mr. Greene, Annapolis—Meihs. Allen, Berry, and S.
Campbell, New-York—Meffrs. Weft, Thomas & Andrews, Blake
and Larken, Bofton—Mr. Hafwell, Vermont—Meffrs. Rice and
Edwards, Baltimore—Mr. W. P. Young, Charlefton.

PLATE 16. *Subscription proposal for* Trials of the Human Heart. *From Rowson,*
Mentoria; or, The Young Lady's Friend, *2 vols. (Philadelphia, 1794), I. PS 2736.R3,*
Clifton Waller Barrett Library of American Literature, Special Collections, University
of Virginia Library

tale itself is so fantastically convoluted, a summary is in order. As it opens, sixteen-year-old Meriel Howard has just left a French convent school, where her supposed mother had placed her (despite the family's being "of a different religion") to save her from her licentious supposed father. Writing to her dear friend Celia Shelburne, still at the convent, Meriel begins a one-way correspondence that will account for most of the novel's 638 pages. She is returning to England, she explains, to attend her ailing godmother, Mrs. Mirvan, and reunite with her parents, whom she has not seen for so long she does not recognize them (in fact, they are not her parents at all). At Mrs. Mirvan's death, Meriel inherits a small fortune, which she will gradually sacrifice to the wiles and compulsions of her libertine father and boorish brother, Richard. The entire family—including Mrs. Talbot, a widow posing as Mr. Howard's relation in order to carry on an illicit affair with him—soon retire to their small estate, where they live on limited funds. Inspired by Meriel's rectitude, Mrs. Talbot calls off the affair and disappears. At the behest of a young neighbor, Miss Dolly Pringle, Meriel begins reading novels, and her judgment declines precipitously. She plans to elope with Dolly's brother, but they are found out, and Mrs. Howard is outraged. While Mrs. Howard is away, Mr. Howard tries to rape Meriel, but she escapes: her family and neighbors interpret her escape as a failed attempt to run off with Master Pringle.[17]

Found senseless in the nearby woods, Meriel gradually regains her sanity; meanwhile, her father is imprisoned for debt and the family "removes" to be near him in London. As her fortune declines in various ill-fated attempts to help her family, Meriel begins to consider "genteel employment." She meets a kindred spirit, Mr. Rainsforth, but the treachery of her envious cousins, Hester and Susan Mossop, puts a stop to their plans to wed. Rainsforth marries an heiress, Miss Kingly, instead, and becomes Mr. Kingly. Meriel redoubles her efforts to save her mother, who grows weaker as the family grows poorer, though at least she finally recognizes the sincerity of her daughter's devotion. Denied references by her haughty aunt, Mrs. Mossop, Meriel can't find work: desperate to feed her mother, she begins to beg. She meets a female procurer and agrees to visit her house the following night, at which point she is prepared for initiation into a career in prostitution. By pleading with her first customer, Mr. Welldon, to spare both her virtue

17. "Miss Shelburne chose to take the veil—I was of a different religion, and have been called into the busy scenes of life" (Rowson, *Trials of the Human Heart,* III, 55). This religion is never specified. Both Catholicism and especially Methodism come in for a fair amount of ridicule (for example, I, 116).

and her mother's life, she inspires him to come to their aid, which he does until the mother's death a few days later. Before leaving town and promptly dying himself, Mr. Welldon places Meriel with a milliner. Here, in addition to making hats, she begins to write verses, for which she is widely mocked; then she is accosted by the head of the household, Mr. Lacour, and must move in with another family, the Newtrams. She begins her own millinery business but, despite a promising beginning, is soon robbed and cheated out of any profit.

Homeless again, Meriel meets a friend of the Mossops, Amelia Sidney, who takes her in. She becomes companion to an elderly heiress, Mrs. Rooksby, meets up with Mr. and Mrs. Kingly, discovers her cousins' earlier deceit in coming between her and Rainsforth/Kingly, and pretends not to care for him in order to preserve his marriage. Mrs. Rooksby and Amelia Sidney persuade her to marry Mrs. Rooksby's wealthy son, Mr. Rooksby, after he is jilted in an attempt to marry his mistress, Clara. Meriel gives birth to a daughter, Clementina, and lives content for a couple of years, until Rooksby, enraged by what he falsely believes to be Meriel's partiality to another man, resumes his affair with Clara. As Rooksby, Clara, and Meriel cross the British Channel to Paris in order to visit the dying Mrs. Rooksby, they meet the Kinglys, and all nearly perish in a shipwreck near shore. Mr. Kingly ties Meriel to the deck, then returns and tears off her clothes to carry her to safety.

Soon after Mrs. Rooksby's death, Mrs. Kingly dies. Meriel returns to England with her daughter and her nurse Deborah, while Rooksby and Clara run through the family fortune in France. Meriel's daughter dies, and Meriel loses her mind; Kingly ministers to her in her distress. Meriel avows her love for Kingly but resists his efforts to persuade her to stay with him while her husband still lives. Panicked that she will relent, she escapes Kingly's lodgings at night to visit her sick and wounded husband in a London prison; on her way there, she is arrested for thievery. The victim, Mrs. Harcourt, attests to Meriel's innocence. Deborah, Meriel's long-faithful nurse and servant, realizes that Mrs. Harcourt is Meriel's real mother, returned from ten years' captivity with "the royal Turk." Accompanying Mrs. Harcourt is her friend, Mrs. Talbot—the same woman who carried out an affair with Meriel's (supposed) father. Meriel is reunited with her birth mother and birth father, a wealthy East-India merchant who had been sent abroad by *his* father in an unsuccessful attempt to prevent his marriage to Meriel's real mother. Shortly thereafter, Rooksby dies; Meriel sets up his mistress, Clara, in a modest lodging in Wales (unlike the two hundred pounds a year people always seem to be getting in this novel, Clara is to make do on ten). A year to the day after the death of Rooksby, Meriel weds Kingly: their family includes Clara's two children with Rooksby and Kingly's two children with his first wife. They all retire to Kingly's palatial digs in Westminster, and Meriel writes Celia a last letter inviting her to join them.[18]

Perpetual Motion

In *Trials of the Human Heart,* character is fate in more than the usual sense. Not only do one's "collective qualities or characteristics" determine one's end, but so do the very "printed or written letter[s]" of one's name. Thus if a personage exists in order to do the protagonist a good turn, he is likely to bear a surname announcing this fact: "Mr. Friendly," perhaps, or Mr. Friendly's friend, "Mr. Welldon." As for those whose motives are more sinister, the reader is similarly warned. What is one to think of the heroine's entirely unpleasant first husband, "Clarence Rooksby," a man with not one but two castles, except that he is not the most important figure on the board? To the attentive reader, a happy ending cannot be far off, thanks to another player with yet greater influence. Yes, his name is "Mr. Kingly," taker of rooks, maker of queens.[19]

The protagonist of this novel is *Meriel Howard,* and the narrative is one in which she learns *how* to *marry.* In that she marries a "king," whose wealth, good taste, and, above all, good manners attest to his refinement, her story is typical of the presumably domesticating effects of sentimental fiction discussed above. Addressing her schoolgirl friend Celia in the last (as the first) letter of the novel, Meriel lets the magic powers of "home" expand to include all who enter her new abode:

> My husband bids me say, should the commotions which at present agitate the Gallic shore, disturb you in your religious retreat; remember, you have a home, to which you can with confidence repair—a home, where you will be received with transport, and where you may consider yourself in the mansion of a sister![20]

Here we see the roof over Meriel's head exerting its full benignant influence. Not only does a home shelter families: it creates them, making sisters out of friends.

18. In *Trials of the Human Heart,* people receive two hundred pounds no fewer than five times (III, 35, 48, 76, 81, IV, 33). Clara gets ten in IV, 169.

19. *Concise Oxford Dictionary of Current English,* 9th ed., s.v. "character."

20. Rowson, *Trials of the Human Heart,* IV, 172.

Disrupting Rowson's seeming equation of sentimental with domestic ideology, however, are the several hundred pages leading up to this last letter. To put the matter bluntly: for a card-carrying representative of sentimental domestic norms, Meriel is away from home a disturbing amount. From her convent school at Bologne, here is where Meriel goes: Bristol; Woodbine Cot; Litchfield; London (including a stop at Fleet Prison, "cheap lodging, on the Surry side of Blackfriars bridge," and a stay with a milliner); "a very neat apartment" in Kensington; Amelia Sidney's house; Harley Street, back in London, where she meets her ill-tempered first husband; Oak Hall, country retreat of said husband; Harley Street; Oak Hall; Dover; Aix; Paris; Harley Street; Glamorganshire; Welbeck Street; Pimlico; Westminster; King's Bench Prison; a London garret; an apartment outside town; Bristol; her newly discovered "dear mother's house," where she is, at last, properly courted; and back to Westminster, to the aforenamed "mansion" she can now call home. What function do Meriel's travels serve? Are they meant only as a reminder of how much better things are back home? Or, more accurately, since Meriel has no home throughout most of the novel, are her travels supposed to remind the reader of how much better things are in the reader's home? As such, Meriel's sojourns would further the project delineated by Bushman and others for the American sentimental novel: making the middle-class residence the site of pleasures previously experienced outside it.[21]

Certainly, there is much in the novel to support such a view, including Meriel's own fascination with furniture. Meriel meets a number of dastardly men throughout her wanderings, but there is one among them—the appropriately named Mr. Welldon—who seems to expect nothing from the generosity he bestows on her, and it is he who indulges Meriel's fascination with objects that can only be considered synecdochic of the domestic interiors they inhabit. When Mr. Welldon provides Meriel with an "apartment," furnished with a "tent bed," a "case of drawers," a "neat dressing case," and a "small trunk," Meriel's delight in these various enclosures is exceeded only by the rapture with which she explores the trunk itself, unveiling item after item (cloth, English poetry, Bible, drawing paper) with an increasing sense of wonder. She then turns to a "light closet that adjoined my bed chamber," where she finds not only a piano but also a "little pocket-book" containing fifty pounds. This is all too much for her, and in the most orgasmic scene

21. Christopher Looby, "George Thompson's 'Romance of the Real': Transgression and Taboo in American Sensation Fiction," *American Literature,* LXV (1993), 651–672, esp. 654.

of the book (save only the one where Mr. Kingly rescues her from the ship-wreck), with a "heart almost bursting," she sinks to her knees by the bed-side, "pour[s] forth" her thanks, and asks that blessings be "showered on" her benefactor (it's too good to omit that her final husband Kingly's real name, you may remember, is "Rainsforth").[22]

Treasures inside a trunk in a back room; an apartment furnished with two cases and a tent bed. At the bottom of the trunk, clues to the drawers, containing a box of crayons and a writing case. Plus a closet and a pocket-book to be opened. What do all these closed-up things, and their observer's pleasure in them, suggest? On one level, by taking pleasure in contained spaces, Meriel is simply reiterating the equation of genteel female subjec-tivity with behavioral and geographic self-circumscription that made Char-lotte's survival depend upon her being at home on her birthday. Yet Meriel's pleasure in the act brings her to an awareness of this imposition, providing her with an image of what might otherwise have remained invisible and thereby lessening the trauma of the existence such restriction also compels. Moreover, in that Meriel is here provided with a rare opportunity to open not one but innumerable boxes, lids, and doors, she also transforms these images of stasis into acts of liberation and release. Mr. Welldon's gift to Meriel thus offers Rowson's readers a variety of countervailing symbolic opportunities.

This game of hide-and-seek can be read as a form of narrative compro-mise, a way to offer women the stuff of creation (money, paper, and cloth) with the least chance of offending the authoritative male reader / subscriber and thereby imperiling others' access to the book at hand. But the game itself is dwelled upon so closely, with so many references to the act of "open-ing," that it spills over its pragmatic, protective function into a rare moment of eroticism. If Rowson's very prose can be said to participate in a cycle of containment and release, then this is a moment of release, exultant and yet "oppressively"—to use a word Meriel employs in the same passage—aware of its transgressive nature.

In the rest of the novel, open boxes transform themselves into open doors, closed boxes into doors that shut Meriel out. Yes, Rowson has her spend a great deal of time outside in the cold so that we may appreciate her hard-won comfort all the more. But her outdoor adventures also comment upon the constraining aspects of her so-called domestic paradise. Moreover, the forced nature of her exodus—Meriel leaves her first home under some duress, escaping, by means of a penknife and a sheet hung out a window,

22. Rowson, *Trials of the Human Heart*, II, 44–46.

sexual assault by the man she believes to be her father—testifies to the absurdity of the assumption that every "lodging" should be a home. Meriel makes the only case she can for a "household . . . organized around a properly affective axis" by refusing to stay put in any lodging that forecloses on this option.[23]

Thus it is of no small significance that, unlike *Charlotte Temple* or the heroines of numerous other early American sentimental novels, from Brown's *Power of Sympathy* to Foster's *Coquette* and Rebecca Rush's *Kelroy,* Meriel—like the more cautious protagonist of Judith Sargent Murray's *Story of Margaretta*—survives past the end of her story. *The Coquette's* Eliza Wharton may eventually wish that she could have heeded the Reverend J. Boyer's creed of calibrating wishes to expectations, but she finds herself not quite up to the task. Rather, her wishes, we have seen, exceed her abilities to manage the forms in which her society returns them to her: as infamy and abandonment. Charlotte, too, has an unfortunate habit of staying put in circumstances that cause her discomfort, whether by continuing to hold a letter she suspects will bring her harm until it is no more than a reflex to open and read its contents or by fainting into the chaise that will take her to New York rather than attending to her very real desire to escape her impending seducer. Only Meriel seems to recognize the value of a well-placed sheet and to entertain the possibility that terror of the unknown may, in fact, obscure a better future.[24]

Meriel's bouts with homelessness do highlight the beautiful home at the end—at which point the reader may crawl inside the chest in all its glory, after a good long scouring of its outer surfaces, to find that things (in anticipation of Susan Warner's *Wide, Wide World* [New York, 1851]) look even bigger from the inside. But the novel gives Meriel plenty of opportunity to wander between locations, and the bad homes she visits on the way to the good are portrayed in sinister enough detail to echo over even her final abode, rendering her faith in its permanence poignant rather than boastful. As a perennial "outsider," ever the sport of a seemingly endless stream of benevolent and not-so-benevolent strangers, Meriel receives far more attention than she does in her final accommodation.

Travel and exile not only provide the conflict in *Trials* but also represent it. That is, movement not only allows for alienation but also defines or articulates it. Put another way, for Meriel Howard, self-proclaimed lover·

23. Glenn Hendler, *Public Sentiments: Structures of Feeling in Nineteenth-Century American Literature* (Chapel Hill, N.C., 2001), 123.

24. Hannah Foster, *The Coquette* (Boston, 1797), 47.

of "retirement, study and domestic employment," motion is quite simply everything. It is what she describes in greatest detail, whether it be offered her (opening boxes); denied her ("It is but seldom I am permitted to go without the boundaries of our garden. . . . I cannot think what my father is afraid of"); or seemingly forced upon her ("To deliberate a moment; was to be lost. . . . The clock had struck three, when convinced of the danger of remaining longer under his roof, I resolved to fly from Kingly. . . . I glided softly down stairs, and opening the street door ventured into the street"). Meriel attends to her sojourns so faithfully, in fact, that at times her report seems arbitrary, as when she responds to her first husband's imprisonment for debt (and rendezvous there with his paramour) by "go[ing] into a room." From transoceanic journey to trip down the stairs, Meriel's definitive state is movement.[25]

Perhaps, then, we should reinterpret Meriel's last letter to Celia, the one where she issues an invitation to join her at home. In order to come "home," Celia would have to do something else first: cross the English Channel, the very body of water that almost swallowed Meriel up before it spit her out again with a new husband to make up for its rudeness. Perhaps travel means so much to Meriel that she cannot bear to give it up, even for marriage. Thus, since she is no longer on the move herself, she passes the baton to her most intimate acquaintance, the one whose experiences she can almost feel as her own and whose retirement she has so long envied. She writes Celia a letter inviting her to get going.

What's So Sentimental?

At this point you may be asking, why not just excise *Trials of the Human Heart* from the sentimental canon altogether? If Meriel remains undomesticated throughout most of the book, doesn't that suggest that this novel, rather than threatening any coincidence of sentimentalism with domesticity, is one where Rowson allowed other generic categories (the picaresque, say, or the gothic) enough play that the final product remains a pastiche? Certainly Meriel is not the only female protagonist in early American literature to indulge in the adventurism associated with the picaresque, although she does so without the "self-parody" that Davidson finds a near-inevitable accompaniment to such flouting of social mores. In 1801, Dorcasina Sheldon, the protagonist of Tabitha Tenney's *Female Quixotism*, burst on the scene from her suburban hideaway "about thirty miles from Philadelphia" and touched down in almost as many locations within that radius as Meriel

25. Rowson, *Trials of the Human Heart*, I, 36, 116, IV, 86, 103.

managed throughout England and France combined. This reading would fit well, in fact, with Rowson's own presumed state while writing the novel. She had just published *Charlotte Temple* to popular acclaim. Meanwhile, she was becoming increasingly aware that her "somewhat disreputable husband" showed little promise of ever becoming the family breadwinner. She had no children of her own but was raising her husband's illegitimate son. Her fame might have given her the confidence to stray from still-inchoate associations between female tranquility and domesticity, whereas her marital situation gave her the motive.[26]

Yet it is wrong to let *Trials of the Human Heart,* and by implication sentimentalism, off so easily. However much this novel appropriates themes of contiguous genres, it performs in an almost exaggerated manner the constitutive tension of sentimentalism as defined here: namely, it continuously relies upon representational excess to compel normative restraint. In other words, this novel invokes "the performance of waste" in order to maintain "the social investment in stability." Many have mistakenly assumed that sentimentalism's normative function prevails, an understandable error when the appeals to rightdoing are so prevalent. But what makes sentimentalism more than a coercive tool—what gives it its potentially disruptive political agency—is that, even when it proclaims the benefits of social conformity, it defies its proclamations through its own exaggerated gestures. Moreover, and particularly for Rowson, it insists that, in a battle between textual figuration and abstract ideation, figure wins. Which is to say, effusion wins.[27]

For example, Meriel has no idea of keeping anything from her parents until she begins reading novels. She starts reading them at the behest of her neighbor, Miss Dolly Pringle, who informs her, "You have a pleasure to

26. Davidson, *Revolution and the Word,* 179; Dorothy Weil, *In Defense of Women: Susanna Rowson (1762–1824)* (University Park, Pa., 1976), 3–4; Tabitha Gilman Tenney, *Female Quixotism, Exhibited in the Romantic Opinions and Extravagant Adventures of Dorcasina Sheldon* (New York, 1992), 4.

27. Joseph Roach, *Cities of the Dead: Circum-Atlantic Performance* (New York, 1996), 123, 148. "The social investment in stability" paraphrases René Girard in *Violence and the Sacred,* trans. Patrick Gregory (Baltimore, 1977). The single most caustic assessment of sentimentalist hypocrisy as a function of its normative pretensions is the following famous passage from James Baldwin: "Sentimentality, the ostentatious parading of excessive and spurious emotion, is the mark of dishonesty, the inability to feel; the wet eyes of the sentimentalist betray his aversion to experience, his fear of life, his arid heart; and it is always, therefore, the signal of secret and violent inhumanity, the mask of cruelty." See Baldwin, "Everybody's Protest Novel," *Notes of a Native Son* ([1955]; Boston, 1984), 13–23, esp. 14.

come, of which at present you can form no idea." Soon she has left behind "natural history," "Rowe's letters," and the other "musty old authors" abhorred by her dissolute father in favor of the tastier fare he can provide. Concomitant with her changed reading habits, her demeanor shifts radically. She starts keeping secrets, wishes to "go into more company," and hopes to "be admired by some fine gentleman." Within a few pages of opening her first "French novel," she has made plans to elope to London with Dolly's brother.[28]

This sequence of events demonstrates perhaps the most shopworn cliché of the period: novels corrupt untrained female sensibilities. More important, it also changes the course of this particular novel, which can now avail itself of sexual acts that would have been unthinkable before Meriel's awakening. Thus, at the precise moment that Meriel entertains her first romantic dalliance with a neighbor boy, her father attempts to rape her. These events subsequently get mixed up in the plot of the novel (in escaping her father, she is assumed to have run off with her lover). But they remain distinct occurrences, both instituted by the novel's sudden taste for the frank depiction of illicit sexual acts formerly treated only obliquely (as with Mrs. Talbot and Mr. Howard's distantly perceived caresses, which Meriel describes only as a "liberty" and an "impropriety"). Whatever *Trials of the Human Heart* may claim to think about nonmarital sex, attempted rape, and incest, it is now ready to issue them forth in abundance; and this change of "Heart" is contingent upon Meriel's first "pleasure to come," that of reading.[29]

This conflation of sexual and textual engagement reoccurs throughout the novel. When Meriel's parents put her under house arrest following her unsuccessful elopement with Pringle, she does not feel the sting of her imprisonment until she is deprived of the power to write by having her paper, pens, and ink taken away. For all her professed penitence regarding her recent filial dishonesty, she immediately persuades her nurse to provide them

28. Rowson, *Trials of the Human Heart,* I, 38, 41.

29. Ibid., I, 17, 38. "Unquestionably, the novel was the subject of considerable cultural criticism," writes Karen Weyler, "particularly during the 1780s and 1790s and especially in periodicals published in New England, but this criticism of the novel needs to be placed in perspective. . . . If nothing else, the sheer number of novels being printed in the United States [about twenty-five in the 1780s, two hundred in the 1790s] illustrates the growing importance of fiction to its readers." Weyler also notes that the "censure of fiction" has been commented upon within virtually every discussion of the novel and that it pertains to British and United States fiction roughly equally. See Weyler, *Intricate Relations: Sexual and Economic Desire in American Fiction, 1789–1814* (Iowa City, 2004), 5, 7.

secretly. In the struggle between ethical (I must obey my parents) and discursive impulse (I must articulate the importance of obeying my parents, even if I have to disobey them to do it), discourse once again triumphs.[30]

As significant as the act of writing is to Meriel, she grants little import to semantic abstraction. In her life, rather, words beget words almost without the intervention of consciousness. Thus, looking back on the letters she wrote her dear Master Pringle in the miasma of that first novel-reading binge, Meriel remembers that they "almost involuntarily" replicated "the very sentiments which I had just embibed." It's easy to contain such comments within the discussion of the perceived danger of novels to naïve young women—a discussion that often fails to note the vast consumption of novels that accompanied this lamentation. (This consumption suggests that the lamentation was as pro forma, for the majority of readers, as Meriel's own repentance despite her willingness to lie again to get more paper.) More significant, however, is the power that Meriel grants to the pen, the written character, the production and reception of text as a physical activity taking place through time rather than as a means to eternal abstractions pertaining to truth or virtue. Meriel reads and writes the way she moves; one act follows another, with little seeming connection or integration of past into future. From this movement of body, pen, and page, moreover, she obtains a pleasurable sense of identity that persists precisely because it resists being relegated to static emblematization of good or evil. In that *Trials,* as an epistolary novel, necessarily partakes of its protagonist's expressive mode, it similarly avoids being reduced to a take-home message (perhaps this is why so few readers took it home in 1795).[31]

In prioritizing textual acts over timeless truths, Meriel demonstrates her author's almost magical faith in the power of discursive form to overdetermine semantic content. This outlook finds its clearest expression in *Mentoria,* a book published in Philadelphia within months of the publication of *Trials.* Rowson directs this work to those young women whose "parents utterly forbid their daughters reading" novels. What makes *Mentoria* not a novel, however, remains unclear. Through the didactic frame of a governess's letters to her absent charges, it retraces familiar ground for the Rowson novel-reader, from seduction and betrayal to autobiographical intimations by the author to emphasis on the Johnsonian credibility of her not-entirely-perfect characters. And, just as *Mentoria's* mere prefatory claim to non-novelhood is said to fit it out for a wider audience than it would otherwise

30. Rowson, *Trials of the Human Heart,* I, 46, 51–52.
31. Ibid., 118.

have merited, the book itself is full of appeals to the power of the shape and sequence of words to stand in for their referential value. Short letters are seen to indicate an overzealous "pursuit of amusement" on the part of the letter writer. Absent prefaces suggest authorial vanity, making prefaces paradoxically an attestation of modesty. Again and again, Rowson as sentimentalist asserts the importance of words to lie not so much in what they signify as in how they proclaim.[32]

Yet, just as Meriel repeatedly avows her distaste for worldly matters while careening from one adventure to another, the how of sentimentalism is rarely in concurrence with the what. One instance of Meriel's professed love of retirement should suffice. Her future first husband, Mr. Rooksby, asks how Meriel is enjoying her stay on his mother's secluded estate. "I think it extremely pleasant, sir," she returns: "It suits the turn of my mind; I am fond of solitude and should be quite happy were I certain of never wandering from this delightful spot, to the gay regions of fashion, folly, and what is in general termed pleasure." This is the same protagonist who describes such "gay" regions in exquisite detail elsewhere for the benefit of her friend Celia. When Meriel accompanies her Aunt Mossop and cousins to a play in London, she spares no effort in depicting "the house, the lights, the brilliant and numerous audience" as well as the many stores she visits before the big night to outfit herself accordingly.[33]

That this productive tension between depiction and proscription grounds sentimentalism is signaled best by Meriel's accounts of reading and attending plays. It seems that her wish to mitigate other people's pain (the proscription of suffering) is generally accompanied by profound delight in the represented pain of others (the depiction of suffering). While perusing "an English novel" by "Mrs. Bennet," which shows "the sorrows of the 'Welsh Heiress,'" Meriel opines that suffering itself can be a pleasure: "The tears stole from my eyes, but they were tears that flowed from a source so pleasing I wished not to stop their course." Her behavior at the play partakes of the same pleasurable indulgence in somatic release. In the midst of all the dazzling finery and practiced gesture, Meriel's inability to conceal her responsiveness to the scenes depicted onstage stands out as starkly as her plain cap with its "knott of white sattin ribbon." "At the pathetic and interesting parts, I could not conceal my emotion," she admits, to the disgust of her cousins, who swear they will never go to a play with her again. Within the terms of

32. Rowson, *Mentoria,* II, 39.
33. Rowson, *Trials of the Human Heart,* I, 109, III, 6.

the novel, however, such transparency receives high marks. Meriel is not so very pretty, others comment, but her near-universal appeal lies in the fact that, as one suitor claims, "Her lovely mind I always find, / Depicted in her face." What Meriel depicts so clearly is nonetheless a complex phenomenon: a simultaneity of pleasure and pain. Meriel's face itself is an exemplary sentimental page.[34]

It has often been noted that sympathetic pleasures feed on the pain of others less fortunate. Whether the sorrow-inducing spectacle takes place at one or two removes—in the world at large or through an aesthetic representation—a degree of alienation, solipsism, voyeurism, and schadenfreude is inevitable on the observer's part. This inconsistency both troubles the apparent ingenuousness of sympathetic display that founds sentimental narrative and calls the consumption of the aesthetic artifact into question. But what if we rethink our emphasis on the forced and fetishized tear, so long the primary synecdoche of American sentimentalism? Rather than take it as a sign of emotional honesty (indicating that the bearer can't hide what she's feeling and that what she's feeling is relatively legible), what if we stop demanding that the tear represent a clear lens between mind and "face" or page, a transparent rendering of a uniform mental state? Instead, might the tear not embody the overdetermined nature of sentiment itself? Moreover, if tears express mental states that are themselves indeterminate, then their use as rhetorical devices becomes less of an issue. Sentimental narrative wouldn't be exploiting the reader by using crying people to make her cry, because crying itself would no longer possess such communicative power. In that case, "virtue in distress," one classic definition of sentimental narrative, might be less significant for its bearing on the moral integrity of either sufferer or witness than for the opportunity it provides both to remain in a state of perpetual agitation. Sentimentalism's pleasure in excess occurs on many more than just the affective levels. And wherever it occurs, it suggests new avenues for resisting circumscription by focusing on the matter rather than

34. Ibid., I, 108–109, II, 151, III, 6, IV, 73–74. Compare these valorizations of pathos with Mrs. Mossop's refusal to visit the home of her recently deceased brother (the man Meriel knows as her father): "You know child my seeing him will be of no use; it will only be hurting my own feelings, with out being of the least service to your father. I never can bear scenes of this kind; my sensibility is so exquisite, that, was I to see my poor brother in this situation, I should not recover it for a month" (II, 15–16). In contrast to the novel's concern with economic exchange, true sensibility, as opposed to the false brand represented here, is willing to expend beyond the possibility of return, to invest in a leaky economy of superfluity.

the message of the text. It thereby reinstitutes an endless cycle of opposition between its own calls to bourgeois self-restraint and the indulgent manner in which they are conveyed.[35]

In an epigraph to *Mentoria,* the author insists, "Detested be the pen whose baneful influence / Could to the youthful docile mind convey / Pernicious precepts, tell loose tales," and concludes, "I would not for the riches of the East . . . sink my Genius to such prostitution." Whatever *Mentoria* may be, its companion text here, *Trials of the Human Heart,* is nothing if not a "loose tale." *Trials* is long, amorphous, and essentially plotless; it loves to talk about sex, money, and—even better—sex for money. Funnily enough, however, its very fascination with the "prostitution" Rowson elsewhere eschews may provide the reader with one avenue to figure out how the book escaped the detestation of both its own author and its many eminent subscribers. How did *Trials* avoid the fate it repeatedly depicted: that of those ruined by their willingness to squander sexual capital in order to live at their ease?[36]

35. The question of what legitimizes the inherently voyeuristic witness of suffering—of the "incongruity between the benevolent human being's utter separation from the object of benevolence" and "the impulse toward merging implicit in the idea of 'sympathy'"—has been central to discussions of eighteenth- and nineteenth-century sentimentalism for some time. Patricia Meyer Spacks argues that sentimental novels' formal inconsistencies constitute narrative acknowledgment of the double significance of the spectacle at the heart of any sympathetic engagement: "Many sentimental novels of the late 18th century . . . struggle to obviate the emotional gap that their reliance on moral spectacle creates." In these novels, "truncations, inconsequentialities, inconclusiveness of plot mirror difficulties of relationship partly constituted by the gap between givers and receivers of benevolence." See Spacks, *Desire and Truth: Functions of Plot in Eighteenth-Century English Novels* (Chicago, 1990), 121, 133. Karen Halttunen also attends to the alienating specularity inherent in eighteenth-century theories of benevolence and their narrative articulations. Noting that "eighteenth-century moral philosophers treated sympathy as a sentiment stirred primarily through sight," she argues, "The convention of spectatorial sympathy at the core of the eighteenth-century literature of sensibility was deeply ambivalent in its treatment of the pain and suffering of other sentient beings. Sentimental sympathy was said to be . . . an emotional experience that liberally mingled pleasure with vicarious pain." See Halttunen, "Humanitarianism and the Pornography of Pain in Anglo-American Culture," *American Historical Review,* C (1995), 303–334, esp. 305, 307, 308. Adam Smith gives an account of how we imitate our own past experience of pain when we feel for the man on the rack; see Smith, *The Theory of Moral Sentiments* (New York, 2002). See also Tom Lutz, *Crying: The Natural and Cultural History of Tears* (New York, 1999).

36. Rowson, *Mentoria,* I, title page.

The reason this book made a modest home for itself in and around 1790s Philadelphia is that it replicated a cultural moment also characterized by a remarkable discrepancy between two competing phenomena: the active public practice of nonmarital female sexuality, prominently including prostitution, and the incipient condemnation of these acts in various print media. This tension between act and edict is the tension sentimentalism revisits as one between medium and message. That American sentimentalism has its roots in an earlier moment than we have commonly paid much attention to is actually fitting; this earlier moment initiated that oxymoronic relationship of print culture to social practice that would become the seminal condition of the sentimental. Setting up an opposition between behavioral restraint and discursive excess, the novel both speaks to a moment when texts reproved what bodies happily did and suggests the manifold potential of both representation and self-representation to exist beyond even their own edicts. As it increasingly engaged in semantic condemnation of a proliferating practice, turn-of-the-century Philadelphia occupied a sentimental moment.

Sentimental Streetwalking

Based on what we have seen of *Trials,* what wasn't American sentimentalism in the 1790s? It wasn't particularly concerned with domesticity as a way of organizing space, behavior, or belief. It wasn't devoid of nonpunitive female sexual pleasure, even outside marriage. And it wasn't a mechanism for converting productive female participants in vanishing household economies into nonproductive ciphers within a developing market capitalist economy. It was global, in the sense of taking place both outside the home and outside the national enclosure; it was highly, if torturously, sexualized, mostly but not exclusively violently; and it was productive, in the sense that it emphasized women's capacities for wage labor and other forms of "useful employment" outside the family. If there is one practice that brings together these three concerns—and that falls out of the American sentimental canon as the nineteenth century progressed—it is that of prostitution. Under this term, I include explicit cases where sex is used to purchase sustenance and other instances when the usually silent relations between female sexuality and material recompense, often hidden through the practice of marriage, are interrupted.

As a British expatriate, Rowson would have been familiar with a culture in which prostitution was valorized, tolerated, pervasive, and public. In London of the eighteenth and nineteenth centuries, "the sex industry was the biggest employer of women . . . after domestic service"; in the 1790s alone, according to the founder of the Thames River Police, fifty thousand prostitutes worked in the city in an atmosphere of relative tolerance and, for some, wealth and celebrity. Arriving in Philadelphia in 1793, Rowson would have been familiar with the city's unusual climate relative to other large coastal cities such as Boston and New York. In 1790s Philadelphia, "sex commerce prospered . . . as part of the expansive, permissive sexual culture and was well integrated into the public and semipublic leisure world of the city." Indeed, "evidence from Philadelphia suggests that, during the transition between the sexual system of the late colonial period and that of the nineteenth century, prostitution took on its most fluid and least exploitative form." This same climate of tolerance might also account for Rowson's warm reception in a variety of less than securely esteemed roles, as actress, songstress, playwright, and novelist.[37]

Simultaneous with this lenient culture of practice, however, a print culture began to emerge that emphasized female sexual restraint as a hallmark of middle-class identity, a sign of female subordination, and a necessary condition for women's role as exemplars of civic virtue. As part of this transition, nonmarital female sexuality came to be represented more negatively in print, even as it was practiced consistent with post-Revolutionary "assertions of individual choice and personal liberties." As publishers began to omit erotica, sexual intrigue, and "bawdy or sexually venturesome women" from newspapers, magazines, and almanacs, nonmarital female sexuality appeared only negatively, either as catastrophic seduction or seduction's frequent consequence, prostitution. Prostitution became a familiar topic in print matter directed at a general readership, inevitably resulting in disgrace and death. Where frank and noncatastrophic depictions of female sexuality did survive, they were either unpublicized and directed exclusively at men (such as the expensive European erotica that now was joined by a few resident productions) or, as we will see in the next chapter, they represented lower-class or ethnic women engaging in humorous behavior depicted as extrinsic to the Anglo-European female subject.[38]

When print culture and sexual practice are as disparate as they were in 1790s Philadelphia, however, it is worth seeking out those particular publications that manage to register a level of internal conflict and contradiction regarding the chastity they supposedly promote. Susanna Rowson, unsurprisingly, led the way with her poem "The Prostitute," which "typified

37. Fergus Linnane, *Madams: Bawds and Brothel-Keepers of London* (Stroud, 2005); Lyons, *Sex among the Rabble,* 278, 279.

38. Lyons, *Sex among the Rabble,* 238, 292, 297–304, 312–322.

the era's prostitute narrative" with its gloomy depiction of an everywoman gone bad. Maria begins life "young," "gay," "sweet . . . and innocent," certainly no worse than many of the "DAUGHTERS OF VANITY" the poem addresses. Thus her progression through the required stages of seduction—unwilling prostitution ("infamous *for bread*"), carefree prostitution ("meets it without dread"), mental and physical decline ("black remorse, and pale disease"), poverty (from "folly's giddy maze" to "casual prostitution" on the cold streets), and moral and physical decay (obscenities spoken in a croaking voice), ending with repentance and death in a poor man's home—clearly inculcated female sexual restraint. One false step, and this could be you.[39]

But even as Maria's appealing nature and innocent beginnings demonstrate her eventual trade as "the inevitable outcome, for all women, of premarital or extramarital sexual behavior," she also represents qualities worth emulation, specifically that of being, like Meriel, "free from disguise." As with seduction narratives of the period, then, her tale does not simply encourage "female sexual inertness" as a necessary feature of female political subordination in the nation-state, though that is one of its functions. Rather, it suggests the problem of self-enfranchisement, the problem of any state formed on the heels of revolution: how to engage in the mutual trust necessary for a social contract while protecting oneself from predators like the one that seduces Maria. How can one remain "free from disguise" while able to detect that quality in others? Thematized in documents as widely varying as Charles Brockden Brown's *Wieland* and *Charlotte Temple,* this question reformulates itself in the tale of the unfortunate prostitute. And as it does, it both tightens the screws on female behavioral improvisation and reminds the contemporary female reader that her circumscription, as both lamented in and encouraged by these tales, is an arbitrary result of the failures of others in her life, those accorded the legitimacy to constitute a polis that merely contains her.[40]

In fact, as with *Charlotte Temple,* Maria's sexual adventures play almost no part in this poem. Blame is reserved for her first suitor (who breaks his vows), her father (who kicks her out of the house), and her female friends (who scorn her). Before she dies, she dedicates an entire verse to questioning the behavior of each—and receives no answer. Whatever this poem says about prostitution and female sexuality, it seems at least as concerned with questioning the conditions that cause the poem to denigrate these constructs as it is with the denigration proper. It's the not-so-very-unfortunate reader

39. Ibid., 305; *Philadelphia Minerva,* July 18, 1795.
40. Lyons, *Sex among the Rabble,* 312.

who ends up chastised: the comfortable witness, here represented as a callous hypocrite. Better to be the prostitute Maria than her friends, lovers, and relations, who have no need to consider the trade and no capacity to sympathize with one who does.

If prostitution is not the worst moral affront in "The Prostitute," it nevertheless remains a marker of the female outcast, in keeping with the tendency of 1790s publications to equate nonmarital female sexuality with social death. *Trials of the Human Heart,* however, further challenges readers used to considering prostitution in purely negative terms by representing it as but one of several viable forms of female economic subsistence. As such, it goes much further than most contemporary works to treat the subject as an experience rather than a spectacle, to evoke what it was like to engage in prostitution in the 1790s rather than merely to witness it. In "The Prostitute," much emphasis is placed on internal and external viewers of poor Maria, from callous acquaintances to poor but sympathetic strangers to the reader herself, who is asked to choose her position from these options. As an epistolary novel, however, *Trials* cares little for the reader or, in fact, for communicative exchange of any kind (almost all the letters are addressed to one friend, who never responds). Rather, it is concerned with how the solitary, if surrounded, Meriel interprets her own changing fortunes to herself. Thus, we are taken step-by-step through the events leading to Meriel's first (and last) professional encounter. We meet the female procurer who introduces her to the practice; we learn exactly what outfit she provides Meriel in which to meet her first client (a brown lutestring nightgown, which she's allowed to keep) and what she feeds her before her assignation.

With every new piece of information, moreover, we are less inclined to view the practice in normative terms and more able to include it among the many other forms of employment Meriel also undertakes in an attempt to feed herself and her ailing mother. Meriel doesn't like being a prostitute, and she's glad her first client frees her of following through on her sexual contract—but she's both willing to try sex for money and perfectly capable of recovering from this encounter as from her many other sexual misadventures. Hence this novel takes up a dominant cultural topos (prostitution as the last resort of the sexually impulsive female) and reworks the terrain in adventurous ways. Like "The Prostitute," *Trials* identifies the aspects of prostitution that make it a feasible, if not an ideal, career for women: economic subsistence, sexual agency, and undomesticated mobility. Prostitution may not satisfy Meriel's quest for *"genteel* employment," and in fact she soon abandons it in her search for less degrading work. But as a form of female "subsistence," it deserves a place. Ultimately, then, *Trials of the Human Heart* is a very hardheaded novel: a testament to what the narrator frequently refers to as the pride due laboring female independence, however obtained.

Moreover, if prostitution itself holds little appeal for Meriel, it nevertheless serves as a metonym for the many other forms of "useful employment" she will attempt with no reluctance whatsoever. In fact, whereas Meriel's peripateticism performs only a covert critique of domestic sanctuary as a necessary condition of genteel womanhood, her emphasis on female earning power is explicit in its challenge to women's prescribed economic dependence and the cultivation of lassitude as a female virtue. She scorns those women, like her cousins the Mossops, "who think it degrading to be able to perform, for themselves, any of the necessary offices of life." She grudgingly admires those, such as her father's erstwhile companion Mrs. Talbot, who reject the office of kept mistress upon realizing, "I have the abilities necessary to earn my subsistence, and they shall be exerted." And she spends most of the novel making good on her early hope to, "by some genteel employment, endeavour to earn subsistence for myself." "In my opinion, the person who has talents, health and spirits to earn a subsistence, is in all respects independent, and there is nothing to me would be more painful, than to eat the bread of indolence."[41]

Much as *Trials* may confront prevailing norms of female dependence, it also participates in the decade's shifting conception of female sexuality. This can be seen most clearly in Meriel's developing sexual persona. Meriel's first affair, carried on secretly at night with the handsome Mr. Pringle, is clearly the result of imprudence, read one way, or passionate yearning, read another. As such, she begins the novel representing, to American readers, a colonial understanding of female sexuality, in which women were seen as more sexually susceptible than men. Later, however, she puts off the erotic consummation of a deep affectual intimacy with her beloved Mr. Kingly for the sake of his kindhearted wife. She has, that is, subjected sexual yearning to self-regulation in pursuit of genteel decency and social harmony. Unlike Charlotte, she has learned to bring intent and action into accord, much as her doppelganger throughout the novel, Mrs. Talbot, begins having "learnt to detest my own vices without making one attempt to eradicate them" and ends in complete (if celibate) "reformation." Both Meriel and Mrs. Talbot end the novel "metamorphosed into the lesser sexual beings"—one through

41. Rowson, *Trials of the Human Heart,* I, 35, 106, 117, 151.

celibacy, the other through long-deferred marriage—as befits the post-Revolutionary model of female sexuality.[42]

Along the way, however (and the way is long), Meriel draws out this transition enough to show its contested nature, suggesting that, even if her own submission remains complete, others (such as the friend she writes at convent school, in many ways the novel's implied reader) may remain disruptive. What, for instance, of the many other unrepentant prostitutes who have shown up along the way? What of the "beautiful, elegant women" in the boxes at the play Meriel attends early on with her cousins, some of whom "come to those public places with no other view than to attract new lovers"? In keeping with the trajectory described above, Meriel hypothesizes that they will follow Maria's path from fortunate concubinage to "walking the streets, subject to the insults of every brutal passenger, and sinking into an untimely grave, under the complicated evils of poverty, sickness and disgrace." Yet in between, they may inspire others the way they do Meriel mere pages later, who "wished myself in the same situation with those victims to vice, if by so doing, I could procure sustenance for my mother." And when they do decline, their downfall will critique, not female sexual integrity, but the unstable conditions of their employment.[43]

The one thing wrong with prostitution in this novel is that it can lose its affiliation with "useful employment" and turn out to possess all the vagaries of another, less systematized form of earning: begging, where nothing is offered but one's suffering countenance and nothing is owed but what the benefactor deems fit at the moment. For all that Meriel claims to rely on her independent labors, much of what she receives in this book is charity. It is this inability to offer something of consistent worth as a female entrant into the eighteenth-century labor market that *Trials* consistently laments. Prostitution, as yet another form of "solicitation," thus represents both the capacity to earn and the more frequent necessity to depend on the kindness of strangers; and when it approaches the latter, it becomes terrifying. Perhaps the scariest sentence in this book is the one where Meriel suggests that she is either going to sell sex or beg: "In this situation, I took a resolution to go out in the close of the evening and solicit the charity of the benevolent." One day not too far off, this very protagonist will be in a position to bestow charity, and giving to the needy will come to seem quite cozy from then on in the Rowsonian oeuvre. While she remains on the soliciting end, however, Meriel's active virtues, although they may testify to her "resolution," also

42. Lyons, *Sex among the Rabble*, 289; Rowson, *Trials of the Human Heart*, I, 21.
43. Rowson, *Trials of the Human Heart*, I, 110–111, II, 26.

repeatedly bring to light the arbitrary denial to early national women of the capacity to earn subsistence.[44]

Early in the novel, Meriel tries her hand at another form of "solicitation": selling some poems. She soon finds herself in much the same situation her prefatory authoress did, standing around amid strangers, getting jeered. Encouraged by a friend "to throw aside the pen, and apply to your needle," Meriel is warned that not only her sex but, more important, her station preclude her success: "The finest turned poem will be entirely overlooked by the world when ushered into it by an obscure author." Even a well-dressed streetwalker may not receive the attention she needs and deserves in the absence of that social station that Meriel can secure only through marriage. The conflation of her various labors—begging, prostituting, making hats, writing verse, and finding a husband—reminds us that the novel's moments of sexual prudery do not insist upon the perils of unchastity so much as they stand in for narrowness of opportunity in all fields available to the "obscure" female. Active virtue is exhausting and frequently futile.[45]

Coda

Catharine Maria Sedgwick, in an 1812 letter to her father, Theodore, described the difference between their two realms of influence. The passage has become central to the analysis of early American gender ideology:

> A life dignified by usefulness, in which it has been the object and the delight to do good, and the happiness to do it in an extended sphere, does, however, furnish some points of imitation for the most limited routine of domestic life. Wisdom and virtue are never at a loss for occasions and time for their exercise, and the same light that lightens the world is applied to individual use and gratification. You may benefit a nation, my dear papa, and I may improve the condition of a fellow-being.

Nancy Cott has cited this passage as evidence of "a broader cultural body of meaning" in which, "denied the incentive and opportunity for economic (and, generally, public) ambition" accorded to men, "women had instead the incentive and opportunity to serve others directly, within family relationships for the most part." Later, Philip Gould would return to the extract. Where Cott emphasized a distinction, he found similarity. "Despite her use

44. Ibid., I, 25.
45. Ibid., II, 63.

of the metaphors of 'cottage' and 'palace,' to distinguish her sphere from her father's," he wrote, "Sedgwick subtly implied a gendered equivalence of their roles." Here we have the two poles of what David Shields refers to as "the domesticity thesis that currently superintends most inquiry into the condition of early national women." Cott points out that women in post-Revolutionary America found themselves increasingly relegated to a home life set off from commercial activity, public assembly, and explicit political enfranchisement. Gould argues that they obtained power nonetheless, for domesticity became the locus of a privatized but publicly traded creed of virtue that they exemplified and administered.[46]

46. Mary E. Dewey, ed., *Life and Letters of Catharine M. Sedgwick* (New York, 1871), 91; Nancy F. Cott, *The Bonds of Womanhood: "Woman's Sphere" in New England, 1780–1835* (New Haven, Conn., 1977), 23; Philip Gould, *Covenant and Republic: Historical Romance and the Politics of Puritanism* (Cambridge, 1996), 67; David S. Shields, *Civil Tongues and Polite Letters in British America* (Chapel Hill, N.C., 1997), xxxi. It is important to note that even those historians most closely associated with such phrases as "republican motherhood" and "separate spheres" went far to emphasize that not all women fit comfortably into these categories. When Cott wrote, for instance, that "the norm for an adult woman remained household occupation" between 1780 and 1835, she was also careful to point out exceptions. Systems such as "putting-out," for instance, made the home central to the "cash nexus" as tasks performed there "prepared the way for the development of manufacturing and the factory system" (Cott, *Bonds of Womanhood*, 21, 24, 25). Linda K. Kerber, who in a preface to the revised edition of *Women of the Republic* upheld the premise that "women's lives were shaped primarily by family obligations" and that the Republican Mother "displayed her politics within the family circle, rather than by entering the public world" as she "integrated political values into her domestic life," noted "isolated exceptions" to women's exclusion from at least pre-Revolutionary political processes, such as "the crowds of women who fought the establishment of smallpox inoculation centers too close to their homes, the women who accompanied Maj. Gen. Braddock's troops as cooks and nurses during the Seven Years' War, the women merchants and traders who signed the famous 'petition' of New York's 'she-Merchants'" (Kerber, *Women of the Republic: Intellect and Ideology in Revolutionary America* [1980; New York, 1986], v–vi, 8, 11). Myriad other historians have discussed a distinction between a male-identified "public" and a female-identified "private" sphere in early national America. Notable among them is Mary Beth Norton, whose *Liberty's Daughters: The Revolutionary Experience of American Women, 1750–1800* (Boston, 1980) was published the same year as Kerber's study. Among "the constant patterns of women's lives," Norton identifies "the small circle of domestic concerns," writing that "the mistress of the household . . . and not her husband, directed the household's day-to-day activities. Her role was domestic and private, in contrast to his public, supervisory functions" (3). Like Kerber, she argues that, in the decade preceding the Revolution, "women's domestic roles took on political significance," not

The consequence granted home in such a world is beautifully conveyed by Sedgwick in a nostalgic look back from the opening pages of her novel *Hope Leslie:*

Home can never be transferred; never repeated in the experience of an individual. The place consecrated by parental love, by the innocence and sports of childhood, by the first acquaintance with nature; by the linking of the heart to the visible creation, is the only home. There there is a living and breathing spirit infused into nature: every familiar object has a history—the trees have tongues, and the very air is vocal. There the vesture of decay doth not close in and control the noble functions of the soul. It sees and hears and enjoys without the ministry of gross material substance.[47]

For this narrator, the objects of home, far from confining the inhabitant, lose their very materiality by means of their familiarity and become animate, signifying presences in the life of a child and that of an adult's memory. They form the elements of language and of self, the dross from which truth is born. No greater power could be imagined, and with woman at its center, no more powerful figure. Sedgwick's paean demonstrates the visionary quality of her earlier observations to her father and stands as a fitting assessment of the near-mystical power of "sentimental domesticity" by the second decade of the nineteenth century.

Strange, then, that in the final words of the novel Sedgwick should describe a female protagonist in terms that far more closely resemble her father's doings and her own eventual course than they do her early self-appraisal. Sedgwick leaves the reader thinking, not on curly-haired Hope and her "end in marriage," but on Miss Downing, the equally beautiful but straight-haired "loser" of their "involuntary competition":

Her hand was often and eagerly sought, but she appears never to have felt a second engrossing attachment. The current of her purposes and

---

least because of the use of economic boycotts against Great Britain (155). See also Janet Wilson James, *Changing Ideas about Women in the United States, 1776–1825* (New York, 1981). For a detailed examination of early national female domestic labor, see Jeanne Boydston, *Home and Work: Housework, Wages, and the Ideology of Labor in the Early Republic* (New York, 1990).

47. Catharine Maria Sedgwick, *Hope Leslie; or, Early Times in the Massachusetts,* ed. Carolyn L. Karcher (New York, 1998), 17.

affections had set another way. She illustrated a truth, which, if more generally received by her sex, might save a vast deal of misery: that marriage is not *essential* to the contentment, the dignity, or the *happiness* of woman. Indeed, those who saw on how wide a sphere her kindness shone, how many were made better and happier by her disinterested devotion, might have rejoiced that she did not

Give to a party what was meant for mankind.

Here, the "wide sphere" over which Miss Downing holds sway approximates Mr. Sedgwick's "world" more closely than it does his daughter's "individual . . . gratification," and the same can be said of the author's own career. Clearly, Sedgwick's own role as a never-married, childless, and celebrated author—her "unconventional choices of spinsterhood and authorship" and the "large number" whose minds she was said to "enlarge"—affiliated her with the donor to "mankind" over "party," with her early appraisal of her father over her own twenty-two-year-old self-assessment. This unexpected end to *Hope Leslie* suggests that, even as the inconsistencies between textual depiction and behavioral practice that characterized the Philadelphia of *Trials's* publication resolved themselves in favor of the texts' more restrictive prescriptions, ambiguity and deviance prevailed, in part through the medium of sentimental literature as practiced by Rowson's successors. The angel in the home might have remained just that—a creature whose reality lay in the effects that believing in her had on those who believed. To whatever degree nineteenth-century women successfully resisted the circumscriptions of post-Revolutionary paternalism, their efforts must be attributed in part to the more chaotic effusions of Sedgwick's forebear.[48]

48. Sedgwick, *Hope Leslie,* ix, xii, 370–371. On Sedgwick's "splendid" career, see Mary Kelley, *Private Woman, Public Stage: Literary Domesticity in Nineteenth-Century America* (Chapel Hill, N.C., 1984), 12–14.

4
DAUGHTERS OF AMERICA

I do not know how it is, but I have strange misgivings hanging
about my mind, that the whole moral as well as political world is
going to experience a revolution. Who knows but our present house
of Representatives, for instance, may be succeeded by members of
the other sex? What information might not the Democrats and grog-
shop politicians expect from their communicative loquacity! I'll
engage there would be no secrets then. If the speaker should happen
to be with child that would be nothing to us, who have so long been
accustomed to the sight; and if she should even lie in, during the
sessions, her place might be supplied by her aunt or grandmother.
— William Cobbett, "A Kick for a Bite"

As previous chapters have demonstrated, a fractious so-
cial realm increasingly relied upon women to provide ideological coherence
in post-Revolutionary America. At the same time, women exercised im-
provisatory skill to influence the socius they were said to merely typify. If
female deference stood for the capacity of a republic to submit to the laws it
made, female endeavor represented the response of those for whom this self-
regulatory ideal made no place as citizens: in a sense, it disrupted the very
capacity of deceptive norms to function upon those they oppressed.

However much women showed up in arenas that did not know how to
figure them—that could not recognize, even when they could absorb, their
presence—there remained one realm in which their exclusion might be said
to be of a piece with their presumed nonexistence: the political, in the strict
sense of that which pertains to the government or state. Christopher Castiglia writes of "the disappointment women faced in the early federal years,
as the situation of women under democracy remained virtually unchanged
from what it had been under British rule." In a polity to which they had
no explicit access through the legitimate mechanisms of the franchise—in
which they could neither vote nor hold office nor own property if married—
how could women be said to behave politically? In answering this question,
scholars have changed our understanding not only of how certain privileged

women thought, felt, and behaved in the early Republic but also of what "politics" means.[1]

Early American political history is often treated more narrowly than most historical topics: it has been called "the last bastion, apparently, of history as the interactions of great men." By focusing on a political culture that includes the behaviors of those excluded from such "interactions," challenges to founders' chic have expanded upon what counts as political history. When considering the activities of those operating outside official channels, however, one quickly moves from political culture to cultural politics: from politics as "pertaining to the state" to politics in the broader sense of "all 'unequal distributions of power.'" Yet early Anglo-American women did not hold back from expressing their views regarding matters of state in pursuit of a less unequal, or at least more self-benefiting, distribution of power.

Indeed, women were not absent from political discussions simply because they did not vote or serve in office. Instead, "women's lack of official political status made them a much sought-after prize. . . . Untainted by self-interest or the pursuit of personal gain . . . women's approval transformed the dross of political machination into the gold of elevated principle." But such power had its limitations. First, it was concentrated among an elite minority of the female population. Second, it depended upon a refusal to take sides. "Once women became as partisan as men, they could no longer function as impartial symbols of moral authority."[2]

Yet female partisanship flourished nonetheless. We have seen from the furor surrounding Rowson's fame that she quickly lost any reputation for

1. William Cobbett, "A Kick for a Bite; or, Review upon Review; with a Critical Essay, on the Works of Mrs. S. Rowson . . . ," *American Monthly Review* (Philadelphia, 1795), in Cobbett, *Peter Porcupine in America: Pamphlets on Republicanism and Revolution,* ed. David A. Wilson (Ithaca, N.Y., 1994), 131; Christopher Castiglia, *Bound and Determined: Captivity, Culture-Crossing, and White Womanhood from Mary Rowlandson to Patty Hearst* (Chicago, 1996), 138; Sharon M. Harris, introduction, in Harris, ed., *Redefining the Political Novel: American Women Writers, 1797–1901* (Knoxville, Tenn., 1995), vii–xxiii, esp. xiii–xx; Rosemarie Zagarri, "Women and Party Conflict in the Early Republic," in Jeffrey L. Pasley, Andrew W. Robertson, and David Waldstreicher, eds., *Beyond the Founders: New Approaches to the Political History of the Early American Republic* (Chapel Hill, N.C., 2004), 107–129; Zagarri, "Gender and the First Party System," in Doron Ben-Atar and Barbara B. Oberg, eds., *Federalists Reconsidered* (Charlottesville, Va., 1998), 118–134; Catherine Allgor, *Parlor Politics: In Which the Ladies of Washington Help Build a City and a Government* (Charlottesville, Va., 2000).

2. See Zagarri, "Women and Party Conflict," in Pasley, Robertson, and Waldstreicher, eds., *Beyond the Founders,* 116, 118, 121.

impartiality; as she aged, her public voice became ever more partisan, not only in stated point of view but in the very print and performance vehicles it occupied. Plays, through which she expressed her earlier political opinions, accommodated a political sentiment that was diffuse enough to please all comers, Federalist and Republican alike. But her odes and dirges celebrating political incumbents demanded explicit Federalist allegiance. Rowson's increasingly outspoken Federalism, even as it supported the party that favored social hierarchy, made it harder to view the women of her day in moralistic terms. With every new rhymed praise of President John Adams, she lost another smidgen of "moral authority"; and with every such loss, she and the intellectual, activist women she represented gained access to more tangible forms of influence.[3]

The implications of the above epigraph thus reach far beyond the congressional halls it invokes. They extend from the narrowly "political" realm to what Cobbett mockingly calls the "moral" one, and from there to the social and cultural practices of the population at large. But the fact that this scene, with its broad social implications, is set at the very fulcrum of post-Revolutionary national government is nevertheless crucial to this chapter. The reason that women have utterly failed in their moral capacity, according to Cobbett, is their demand not merely for a public but also an explicitly political voice, not merely for acceptance in print but also for acceptance in Congress. It is the attempt to influence, rather than merely emblematize, the processes of national self-determination that Cobbett marks as profoundly disruptive for women and that Rowson finds essential both to their and the nation's well-being.

The following pages examine those aspects of Rowson's works (drama, oratory verse, song) that address women's capacity to participate in matters of state—from war to the passage and enforcement of law—with particular attention to sexuality and sexual difference. Not surprisingly, Rowson chose performance-based vehicles for the exploration of political topics. Most of her discussions of American government are meant to take place in public spaces and among large groups; they occur in dramatic pieces enacted before the largest theater audiences of North America (including Philadelphia's Chestnut Street Theatre and Boston's Federal Street Theatre), in songs sung in company throughout the Northeast, and in poems recited

3. Introduction, and Zagarri, "Women and Party Conflict," both ibid., 1, 2, 6, 10, 108, 109. See also Joan Wallach Scott, "Women's History," in Scott, *Gender and the Politics of History* (New York, 1988), 26.

during public orations commemorating figures and events of national import. Indeed, Rowson's political verses were written with public recitation in mind—her *Miscellaneous Poems* interrupts a Washington elegy to note which portion of it was recited by Josiah Bartlett in his oration commemorating Washington's death.[4]

Because they concern themselves most outwardly with women's political role in the United States, Rowson's plays will be the focus of this chapter. Through their outspoken participation in the consolidation of nationalist sentiment, these works champion a voluntaristic model of American citizenship in which convictions, rather than received traits such as sex or birthplace, determine one's eligibility to participate in national self-governance. Rowson's plays are full of women who become American by learning to believe the right things, just as Rowson herself found widespread acceptance through her expert manipulations of patriotic virtue on stage and in print. This technique served her well in at least two ways. An emphasis on abstract belief over material origin made the author-actress's own inconvenient genealogy, including her loyalist family ties and her recent British residence, seem less suspect and thus helped legitimate her presence before potentially hostile American audiences. At the same time, the emphasis on American citizenship as a construct based in belief, as opposed to origin, freed Rowson from having to choose between her English past and her American present, as long as she expressed adequate sympathy for American causes. It thus preserved her status as the perennial English expatriate, an image that we have seen she also took care to maintain, even years into her second American residence, as a claim on both exoticism and legitimate gentility.

Celebrating the young Republic's capacity to determine its own destiny, as well as the corollary potential of all who share in that vision to join its celebration of Independence, sets these works up to include female enfranchisement almost as an afterthought. Here, one must tread carefully. As we saw from the poem "Rights of Woman," discussed in Chapter One, Rowson was partial to a duty-bound notion of female rights: the right to serve others, primarily truant husbands and ailing fathers. Even her female revolutionaries find motivation in a yearning for the well-being of their menfolk or, alternatively, discover their capacity for self-sacrifice as a function of their republican politics. But there is no denying that Rowson's frequent atten-

4. Susanna Rowson, *Miscellaneous Poems; by Susanna Rowson, Preceptress of the Ladies' Academy, Newton, Mass.* (Boston, 1804), 44–54, esp. 53.

tion to current national and international crises, from the Algerian crisis to the Whiskey Rebellion to fears of French invasion, both represents women in positions of political authority and stands as an important rhetorical instantiation of female political agency.[5]

In contention with this emphasis on individual and national self-determination as a means to greater female political influence, Rowson's plays also call upon "ascriptive" categories of identity. This term denotes qualities of perceived identity that, contrary to the voluntaristic model of citizenship described above, are rooted in "apparently immutable characteristics." Challenging the self-aggrandizement evident in much of Rowson's work, where seemingly immovable obstacles and overwhelming odds fall before the all-powerful sway of the properly self-governing female heroine, this strand emphasizes, and indeed takes solace in, that which a person simply cannot get beyond.[6]

Despite such ascriptive characters' frequent abjection, Rowsonian drama nevertheless figures both playwright and audience members through them. In particular, Rowson's two surviving plays, *Slaves in Algiers; or, A Struggle for Freedom* and *The Volunteers,* grant the capacity for sexual pleasure to nonwhite, non-Christian women in a manner that both affirms Anglo-American women's superiority to carnal impulse and invites their temporary identification with these lesser figures. Through the staged spectacle of the sexualized female Muslim and Native American, Anglo-American female audiences can thereby engage the very forms of desire against which they simultaneously articulate their political agency.[7]

We cannot, therefore, understand these works' hierarchies of personal

5. Ibid., 98–104, esp. 103.

6. Usually, these qualities exist in those who are being witnessed, not in the viewers: usurious Jews, drunken Spaniards, and North African Muslim potentates, stock figures of the British stage tradition that so thoroughly informs Rowson's American plays. Even when these characters have a voice, the assumption is generally that the viewer should picture himself gazing at the speaker rather than imaginatively occupying his or her point of view, as one might be inclined to do with a more heroic figure. Quoted in Elizabeth Maddock Dillon, *"Slaves in Algiers:* Race, Republican Genealogies, and the Global Stage," *American Literary History,* XVI (2004), 407–436, esp. 408. On Rowson's "ethnic typing" as a sign of her debt to British plays, see Jeffrey H. Richards, *Drama, Theatre, and Identity in the American New Republic* (Cambridge, 2005), 8.

7. Susanna Rowson, *Slaves in Algiers; or, A Struggle for Freedom* . . . , in Amelia Howe Kritzer, ed., *Plays by Early American Women, 1775-1850* (Ann Arbor, Mich., 1995), 55–95, esp. 93–95, epilogue; Rowson, *The Volunteers: A Musical Entertainment, as Performed at the New Theatre, Composed by Alex Reinagle* . . . (Philadelphia, 1795).

and social worth—their class, regional, and, most important, ethnic politics—as either fully instrumental (racialized others sacrificed for the sake of a consolidated corporate national identity) or merely ephemeral in the context of her substantive plea for transatlantic amity. Rather, it is the play between the malleable and the fixed, the hierarchical and the horizontal, the ascriptive and the self-determining, that accords Rowson's complex negotiation of American women's political role in the new Republic both its instructive power and its capacity for lament, both its utopian and its memorial roles.

This figuration may help reconcile a persistent point of contention regarding the role of *Slaves in Algiers* within transatlantic early American studies. Emphasizing the voluntaristic aspects of the drama, Philip Gould argues that "race is a motile term largely synonymous with culture." He identifies a "flexible model of racial identification," wherein "the fate of each character depends upon his or her ability to embrace the enlightened form of Christianity that is the thematic focus of the play." He concludes, "The play suggests that 'Moriscan' and 'Christian' identities are less a function of genealogy than of sensibility," as "all racial and national identifications become the function of feeling—the only category, it would appear, that the play naturalizes."[8]

In taking up the play's "ascriptive" qualities, Elizabeth Maddock Dillon agrees that the primary impetus of the play is creating "coherence." But where Gould figures a transatlantic sensibility, Dillon emphasizes an opposition between those within and those without the national border, arguing that "racialization in this period is less aimed at identifying the *Other* as different and therefore undesirable than at creating a broad national coherence out of a group of individuals with primarily local attachments." The difference in emphasis here is significant. Where Gould sees the play working to salvage a transatlantic British-American identity so as to allow for effective and self-approving participation in a global commercial sphere, Dillon looks to a geographically delimited if "broad national coherence" formulated within a "distinctly global geography." Gould sees the play attempting to overcome antagonism in the service of transatlantic coherence; Dillon sees it instituting transatlantic antagonism in the service of national identity. For Gould, the play makes friends of potential enemies. For Dillon, it finds enemies so as to figure a group of assembled strangers as friends. But we can, by focusing on the sexuality that Cobbett found so useful in rendering

8. Philip Gould, *Barbaric Traffic: Commerce and Antislavery in the Eighteenth-Century Atlantic World* (Cambridge, Mass., 2003), 104.

women unfit for political incorporation, reconcile these countercurrents in the play's treatment of gender and race.[9]

This focus is made easier by the fact that Rowson, in keeping with her contemporaries, loved to figure the difference between responsible self-regulation and dissolute self-indulgence by playing on that between political "liberty" and sexual "license." Generally, it would seem that women proved their utter unlikeness to the figures of Cobbett's universe (or that of Woll-stonecraft's excoriators) by sacrificing their sexual capacities for the sake of their political enfranchisement. They thus became the opposite of Charlotte Temple as she was understood at the outset of this book: Charlotte possesses no capacity for self-articulation and hence falls prey to the uses to which others put her empty shell of a body. Rowson's female political martyrs, in turn, possess so finely articulated a sense of their identity and its place

9. In concentrating on how the play constructs national identity against outsiders, as opposed to in sympathy with estranged former fellows, Dillon's study is highly attuned to the play's use of racial ascription to institute social hierarchy. Thus "whiteness (rather than social status or property ownership) became an increasingly important component of white women's political authority," and more generally, "race an increasingly important signifier of difference." In sum, "Rowson redraws the boundaries of the republic such that race (rather than gender) becomes a primary line of demarcation between the interior and the exterior of the republic" (Dillon, *"Slaves in Algiers," American Literary History*, XVI [2004], 407, 408, 413, 417, 423). Michael Hardt and Antonio Negri describe "the mechanisms of colonial racism that construct the identity of European peoples in a dialectical play of oppositions with their native Others." "The concepts of nation, people, and race are never very far apart" (Hardt and Negri, *Empire* [Cambridge, Mass., 2000], 103). Eve Kornfeld explains how cultural identities form as a series of what Edward Said calls "contrapuntal ensembles":

> The categories of identity constructed in these learned and popular narratives are taken to be divinely ordained, immutable, or natural, determined by biological or psychological heredity. They acquire the status of knowledge, even of self-evident fact. This fixity is precisely their strength: once established, the cultural categories lend stability and teleological justification to profoundly unstable and contestable identities and relationships of power. Individuals within the dominant social group may then inhabit their usurped imperial space comfortably, with a sense of cognitive coherence and political consensus or hegemony. The representation of the Other is therefore a crucial element in the construction of identities and in the constitution of social power through knowledge.

(Kornfeld, "Encountering 'the Other': American Intellectuals and Indians in the 1790s," *William and Mary Quarterly*, 3d Ser., LII [1995], 288; Edward W. Said, *Culture and Imperialism* [New York, 1993], 52).

within a larger sociopolitical construct that they willingly sacrifice sexual gratification to this higher law; they forestall longed-for marriages, offer their bodies to unfeeling dictators, and let lovers return to former relationships. Such gestures indicate that they have realized both the importance of republican citizenship and their capacities to attain it through personal sacrifice to the greater good, regardless of the charges of men like Cobbett.

But a sense of perpetual castigation nonetheless clouds their exertion of these new skills. For if male self-denial for the public good left room for sexual dalliance (witness Franklin's *Autobiography* as well as its corrupt mirror image, Stephen Burrough's *Memoirs*), a political voice for women was yet more costly. Over the course of the 1790s, female sexual legitimacy increasingly occurred only within marriage. But for the women who "influenced the structure of political power or the dynamics of political action" in Rowson's oeuvre, even marriage didn't suffice. Female political activists, rather, are best served by lifelong chastity.[10]

It is within this frame that figures of national, religious, and ethnic alterity obtain limited agency. Since they get to try on, albeit temporarily, sexualities denied the white Anglo-American Christians without suffering cruel fates in response, they end up serving as the only locale in Rowsonian drama where sexual play takes place. And the gratification extends to the audience. When Spanish captives get drunk and reminisce about the ladies who won't have them, or when Moriscan (Moorish) young women get a crush, the audience is invited to try on their sensations, if only within the temporal and spatial bounds of the theater and if only in the realm of fantasy.

Thus whereas racial ascription allows Rowson to establish white Anglo-Christian America as a haven of gender equality through its hierarchical relation with other nations, religions, and ethnicities, gender nevertheless plays both a stabilizing and disruptive role in this hierarchy. It is through temporary identification with Native American, Islamic, and half-Jewish women that female Americans experienced a frank valorization of erotic pleasure that was increasingly stigmatized as the nineteenth century approached. Whatever ethnic condescension was involved, envy and longing also played a part, and, with them, the implicit critique of an Anglo-American culture that made female active virtue ever more dependent upon inactive libido.

10. Clare A. Lyons, *Sex among the Rabble: An Intimate History of Gender and Power in the Age of Revolution, Philadelphia, 1730–1830* (Chapel Hill, N.C., 2006); Zagarri, "Women and Party Conflict," in Pasley, Robertson, and Waldstreicher, eds., *Beyond the Founders,* 108.

The following discussion will proceed in three stages. The first attends to how female sexuality was used to respond to women's potentially disruptive political influence after the Revolution; it also addresses the complex and shifting relationship of female political affiliation and partisan politics during the 1790s. The second stage focuses on Rowson's plays (one complete, one partially extant, and one detailed in an extensive newspaper review) to show how her political views play out in a forum that, through its emphasis on embodied spectacle as opposed to textual narrative, foregrounds gender, racial, class, and geographic difference in relation to sexual practice. The last section addresses her verses about federal policy and national leaders to see how they recast female political agency from within a genre in which both speaker and audience are figured as male. Rowson's political verse attempted to influence the electoral decisions of white men. That at least one such composition ended up being edited for performance in ways that minimized its partisan effectiveness only attests to how much resistance even such mediated forms of female political agency inspired.

Sexual Politics and Federalist Feminism

From Mary Wollstonecraft to Meriel Howard, as we have seen, assertive women of the 1790s increasingly risked having their active virtue, or "passion for pursuing the public good," conflated with sexual degeneracy in the manner that Cobbett attempts above. Whether female entrance into the early national public sphere took place through authorial endeavor, political association, itinerancy, wage labor, or some combination of these, individuals such as Rowson, her sister authors, and many of her audience members and readers confronted charges of pervasive impropriety that extended from the particular acts in question to the actors' overarching personal identity. To be a publicly active woman in the 1790s, as the epigraph makes only too clear, was to open oneself to accusations of sexual laxity; and to be sexually lax as a woman was to lose any claim on moral authority. The more a woman of this period was perceived as driven by lustful urges, the more her consciousness was seen as a function of her corporeality and hence the less subject to self-regulation. To put it bluntly, perceived sexual laxity calcified female identity itself, rendering it part of the object world. One might write or not write, earn or not earn, move within and without the domestic enclosure. But sexual degradation was permanent, because it spoke to the unchanging fact of the body and gave that body a majority share in personhood. Charges of sexual indiscretion were thus particularly effective in cases, such as the one Cobbett describes at the outset of this chapter, where the cause for alarm was explicitly political in nature because they rendered women dysfunctional within post-Revolutionary rhetoric of individual and national self-determination and hence justified their exclusion from the perquisites of republican citizenship. Sexualizing all forms of female participation in the public sphere was thus a useful mechanism for denying women political agency within the young nation.[11]

Pregnancy, as discussed in the first chapter, was a particularly resonant sign of female dependence within a culture that placed a premium on independence. Thus when Cobbett envisioned women giving birth in Congress, he dropped two of the most important and conflicting symbols of the early national period into one ideological glass beaker. What was the House of Representatives, after all, if not a hallowed space for the processes of national self-determination? And what was the female womb if not a final, secret refuge from the more terrifying implications of this myth: a space where the body did its own work, unresponsive to the promptings of the mind? For an ardent Federalist—indeed, an unrepentant British loyalist—such as Cobbett, the image of women giving birth in Congress was doubly significant. First, it demonstrated the ludicrousness of giving women a political role in the new government, as their "communicative loquacity"—the verbal equivalent of their rampant sexuality, itself evident from all the childbirth taking place—rendered their statements meaningless. Women might say as much as they liked; as creatures that had to time their utterances around their genital productions, their words had little more worth than the inarticulate groans of a laboring body. Second, although the notion of childbirth in the United States Congress made that of a politically articulate woman laughable, it also exposed the legislative branch itself as constructed on only the most tenuous grounds. Sexual decadence thus both pertains to women in particular in this passage and stands for the vulnerability of an entire nation premised on the capacities of its citizenry to govern themselves. Cobbett here reminded his readers: you've already had one revolution; now, how are you going to prevent sexual anarchy?[12]

11. J. G. A. Pocock, *The Machiavellian Moment: Florentine Political Thought and the Atlantic Republican Tradition* (Princeton, N.J., 1975), 472. Elizabeth Maddock Dillon aptly parses this passage as "a scene in which the political order is disrupted by the presence of a female body that cannot function autonomously" (Dillon, *The Gender of Freedom: Fictions of Liberalism and the Literary Public Sphere* [Stanford, Calif., 2004], 13). Nancy Isenberg cites another satiric account of public birthing, from the *New York Herald*, 1852, as evidence of women's presumed subjection to their physical nature (Isenberg, *Sex and Citizenship in Antebellum America* [Chapel Hill, N.C., 1998], 42–43).

12. Keith Arbour, "Benjamin Franklin as Weird Sister: William Cobbett and Fed-

As a sign of the difficulty of containing Revolutionary sentiment, one form of succession engenders another in Cobbett's passage in a veritable world upside down. Once women take over, they must also stand in for one another when the demands of their corporeal station preclude them from active debate. Interchangeability in turn suggests indistinguishability; clearly, women's common status as breeders has a far more definitive impact on their identity than anything one or another of them might say. Granted, Cobbett's assumption that a female United States representative's "place might be supplied by her aunt or grandmother" suggests that he is not the best equipped to evaluate an author such as Rowson, since he does not believe in the distinctiveness of female voices in the first place. Like the "sage critic" from our last chapter, he is destined to find merely what he seeks. But to leave the matter at this would be to miss the point of his attack. By subjecting a widely published female author to ridicule in a manner that conflates the acts of writing and public speaking, Cobbett indicates the threat that women and other disenfranchised groups were seen to pose to a tenuous American political order and thus the climate of anxiety and hostility within which authors such as Rowson were operating.

Keeping women out of office thus became a test not only of female incapacity but also of national legitimacy. Misogyny and other forms of derision based on maintaining social hierarchy expressed fears of imminent national dissolution. On the one hand, "pseudo-aristocratic Americans were afraid . . . that women and African Americans would, with democrats' help, successfully apply the Revolutionary ideology of inalienable equal rights to themselves . . . and that as a result [pseudo-aristocratic Americans] would never again be able to behave as they pleased." On the other, keeping women out of power was but one more fear-based response to signs of fault lines in the national edifice itself, as the French Revolution grew more radical and Americans of all stations seemed ever more ready to follow its lead in emphasizing equality over liberty. In 1776, the Declaration of Independence proudly proclaimed, "All men are created equal." But in 1791, the French Declaration of the Rights of Man and of Citizen argued, "Men are born and always continue free, and equal in respect to their rights." The change from equality as doing away with "privileges of birth" to the "leveling-down mentality" of the French Revolution was significant, and some Americans were scared enough to pen parodies of the French national anthem that frankly avowed their fears of French invasion. The 1790s, then, constituted a decade

---

eralist Philadelphia's Fears of Democracy," in Ben-Atar and Oberg, eds., *Federalists Reconsidered*, 185.

obsessed with the fragility of the Union. For women to enter political office both threatened the naturalized order of things and symbolized the very real possibility that an expanded franchise might burst the bounds of republican coherence.[13]

It has been argued that the censure of female political rights through intensifying separate spheres ideology in the early nineteenth century is miscast when it is viewed as a preventive measure. What if, instead, mockery such as Cobbett's was a response to a very real assertion of female political presence in the 1790s? This interpretation becomes quite persuasive when one considers the popularity of print satires in which the joke is on women who encroach upon "the masculine marks of citizenship."[14]

Consider, for instance, the number of jokes about female "obedience" that made the rounds during the early years of the decade, to which Rowson would contribute in the epilogue to *Slaves in Algiers*. The fad might have begun with a "satirical letter" from Benjamin Franklin's grandson, Benjamin Franklin Bache. In this letter, Thalestris (a woman) overhears a group of young women discussing their plans to take up militia duty. She responds, "Upon my word, I long for this happy change of affairs. We shall then expunge the odious *obey* from the wedding ceremony." Thalestris continues into a blissful fantasy of holding her husband at gunpoint. Soon enough,

13. Ibid., 183, 185, citing William Doyle, *The Oxford History of the French Revolution* (New York, 1989), 318–319; Cobbett, "Kick for a Bite," in Cobbett, *Peter Porcupine in America,* ed. Wilson, 131. Parodies of "La Marseillaise" included one by Rowson, to be discussed ahead, as well as Josiah Dunham, "A Parody of the Marseilles Hymn, as Sung at the Late Celebration at Hanover," in "Oration, for the Fourth of July, 1798; Delivered in the Meeting-House, in the Vicinity of Dartmouth-College . . ." (Hanover, N.H., 1798), 15, Early American Imprints, 1st Ser., 48415. Dunham's parody was reprinted in the *Green Mountain Patriot,* Feb. 7, 1799.

14. Isenberg, *Sex and Citizenship,* 13, 43. According to Zagarri, the 1790s witnessed a real increase in women's political participation: "The notion of gendered spheres gained prominence at the very time that women were participating in politics to a greater extent than ever before. The coincidence is not accidental. At the very least, the tension between an apolitical feminine ideal and the realities of partisan politics may account for the increasingly strident denunciations of 'female politicians' found in the prescriptive literature of the early nineteenth century. . . . Thus while historians usually portray separate spheres ideology as a tool that was used to prevent women from entering politics, it may in fact have represented something else: a conservative reaction against women's more extensive involvement in the nation's political life. Through their participation, women had helped create the problem of party politics. Now, by leaving, they would help resolve the conflict" (Zagarri, "Women and Party Conflict," in Pasley, Robertson, and Waldstreicher, eds., *Beyond the Founders,* 110, 118, 121–123).

she and like-minded "absolute mistresses" "govern the state" and "set up a FEMALE EMPIRE" throughout the Western Hemisphere. Not surprisingly, Cobbett contributed his own joke on the subject. Commenting that "the *reformers* of the *reformed church,* have been obliged (for fear of losing all their custom) to raze the odious word *obey* from their marriage service," Cobbett wonders that "they had not imposed it on the husband; or rather . . . dispensed with the ceremony altogether; for most of us know, that in this enlightened age, the work of generation goes hummingly on, whether people are married or not." Like Bache, Cobbett speaks to an association between female equality, sexual permissiveness, upendings of hierarchy, and pervasive social disorder that seems to have saturated the cultural consciousness from 1791 to 1795.[15]

In opposition to the views of Cobbett and his ilk stands a widespread practice of Federalist-affiliated female participation in national politics, in which Rowson's plays and verses participated. Although it may seem counterintuitive, there is a case to be made that "the social conservatives of the early republic proved to be more progressive concerning women than their putatively more liberal rivals." The most influential claims for improvements in female education, the parenting of daughters, and the structure of marriage came from staunchly Federalist female authors and public figures such as Judith Sargent Murray, Annis Boudinot Stockton, and Abigail Adams. During their brief period of enfranchisement in New Jersey, women tended to vote Federalist. And women tended to find a warmer welcome in Federalist-themed events than Republican.[16]

Why was the Federalist Party, which in general worked to maintain social hierarchy, more conducive to claims for gender equality than the Republican Party, which worked to expand the white male franchise? This irony can be understood as a result of the constraints that developed in response to expansions of the franchise in this period. Because the Republicans focused on actualizing the potential equality of all white men, regardless of wealth, geographic locale, or station, they tended to be dismissive of the capacity of nonwhites and women. This attitude was partly a matter of mere inattention; thus Jefferson could freely admit that, despite making education the primary focus of his retirement years, educating women "has never been

15. *New-York Packet,* Jan. 29, 1791; Cobbett, "Kick for a Bite," in Cobbett, *Peter Porcupine in America,* ed. Wilson, 131.

16. Zagarri, "Gender and the First Party System," in Ben-Atar and Oberg, eds., *Federalists Reconsidered,* 119; David Waldstreicher, *In the Midst of Perpetual Fetes: The Making of American Nationalism, 1776–1820* (Chapel Hill, N.C., 1997), esp. 167.

a subject of systematic contemplation with me." Many have argued, however, that this viewpoint also had a more deliberate aspect. Republicans countered charges of radical extremism by emphasizing the natural limits to their egalitarianism through the exclusion of women and nonwhites. And they created material opportunities for their target population precisely by denying them to those outside their primary frame of reference. The result was that "some white women and African Americans who could vote in the early 1790s no longer could after the 'Republican Revolution' of 1800."[17]

On the other hand, Federalism's greater tolerance for gender reform similarly depended upon exclusion, since it extended only to those women who were part of the financial, social, and ethnic elite that the party found worthy of serious consideration. Because the Federalists embraced hierarchy, they were not threatened by offering a clearly demarcated role to women: not only were the rights contained within that role based on a deferential model of gender relations, but they extended only to women of a certain station. It was perfectly acceptable for female Federalist authors, who were educated and articulate, to write passionately in support of female causes. But there was no systematic attempt by the Federalist Party to alter the condition of women of all stations.[18]

Rowson's political affiliations during her first decade in the United States are not a matter of common consent. Since she made no clear statement of party allegiance until about 1798, when she began to publish poems glorifying Federalist leaders, many have looked to her early supporters and detractors to align her in general terms with Republican interests. John Swanwick, Rowson's greatest champion, was a new Democratic-Republican senator at the time he defended her in print, whereas Cobbett "donned high Federalism" upon his arrival from England to become "a bellwether of the most reactionary politics." Based on these men's politics, then, it would seem that Rowson, too, favored a Republican worldview. The history of the American theater, however, suggests an alternative possibility.[19]

17. Zagarri, "Gender and the First Party System," in Ben-Atar and Oberg, eds., *Federalists Reconsidered,* 132; Joseph J. Ellis, *Passionate Sage: The Character and Legacy of John Adams* (New York, 1993), 187; Dillon, *"Slaves in Algiers," American Literary History,* XVI (2004), 413.

18. For a convincing challenge to the idea that Federalism offered a surer platform for early American female political activity than did Republicanism, see Kate Davies, *Catharine Macaulay and Mercy Otis Warren: The Revolutionary Atlantic and the Politics of Gender* (New York, 2005), esp. 294, 309.

19. Dillon, *"Slaves in Algiers," American Literary History,* XVI (2004), 412, 430 n. 9; Arbour, "Benjamin Franklin as Weird Sister," in Ben-Atar and Oberg, eds., *Fed-*

"A Company of English Comedians Had Arrived"

Theater was a highly inclusive medium in the 1790s. Like the many novels Rowson had published by the time her first play was staged in June 1794, early national theatrical performance welcomed "audiences of differing social and economic classes who were beginning to clamor for the right to shape America's cultural identity," with the important difference that it put them all in one place, bringing "divergent groups face to face under the same roof." When Rowson's first troupe, Thomas Wignell's New Theatre Company, returned to Philadelphia's Chestnut Street Theatre in 1793 following that city's yellow fever epidemic, they were met with widespread enthusiasm, as described by the narrator of Charles Brockden Brown's *Ormond*.

> Meanwhile, the dominion of cold began to be felt, and the contagious fever entirely disappeared. The return of health was hailed with rapture by all ranks of people. The streets were once more busy and frequented. . . . Public entertainments were thronged with auditors. A new theater had lately been constructed, and a company of English comedians had arrived during the prevalence of the malady. They now began their exhibitions, and their audiences were overflowing.

Here, dramatic performances in which Rowson acted and sang, and a few of which she authored, are seen as the very proof of a city's returning health, its capacity to mix "all ranks of people" in one great "overflowing" rapture.[20]

As a forum for urban diversity, theater was a likely venue for the advocacy of female rights. The dramas performed on Philadelphia, New York, Boston, and Baltimore stages fostered numerous and diverse claims for gender equality. As Faye Dudden summarizes in her study of women in nineteenth-century American theater, "the early playhouse was . . . a contested arena where men were dominant but never in control, where women found the cultural authority of audience members, the economic independence that came from the actress's work, and even a limited entrée into politics." And Amelia Howe Kritzer notes "the frequency with which [early American

eralists Reconsidered, 187; Susan Branson, *These Fiery Frenchified Dames: Women and Political Culture in Early National Philadelphia* (Philadelphia, 2001), 115.

20. Heather S. Nathans, *Early American Theatre from the Revolution to Thomas Jefferson: Into the Hands of the People* (Cambridge, 2003), 83; Charles Brockden Brown, *Ormond; or, The Secret Witness,* ed. Mary Chapman (Toronto, 1999), 93–94.

plays'] action centers on a female character's interaction with and influence upon a major historical event."[21]

In that it makes women central to the outcome of the nation's first true international crisis, *Slaves in Algiers* may be the paradigm of such a play, but it was not alone in proposing unlikely gender roles for women. Judith Sargent Murray's *Traveller Returned,* first performed at the Federal Street Theatre in 1796, featured an intellectual mother who would rather read about how a substance called "phlogiston" is derived from the sun than interact with her daughter. And the prologue to British playwright Elizabeth Inchbald's *Everyone Has His Fault,* performed at Philadelphia's New Theatre, gently pokes fun at the audience's expectation of a male author while lodging a plea for female education. Mentioning Wollstonecraft's *Vindication of the Rights of Woman,* the prologue takes up the prevalent theme of female obedience. Although "women may make too free—and know too much," those who have had the opportunity "to cultivate that useful part— the mind" have both wit and the ability to "use it well," thereby deserving to have their work performed alongside that of male authors.[22]

For all its inclusiveness regarding audience, performer, and subject matter, however, early national theater was indebted to an elite economic agenda that was primarily Federalist. Boston finally made way for theater among its "legitimate amusements" because, as Federalists came to dominate the city in the 1790s, they overwhelmed a primarily Democratic-Republican opposition. Federalist participation was crucial to overturning an American antitheatrical bias that ranged from Puritan theocracy to the Constitutional Convention's ban on theatrical productions. This participation represented the interests of "a new post-war elite, intent on launching a system of banks, corporations, and cultural institutions that would place them on the world stage." Federalist shareholders sponsored both Philadelphia's Chestnut Street and Boston's Federal Street theaters.[23]

21. Faye Dudden, *Women in the American Theatre: Actresses and Audiences, 1790– 1870* (New Haven, Conn., 1994), 4, 5; Kritzer, introduction, in Kritzer, ed., *Plays by Early American Women,* 2.

22. Judith Sargent Murray, *The Traveller Returned,* in Kritzer, ed., *Plays by Early American Women,* 97–136, esp. 11; "Prologue, by the Rev. Mr. Nares, Spoken by Mr. Farren," in [Elizabeth] Inchbald, *Every One Has His Fault: A Comedy, in Five Acts, by Mrs. Inchbald, Mark'd with Alterations (by Permission of the Managers) by William Rowson, Prompter* (Philadelphia, 1794), 3–4, Early American Imprints, 1st Ser., 27154.

23. Richards, *Drama, Theatre, and Identity,* 301; Nathans, *Early American Theatre,* 6, 7, 50–55. The chapter "I Can Do Everything with Money and Nothing Without:

PLATE 17. *"Philadelphia Theatre, in Chesnut St." 1807. Engraving by M. Marigot.*
Print and Picture Collection, The Free Library of Philadelphia

The Federalist funding of theater was part of a larger economic agenda
that favored American commercial expansion. We might define the late-
eighteenth-century American imperialist impulse as follows: "To export . . .
the practices and values of laissez-faire capitalism to convert people into
consumers and thereby expand markets." Elsewhere, Rowson exemplified
this practice in depicting the triumph of sailors returning home to share in a
rousing celebration of "America, Commerce, and Freedom." The predations
upon American shipping interests in the Mediterranean Sea that formed the
basis for *Slaves in Algiers,* then, presented a topic tailor-made for a proto-
Federalist argument linking global commerce, female rights, and Ameri-

The Pennsylvania Federalists Take Control" is of particular relevance. See also S. E.
Wilmer, *Theatre, Society, and the Nation: Staging American Identities* (Cambridge,
2002), 56. The Haymarket, a rival Democratic-Republican establishment, was built in
Boston shortly after the Federal Street Theatre.

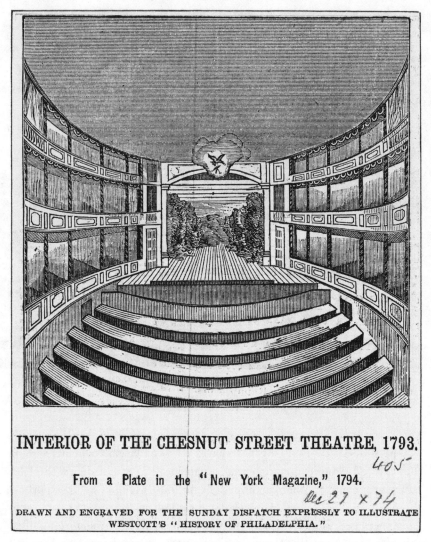

INTERIOR OF THE CHESNUT STREET THEATRE, 1793.

From a Plate in the "New York Magazine," 1794.

DRAWN AND ENGRAVED FOR THE SUNDAY DISPATCH EXPRESSLY TO ILLUSTRATE
WESTCOTT'S "HISTORY OF PHILADELPHIA."

PLATE 18. *"Interior of the Chesnut Street Theatre." 1793. Print and Picture Collection,
The Free Library of Philadelphia*

can national unity. And understanding the Federalist context of a play that, on its surface, presents no obvious partisan argument—and in fact went to great lengths to please a bipartisan audience—makes sense of the seeming inconsistency between its claims for gender equality and its championing of a globalized sociopolitical hierarchy.[24]

Key to Rowson's message is the ability to differentiate between deference, or chosen submission, and subjection, or involuntary submission. In the former, Rowson finds the key to civilization; in the latter, the mark of barbarism. Asking no more, really, than that the Anglo-American men of this play offer Anglo-American women the right to choose their obedience, the drama offers as a reward the skill these women then show at teaching the same right to their unenlightened Algerian brethren. Thus for all that the Christian captives of *Slaves* have to teach their Moorish captors, the Moors in their initial ignorance also deliver a message to the audience regarding the importance of treating American women as independent beings. Do right by your wives and daughters, the play informs the social conservatives behind the theater's fortunes and the new nation's fledgling government, and you will also do well by them—not only at home but in North Africa and beyond.

Thus does a region that in fact posed a significant threat to American shipping interests come to serve as Rowson's prototype for a subject state in the making, one that awaits only the influence of the female American to show it how to choose its subjugation. *Slaves in Algiers* thereby suggests that including women in United States political culture not only will accord with female deference but will also help prop up a "Standard of Liberty," to cite another Rowson composition, that depends on the establishment of United States dominion throughout the globe. The character named Olivia summarizes this conflation of global American dominance with female citizenship in the final lines of the play, asking that "freedom spread her benign influence through every nation, till the bright Eagle, mixed with the dove and olive branch, waves high, the acknowledged standard of the world." *Slaves in Algiers* both fantasizes an eighteenth-century world in which women start revolutions and sway despots and provides a ready vehicle for

24. John Carlos Rowe, *Literary Culture and U.S. Imperialism: From the Revolution to World War II* (Oxford, 2000), xi. The song commonly known as "America, Commerce, and Freedom," after the last line of its chorus, first appeared as "New Song, Sung by Mr. Darley, Jun., in the Pantomimical Dance, Called the Sailor's Landlady: Words by Mrs. Rowson, Music by Mr. Reinagle" (Philadelphia, 1794), Early American Imprints, 1st Ser., 27648.

the fantasy in the shape of a subject population ready for tutelage by their fair captives.[25]

Daughters of America, Slaves in Algiers

Slaves in Algiers was part of a self-conscious flurry of American literary nationalism in the wake of the international relations predicament known as the Algerian crisis and remembered today as a first step toward the Tripolitan War of 1801–1805. When the Treaty of Paris ended British protection of American shipping interests in 1783, Barbary corsairs from the North African states of Tripoli, Algiers, Tunis, and Morocco began attacking American ships in the Mediterranean. The Barbary States demanded tribute to halt the attacks, which the United States government begrudgingly paid. But the situation did not resolve itself. In 1793, for instance, the same year Susanna Rowson and her husband William arrived in Philadelphia, Algerians seized the brig *Polly* on its way from Boston to Cádiz. Between 1784 and 1815, more than a dozen American ships, from the *Betsey* to the *Philadelphia,* were captured by vessels from off the North African coast, and more than four hundred American sailors were imprisoned—some for as long as eleven years. Those addressing the Barbary captivity crisis in print included Benjamin Franklin, Tabitha Tenney, Royall Tyler, and Maria Pinckney. In 1794 alone, the year that *Slaves in Algiers* was first performed, Mathew Carey published his *Short Account of Algiers,* and Daniel Saunders' *Travels and Sufferings* began a run that went into six editions.[26]

25. Susanna Rowson, "The Standard of Liberty," in Rowson, *Miscellaneous Poems,* 94–97; Rowson, *Slaves in Algiers,* in Kritzer, ed., *Plays by Early American Women,* 93.

26. A month before his death, Benjamin Franklin, in his last published hoax, wrote a satirical letter in the voice of Sidi Mehemet Ibrahim, a proslavery Algerian pirate: "To the Editor of the Federal Gazette," *Federal Gazette, and Philadelphia Evening Post,* Mar. 25, 1790, Early American Newspapers, 1st Ser., 1690–1786. In Tabitha Gilman Tenney's *Female Quixotism,* the protagonist Dorcasina, like Franklin, uses the Algerian crisis to argue against slavery in the United States. To her servant Betty's comment, "Perhaps . . . Lysander and his father treat their slaves well, and they live comfortable and happy," Dorcasina replies, "Comfortable they may be . . . but slavery and happiness are, in my opinion, totally incompatible. . . . They complain of the idle, thievish, unfaithful disposition of their slaves; but let the proprietors in their turn, be degraded to servitude, let them be made prisoners by the Algerines, let them have task-masters set over them, to drive them out to labour in herds, like the beasts of the field; then should we see whether they would be more faithful or more industrious than the wretched Africans: then should we see whether, after a number of years had elapsed, and they knew their servitude would terminate but with life, their minds would not become

Meanwhile, "American public opinion was enraged" by "an irresolute Congress which had haggled about moderate sums of money while the national honor was trampled." Jefferson wrote as early as 1786 that he "thought it would be the best to effect a peace through the medium of war" as opposed to "a peace bought with money." Both perspectives were reflected in Congress over the following decade, with recommendations for "naval force" alternating with appropriations for ransom funds. Neither was fully successful. The enslavement of white Americans off the north coast of Africa thus constituted the nation's first international crisis in the fullest sense of the term: not only were Americans in trouble abroad, but the United States government was losing face at home.[27]

If we trust Rowson's claim in the preface to *Slaves in Algiers* that she took two months to complete the drama, she would have begun writing immediately after the government's first act of defiance: on March 27, 1794, President Washington signed the Navy Act, authorizing the construction of six American warships. (Perhaps this uncharacteristic decisiveness is why Edward Watts writes that *Slaves in Algiers* was one of several books "whose intent was to educate the American public about the Algerians in such a way that the government's response to the crisis seemed the only possible solution.") But despite the apparent impetus this highly popular gesture gave to her choice of a topic, Rowson was no more consistent than the United States government in her policy recommendations. Several "solutions" were on the table, and the feat of Rowson's play was to present them all as worthy responses without addressing their incompatibilities.[28]

degraded and vicious with their situation." See Tenney, *Female Quixotism: Exhibited in the Romantic Opinions and Extravagant Adventures of Dorcasina Sheldon*, ed. Jean Nienkamp and Andrea Collins (New York, 1992), 8–9. Probably the most lastingly influential work on this topic is Royall Tyler's novel, *The Algerine Captive; or, The Life and Adventures of Doctor Updike Underhill, Six Years a Prisoner among the Algerines*, ed. Don L. Cook ([1797]; New Haven, Conn., 1970). Maria Pinckney included the proslavery play *The Young Carolinians; or, Americans in Algiers* in [Sarah Pagson Smith], *Essays, Religious, Moral, Dramatic, and Poetical: Addressed to Youth; and Published for a Benevolent Purpose* (Charleston, S.C., 1818), 58–111.

27. James R. Lewis, "Savages of the Seas: Barbary Captivity Tales and Images of Muslims in the Early Republic," *Journal of American Culture*, XIII, no. 2 (Summer 1990), 75–84, esp. 75–76; Paul Baepler, ed., *White Slaves, African Masters: An Anthology of American Barbary Captivity Narratives* (Chicago, 1999), 7–9; Glenn Tucker, *Dawn Like Thunder: The Barbary Wars and the Birth of the U.S. Navy* (Indianapolis, 1995), 57, 58, 71, 74.

28. Edward Watts, *Writing and Postcolonialism in the Early Republic* (Charlottesville, Va., 1998), 74.

Rowson's "Play, Interspersed with Songs," as the title page of the printed volume announced, had something for everyone. First performed June 30, 1794, at Philadelphia's Chestnut Street Theatre, it had an unlikely plot "cobbled together from stock elements inherited from British drama," with the significant exception that there were "no British plays before Rowson's with Americans in North Africa." As is held to be true of most English and American plays of this period (including, for instance, Murray's *Traveller Returned,* with its conventional long-lost reunions and multiple marriages), *Slaves* was "influenced primarily by other plays," significant among them Aaron Hill's *Zara,* a popular translation of Voltaire's *Zaire* that Rowson must have seen while still in England. Like *Zara, Slaves in Algiers* centers around an Islamic ruler who holds a Christian man captive and whose daughter offers to marry the dey in order to obtain her father's freedom. *Zara* ends tragically, with the liberation of the captive but the death of the daughter. As a musical comedy, however, *Slaves* depicts the captives' release with no more than a brief struggle offstage. It also, as was de rigueur for American female-authored dramas of the period, ends with a highly unlikely family reunion between Constant, the senior captive, Rebecca, his long-lost wife and the most articulate spokesperson for American liberty, and their daughter Olivia and son Henry.[29]

As Jeffrey H. Richards points out, several details from *Zara* reappear in *Slaves* with almost no change, including repeated names (Selima) and character relationships. Unlike Richards, however, who suggests that *Zara* reappears in the role of Olivia, I would propose that *Slaves* takes *Zara*'s key qualities and distributes them among three female characters. Olivia takes on the role of sacrificial daughter; the half-Jewish, English-Algerian captive Fetnah replicates *Zara*'s multifaceted religious and geographic heritage and, like her, describes it to a servant named Selima in the first act; and Zoriana, the dey's daughter, has the closest-sounding name and the same unparalleled beauty. Given that *Slaves,* in an instance of what Carroll

29. Richards, *Drama, Theatre, and Identity,* 5, 145, 153; Rowson, *Slaves in Algiers,* in Kritzer, ed., *Plays by Early American Women,* 93; Murray, *Traveller Returned,* ibid., 97–136. Dryden's *Don Sebastian* was also influential, as was an episode from Cervantes's *Don Quijote* that Rowson mentions in the prologue. Another influential play worth mentioning as a potential source for *Slaves in Algiers* was Eliza Haywood's *Fair Captive: A Tragedy,* first staged and printed in 1721. Set in Constantinople, this play features a "Grand Visier" named Mustapha who loves a beautiful Spanish captive, Isabella, and wishes not to ransom her (Margarete Rubik and Eva Mueller-Zettelman, eds., *Delarivier Manley and Eliza Haywood,* vol. I of *Eighteenth-Century Women Playwrights* [London, 2001], 105–160).

Smith-Rosenberg terms "interracial comity," represents Muslim women in sexualized yet highly sympathetic terms so as to allow its Anglo-American audience a degree of erotic license, it is significant that the play derives three characters of disparate religions and ethnicities out of one woman.[30]

In her novels written before *Slaves,* Rowson had honed the skill of appealing to diverse audiences. In *Charlotte Temple,* whose first two American editions appeared the same year *Slaves* was first performed, the narrator addresses a variety of implied readers. She not only has tender asides for the matrons and young girls whose fates are wrapped up in the tale but also gibes for the skeptical men and boys who might be reading over their shoulders. In her first play, Rowson again courted the widest possible audience by reconciling a number of opposing viewpoints on a sensitive political matter into one blockbuster of an encomium on American patriotism. In soliciting contributions to a ransom fund in a prologue, the play satisfied those who sided with an accommodationist view of the matter: that America, like its fellow European nations, should cede to the monetary demands of the Barbary States. By staging a captive rebellion, *Slaves* simultaneously gave vent to the militaristic perspective, which held that, without a navy to back up the terms of any agreements between the United States and North African governments, ransom wouldn't work. Given that Rowson wrote the play for her benefit night, at which she kept all net proceeds, her skill at appealing to the largest possible audience would have served her particularly well.[31]

30. Richards, *Drama, Theatre, and Identity,* 153; Carroll Smith-Rosenberg, "Subject Female: Authorizing American Identity," *American Literary History,* V (1993), 481–511, esp. 500. Gould notes that Fetnah is listed as a "Moriscan" in the dramatis personae, although in the play she exclaims, "Lord, I'm not a Moriscan" (Gould, *Barbaric Traffic,* 104).

31. Benilde Montgomery claims that "Rowson's position in the national debate, too, is clear: she favors the continued payment of ransom and opposes any new war" (Montgomery, "White Captives, African Slaves: A Drama of Abolition," *Eighteenth-Century Studies,* XXVII [1994], 615–630, esp. 619). But the play clearly meets Lewis's definition of the "propagandistic" Barbary captivity narrative, which "invites the reader to take up a heroic task" ("Savages of the Seas," *Journal of American Culture,* XIII, no. 2 [Summer 1990], 77). For Eve Kornfeld, the play "was a political act, both in its attempt to stimulate greater American activity, and in its figurative lifting an arm for liberty" (Kornfeld, "Women in Post-Revolutionary American Culture: Susanna Haswell Rowson's American Career, 1792–1824," *Journal of American Culture,* VI, no. 4 [Winter 1983], 56–62, esp. 58). Branson notes that the play "was intended to be a box office draw" (*These Fiery Frenchified Dames,* 112). Richards observes that such apparent profiteering was in fact typical of theater of the period: "In the late-eighteenth-century theater, characters that we might view as quintessentially American might be acted

If the technique of manufacturing foreign crisis to minimize domestic party strife was no stretch for Rowson, the play's other great act of peace-making presented a greater challenge. Shortly before *Slaves in Algiers'* premiere, England had negotiated a treaty between Algiers and Portugal so as to allow greater Algerian access to the Atlantic. Since Americans would not have been captured by Algerian corsairs in nearly as great numbers were it not for this treaty, the depiction of United States citizens in North African captivity could easily have translated to a covert critique of British naval policy relative to the United States. The Jay Treaty, signed November 19, 1794, four months after the play's debut performance in Philadelphia, suggests the importance the Federalist administration placed on Anglo-American affiliation, whereas the "widespread, even violent, opposition" to the treaty upon its being made public in 1795 indicates the popular loathing this apparent favor-currying aroused. *Slaves* would have taken a safer route, then, had it portrayed a British villain.[32]

But *Slaves in Algiers* does not condemn the British (nor could it, with Rowson a recently arrived British immigrant) so much as argue for unity and mutual forgiveness in the name of an Anglo-American commercial imperium. As a result, not only are Federalist and Democrat indistinct entities within the drama, but so are English and American. Again, novelistic precedent existed. In *Slaves in Algiers,* Rebecca, the captive matriarch, sums up the American ethos in reference to her son Augustus—"Must a boy born in Columbia, claiming liberty as his birthright, pass all his days in slavery?" By the end of the play, the meaning of "liberty" has expanded, as the American mission metamorphoses from obtaining the release of the protagonists to awakening their former captors to their own metaphoric enslavement. But in 1789, five years before the first production of *Slaves in Algiers,* Rowson, still in England, had anonymously published a novel that also made use of international tensions in the Mediterranean. And in *Mary; or, The Test of Honour,* liberty, far from having an American patent, belongs to Great Britain. The novel's eponymous heroine, an orphan about to be married off to a lout, stakes the British claim:

Yes (retorted Mary), you will see, that I am a free born Englishwoman, and that I have spirit enough to assert those rights which nature and

---

by persons whose commitment to America was more monetary than anything else" (Richards, *Drama, Theatre, and Identity,* xx).

32. Gould, *Barbaric Traffic,* 88, 90, 99, 179; "Theatrical," *Massachusetts Mercury,* Apr. 21, 1797.

my country allow me, while my actions are innocent, and my wishes guided by prudence and virtue, I shall think no person has a right to assume a tyrannical sway over me, or dictate to me whom I shall visit, or what friends I shall receive.

Months later, after Mary and her destined mate Stephen have been introduced, torn apart, reunited on the high seas, shipwrecked, rescued from a deserted island after living on oranges, and had their vessel boarded by Algerian pirates, Stephen takes charge with a similar call to "those rights which nature and my country allow me." "Now is the time for victory," he exhorts his British companions; "all who love liberty, follow me!"[33]

In ascribing the selfsame virtue, in two different books, to two recently warring nations, Rowson went beyond the conciliatory abilities demonstrated in her attempt to satisfy pacifist and militarist viewpoints simultaneously in the pages of her only fully extant play. She opened herself to charges of opportunism, hypocrisy, and, worse, charges that Cobbett, we have seen, was only too happy to bring without even knowing that *Mary* existed. He suggested that "her sudden conversion to republicanism, ought to make us look upon all her praises as ironical" and excoriated those who make self-serving use of liberty. For Rowson's sake, one can only be glad that he remained ignorant that she devoted not one but two sets of pages to this "dear word."[34]

Rather than respond to the play according to the terms Cobbett set for appraising Rowson (was she a true patriot or merely an opportunistic conniver?), it is possible to read *Mary's* blend of female equality and political liberty as a useful entrée into how Rowson's more widely known American play stakes its claim for female rights. The first thing to realize is that "liberty" itself was a useful term in reconciling opposing points of view. If "the cure . . . for Party Rage is a play," then it helps if the play, like *Slaves* and *Zara*, "makes liberal use of the word 'liberty' in a generic way and associates it with basic English values, regardless of political party." In keeping with Rowson's conciliatory approach to both the Algerian crisis and her audience, this was a concept that could easily accommodate fractious elements of a theater audience.[35]

33. Rowson, *Slaves in Algiers,* in Kritzer, ed., *Plays by Early American Women,* 62; Rowson, *Mary; or, The Test of Honour* (London, 1789), I, 34–35, II, 51.

34. Cobbett, "Kick for a Bite," in Cobbett, *Peter Porcupine in America,* ed. Wilson, 129, 133.

35. Richards, *Drama, Theatre, and Identity,* 147, 150.

In addition, *Mary* uses "liberty" in a way that illuminates *Slaves'* subsequent appropriation of the term. It could be argued the word meant something different in its British and American contexts. Mary, who wishes only to choose her own husband and, in pursuit of that goal, to determine her own "friends" and "visits," might have intended "negative liberty," pertaining to that which respected the individual, whereas the American captives, as newly independent citizens who found themselves pawns in an international crisis, had "positive liberty" in mind, having to do with the enfranchisement of a people. In that case, *Slaves* would be paying the United States a compliment by suggesting that the U.S. accomplished for a nation what England had up to that point understood in a more limited context.[36]

Another way of interpreting *Mary's* very personal understanding of liberty is as a gender-based practice that *Slaves* furthered quite effectively. In this case, Mary took an abstract concept and made it concrete to her readers. Whether or not the concept of political liberty meant much to the average novel reader, the thought of not being able to live daily life according to one's own precepts struck a chord, and it was women, precisely because they were confined to the mundane, who could make this transition from the abstract to the particular stick. Similarly, in *Slaves,* the word "liberty," although on virtually every page, is almost always spoken by women, suggesting that the play also used women's association with the concrete to intensify the affective power of perhaps the decade's (and American stage's) most omnipresent word. Since *Slaves'* agenda had little to do with American triumph over British naval and commercial policy and a great deal to do with expanding the rights of Anglo-American women like Rowson, whether newly arrived or not, *Slaves* thus gained, rather than lost, by appropriating a long tradition of British liberty lore. Nevertheless, the proximity of these two calls for female agency premised on distinct and often-oppositional national identities should remind readers today not to naturalize *Slaves'* rampant American patriotism.[37]

36. According to Gordon S. Wood, negative liberty is "the personal liberty and private rights of the individual"; positive liberty is "participation in government." Wood cited in Gary L. McDowell and Sharon L. Noble, eds., *Reason and Republicanism: Thomas Jefferson's Legacy of Liberty* (Lanham, Md., 1997), 120.

37. As Joseph C. Schöpp writes, "It was Rowson's deliberate strategy to replace the 'unfeeling world' of a hierarchically structured patriarchy by a world of affection in which women as its custodians could play a central role" (Schöpp, "Liberty's Sons and Daughters: Susanna Haswell Rowson's and Royall Tyler's Algerine Captives," in Klaus H. Schmidt and Fritz Fleischmann, eds., *Early America Re-explored: New Readings in Colonial, Early National, and Antebellum Culture* [New York, 2000], 291–307,

In fact, *Slaves'* over-the-top celebration of all things American helps its triumphant Anglo-American women deliver a very specific critique of their new nation. Despite the play's complacent fantasies regarding the beneficent effect of American might on those who brush up against it, its nationalist rhetoric, self-satisfied though it may be, is spoken by female characters and thus takes on a resonance it might not have held had the speakers stood to benefit more clearly from the wonders they described. One has the sense that the play's American women had to leave their nation even to speak its most self-congratulatory lines, and their words thereby assume an ironic aspect, with Algerian captivity obtaining a certain likeness to their situation in the United States even as they used their captivity to champion American liberties.[38]

No hint that Algiers is a distinct geographic realm with its own topography disturbs this likeness. Rather, for a play that takes place in a foreign land, *Slaves* presents a strangely sparse image of territory that would no doubt have made a striking impression on its captive inhabitants. One might attribute this instance of a "debased Oriental setting" in part to Rowson's obvious lack of familiarity with the landscape she described if not for the dozens of accounts that circulated regarding the region, including one penned by her own printer, Mathew Carey. Indeed, Rowson published *An Abridgment of Universal Geography* in 1805 and gave the Barbary States four large pages, situating each country exactly, providing climatological and zoological information, and describing religious practices (despite the general "oppression of their government," "all foreigners are allowed the open profession of their religion"), exports ("leather, fine mats, embroidered handkerchiefs, and carpets"), and more. In addition to providing a wealth of information lacking in the play, *An Abridgment of Universal Geography* illuminates an important motive behind this slighting treatment, as well as behind Rowson's negative portrayal of the region's inhabitants in both textbook and play. For the Barbary States represent a catastrophic vision of the American future. Like the United States, with its conceit of itself as

---

esp. 297). A later Rowson play was more willing to malign the English for patriotic effect. *The Americans in England; or, A Lesson for Daughters* casts its seducer as an English aristocrat who, "having ruined his fortune by dissipation and gaming, and obliged to quit his native land, repairs, under the assumed name of Ormsby, to *New England*." See "Theatrical," *Massachusetts Mercury,* Apr. 21, 1797.

38. On the play's protest against women's circumscribed position after the American Revolution, see Amelia Howe Kritzer, "Playing with Republican Motherhood: Self-Representation in Plays by Susanna Rowson and Judith Sargent Murray," *Early American Literature,* XXXI (1996), 150–166.

a Roman republic reborn, *An Abridgment* makes clear that "it can scarcely be doubted, that the countries which contained Carthage, and the pride of the Phoenecian, Greek, and Roman works, are replete with the remains of antiquity." Now, however, "they lie scattered, amidst ignorant, barbarous inhabitants." Present civilization, then, is no protection against a return to barbarity and may in fact, through luxury and over-refinement, invite such a fate. Rowson's lack of attention to anything unfamiliar that might have presented itself to her captives' view, then, can be far more readily attributed to the play's insistence that nothing of import would (or should) survive contact with these captives, since all was to be folded eventually into a strict republican self-governance that could not only protect the United States against such a fate but spread its formula for civilized "liberty" through-out the globe. Rowson would elaborate on this project in her later political verse.[39]

The play does not content itself merely with wresting power from the Algerians and bestowing it upon their Anglo-American former captives. It also insists that the Algerians want what the Americans have to sell. In a telling example of "the sentimentalization of political authority," wherein readers come to believe in the notion of personal agency at the very moment they have finally sacrificed it once and for all, the Moors of the play not only experience subjugation but come to look upon it as a new kind of freedom. The cruelest irony of Rowson's drama is that, when the dey and his under-lings are forced to give up their prized possessions, they consider themselves to have profited. These possessions are the Euro-American prisoners, who could have commanded, in historical fact as well as national literary fan-tasy, a pretty penny in ransom funds. In freeing the prisoners, the repentant kidnappers profit, they believe, not in material terms but rather because

---

39. Rowson, preface to *Slaves in Algiers,* in Kritzer, ed., *Plays by Early American Women,* 56–57; Rowson, *An Abridgment of Universal Geography, Together with Sketches of History Designed for the Use of Schools and Academies in the United States* (Boston, [1805]), 144–146; Gould, *Barbaric Traffic,* 33, 88. Joe Snader describes the mood of the play as follows: "Both the debased Oriental setting and the plot of subjugation and escape enforce an expansionist ideology by suggesting that autonomous and self-reliant Western captives possess a natural right and ability to resist and control the alien cul-tures that have enslaved them" (Snader, "The Oriental Captivity Narrative and Early English Fiction," *Eighteenth-Century Fiction,* IX [1997], 267–298, esp. 268). On actual captives' narratives that Rowson might have come across, see Fuad Sha'ban, *Islam and Arabs in Early American Thought: The Roots of Orientalism in America* (Durham, N.C., 1991), 76.

they have learned from their victims "how to practice what is right." Thus Rowson portrays the dey's entourage in a celebratory mood as they sacrifice both personal freedom and cultural independence. They express only gratitude to the "generous conquerors" with whom they have just exchanged jewels of inestimable value (territory, the income allowed by ransom, and a distinct worldview) for trinkets (a word—"freedom"—and the capacity to bestow it upon their only remaining underling, Ben Hassan).[40]

Rowson's achievements in the realm of gender equity are thus purchased at a cost to those whose vanquishing and conversion stand as proof of Anglo-American female righteousness. As Rowsonian heroines wrest their fates from the grip of circumstance to transform themselves from beggars to queens *(Trials of the Human Heart)*, from crazed single mothers to beloved martyrs *(Charlotte Temple)*, from widows to newlyweds *(Slaves in Algiers)*, and from captives to generals in a liberating force, their non-Christian counterparts, though similarly marked for change, seem to lose, rather than gain, in distinctiveness. Moreover, in that the Algerian men in Rowson's play conveniently come to share their opponents' values at the exact moment of the latter's armed takeover, the play appeals to a persuasion rendered the less independent by the simultaneous imposition of force.[41]

Furthering the drama's recourse to determinism in the service of a voluntaristic model of female citizenship, *Slaves* features many characters whose behavior is said to proceed from their geographic origins, either for better or for worse. According to the play's template for patriotic virtue, it isn't supposed to matter where one is born, only what one believes. Rebecca, as usual the mouthpiece for right thinking in the play, espouses the drama's supposed internationalism: "I am an American; but while I only claim kinship with the afflicted, it is of little consequence where I drew my first breath." Nevertheless, birthplace is mentioned obsessively throughout the first few pages as a means of depicting character. And as it turns out, in line with Rowson's

---

40. Rowson, *Slaves in Algiers,* in Kritzer, ed., *Plays by Early American Women,* 92, 93; Gould, *Barbaric Traffic,* 103.

41. Here, Rowson supports what Samir Amin calls the ideology of "universalism": "The new rationality calls for the democratic management of society and the supremacy of reason and gives rise, *by force of conquest,* to a unification of aspirations for a certain type of consumption and organization in social life" (emphasis added) (Amin, *Eurocentrism,* trans. Russell Moore [New York, 1989], 72). Islam is a particularly compelling vehicle for Western self-articulation given what Edward W. Said calls its "uneasily close" relationship with Christianity and its exception from the "continuous history of unchallenged Western dominance" of the rest of the Orient (Said, *Orientalism: Western Conceptions of the Orient* (1978; New York, 1995), 73, 74.

inability fully to render her Algerian characters—especially male—northern climes produce freer subjects and richer subjectivities. Rebecca's Algerian companion Fetnah, for instance, despite being "educated in the Moorish religion," turns out to be so good at learning what Rebecca has to teach because she "was not born in Algiers" and instead drew her "first breath in England." As a woman, it seems, Fetnah is capable of any self-transformation; but as an Algerian, she would have found Rebecca's teachings rocky going, so it is convenient that she turns out to be half-British (not insignificantly, on her mother's side). When Fetnah says of Rebecca, then, that "[she] came from that land where virtue in either sex is the only mark of superiority. She was an American," she sums up a central paradox of the play and of early national self-awareness within a global context. Apparently, one must hail from a very particular geographic locale to understand that circumstances of birth are irrelevant to determining individual worth.[42]

42. Rowson, *Slaves in Algiers,* in Kritzer, ed., *Plays by Early American Women,* 60, 61, 90. The clearest articulation of the correlation of personal worth to Anglo-American proximity in the Rowson canon occurs in *An Abridgment of Universal Geography,* which posits New England as the global center of moral authority and female worth, emphasizing widespread education and minimizing extremes of wealth and poverty. Although *An Abridgment* takes a great deal of material directly from Jedidiah Morse's popular *American Geography,* Rowson adds a telling sentence to his praise of Massachusetts: "For besides those already mentioned, there are academies sprinkled over the whole state, founded by the liberal donations of some of its late wealthy and judicious citizens, who, sensible of the necessity of education to render happy and prosperous any state or commonwealth, have, highly to their honour and credit, bequeathed part of their riches to promote so desirable an end." Rowson's position as director of a Boston-area academy no doubt played a role in this addition. Rowson identifies Morse by last name only in the preface, along with William Guthrie and John Walker. She also refers to William Robertson's *History of America* and the works of Abbe Raynal and alludes to Lady Mary Wortley Montagu, author of the "Letters, during Mr. Wortley's Embassy to Constantinople, 1716–18," as a "celebrated female traveller" in her discussion of Turkey. See Rowson, *Abridgment of Universal Geography,* 98, 177; Morse, *The American Geography; or, A View of the Present Situation of the United States of America,* 3d ed. (Dublin, 1792). On geography textbooks in the early national period, see Martin Brückner, "Toward a Morphology of National Geography Books," in his *Geographic Revolution in Early America: Maps, Literacy, and National Identity* (Chapel Hill, N.C., 2006), 146–158.

I will provide here just one example of Rowson's variations on Morse, which are fascinating and deserve further study. In the section on Lapland, many of the sentences are identical, or vary only in word order (Morse's "travels with a reindeer in a sledge" to Rowson's "travels in a sleigh, drawn by reindeer"). But Rowson significantly omits a portion from Morse's last paragraph on Lapland: "but it is understood to be the busi-

Further, the drama mocks those whose feeble attempts to escape their beginnings or put on airs only exacerbate the innate correspondence between their circumstances of origin and their true nature. Rowson sounded this theme in her attempts to distinguish between the deserving and the undeserving poor, as in *Mary,* where the evildoers are sure to be recognizable—like Mary's guardian's wife, Mrs. Fentum—from their aspirations to rise above their station. Here, however, to be poor and ambitious is not to be evil, or at least not seriously so, but rather comic. Consider, for instance, the Spanish captive Sebastian, who takes to the bottle a little too frequently. On one such occasion, he mistakes another of the play's objects of ridicule, the aforementioned Ben Hassan, for a worthy romantic partner, owing in part to the fact that Hassan has dressed as a woman in order to escape the dey and his guards. (Hassan, it bears mention, has been tricked into this absurdity by the American Frederic, who convinces him that the dey has caught on to his concealment of American slaves.) Their subsequent foolery is predictable, being that Ben Hassan started out selling "pepper-mint drops" and Sebastian descends from a laundress and a barber. Only these men sing the songs that allow the drama to "excite a smile," in Rowson's prefatory hope. Similarly, only Sebastian wishes to claim "the law of retaliation" against the dey and his cohorts at the end of the play, in a final demonstration of his inability to perform adequately as an American citizen.[43]

Thus there is a struggle between an appeal to our capacity for adaptation to changing circumstance and a shrinking from its risks through reference to innate characteristics—either of perceived national origin, such as the American love of liberty, or of ethnically marked and class-based personal tendency, such as a Jewish merchant's greed and deception or the drunken debauchery of a Spanish laundress's son. The result is that certain groups remain steadfast in order to serve as the poles toward and away from which the changeable characters tend. Rebecca, Constant, and Frederic, whose fortune it is to be white, Christian, and American, exemplify enlightened self-determination, whereas Ben Hassan and the servant Sebastian merely show forth their destined degradation the more they attempt to supersede it.

In between stands the North African Moor. The energy of the play stems

---

ness of the men to look after the kitchen, in which, it is said, the women never interfere." Without this addition, Rowson's last paragraph simply reads, "There is very little difference between the habits of the men and the women" (*Abridgment of Universal Geography,* 25, 26).

43. Rowson, *Slaves in Algiers,* in Kritzer, ed., *Plays by Early American Women,* 57, 65, 75, 79, 92.

not only from the white Christian Americans' attempt to resume their right-ful position as determiners of, rather than objects within, "the discursive strategies of empire" but also from the need to fix the Muslims' stance within such a framework. At times the Algerian men, with their "whiskers" and "great beetle brows" and their voracious sexuality, seem merely one more caricature in the play's stable of characters degraded by their inability to rise above appetite. At others they are given the opportunity to move from the position of viewed objects to that of active moral agents by adopting the values of their American slaves. It comes as no surprise that the key figures in this transition are, not the dey, but his female dependents.[44]

Manufacturing Liberty

Those familiar with Rowson only from *Charlotte Temple* might be sur-prised by the humor and energy to be found among the playwright's female personae. Where Charlotte's signature gesture was collapse, women such as Rebecca, Olivia, Zoriana, and Fetnah respond to their captivity, albeit of a very different sort from Charlotte's, with outspoken defiance. And although they are accompanied by a host of husbands, sons, lovers, and would-be swains, the adventure is indubitably theirs to lead. Women raise the money to buy the necessary arms; they assist in organizing the overthrow; they initiate the escape; and, perhaps most important, they utter the words that persuade their former captors to change their ways.[45]

Although women foster liberty, they do not often experience it without compromise. Instead, there is a strange admixture of independence and self-sacrifice in the female characters' actions and correspondingly in Rowson's model of female citizenship. The single most dramatic political gesture in the play is Olivia's proffered marriage to the dey—accompanied by her threatened subsequent suicide—in exchange for the freedom of her captive father. "Let me alone be the sacrifice," she pleads to Muley Muloc. Rowson's female Americans thus prove their eligibility for enfranchisement by testing their skill at the less pleasant aspects of republican citizenship.[46]

44. Snader, "Oriental Captivity," *Eighteenth-Century Fiction,* IX (1997), 267–298, esp. 268; Rowson, *Slaves in Algiers,* in Kritzer, ed., *Plays by Early American Women,* 60.

45. Walter J. Meserve, *American Drama to 1900: A Guide to Information Sources* (Detroit, Mich., 1980), 116. Adds Schöpp: "While Columbia's sons, verbally declaiming their liberty creed, play a rather peripheral role in Rowson's play, it is the daughters who move to center stage and become liberty's real agents" (Schöpp, "Liberty's Sons," in Schmidt and Fleischmann, eds., *Early America Re-explored,* 295).

46. Rowson, *Slaves in Algiers,* in Kritzer, ed., *Plays by Early American Women,*

What of the paradoxically situated North African woman? Like her American sisters, she plays a central role in the uprising. Far quicker than her male compatriots to adopt the signature love of liberty, she is essential to the American project of "educating" her fellow North African men. At the same time, she takes on some of the North African's taboo sexuality and is able to speak openly of her loves and lusts in a way her white female companions are not. As such, she allows her audience to enjoy imaginative indulgence in a lust they can then defer. As if to emphasize the risks of enacting this erotic independence outside the theater, however, the fate of the North African woman is unduly severe in an implicit act of atonement. In the end, Rowson's North African women show the ironic depth of their self-determinism by taking the self-sacrificial posture of the American woman to a new extreme.

The sexualization of North African figures pervades the entire drama and includes men. The play opens upon two competing articulations of this practice. The first scene introduces the Algerian slave Fetnah, "chosen favorite of the Dey," lamenting her confinement as she awaits an evening visit from her captor. As she explains to fellow slave Selima, her father, Ben Hassan, a Jewish convert to the Muslim faith and the owner of several Barbary pirate corsairs, sold her into slavery. Fetnah has recently discovered her longing for liberty under the mild tutelage of Rebecca. We next encounter Rebecca herself, reading a book and commenting aloud upon the "spark of intellectual heavenly fire" her activity inspires. She begins to soliloquize about her long-absent husband and enslaved son, when Ben Hassan enters her quarters. He begins, in heavy dialect, to alternate demands for a ransom he has in fact already received with equally illegitimate sexual propositions. Justifying his proposed amour through the conflation of political liberty with sexual license ("Our law gives liberty in love. You are an American and you must love liberty"), he allows Rebecca to introduce in response one of the signal themes of the play: that American Independence is dependent upon female self-regulation and, in particular, sexual restraint. Thus, drawing herself up to show forth in all her innate American matriarchal

88. Mary Anne Schofield suggests the vexed nature of Rowson's notion of feminine agency by paralleling three quite-unlike forms of "subversion": "Fetnah rebels against her father; Zoriana rebels against the patriarchal structure of Algeria by rejecting her oppressive religion; Olivia rebels against her fate by planning suicide" (Schofield, "The Happy Revolution: Colonial Women and the Eighteenth-Century Theater," in June Schlueter, ed., *Modern American Drama: The Female Canon* [Rutherford, N.J., 1990], 35).

authority, Rebecca puts a stop to the interloper's buffoonish prattle: "Hold, Hassan. Prostitute not the sacred word by applying it to licentiousness." Hassan's attitude marks him as unfit for the voluntaristic model of American citizenship Rowson both advocates within the play and exemplifies by means of it. Beginning with this proclamation, the play nicely anticipates the charge Cobbett brought against the kind of republic that would tolerate a performance of *Slaves in Algiers:* that according women a public voice both equates with and results in rampant sexual degeneracy. In opposition to his visions of social corruption figured as disorderly copulation, Rebecca and her fellow American slaves present a world in which the heady freedoms of political self-determination are kept in check by the equally strongly asserted female capacity for sexual self-denial.[47]

The play then presents increasingly onerous articulations of this dictum while bifurcating along a racialized divide between Anglo-American Christian female slaves and their non-English, non-Christian counterparts. Female American captives' facility at just saying no for the betterment of their nation seems painless enough at first. Hassan, after all, is both repulsive and reprehensible within the terms of the drama. But the enactment of an explicitly politicized female self-denial becomes ever more challenging as the play progresses. The difficulties are of two kinds. For white women such as Rebecca's long-lost daughter, Olivia, coincidentally enslaved in the same palace, the proposed sexual union that must be resisted is so repugnant as to make suicide a kinder alternative. For female Algerians enrolled in Rebecca's school of the Americas, meanwhile, the story is quite different. Possessed, unlike their chaste white teachers, of a natural "liberality," these characters' challenge is to resist an acknowledged erotic impulse for reasons that themselves seem none too inviting.[48]

To fully understand this dynamic, let us conclude our discussion of the play with a detailed look at two of its most compelling characters, Zoriana and Fetnah. Zoriana highlights the North African characters' status as lighter-skinned non-Europeans by being overtly based on Zoraida, the captive's love interest in Cervantes's *Don Quijote.* Zoraida is the "fantastically beautiful" daughter of a "highborn and rich Moor," whose "singularly white hand" is fond of dropping scads of money out of her bedroom window for the captive to use to free himself and take her with him. Like Rowson's Zoriana, whose beauty is also connected to her being both "fair" and "Mori-

47. Rowson, *Slaves in Algiers,* in Kritzer, ed., *Plays by Early American Women,* 59, 62–63.

48. Ibid., 69, 70.

scan," Zoraida has converted to Christianity under the influence of one of her father's female slaves and is frank in averring her love. Although Rowson takes the most explicit physical contact between Cervantes's Zoraida and the captive—in which she pretends to faint into his arms in order to avoid her father's wrath—and attributes it to the more playful and obstreperous Fetnah, Zoriana shares her Cervantean corollary's "liberality," her willingness to link her fate to that of a stranger and a slave by waving a stick out her bedroom window with a white handkerchief attached, containing a letter and a bundle of coins. After frankly confessing her "tenderer passion" to Henry and learning he is already betrothed to Olivia, Zoriana continues to acknowledge her attraction ("that I loved your Henry I can without a blush avow") while using her Christianity to transform lust into something new ("but 'twas a love so pure that to see him happy will gratify my utmost wish"). Managing to perform what she calls "a Christian's duty," however, she continues to experience contrary impulses: "My disappointed heart beats high with resentment," she admits, and in an "aside" she notes that she is "wretched" as Henry and Olivia are "blest." Zoriana thus walks a line between the sexless Christian virtue of what Cervantes would call the "high-born" white women in the drama and the carnal indulgence of the Jews and servants. She joins the comic figures in showing forth language's more sensual aspects by performing two of the drama's songs, albeit in a melancholy mode, while modeling her white companions' proclivity to instructive martyrdom by giving up her man. Zoriana invites subversive vicariousness precisely because she possesses the capacity to renounce such behavior before the evening's end.[49]

The half-British, half-Moorish Fetnah is even more sexually frank. The play's most physically courageous character, during most of the play, as "the

49. Rowson, *Slaves in Algiers,* in Kritzer, ed., *Plays by Early American Women,* 68–71, 85; Miguel de Cervantes, *Don Quijote: A New Translation,* ed. Diana de Armas Wilson, trans. Burton Raffel ([1605]; New York, 1999). The preface to *Slaves in Algiers* acknowledges that "some part of the plot is taken from the Story of the Captive, related by Cervantes, in his inimitable Romance of *Don Quixote.*" Erin Webster Garrett refers to Cervantes's Zoraida as a woman "half Moor (the body) and half Christian (the soul)" who "enters into self-imposed exile from her home culture in order to actualize a hidden and purportedly European self" (Garrett, "Recycling Zoraida: The Muslim Heroine in Mary Shelley's *Frankenstein," Cervantes,* XX, no. 1 [Spring 2000], 133–153, esp. 141). Julie Ellison writes, "The Moor, representative of sophisticated Mediterranean rim cultures, thus takes on some of the erotic possibilities of the mulatto in U.S. antebellum novels and is easily assimilated to sentimental or romance plots" (Ellison, *Cato's Tears and the Making of Anglo-American Emotion* [Chicago, 1999], 48–49).

spokesperson of [Rowson's] most radical ideas," Fetnah gives credence to the concept that the men in the play "claim superiority in words, while the females, by their deeds, demonstrate their intelligence and bravery." She is the mouthpiece for many of the signal republican themes of the drama, including its insistence that liberty is preferable to luxury (into the midst of reflections on the weather, she is fond of dropping lines like "'Tis a delightful garden, but I believe I should hate the finest place in the world, if I was obliged to stay in it whether I would or no") and its incipient feminism ("in the cause of love or friendship," she notes before setting off to rescue the captives, "a woman can face danger with as much spirit, and as little fear, as the bravest man amongst you"). Fetnah also embodies Rowson's "boldness in the treatment of female sexuality," whether describing the dey's "huge scimitar," wishing out loud that "some dear, sweet, Christian man would fall in love with me," or professing her attraction to the first such man to present himself after overhearing her wish: the "pilgarlic" (bald) Frederic. Dressing as a man in order to escape the palace, rescue her "dear instructress" Rebecca, and elope with her new beloved, Fetnah then initiates the chain of events that results in the captives' release and their captors' conversion.[50]

At the end of the play, however, she becomes its greatest study in contrasts. She turns into what she so admires, an American woman, not through escape or overthrow, but rather through an act of self-sacrifice that is an exact duplicate of the one originated by Olivia. It is the close of the evening; the Americans are free and offering certain of their African captors the opportunity to accompany them home, including Fetnah but with the notable exception of her father, Ben Hassan. Up to this point Fetnah is willing to defy the dey, dress as a man, escape the palace, and hitch up with a virtually unknown American man in order to "fly, together, from this land of captivity to the regions of peace and liberty." Now, however, she surprises everyone by placing filial duty ahead of personal freedom. Arguing that "while my father was rich and had friends, I did not much think about my duty; but now he is poor and forsaken, I know it too well to leave him alone in his affliction," Fetnah, whose first words have to do with her loathing for pretty cages, declines the Americans' invitation and decides to remain in captivity with the play's single most despicable character. Foregoing both her romantic dalliance with Frederic and an opportunity to join her admired friends on

50. Zoe Detsi-Diamanti, *Early American Women Dramatists, 1775–1860* (New York, 1998), 67; Sally Burke, *American Feminist Playwrights: A Critical History* (New York, 1996), 18, 19, 59, 73, 74; Rowson, *Slaves in Algiers,* in Kritzer, ed., *Plays by Early American Women,* 67, 72, 80.

their return to the United States, she becomes more American than ever she could have become merely by getting on a boat. Thus the Muslim women of *Slaves in Algiers* do not participate in the final good fortune of their American compatriots, who come to deserve their happy fates simply by being willing to give them up, whereas Zoriana and Fetnah's sacrifices have to be seen to be believed. Fetnah's rhetoric reflects this duality by progressing from giddy rhyme ("no bolts and bars, no mutes and guards, no bowstrings and scimitars") to ponderous prose reflections on "duty."[51]

If Fetnah's fate distinguishes her from the Anglo-American female characters of the play, it links her importantly with late-eighteenth-century female audience members in Philadelphia, Baltimore, and New York. For in choosing her onerous submission, she mimics the elite practice of deferential self-determination that Rowson made available to a wider American female populace. As an emblem of female liberty, Fetnah begins the play deliciously suggestive of eroticism, or "license." She then stages a militaristic overthrow that recasts "liberty" as the legitimizing ground for American global capitalism. Finally, she sacrifices her personal freedom as a salve to audience members concerned that female political agency posed a threat to their patriarchal world order. Daughters, she promised, would continue to defer to fathers, just as Muslims would forever defer to the Constants and Frederics of the Northern Hemisphere.

In sum, Rowson, who played Olivia onstage, made America's imperial potency abroad dependent upon female emancipation at home while articulating the self-imposed limits these "free" women would undoubtedly adhere to as a comfort to those who, like Cobbett, foresaw anarchy in a gender-inclusive polis. She thereby both flattered her audience and, by the obvious discrepancies between the position of the women in the story she told and in the one taking place back home, suggested that the enfranchisement of women was crucial to the realization of the play's dream. Those who wished to lay claim to national authority in a global context were thereby required to embrace a program of increased female agency—whereas those who welcomed female liberty were required to envision it as the self-sacrifice expected of true republicans. Making the celebration possible were the myriad characters for whom choice was never an option.

If focusing on the insistent divide between Moorish and white, Spanish and English, Jewish and Protestant words, fates, and worths allows us to situate the drama in its historical, political, and cultural moment, doing so

51. Rowson, *Slaves in Algiers,* in Kritzer, ed., *Plays by Early American Women,* 73, 77, 93.

without also attending to the dialectical process by which whites identified with their so-called inferiors limits that endeavor. Rowson hints at the capacity for Anglo-American female sexual play under an assumed name in her onstage delivery of the epilogue to *Slaves*. And she develops this experiment in a partially surviving play.[52]

Voluntary Association

In 1795, the Federal Street Theatre staged a Rowson ballad-opera called *The Volunteers*. This piece survives only as a vocal score, with words by Rowson and music by Alexander Reinagle. Just as *Slaves in Algiers* concerns itself with the Washington administration's first international crisis, *The Volunteers* addresses the first domestic one. During the Whiskey Rebellion of 1794, the president called out fifteen thousand militiamen from four states to suppress western Pennsylvania's rebellion against a distillery tax levied by Congress. Like its predecessor, *The Volunteers* employs the crisis to patriotic effect while staging Anglo-American political virtue in relation to a racialized other. Since the Whiskey Rebellion took place on native soil, Native American characters in this drama perform the ambivalent ethnicity previously assigned to the Algerians. In both cases, however, sexual politics and ethnic condescension intersect in important and troubling ways.

If *Slaves in Algiers* made gender equality dependent upon ethnic hierarchy, *The Volunteers* allows at least one of its nonwhite characters some independent worth. Since the full text of the play has been lost, it must be interpreted only provisionally. But what remains suggests two related developments from the previous play. First, *Slaves in Algiers'* fascination with sexual promise, threat, and loss gives way here to a more exclusive focus on the potential for female communion inherent within these dynamics. Second, *Slaves'* tendency to chart ethnic difference along a moral continuum is here in at least temporary abeyance.

Early in the score, two young women lament their departed lover in one voice: "I'll talk of all my Lovers charms his honor love and truth. The pitying powers to my arms restore the much lov'd Youth." Their words are identical throughout the duet. But in solo performances immediately prior to this song, we learn about their differing responses to their similar pre-

---

52. Fetnah's sacrifice is consistent with the feminist perspective that "in contesting with white men for a liberal humanist subjectivity, nineteenth-century white women joined with them in espousing Europe's imperial venture and, in so doing, denied subjectivity to women of color." See Smith-Rosenberg, "Subject Female," *American Literary History*, V (1993), 481–511, esp. 500.

dicament. Aura, a young, Anglo-American woman torn between her inclination for "dear Harry" (presumably off quelling the Whiskey Rebellion)
and her mother's preference for a "rich old miser" aiming to take her to
church Thursday next, stays in one spot, patiently awaiting Harry's return
("Come tell me that thy faithful heart, does still with tender passion glow").
Meanwhile, Omeeah—a Native American woman also smitten by an absent
soldier whom she knows only as "Dear Yankoo"—takes action: "O'er craggy
rocks I'll eager climb / thr'o dreary wastes I will pursue thee." Anyone who
has ever set off in quest of a missing companion only to be frustrated by that
person's like-minded decision to roam—or, conversely, anyone who's stayed
rooted to the spot while the other person remains similarly immobilized—
knows that, when two people are inadvertently separated, it's best for one
to loiter and one to search. But the question invariably asserts itself: who
should do which? Without the libretto, we do not know which, if either,
romantic strategy prevails or even whether the gentleman in question is, as
another Rowson lyric puts it, "worth the trouble." But if the "Duetto" frus-
trates the play's romantic search, it also leads us to alter our investigation
in important ways. It introduces the possibility that these two women, in
their willingness to harmonize their quest across a profound ethnic and cultural divide, might share something more important than with their absent
suitors.[53]

   Their cooperation is all the more surprising given the possibility that
they are singing about the same man. And there are suggestions to this
effect beyond their mutual fondness for the adjective "dear." The most significant indication that the two singers share the same romantic interest is
that the racially charged love triangle is a favorite device of Rowson's, as
seen above with Zoriana's dilemma. Even more telling is an incident from
Rowson's historical novel, *Reuben and Rachel* (1798), published three years
after Aura and Omeeah took to the stage. Here, two young women, one
Native American and one Anglo-American, are in love with the same man.
"Eumea," daughter to a Mohawk chief and a half-French mother, commits
suicide after Reuben, whom she has rescued from captivity and from whom
she has been instructed in all things European at her mother's request, weds

53. No text has been found from the third and fourth of Rowson's plays, *The American Tar; or, The Press Gang Defeated,* performed in 1796 and probably never published,
and *Americans in England; or, Lessons for Daughters,* performed in 1797. Rowson,
Volunteers, "Duetto," 10–12; Rowson, "He's Not Worth the Trouble," in J. Hewitt, com-
poser, *The Songster: Containing a Selection of the Most Approved Patriotic and Comic
Songs* (Haverhill, Mass., 1817).

one Jessy Oliver. "Omeeah" is enough like "Eumea" to establish both the former's status as a Native American and the likelihood that the two share the same problem. Disturbing this likelihood, however, is the fact that "Yankoo," despite sounding like "Yankee," is also the name of a Native American character in *Reuben and Rachel*.[54]

At the very least, Omeeah and Aura's identical lyrics highlight the fact that their lovers' return depends not only on the ravages of war but also on the fidelity of distant young military men. That is, each woman increases the other's likelihood of actually having to do herself in should her lover be denied her. Yet the duet occurs despite the romantic threat it only intensifies. Evidently, these women prefer an opportunity to share their suffering, even at the risk of increasing it, to a safer but silent solitude.

The interracial comity remains lopsided. In *Reuben and Rachel,* Eumea's mother wants nothing more than to have her instructed in European "language, customs, manners and religion." In this context, even Eumea's love for Reuben can be seen as yet another emulation of Christian white womanhood. In *The Volunteers,* the assumed superiority of the Anglo-American manifests itself in the vocal score's very architecture. Omeeah gets one solo song, Aura two; Omeeah sings beneath Aura, supporting her treble flights with lower tones; Omeeah may not even know her lover's given name. In this world of sentimental communion, then, certain subject positions remain implicitly superior to others.[55]

Regardless of how we view the two singers' thematic counterpoint, however, the fact that their relationship takes discursive precedence—at least in

54. Susanna Rowson, *Reuben and Rachel; or, Tales of Old Times: A Novel* (Boston, 1798), II, 293, 295, University of Virginia, E-Text Center, Early American Fiction Collection (1789–1875), http://etext.lib.virginia.edu/eaf/authors/shr.htm. James H. Cox, Carroll Smith-Rosenberg, and Eve Kornfeld focus on *Reuben and Rachel* to investigate Rowson's representation of Native American culture; see Cox, "The Power of Sympathy: European American Women Novelists Imagine Indigenous Absence," *American Transcendental Quarterly,* N.S., XV (2001), 191–207, esp. 193, 197; and Smith-Rosenberg, "Subject Female," *American Literary History,* V (1993), 500. For Kornfeld, *Reuben and Rachel* participates in both sides of a dual process wherein "the natural simplicity of the 'savage' can appear as humanity or barbarism" (Kornfeld, "Encountering 'the Other,'" *WMQ,* 3d Ser., LII [1995], 287–314, esp. 296). Steven Epley suggests that Rowson drew heavily from the legend of Inkle and Yarico in *Charlotte Temple* (Epley, "Alienated, Betrayed, and Powerless: A Possible Connection between *Charlotte Temple* and the Legend of Inkle and Yarico," *Papers on Language and Literature,* XXXVIII [2002], 200–222). The stories of Eumea and Omeeah retell this legend even more exactly.

55. Rowson, *Reuben and Rachel,* II, 295, 361.

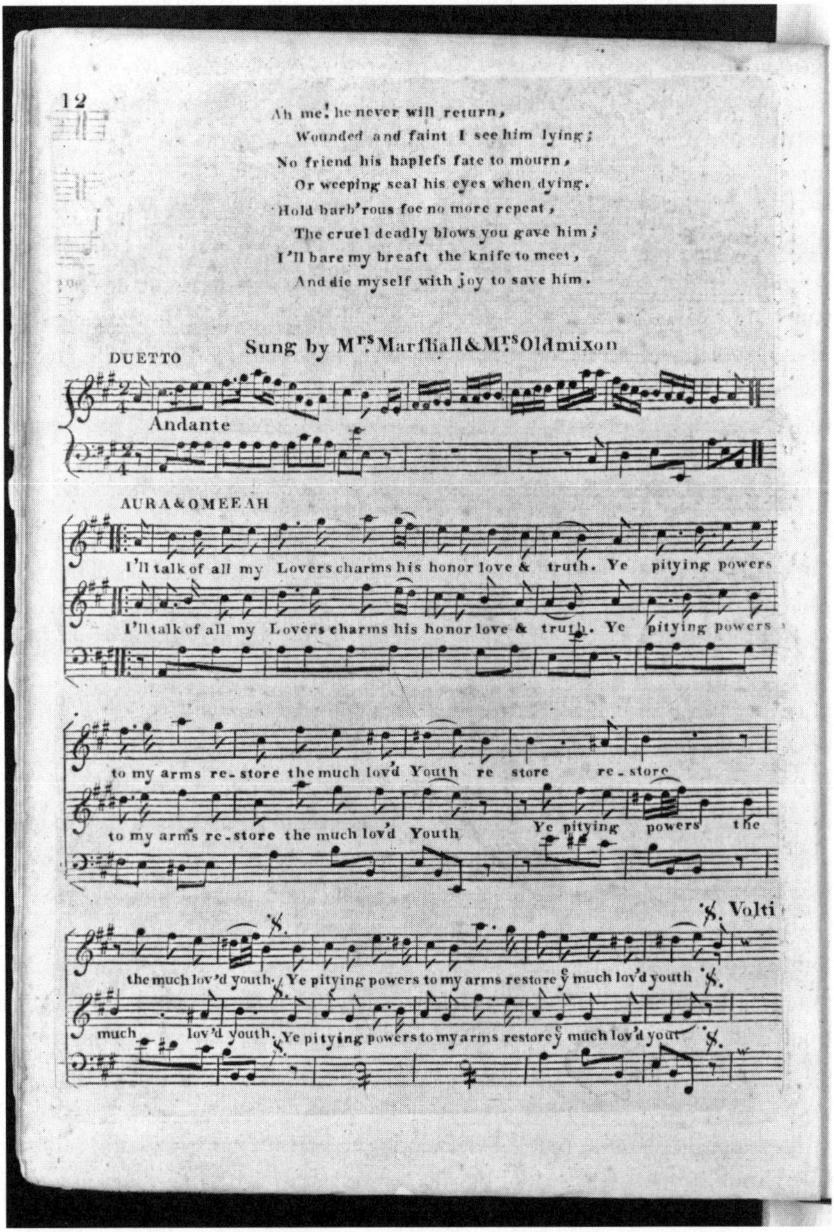

Ah me! he never will return,
Wounded and faint I see him lying;
No friend his haplefs fate to mourn,
Or weeping seal his eyes when dying.
Hold barb'rous foe no more repeat,
The cruel deadly blows you gave him;
I'll bare my breaft the knife to meet,
And die myself with joy to save him.

DUETTO Sung by Mrs Marfhall & Mrs Oldmixon

Andante

AURA & OMEEAH

I'll talk of all my Lovers charms his honor love & truth. Ye pitying powers

I'll talk of all my Lovers charms his honor love & truth. Ye pitying powers

to my arms re-store the much lov'd Youth re store re-store

to my arms re-store the much lov'd Youth Ye pitying powers the

§ Volti

the much lov'd youth. Ye pitying powers to my arms restore ÿ much lov'd youth §.

much lov'd youth. Ye pitying powers to my arms restore ÿ much lov'd yout §.

PLATE 19. *Vocal score for Rowson,* The Volunteers: A Musical Entertainment, as Performed at the New Theatre, Composed by Alex Reinagle *(Philadelphia, 1795).* *Library of Congress, Prints and Photographs Division*

the surviving text—over an imagined communion with a faintly rendered male figure has far-reaching implications. Omeeah's exclusion from full participation in the prevailing discourse ("I'll seek . . . one whose name I know not"), side by side with Aura's potential entrapment in the rites of patriarchal romance as her mother schemes to hand her over to an aging miser, speaks to the transatlantic author's acknowledgment that both exile and inclusion have their disadvantages. Although each woman's story alone makes for a rather standard dilemma and illuminates predictable issues (the fragility of female integrity before romantic love in a patriarchal culture), the two stories together highlight a far more philosophically rich set of issues, ranging from the potential for female comradeship in the face of heterosexual loss to the tenuous nature of a social fabric woven from discrete individual expectations.

"Future Story"

In the vocal score to *The Volunteers,* sexual union remains a marginal but nevertheless informing presence in a play based on current affairs. The next phase in Rowson's performance-oriented work involves yet a further investment in political crises but a temporary escape from both gender difference and sexual yearning. Instead, Rowson develops an abstract, male-identified poetic persona, as if to join the pantheon of classical deities with which these works demonstrate her familiarity and kinship. Rather than apologize for her limited training as a female author—a pose familiar to us from her novel prefaces—Rowson's later works in the decade, mostly poems, proudly display a rather considerable knowledge of and facility with a masculinist lore emphasizing the classical thematology of a Roman republic reborn.

If Rowson's novels constituted an imagined community of female readers and her drama spoke to a mixed-sex audience in terms of their particular gendered interests, her verses—read, spoken, and sung—also united participants. Not only did the poems address topical themes, but they were often performed as part of various public events. Her most lastingly influential ditty, known as "America, Commerce, and Freedom" for the last line of its chorus, has often been acknowledged as a rallying cry for a fledgling liberal public on its way to identifying personal gain with the common good, figured both within and across national boundaries. But many other songs also entered into the public realm in response to much-discussed military and political events, including the death of George Washington in 1799. The frequency with which Rowson's political verse was printed in collections dedicated to commemorating "the father and friend of his country" suggests her participation in a discourse of remarkable "expressive homogeneity"; the result of its role in constituting a "national affect, distributed among particular but not isolated persons." Moreover, numerous notations throughout the *Miscellaneous Poems* detailing what portion of which poem was spoken where and by whom indicate a degree of authorial pride in the part her verses played in the formation of national sentiment.[56]

Most of Rowson's explicitly political verses were written and performed between 1798 and 1800, during the earliest years of her Young Ladies' Academy in Boston. What led to this rather intense outpouring of support for the Federalist establishment? The most obvious answer, and one in keeping with Rowson's career path more generally, is that poems supporting the status quo reflected her desire to enter the ranks of Boston society. During Rowson's move from Philadelphia, now in its last years as a national capital, to Boston, something changed in her narrative self-presentation. For the first time, this mistress of conciliation became willing to take on unpopular points of view within the larger nation in order to win the approval of a more narrowly defined audience of Federalist leaders and their sympathizers. Since Rowson no longer earned her living from the wide swath of individuals able to pursue the "legitimate amusements" of novel or stage but rather from those few able and willing to send their daughters to private academies, it was to her benefit that she opposed the broader public will in this case. In this sense, her move from more universal to selective concilia-

56. Max Cavitch, "The Man That Was Used Up: Poetry, Particularity, and the Politics of Remembering George Washington," *American Literature,* LXXV (2003), 247–274, esp. 251. The national song "Truxton's Victory," subtitled "A Naval Patriotic Song, by Mrs. Rowson of Boston," was printed as a broadside in 1799 (Early American Imprints, 1st Ser., 49493). And her birthday ode to Washington, later published in her *Miscellaneous Poems,* was titled "Song: Written for the Celebration of the Birth Day of George Washington, Esq., and Sung on That Occasion, in Boston, February 11th, 1798." Rowson's work also featured prominently in the public outpouring in response to the death of George Washington, with at least three works appearing in 1800 alone. Ten lines from her "Eulogy to the Memory of George Washington" were included in an oration "delivered . . . before the inhabitants of Charlestown," Massachusetts, on February 22, 1800. The same year, an ode was included in *Hymns and Odes, Composed on the Death of Gen. George Washington . . . and Dedicated to Those Who Please to Sing Them!* ("Father and friend of his country" is from the full title to this collection.) This collection was meant for the use of "religious and social assemblies," and the readers were invited to "select whatever suits them best, and mourn the man of the age in sublimest strains." Finally, a "Dirge," scored for music, appeared in *Sacred Dirges, Hymns, and Anthems* commemorating the great man's death (1800).

tion betrayed a consistent regard for her public reputation as it pertained to her professional goals.[57]

Thus, however much of a peacemaker Rowson the playwright was in the middle years of the decade, by the late 1790s, Rowson the poet was an ardent and self-conscious Federalist, fiercely dedicated to maintaining the legitimacy of a party increasingly threatened by partisan opposition and citizen unrest in the wake of the unpopular Alien and Sedition Acts (1798). By this point, Rowson was no longer a newly arrived immigrant in pursuit of popular affection as an actress and playwright but rather a well-known member of a "Federalist-dominated stage," the Federal Street Theatre. Soon after, she was educating the daughters of the city's, and the nation's, elite. Where once she found it necessary to beg her readers for lenience, then, on both a personal level and as a representative of a hostile nation, she now attempted to secure public confidence within a distinct geographic context and historical moment, proclaiming as "high" a Federalism as her fiercest detractor—and with it, a forthright anglophilia. Correspondingly, she evinced outspoken disdain for French political and cultural interests, another sure audience-pleaser as Federalist and Republican alike became ever more afraid of Jacobin infiltration.[58]

As the letter that opens this book demonstrates, Rowson did not merely trumpet convenient political views when it served her public image to do so. She also demonstrated intense political affiliations in her private correspondence. Political verse appealed to Rowson during this period not only for its social advantages but because it was a genre that, contrary to her theatrical career, offered her the opportunity to write from an implicitly masculine perspective even as she claimed authorship with her own well-known female name. There are, in fact, no blushes or appeals to gender at all in these verses. Instead, Rowson assumes a radically gender-neutral poetic persona to trumpet the accomplishments, present and future, of the "sons of Columbia." In doing so, moreover, she demonstrates an easy familiarity with the very branches of knowledge that she so often claimed ignorance of in the prefaces to her novels. Finally, writing odes, dirges, and parodies about current events and civic leaders offered a unique opportunity to affect the decisions of those who could vote and hold office. Topical verse not only demonstrated the author's stake in the fate of her nation; it also could directly influence electoral outcomes.[59]

57. Richards, *Drama, Theatre, and Identity,* 301.
58. Ibid., 86.
59. Patricia L. Parker, *Susanna Rowson* (Boston, 1986), 19. This argument contra-

Rowson's political poems exemplify what J. G. A. Pocock calls "the age's intense and nervous neoclassicism," frequently representing the United States as a republic reborn from the ashes of Greece and Rome. In her epic "Standard of Liberty," Jove sends the Roman eagle, expelled from its fallen empire, to circle the skies until Columbia comes into view, where it can finally land. But unlike its corrupt predecessors, Columbia promises to remain timeless and eternal: "Nor fear thou e'er shalt be expell'd again: / Columbia's Standard ne'er shall know a stain." To capitalize on this eternal good fortune, however, the United States must unify under Federalist rule, which through its embrace of hierarchy at home and abroad can prevent Rome's fall to luxury, pride, avarice, "and every vice beside." Rowson's paeans to eternal Columbia, then, inevitably depend upon the rout of Republican dissent.[60]

If in 1794 Rowson could still represent Barbary pirates as most directly accountable for harassment of Americans on the Atlantic, by 1796 both England and France were actively engaged in harassing American ships. Diplomatic crises with France were particularly intense, beginning with the radical violence of the Committee of Public Safety in 1793 and 1794, which intensified domestic party strife. In 1797, the French Directory refused the American envoy, Charles Cotesworth Pinckney, sent to replace James Monroe. As Republicans were shut out of negotiations for a subsequent mission, Federalist President Adams and Republican Vice-President Jefferson almost immediately gave up any possibility of mutual consultation in matters of state, despite the fact that both parties were eager to halt French hostilities. Meanwhile, French seizures of American ships continued, and the Directory declared, in a curious about-face to the *Slaves in Algiers* plot, that any vessels carrying British goods would be treated as pirates. It was in the context of these two signal crises—a "quasi naval war with France" and the resumption of party strife within the administration—that Rowson composed the militaristic verses discussed below. Her work is thus typical of how Federalists used the bloodshed of the Reign of Terror to discredit

---

dicts Rowson biographer Dorothy Weil's observation regarding Rowson, "the poet and lyricist," that "the author's miscellaneous works reveal a point of view consistent with that of the novels and texts . . . the speaker is . . . the same mentor appearing in the other works" (Weil, *In Defense of Women: Susanna Rowson (1762-1824)* [University Park, Pa., 1976], 154). This may be true of much of Rowson's verse: it is not true of the works discussed here.

60. Pocock, *Machiavellian Moment,* 466; Rowson, "Standard of Liberty," in Rowson, *Miscellaneous Poems,* 94-97; "Strike, Strike the Chord, Raise, Raise the Strain," in Elias Nason, *A Memoir of Mrs. Susanna Rowson . . .* (Albany, N.Y., 1870).

Republican sympathizers, even as Republican leaders struggled to distance themselves from French revolutionary excesses by repudiating the new and more radically egalitarian Democratic-Republican societies.[61]

The "Parody on the Marseilles Hymn, Adapted for the Sons of Columbia," based on the French national song composed in 1792, lambastes American Republicans as agents of Jacobin dissent. This poem likely dates to about 1798, when another parody of the Marseilles hymn was performed and published as part of Josiah Dunham's Fourth of July oration in Hanover, New Hampshire. Like Dunham's, Rowson's parody addressed "Columbia's Sons," claiming that the triumph of American liberty over slavery depends upon the defeat of "Gallic tyrants." Although both figure the French threat as an approaching storm, the more militaristic Dunham verses maintain a strict boundary between "usurping Frenchmen" who threaten to "invade our peaceful shore" and the "injur'd Freemen . . . all hearts resolv'd" who oppose this encroachment at all costs.[62]

In contrast to Dunham's lust for carnage, expressed through repeated calls to "the avenging sword unsheathe!" Rowson's parody appeals to more ethereal impulses, such as how the person reading or singing these verses wishes to be remembered by his nation. In a gesture familiar to readers of her political poetry, she appeals to a nationalist sentiment figured, not as victory in battle per se, but rather the capacity such victories grant Columbian sons to exist in memory. The song commands them to "awake to glory," not through combat alone, but rather by maintaining a national unity that will allow them to "transmit your name to future story, / As learned, gen'rous, brave and wise."[63]

With this shift from mere military victory to subsequent unity comes a destabilization of the boundaries between friend and foe. How exactly is unity to be attained, when Jacobin agents have the ears of untrustworthy native residents? Insisting that both the French and the Francophilic must be opposed at all cost, the "Parody" suggests that Jacobin agitators and Republican dissidents are indistinguishable. It thereby sets the tone for later Rowson verse by making evident that pleas for "unity" are really pleas for

61. James Roger Sharp, *American Politics in the Early Republic: The New Nation in Crisis* (New Haven, Conn., 1993), 163, 164.

62. Susanna Rowson, "Parody on the Marseilles Hymn, Adapted for the Sons of Columbia," in Rowson, *Miscellaneous Poems,* 186–188; Dunham, "Parody of the Marseilles Hymn," in "Oration, for the Fourth of July," 15.

63. Rowson, "Parody on the Marseilles Hymn," in Rowson, *Miscellaneous Poems,* 186–188. The Marseilles Hymn was also published in New York and Philadelphia.

Federalist dominance, as it celebrates the urge to stamp out enemies both within and without the national boundary. If "Columbia's Sons" wish to be remembered, the song suggests, they had best look out for traitors close to home:

> Shall pois'nous reptiles, mischief brewing,
> With cringing knaves, a lawless band,
> Spread disaffection through the land,
> While mean and selfish schemes pursuing?
> . . .
> The breath of demagogues is howling,
> Their threat'nings gleam along the sky.
> And shall we tamely hear it roaring,
> Th' horizon with dark clouds o'erspread;
> While Liberty, with drooping head,
> See's democratic despots soaring?

Lest the point be missed that these "demagogues" might be posing as peaceful neighbors, the parody concludes by spurring on Liberty's children to remain "victorious" over "insidious friends." Hence the violence eschewed at its outset is reinscribed in relation to the project of rooting out internal dissent.[64]

Another song by Rowson, honoring an early naval victory and published as a broadside in 1799, focuses more explicitly on the enemy without. Like the Marseilles parody, this song uses martial victory as a platform for rumination on just how national sentiment is configured; and again, the capacity to project the national present into a future it determines plays a crucial role. This time, however, the song grants itself a constitutive, as opposed to merely instructive, role in this rhetorical process. "Truxton's Victory" celebrates the recent victory of the U.S. Navy frigate *Constellation,* under the command of Commodore Thomas Truxton, over the French ship *L'Insurgent* in a Caribbean sea battle. "Truxton's Victory" does employ the terminology of death's preferability to slavery, but in this case, the "knaves" that so conveniently rhyme with "slaves" are clearly French insurgents, not American sympathizers.

> Tho' Gallia through Europe has rush'd like a flood,
> And delug'd the earth with an ocean of blood;

64. Ibid., 186, 187.

While by *faction* she's led, while she's govern'd by *knaves,*
We court not her smiles, and will ne'er be her slaves.

To secure domestic autonomy and resist enslavement to false precept, the piece offers poetic "tribute" as a surrogate for the craven monetary tribute demanded by the French for American rights to Atlantic commerce:

Tho' *France* with caprice dares our *Statesmen* upbraid,
A tribute demands, or sets bounds to our trade;
From our young rising *Navy* our thunders shall roar,
And our Commerce extend to the earth's utmost shore.
. . .
Then raise high the strain, pay the tribute that's due
To the fair Constellation, and all her brave Crews
Be Truxton rever'd, and his name be enroll'd
'Mongst the Chiefs of the Ocean, the Heroes of old.

Patriotic verses such as the Marseilles parody and "Truxton's Victory" not only describe the dangers attendant upon military weakness and internal dissent but, in true mercantile Federalist style, figure the reward for military strength in terms of "extensive commerce." These martial airs thus helped constitute a national sentiment, figured in classical rhetoric, against the predations of Republican pretenders.[65]

During this same period, Rowson also worked to secure national unity through her participation in the national pastime of praising favored political leaders in meter and rhyme. Among these compositions were birthday odes to John Adams and George Washington as well as at least two eulogies and one dirge for Washington. Rowson's academy was eventually to join in the commemoration, with students transcribing Washington elegies and using Washington memorial prints to learn needlework.[66]

Writing before the passage of the Alien and Sedition Acts, Rowson celebrated Washington's birthday in a "Song. Written for the Celebration of the Birth Day of George Washington, Esq. and Sung on That Occasion, in Boston, February 11th, 1798." Its refrain associates liberty with order, and "independent" is figured as free "from anarchy." The song also expresses the hope that the nation will remain "from oppression secure." In the name of such security, measures were soon to be imposed that in fact seemed suffi-

65. Ibid.; Rowson, "Truxton's Victory."
66. Cavitch, "Man That Was Used Up," *American Literature,* LXXV (2003), 264.

ciently "oppressive" to many that they helped bring the Federalist era to an end with the election of Jefferson in 1800.[67]

Rowson made her sympathies with the Alien and Sedition Acts more evident in a poem dedicated to the man who signed them into law in July 1798. Ostensibly based upon similar laws in the United Kingdom and Canada in response to the threat of French radicalism, the massively unpopular acts aimed to silence Jeffersonian opposition through deportation, citizenship restrictions, and censorship. Rowson's "Ode on the Birthday of *John Adams, Esquire, President of the United States of America, 1799*" returns to the thematic structure of the martial airs while maintaining her commitment to Federalist rule even as it began to unravel. After reading about "great *Alcides, Jove*'s immortal son," the speaker wonders, "Where in these degenerate ages, / Can we a mortal find, / Like this recorded by the sages?" *Liberty* soon appears with an answer: "Columbia boasts . . . An equal hero's birth" in "ADAMS, greater far than [Alcides]." Adams's greatness turns out to reside in his capacity to maintain unity through force: he "trod base detraction to the earth" and "enforc'd the laws, / That made his country free." This reference to Adams's failed attempts to enforce the Alien and Sedition Acts goes against historical fact, since during the Adams presidency no aliens were actually deported, and only ten people were ever convicted of sedition. But it demonstrates Rowson's allegiance to the current administration by aligning Columbian might with the maintenance of Federalist rule through the enforcement of unpopular law.[68]

Why was Rowson so interested in writing poems about influential political figures between 1798 and 1800? It provided a doubly excluded (British and female) nonvoter the most direct route available to influence the political maelstrom engulfing the country in one of the most contentious presidential elections to date, the election of 1800. Interestingly, however, even when these verses informed contemporary debates through performance, excerpt, and inclusion in anthologies, they were subject to alteration in ways that minimized the pertinence of their commentary. This is nowhere more evident than in Rowson's longest, most-discussed, and most complex political verse, the "Eulogy to the Memory of *George Washington, Esquire*." As mentioned in an editorial insert to the "Eulogy" in *Miscellaneous Poems* in 1804, Josiah Bartlett performed ten lines from this poem in his oration com-

67. Susanna Rowson, "Song: Written for George Washington," in Rowson, *Miscellaneous Poems,* 60–61.

68. Susanna Rowson, "Ode on the Birthday of *John Adams,* Esquire, President of the United States of America, 1799," ibid., 32–39.

memorating Washington's death, on the day Congress specified for communal mourning, February 22, 1800. Bartlett, however, emended Rowson's text in several significant ways.

Rowson wrote:

Let this reflection dry a nation's tears,
He died as ripe in glory as in years;
And tho the loss of W is great,
ADAMS remains to guide the helm of state;
And would you prove the hero's memory dear,
Learn his last parting precepts to revere.
My friends, my fellow-citizens, said He,
Be still unanimous, be great and free;
For know, a state may soon be rendered weak
By foreign faction or by private pique;
Let not corruption e'er your judgment blind;
Preserve with care an independent mind;
Support, revere the laws; believe me, friends,
Your all on unanimity depends.
By faction, all would be to chaos hurl'd;
Be but united, and defy the world.

The contemporary reader is to be comforted for the loss of Washington by the fact that "ADAMS remains to guide the helm of state"; but in an election year, perhaps, Josiah Bartlett felt these lines compromised the authority of his oration. Whatever his reasoning, in quoting the "Oration," Bartlett skipped these two lines, going directly from "as ripe in glory as in years" to "would you prove the hero's memory dear." His quotation thereby takes an implicit suggestion to vote for Adams as an act of filial allegiance to the first president and transforms it into a more general paean to avoiding internecine conflict. Omitting the following four lines that end with "private pique" and substituting "contention" for "corruption," the excerpted verse greets the assembled audience as a global appeal to good behavior rather than the specific attempt to influence an election that it once was.[69]

What, then, does it avail the female authority on matters of state, capable of rendering them in verse spoken and sung, that she knows to invoke clas-

69. Susanna Rowson, "Eulogy to the Memory of *George Washington,* Esquire," in Rowson, *Miscellaneous Poems,* 44–54.

sical precedent as a platform for yet greater Columbian triumph? The poet claims not to envy Homer, who got to "sing the chiefs of Greece": she, after all, gets "matchless Washington." But however eloquently the female poet might stake her claim in a "united" nation, her attempts will be read through the ameliorative frame of literary discourse, itself a poor cousin to direct enfranchisement. Hence we might read the end of this brief phase in Rowson's authorial history as a reaction not only to a realigning election but also to the limits of print discourse to serve as a functional surrogate for the right to deliver, not merely be excerpted in, political orations.

On later occasions, Rowson ensured that no such misquotation could occur. Subsequent recitations of her work usually proceeded from the mouths of her own students, assembled for public exhibitions of the Young Ladies' Academy. Rowson's last novel emerges from this world to suggest alternative avenues for female civic empowerment to the realms of print and theater. It would seem that Rowson's last published works followed upon a foray into political discourse that, although it might have originated in little more than a desire for social position, resulted through its very frustrations in a concept of the female subject capable not only of accommodating post-Revolutionary reinscriptions of paternalistic authority but also of creating alternative spaces—schools and charitable institutions prominent among them—that functioned according to a different logic. It is to this logic that we will turn in this study's last chapter.

Epilogue

In the epilogue to her only completely surviving play, *Slaves in Algiers; or, A Struggle for Freedom,* Rowson famously addressed her female audience members as follows:

> Well, ladies, tell me: how d'ye like my play?
> "The creature has some sense," methinks you say;
> "She says that we should have supreme dominion,
> "And in good truth, we're all of her opinion.
> "Women were born for universal sway;
> "Men to adore, be silent, and obey."

The last two lines of this passage have often been taken out of context as an easy way of demonstrating Rowson's dedication to obtaining greater power for women of the early Republic. Such a reading, however, overlooks several things. It is a misreading of the play itself to suggest that it "says that [women] should have supreme dominion." In fact, *Slaves* takes women to new depths of self-sacrifice in the service of fathers, sons, lovers, and friends. This statement, then, is best interpreted as yet another sally in the battle of the sexes raging through popular print and performance culture at this time: a pointed joke, but a joke nonetheless. Making clear through exaggeration that obtaining "supreme dominion" is not the play's true agenda, *Slaves's* epilogue minimizes any potential antagonism from audience members unused either to female playwrights or female revolutionaries such as those whose onstage adventures have just come to an end. Rowson's subsequent enumeration of the activities contained within women's "universal sway" offers further comfort: beguiling sorrowful parents, cheering afflicted husbands, humoring and forgiving truant ones, and generally engaging in women's duty-bound notion of rights in the early Republic.[70]

The context in which this claim is made suggests that Rowson not only exaggerates women's authority here but also gently parodies herself. Before entering the stage, she responds to a prompter's urgings that she hurry, by proclaiming herself "in such a flurry" that she "must stop a moment just for breath!" Through her tardy, disheveled, and breathless entrance, she suggests both broad comedy and a degree of sexual innuendo. In light of this innuendo, the "sway" she jokingly claims for women clearly also has intimations of dominant erotic play. Moreover, by putting the subsequent claim to "supreme dominion" in the mouths of her female audience members ("methinks you say"), she includes them in her jest, attributing the same subversive spirit to them. As such, she grants them a degree of the humorous sexual license that she herself enacts.

How might we reconcile the drama's near-saintly white English emblems of decorum with Rowson's own flirtatious final turn, which was significant enough to be included in the published version of the play above the words "Written and spoken by Mrs. Rowson"? How, that is, might one reconcile her performance as Olivia to that of a disheveled playwright? Rowson's final appearance suggests that the contemporary American female audience members might have seen themselves not only in their playwright but also in other sexualized figures of more pronounced alterity. This imaginative commitment occurred both wishfully, as when Fetnah got to sing about her liberal attitudes toward love, and shamefully, when it became clear that the Moriscan women's fates were in many ways more akin to American women's current condition than were those of white female characters onstage.

70. Rowson, *Slaves in Algiers,* in Kritzer, ed., *Plays by Early American Women,* 93–95.

However it was perceived, Rowson's curtain call must have won her audience over. She appeared again to deliver the epilogue to her now-lost comedy of 1797, *The Americans in England; or, A Lesson for Daughters,* on April 18, 1797. According to a theatrical notice in the *Massachusetts Mercury,* "the applause was so great, that it was above a minute before she could attempt to speak, and her exit was followed by three distinct plaudits."[71]

At what point does cultural politics become political culture? When do standing ovations for a favored entertainer constitute a political body? Despite Cobbett's censure and her audience's praise, Rowson neither entered Congress nor married a politician. And her attempts to influence electoral outcomes directly by providing the text for public orations backfired when those who spoke her words changed them to minimize their strategic import. Rowson was welcome to express her support for those in power, but she was unlikely to alter governmental practice in any tangible way. Nevertheless, an opportunistic, socially conservative, and white Anglo-Protestant supremacist author, who frequently tailored her political views to the attainment of social stature, did indeed fashion a political culture out of her cultural politics. She did so by exhorting her mixed-sex audience to pay attention to national and international affairs of state and to assume women's relevance to governmental affairs that largely denied their existence. And she did so through her mastery of a variety of print vehicles that assembled individuals into like-minded public assemblies. Less important than the specifics of Rowson's partisan allegiance, then, may be the skill with which she purveyed her views to the largest possible number of people. Rowson started from the premise that every respondent to a text should consider herself in the company of every other; and she felt it her duty to bring this company

71. Ibid., 93–94. According to the detailed summary presented in the *Massachusetts Mercury, The Americans in England,* like *Slaves,* went heavy on didactic melodrama. It reprised the story of *Charlotte Temple,* with Courtland, a dissolute English aristocrat on the run from his gaming debts in New England, as the seducer. He persuades his conquest, Melissa, to travel with him to England in expectation of an honorable marriage. There, he installs her in a "house of ill fame" and begins to pursue a wealthy bookseller's daughter. Despite its extravagant melodrama, the play is allowed to finish up as a comedy because Melissa preserves her virtue, Courtland's treachery is discovered, and the four sympathetic young characters end up happily married. Thus, if Rowson began this epilogue in something of the playful mood that characterized her previous delivery, she would have established a pattern of narrating a cautionary tale from the perspective of a light-hearted, self-deprecating authorial persona. Clearly, audiences responded to this formula, as attested to by "the reiterated and unequivocal bursts of applause with which [the comedy] was received." See "Theatrical," *Massachusetts Mercury,* Apr. 21, 1797.

into a harmony of conviction. As such, she was a born politician, with all the label's positive and negative connotations, in a republic on its reluctant way to establishing some form of democracy. The culture she informed was ever less able to sustain the emblematic status of women who preferred, like her, to enter the fray.

Chapter opening

chapter **5**

NOVEL SCHOOLROOMS

> *I shall be employed about things, not words.*
> —*Mary Wollstonecraft,* A Vindication of the Rights of Woman

In 1787, in a lecture at the Young Ladies' Academy of Philadelphia, prominent citizen, physician, and esteemed University of Pennsylvania chemistry professor Benjamin Rush delineated the benefits of a pragmatic education for American women. Favoring bookkeeping and geography over French, vocal music over instrumental—and history, travels, poetry, and moral essays over the British novel—Rush exhorted his listeners to prepare to play a crucial role in determining a national character as distinct from Britain's. Unlike the British, Rush argued, Americans' sentiments ranged within modest bounds. Rather than form female education on a model that did not suit "our present manners," best "to study our own character . . . and to adopt manners in every thing, that shall be accommodated to our state of society, and to the forms of our government." In particular, as far as female education went, it was "incumbent upon us to make ornamental accomplishments, yield to principles and knowledge, in the education of our women." The whole nation would benefit: "Let the ladies of a country be educated properly, and they will not only make and administer its laws, but form its manners and character."[1]

The stated potential of female education to work to the national benefit speaks to "the discursive foundation of national legitimacy" in the United States. Women, and in particular married women (such as Rush rightly assumed many Ladies' Academy students would soon be), did not own much else besides their words. Eighteenth-century Anglo-American marriage was an economic institution characterized by the English common-law system of coverture, in which "rights to women are held by men" and "women are in no position to realize the benefits of their own circulation." In practical

---

1. Benjamin Rush, *Thoughts upon Female Education, Accommodated to the Present State of Society, Manners, and Government, in the United States of America*. . . . (Boston, 1787), 12, 20, Early American Imprints, 1st Ser., 20691. Rush was also a founder of the Philadelphia Young Ladies' Academy.

terms, this meant that "married women could not own personal property in their own names, could not make contracts, including for the management of any realty, wills, or even for their own labor, and could not, with few exceptions, appear in court. Coverture, therefore, not only deprived women of property, the most significant source of power and status in early modern society, but it also denied them access to the legal system." In this regard, the Revolution was no revolution at all for women, since "in one way or another, everything women owned before marriage became their husbands' afterwards." Thus to claim women's importance to the national project was to foreground the significance of utterance over object in constituting the new Republic.[2]

If women represented the promise behind a discursively founded national legitimacy, however, they also possessed the power to subvert it. For Rush, this disruptive capacity was implicit in "that passion for reading novels, which so generally prevails among the fair sex." Far from training readers in "acts of humanity," novels excited an "abortive sympathy" that "blunts the heart to that which is real," wasting women's communicative powers on specters rather than flesh and blood. Lest one wonder whether Rush included Rowson's work among these "British novels," he specifies her most influential heroine by name: "Hence, we sometimes see instances of young ladies, who weep away a whole forenoon over the criminal sorrows of a fictitious Charlotte or Werter, turning with disdain at two o'clock from the sight of a beggar, who solicits in feeble accents or signs, a small portion only, of the crumbs which fall from their fathers' tables." Although these individuals might have stepped right out of one of the novels he cautions his audience against (the Mossop sisters, perhaps?), the fact remains that, despite his own evident comfort with sentimental discourse, Rush did not find such fare suitable for young ladies.[3]

2. Christopher Looby, *Voicing America: Language, Literary Form, and the Origins of the United States* (Chicago, 1996), 15; Rush, *Thoughts upon Female Education,* 6; Gayle Rubin, "The Traffic in Women: Notes on the 'Political Economy' of Sex," in Joan Wallach Scott, ed., *Feminism and History* (Oxford, 1996), 105–151, esp. 118, 124; Karin Wulf, *Not All Wives: Women of Colonial Philadelphia* (Ithaca, N.Y., 2000), 3; Marylynn Salmon, *Women and the Law of Property in Early America* (Chapel Hill, N.C., 1986), xv, 41.

3. Rush, *Thoughts upon Female Education,* 12. "Werter" probably refers to *The Sorrows of Young Werther (Die Leiden des jungen Werthers),* by Johann Wolfgang von Goethe, first published in 1774. Susan Scott Parrish observes that a mid-eighteenth-century naturalist, Griffith Hughes, "included women in his audience and in the hetero-

The power of women and their novels to do harm bespeaks the skepticism that lurked behind the hope that a nation might "declare" itself into being. The Declaration of Independence was "at once *referring* to the nation-state (as if it already existed) and *instituting* it (since it did not yet exist), creating by the Declaration the independent political entity that was the only legitimate author of that Declaration." And even if language could magically establish what it claimed was already "self-evidently" true, it was less successful at erasing what it claimed was false, since it tended to invoke the very thing whose absence was specified. Thus, although it was entirely possible to start a revolution by means of performative utterance, it was hard to contain the energies unleashed thereby—to stop people from throwing off the shackles of precedent or authority merely by saying, "Stop it." Stop what? By specifying what "it" was, the prohibitive utterance necessarily put into the world the very thing it would eradicate. And novels in particular placed a premium on the capacity of language to create what it described. This is why Rush considered "moral essays," and not novels, legitimate reading for young women. (It is probably also why novels remained more popular than moral essays.) And this is why novels spoke to women in particular, who were already living the less-salutary effects of the American Revolution and knew intrinsically, therefore, the capacity of language to betray its own promises. By manipulating this register of contradiction, we have seen, Rowson served the women of the new Republic well, teaching them that, if language did not always deliver on its claims, it nonetheless offered many opportunities—subtle and not so subtle—for subversion and subterfuge.[4]

---

social scene of natural history, yet he delineated for them a distinct relationship to nature and to knowledge, associating men with natural philosophy and its central attribute of disinterested curiosity and associating women with imagination, artifice, and the need for improvement." This outlook presages Rush's above, in that it both includes women in the audience and the "scene" of advanced education, but finds them peculiarly susceptible to the dangers of a genre that cultivated "imagination" and "artifice," and, moreover, suggests that they "need . . . improvement." See Parrish, *American Curiosity: Cultures of Natural History in the Colonial British and Atlantic World* (Chapel Hill, N.C., 2006), 174.

4. Looby, *Voicing America,* 23. Gillian Brown linked this crisis in self-authorization to the early national emphasis on distressed female bodies: "The oft-noted late-eighteenth-century feminization of sensibility worked to contain specters of consent in female bodies. Representations of anxieties about, and hopes for, the nation founded upon consent accordingly took the form of narratives about women in trouble." Although I agree that such narratives served this purpose, I focus here on what they did for the women themselves, whose concerns were often more local and immediate than

By the time Rowson got to her last novel, which was being announced in the papers as shortly forthcoming even as she approached death, she seemed finally to have taken Rush's chastisement to heart. Tiring of indirection, she attempted to write a novel that did exactly what it said. To our benefit, perhaps, and despite the many safeguards the novel instituted, she was unable to control her production as well as she might have liked, and not only because she died before it could be published. For, like its parent text *Charlotte Temple, Lucy Temple* introduces the things it eschews to salutary effect. If Charlotte's passivity was as deeply inviting as it was rigorously disavowed, Lucy's emphasis on personal, and particularly erotic, sacrifice for the good of the community makes itself known in a novel imbued with a selfish fascination with wealth and a sense of immense, unreciprocated longing. For all that *Lucy Temple* championed the virtues of celibate public service as a worthy alternative to marriage for Rowson's own graduating students, it also taught female readers to acknowledge both the significance of financial well-being and the erotic longing that contemporary expectations were channeling into the very act—marriage—that would take their financial future out of their hands.[5]

In 1797, the same year Rowson last appeared on stage, she opened Mrs. Rowson's Young Ladies' Academy in Boston. Between 1805 and 1822, when she retired from the academy just two years before her death, she wrote and published four textbooks, a series of biblical dialogues, and a

---

the fate of the nation, precisely because they were being used to articulate that fate. In this regard, I see women as part of "the multitude" in Michael Hardt's and Antonio Negri's extension of the contradiction Looby names from the nation to the people: "The identity of the nation and even more so the identity of the people must appear natural and originary. We, by contrast, must de-naturalize these concepts. . . . Although 'the people' is posed as the originary basis of the nation, *the modern conception of the people is in fact a product of the nation-state,* and survives only within its specific ideological context. . . . The people is somewhat that is one, having one will, and to whom one action may be attributed; none of these can be properly said of the multitude. . . . Whereas the multitude is an inconclusive constituent relation, the people is a constituted synthesis that is prepared for sovereignty." See Brown, *The Consent of the Governed: The Lockean Legacy in Early American Culture* (Cambridge, Mass., 2001), 112; Hardt and Negri, *Empire* (Cambridge, Mass., 2000), 103.

5. Rowson died March 2, 1824. On March 8, 1823, the *Providence Patriot* ran a "literary" notice announcing that "Mrs. Rowson, of Massachusetts, author of that interesting novel, 'Charlotte Temple,' is now employed in preparing for the press a sequel to that tale, entitled 'Charlotte's Daughters, or the Three Orphans.'" Unless otherwise specified, references to *Lucy Temple* throughout this chapter will be to Susanna Rowson, *Charlotte Temple and Lucy Temple,* ed. Ann Douglas (New York, 1991).

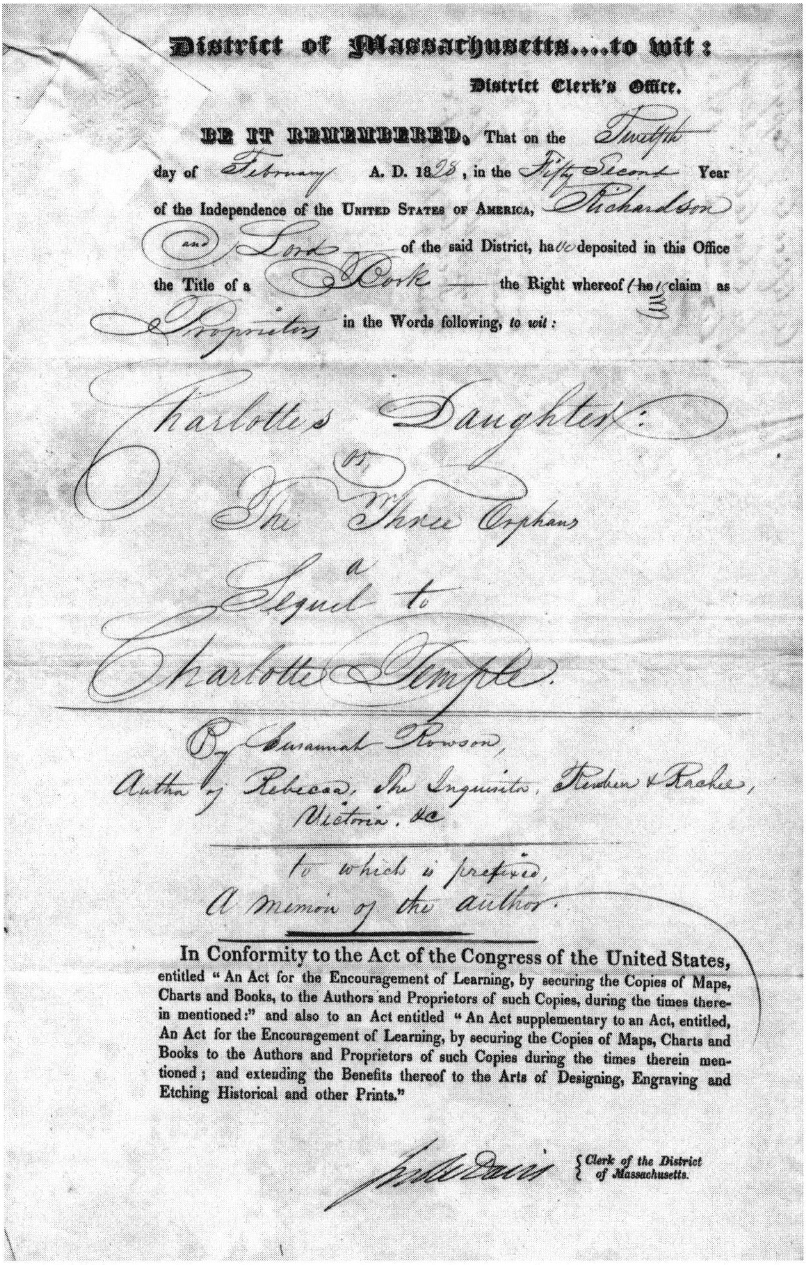

PLATE 20. *Copyright agreement for Rowson,* Charlotte's Daughter;
or, The Three Orphans *(Boston, 1828). Papers of Susanna Rowson, MSS 7379,*
Clifton Waller Barrett Library of American Literature, Special Collections,
University of Virginia Library

collection of recitations from the academy's yearly exhibitions. Despite her claim in the preface to *Reuben and Rachel; or, Tales of Old Times* (1798) that she was done with novels, she also wrote one. First appearing posthumously in 1828 as *Charlotte's Daughter; or, The Three Orphans,* with a memoir of the author by her friend Samuel Knapp, the novel went through some thirty-one editions (and several titles) to become Rowson's second most popular work, generally known as *Lucy Temple.* (Critics generally accord her *Rebecca; or, The Fille de Chambre* the honor of being the second most popular work during her lifetime.) Allusions throughout the novel suggest that it was written toward the end of her career directing the school. For instance, she includes a reference to "the cause of the orphan, and . . . the widow" commensurate with her participation in the Fatherless and Widows' Society, of which she was elected president in 1820. That *Lucy Temple* is unabashedly didactic, and that its protagonist becomes a teacher, does not surprise.[6]

Where earlier Rowson works such as *Trials of the Human Heart* and *Slaves in Algiers* seemed to protest too much in announcing their reformative intent between embraces, no one could accuse this novel of being too sexy. In fact, here the author doesn't concern herself much with chastity— or its loss—at all; she's far too busy documenting the financial affairs of her protagonists. In *Lucy Temple,* the worst thing a young woman can give up is, not her virginity, but her passbook. Nor is this merely a novel about the management of money—it concerns economy at every level. One key to the emotionalism characteristic of a sentimental narrative such as *Charlotte Temple* is that the reader is encouraged to identify strongly with a single, threatened protagonist. This novel, however, has three. Readers are invited to diversify their emotional investment instead of having a single and none-too-reliable object of attachment monopolize their sympathies. If we think of "economy" in its wider sense as "the organization, internal constitution, apportionment of functions, of any complex unity," and we think of a book as one such "complex unity," the novel thus operates at a formal level in a way that reflects its thematic concerns. Just as it harps endlessly about the

---

6. The *Christian Watchman and Baptist Register* announced that "Susannah" Rowson was chosen as president of the Fatherless and Widows' Society at its fourth annual meeting and first public celebration (Oct. 14, 1820). During the Revolution, the British had donated proceeds from their Boston theatrical productions to the "Widows and Children of the Soldiers." Rowson's theatrical background, then, might have placed her in good stead with this association. See Jeffrey H. Richards, *Drama, Theatre, and Identity in the American New Republic* (Cambridge, 2005), 149; Ellen B. Brandt, *Susanna Haswell Rowson, America's First Best-Selling Novelist* (Chicago, 1975).

best way to distribute limited resources, either to make a poverty-stricken existence tolerable or a wealthy one just, it makes us prudent readers.[7]

Lucy Temple emphasizes economy three ways: semantically (using monetary signifiers), normatively (phrasing moral worth as a matter of correct expenditure and creating a closed system in which charitable giving correlates with behavioral modification on the part of the recipient), and structurally (in the system of attachments it invites between its implied reader and its three main characters). At the first level, the book loves cash: coins and bills lie strewn across its pages. At the second, the ethical value the novel ascribes to financial transactions is apparent not only in its substitution of financial for sexual expense as the signature trope of female depravity but also in its linking of charitable giving to moral reform. Finally, the novel's contract with its reader emphasizes measured and diversified attachment over large-scale investment in a single source, in pursuit of a system of affectual exchange in which the participants are protected against devastating loss. This chapter, then, discusses money in the book and the book as an economy in the term's definition above. As it turns out, however, the two—economy in the book and the book as economy—don't sit comfortably together, since the lavish discursive expenditure of the former contradicts the novel's symbolic and structural emphasis on thrift. And it is this discomfort that saves the book from its otherwise justly deserved reputation as a "conservative" text whose main agenda is self-regulation on the part of its female readers.[8]

By attending to the substitution of money, in *Lucy Temple,* for the sex alluded to in both *Charlotte Temple* and the novel of seduction that early work obliquely engaged, we come to appreciate the depth of the author's yearning late in life for a satisfactory model of human intimacy to stand in for the treacheries of "gender, obligatory heterosexuality and the constraint of female sexuality." To a certain degree, Lucy Temple's dedication to learning—and *Lucy Temple's* dedication to teaching—money management skills to single women did, in fact, substitute a more reliable model for relating to the outside world than the asymmetrical economic and affectual exchanges of "heterosexual unions [insured] by means of economic interdependency." But these educational activities also reinscribed the very excesses they meant to evade. And it is in these reinscriptions that we finally and perhaps only temporarily escape the introjection of authority commonly said to attend

7. *Oxford English Dictionary,* 2d ed., s.v. "economy"; Susanna Rowson, *Lucy Temple: Charlotte's Daughter,* ed. Christine Levenduski (Albany, N.Y., 1992), 259.

8. Karen Weyler, *Intricate Relations: Sexual and Economic Desire in American Fiction, 1789–1814* (Iowa City, 2004), 81.

upon the nineteenth-century domestic world of maternal regulation. *Lucy Temple* pays perhaps unwitting tribute to the possibility that knowledge and power are not completely conflated in the bourgeois subject, to precisely the degree that the novel's plan to make affectual exchange (here tracked by the sign of the coin) the basis for knowledge (here phrased as the capacity for measured attachment) fails.[9]

This chapter makes a case for how Rowson's experiences as a pedagogue informed her last published work, allowing it to teach in new ways while maintaining the Rowson novel's signature productive tension between cautionary diatribe and invitation to indulgence, between that which it warned against and that which it performed. In *Lucy Temple,* the medium of exchange is money as opposed to sexual fluids, and the tension is between monitory calls to thrift and its mess of financial signifiers. But if Rowson, in profound disillusionment with heterosexual economies of affect, turns away from romantic attachment once and for all in her last book, she does not thereby give up on the salvific force of love. Rather, she locates sustaining and ardent affection, not in marital relationships, but in the exchanges of the schoolroom.

Exploring Rowson's teaching methods and experiences will show how she reconceptualized female education as dependent upon a passionate attachment between teacher and student, one capable of fostering innovative learning as well as willing obedience. The chapter will then demonstrate how this pedagogical model informs the didacticism of her last novel. Rowson can't resolve the tension between the descriptive and normative registers of the early American novel, but she can make use of this paradox to suggest that, far from treating desire as an obstacle to independent learning, we would do well to treat the two in uneasy but profound alliance.

Paralleling the tension between edict and depiction characteristic of the Rowsonian novel, literate Anglo-American women between 1790 and 1830 experienced a disjunction at the heart of their everyday existence. On the one hand, they were increasingly present in public life: as wage earners, as authors, editors, and teachers, as participants in a wide variety of so-

9. Rubin, "Traffic in Women," in Scott, ed., *Feminism and History,* 121, 122. Maternal regulation is emblematized in such influential models of intersubjectivity as Jay Fliegelman's "soft compulsion" and Richard Brodhead's "disciplinary intimacy," discussed ahead. See Fliegelman, *Declaring Independence: Jefferson, Natural Language, and the Culture of Performance* (Stanford, Calif., 1993), 40; Brodhead, *Cultures of Letters: Scenes of Reading and Writing in Nineteenth-Century America* (Chicago, 1993), 21.

cial affiliations, including benevolent societies (such as the Fatherless and Widows') and reading groups (such as the reading class that probably discussed Rowson's "Sketches of Female Biography"). We have seen throughout this book, however, that along with women's increasing public presence occurred an equally intense privatization of the domestic sphere in which economic consumption was emphasized over production and where wifehood and maternity were seen to show forth women's innate capacity for sympathy and nurture, creating a refuge from the competitive ethos of the commercial realm. As Elisabeth Anthony Dexter argued persuasively two generations ago:

> It seems certain that a larger proportion of women worked outside their homes in the years after 1776 than earlier, and that a number of new opportunities were gradually opened to them, but that new restrictions and handicaps developed also. A working woman of—say—1760, was considered simply on her own merits. After 1800 or thereabouts, such a woman was self-conscious, and her neighbors critical. She was no longer just an individual trying to earn a living; she was a female who had stepped out of the "graceful and dignified retirement" which so well became her sex. Her emergence might be praised or blamed; it could not be taken as a matter of course.

And G. J. Barker-Benfield a generation later:

> At the beginning of the nineteenth century in America . . . the urban, trend-setting women, the "women of the future," were placed in a difficult position, caught between new possibilities and the need for a response to the special demands that men made of them. Industrial growth and the phenomenal shaping of American history in the nineteenth century were inalienable from the male attitude that demanded not only that the two styles of life, male and female, be separate, but that women should remain subordinate, and in the home.[10]

10. On female wage earning, see Marion Rust, "Measuring Pleasure: Susanna Rowson and Sentimental Agency, 1754-1817" (Ph.D. diss., Stanford University, 1997), 103. On the reading group mentioned above, see Mary Kelley, *Learning to Stand and Speak: Women, Education, and Public Life in America's Republic* (Chapel Hill, N.C., 2006), 200-201; Susanna Rowson, "Sketches of Female Biography," in Rowson, *A Present for Young Ladies, Containing Poems, Dialogues, Addresses, Etc. Etc. Etc. . . . .* (Boston, 1811), 83-122. Mary Beth Norton describes the significance of voluntary societies to nineteenth-century American northern women; see her *Liberty's Daughters:*

If there was one area in which these tensions made themselves most evident early in the century, it was female education. Here, too, radical changes took place over the course of thirty years. In the early Republic, only a small percentage of the national population received any higher education. By 1830, the United States boasted 182 female academies and at least 14 female seminaries. (The term "academy" generally referred to any school that offered more than the reading, writing, and ciphering offered in the common schools.) Rowson's school for girls, though among the earliest, was preceded by others, important among them the Young Ladies' Academy of Philadelphia, founded in 1787, and Sarah Pierce's Litchfield Female Academy, founded in 1792. In general, the students at these schools ranged from about twelve to twenty and stayed about three years.[11]

Between the 1790s (Charlotte's decade) and the 1820s (Lucy's), significant changes took place in the lives of these students. The post-Revolutionary elite was able to posit white Americans as a single community in which middling and lower orders deferred to them. Female schooling largely operated to maintain this sense of entitlement and unity through the teaching of "social accomplishments," from music and drawing to French and penmanship (some early republican academies taught a particular, exclusively female orthography drawn from Italian). The "performance of sociability" was tantamount. In this context, female authority, although not as great as male, was based on sameness with men, and heterosocial spaces dominated the social landscape.

By 1820, however, white Americans could no longer see themselves as one. As civil society became less coherent, it also became more recognizably

The Revolutionary Experience of American Women, 1750–1800 (1980; rpt. Ithaca, N.Y., 1996), 306–307. On the household's relationship to consumption, see Lori Merish, *Sentimental Materialism: Gender, Commodity Culture, and Nineteenth-Century American Literature* (Durham, N.C., 2000). On sentimentalized domesticity as a means of rationalizing capitalist economic practice, see Gillian Brown, *Domestic Individualism: Imagining Self in Nineteenth-Century America* (Berkeley, Calif., 1990). For an examination of the complicity of hegemony and resistance in nineteenth-century domesticity, see Lora Romero, *Home Fronts: Domesticity and Its Critics in the Antebellum United States* (Durham, N.C., 1997). On changing patterns of female sexuality, see Clare A. Lyons, *Sex among the Rabble: An Intimate History of Gender and Power in the Age of Revolution, Philadelphia, 1730–1830* (Chapel Hill, N.C., 2006); Elisabeth Anthony Dexter, *Career Women of America, 1776–1840* (1950; Clifton, N.J., 1972), 219; G. J. Barker-Benfield, *The Horrors of the Half-Known Life: Male Attitudes toward Women and Sexuality in Nineteenth-Century America* (1974; New York, 2000), 20.

11. Kelley, *Learning to Stand and Speak,* chap. 3, esp. 67.

variable, including women in acknowledged leadership roles as teachers, authors, editors, and members of benevolent and reform societies. Over the course of thirty years, female authority came to be based increasingly on women's difference from men, and homosocial spaces began to dominate the social landscape. As the self-defined elite expanded to include more and more of the middling sort, attaining the behavioral requirements that connoted genteel womanhood became possible to a wider spectrum of the population—and also became more incumbent as punitive measures against the truly poor intensified. With their relative geographic and class-based diversity, female academies trained young and primarily Anglo-American women in the requirements of the new democratic gentility, in which the performance of selfless benevolence and charitable obligations took precedence over ornamental displays of taste and refinement and in which genteel behaviors both oriented themselves toward aiding the less affluent and affirmed the bearer's elite status.[12]

In sum, early national academy education and the activities it sponsored both expanded the scope of genteel feminine influence and maintained a sense of distinction from the lower orders. It schooled women in how to function in the public sphere, that middle ground between family and nation-state, and helped them negotiate the contradictions between their greater public presence and increasing behavioral constraints. It began to fulfill the promise of Wollstonecraft's early call to female educational parity, so popular among American women in the first half of the 1790s, while allowing these same individuals to deride her once her published life history was seen to contradict conservative norms of wife- and motherhood that the schools did not explicitly challenge. More than any other site, female acade-

12. Lynne Vallone writes that, beginning in the nineteenth century, "economic and social conditions . . . enabled women to spend more time in relieving the wants of the poor and offered them greater opportunities to wield their feminine influence outside of the home. . . . Popular ideologies of femininity . . . stressed that the woman . . . was especially suited to perform charitable works as an extension of the domestic ideology that kept her arts in the home" (Vallone, *Disciplines of Virtue: Girls' Culture in the Eighteenth and Nineteenth Centuries* [New Haven, Conn., 1995], 16–17). On the transition from heterosocial to homosocial institutions in the early nineteenth century, see Kelley, *Learning to Stand and Speak,* 53–54. On pre- and post-Revolutionary elite sociability, see David S. Shields, *Civil Tongues and Polite Letters in British America* (Chapel Hill, N.C., 1997); and Carla Mulford, introduction, in Mulford, ed., *Only for the Eye of a Friend: The Poems of Annis Boudinot Stockton* (Charlottesville, Va., 1995), 1–57. On intensifying strictures against the poor, see Richard L. Bushman, *The Refinement of America: Persons, Houses, Cities* (New York, 1992), 279.

mies exemplified the incompatibility between women's expanding influence and an increasing emphasis on domestic containment and self-regulation, even as they taught their students how to negotiate this turmoil.[13]

Thus the world that *Lucy Temple* inhabits looks quite unlike its forebear's, in that it possesses two extremes that were only amorphous during the time that *Charlotte Temple* was introduced in the United States. First, women have become an acknowledged public presence, especially as teachers and purveyors of charitable reform. Charlotte's boarding-school instructors were only shadowy figures, both to the reader and to the students they failed to supervise. By Lucy's day, however, teaching has become both a personal means to escape despair and a social identity granting unmarried women recognition and respect in the absence of marriage. Similarly, Charlotte's childhood home is but a distant memory, and although she yearns for it, the novel provides little detail about it or any subsequent residence. By the time the orphaned Lucy finds shelter in her uncle's cottage, the significance of home has expanded, all but determining the perceived worth and well-being of its inhabitants. Thus Lucy and her adoptive sisters learn all they need to survive in the world at large within its walls and from its resident benevolent patriarch, Mr. Matthews.

As the surprising fact that Matthews is a "Mr." begins to suggest, however, turning the Matthews residence into the primary source of its charges' education can be read two ways. On the one hand, the Matthews home school could be said to emblematize a domestic discourse that places the welfare of the nation at the feet of its domestic caregivers. On the other, the novel could be offering the female academy as a surrogate for a home life that isn't all it's cracked up to be. Appointing the asexual but undeniably male Mr. Matthews as guardian, then, both highlights the nondomestic aspects of his so-called home and suggests that domestic spaces themselves need not operate according to a strict gender binary. Similarly, by emphasizing financial thrift, the novel prepares its charges to supervise their homes wisely and suggests that money management is an important skill to women intent on avoiding the economic entrapment of marriage.

13. "No matter if women were accorded educational opportunity," Kelley states, "they were still denied the Enlightenment's promise of self-actualization. Instead of using for themselves 'the richest of earthly gifts' . . . they were expected to place their learning at the service of two families, the family they had constituted in taking husbands and bearing children and the family that had been constituted for them in the establishment of an independent United States" (Kelley, *Learning to Stand and Speak,* 49). On expanding academy attendance and resultant self-definition against both aristocratic and vulgar orders, see 4, 23, 28, 31, 80.

What characterized the female intellectual communities that Rowson helped create and thematized in her last novel? Rowson's curriculum seems to have occupied a middle ground between the basic course offerings of the earliest academies and the later advances led by schools such as Pierce's Litchfield Academy, as well as between the ornamental skills that characterized early republican education and the pragmatic skills emphasized by theorists such as Rush. Like almost every academy of the period, hers offered reading, English grammar, writing, history, arithmetic, and geography. She placed particular emphasis on geography, not only producing two textbooks on the subject but also emphasizing it in advertisements for the school. Amid a three-tiered system of course offerings, one announcement specified that those who "take lessons in Painting only" might also "study Geography, and the use of the Globe, without any additional expense." Rowson never ventured into the natural sciences, rhetoric, logic, or advanced mathematics that Pierce introduced to her academy after 1814, when female academies began to adopt a similar curriculum to male colleges. (Female academies, however, rarely taught Latin, which meant that they de facto were the first to modernize the college curriculum.) Instead, she placed a continued emphasis on the ornamental accomplishments derided by Rush. The academy offered electives in painting landscapes, flowers, and figures; music was taught two days a week, and dancing occupied another two afternoons.[14]

However much Rowson's school emphasized its role in teaching women to exert influence from within the domestic realm, either through service or ornament, it also enabled other, more direct forms of entrance into the public sphere. Often, these consisted of associational activities that began at the school and were then carried on in varied manners afterward. Student exhibitions, a common feature of many female academies, were a highlight of Rowson's year. They were advertised in the local press and reported upon faithfully. Female academy schooling was crucial to the growth of organized benevolence between 1797 and 1820, and in this Rowson's academy was also typical. Rowson modeled such activity through her participation in at least two voluntary societies.[15]

14. *Columbian Centinel. Massachusetts Federalist* (Boston), May 30, 1807, 3; Kelley, *Learning to Stand and Speak*, 91–92.

15. Reports on Rowson's academy exhibitions appear in the *Massachusetts Mercury,* Nov. 5, 1799, and Oct. 7, 1800; *Boston Weekly Magazine,* Oct. 30, 1802; *Boston Weekly Magazine,* Nov. 23, 1802, Oct. 29, 1803, and Oct. 20, 1804; *Gazetteer* (Boston), Nov. 2, 1803; and *New-England Palladium* (Boston), Nov. 30, 1810. By 1816, in addition to her work with the Fatherless and Widows' Society, Rowson was also a member of the Prayer Book and Tract Society, whose first anniversary she celebrated by writing

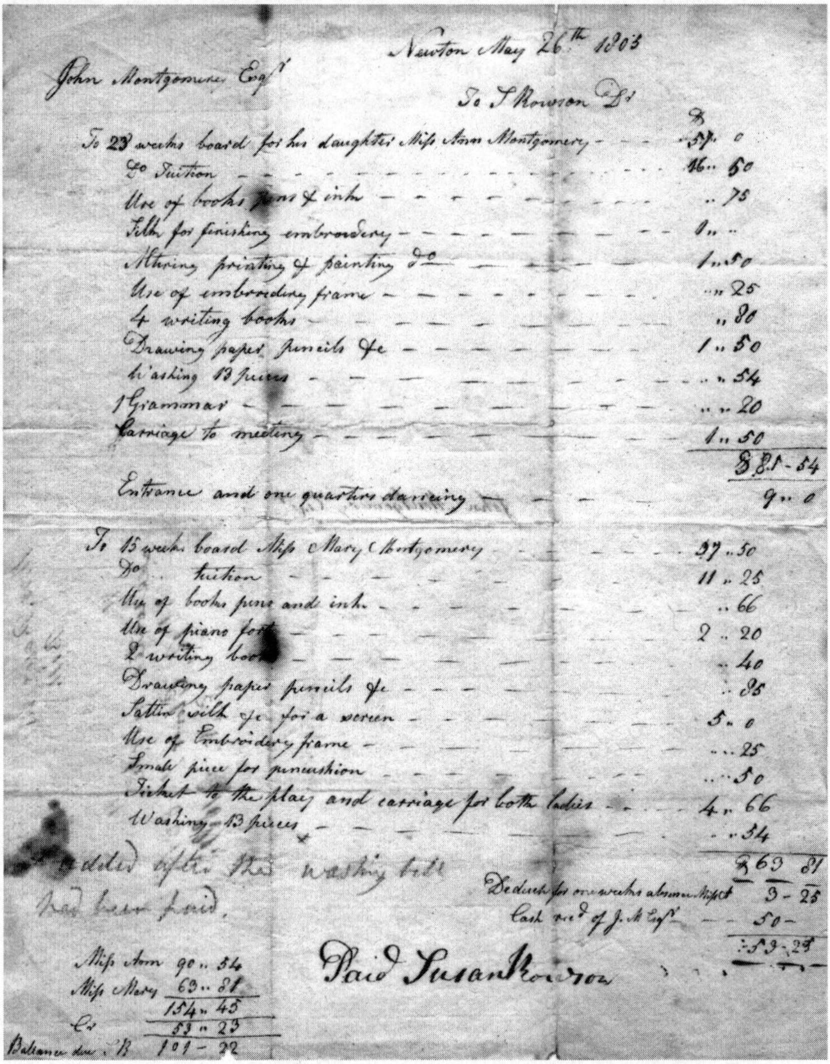

Newton May 26th 1803

John Montgomery Esqr

To S Rowson Dr

	$
To 23 weeks board for his daughter Miss Ann Montgomery	57. 0
Do Tuition	16.. 50
Use of books pens & ink	.. 75
Silk for finishing embroidery	1.. ..
Altering printing & painting do	1.. 50
Use of embroidery frame	.. 25
4 writing books	.. 80
Drawing paper pencils &c	1.. 50
Washing 13 pieces	 54
1 Grammar	 20
Carriage to meeting	1.. 50
	$81-54
Entrance and one quarters dancing	9.. 0
To 15 weeks board Miss Mary Montgomery	37.. 50
Do tuition	11.. 25
Use of books pens and ink	.. 66
Use of piano forte	2 .. 20
2 writing books	.. 40
Drawing paper pencils &c	.. 85
Sattin silk &c for a screen	5.. 0
Use of Embroidery frame	.. 25
Small piece for pincushion	.. 50
Ticket to the play and carriage for both ladies	4.. 66
Washing 13 pieces	.. 34
	$63 81
Deduct for one weeks absence Miss A	3 - 25
Cash recd of J. M. Esqr	50-
	53-25

Added after the washing bill had been paid.

Paid Susan Rowson

Miss Ann	90.. 54
Miss Mary	63.. 81
	154.. 45
Cr	53.. 23
Ballance due S R	101 - 22

PLATE 21. *John Montgomery's tuition bill for Susanna Rowson's academy. 1803. Papers of Susanna Rowson, MSS 7379, Clifton Waller Barrett Library of American Literature, Special Collections, University of Virginia Library*

More than most academies of the period, Rowson's contributed to another important aspect of public life for early-nineteenth-century women, namely, participation in discursive institutions. Rowson's school received mention at least a dozen times in newspapers between 1803 and 1824. As a frequent contributor to and possible editor of the *Boston Weekly Magazine* and contributor to the *New England Galaxy* during her tenure at the school, she possessed further opportunity to link the three forms of professional activity most open to women during this period: writing, editing, and teaching. Furthermore, she was among those preceptors to write a variety of materials for the use of her own and other female academies, including dramatic recitations, commencement addresses, and textbooks. (Rowson's closest companion here was Sarah Pierce, who, like Rowson, wrote short plays, commencement addresses, and lyric verse and whose *Sketches of Universal History* [1811] was widely used in schools. Novelist Tabitha Tenney also wrote *The New Pleasing Instructor* [1799], which "combined short essays and poetry with dialogues and dramatic pieces intended for schoolroom performance.")[16]

Female intimacy, the last form of associational activity fostered by Rowson's school, was also no doubt the most nebulous. But letters between women after leaving the academy suggest that many lasting ties were formed there. Dispersed throughout the Northeast, several women remem-

---

an ode and a hymn for it (Papers of Susanna Rowson, 1770–1879 [hereafter cited as Rowson Papers], MSS 7379, Clifton Waller Barrett Library of American Literature, Special Collections, University of Virginia Library, Charlottesville, Va.). On the link between academy education and organized benevolence, see Kelley, *Learning to Stand and Speak,* 29, 32, 73, 108–109, 278.

16. Lisa L. Moore, "The Swan of Litchfield: Sarah Pierce and the Lesbian Landscape Poem," in Thomas Foster, ed., *Long before Stonewall: Same-Sex Sexuality in Early America* (New York, 2007), 1–3; Joseph Fichtelberg, "Uncivil Tongues: Slander and Honour in Susanna Rowson's *Trials of the Human Heart,*" *Eighteenth-Century Fiction,* XVIII (2006), 425–451, esp. 433. Fichtelberg argues that the performative aspect of the dialogues and dramatic performance entailed "learning . . . moral lessons . . . not simply absorbing but literally enacting them, a citational process intended to shape a nation's mores." As my discussion ahead of Rowson's own dialogues and dramatic pieces for students suggests, in Rowson's case the "moral lessons" were rendered difficult to "absorb" by the fact that they usually contained multiple, conflicting perspectives.

Rowson's several pedagogical publications include: *A Spelling Dictionary* (1807); *A Present for Young Ladies* (1811); *Exercises in History, Chronology, and Biography* (1822); *Biblical Dialogues between a Father and His Family* (1822); and two geographies, the introductory *Youth's First Steps in Geography* (1818) and the mammoth *Abridgment of Universal Geography* (1805).

bered each other well some thirty years afterward, when Rowson's second biographer, Elias Nason, came calling, and were able to help him find one another. These letters also show that, from the vantage point of those who had married, borne children, or cared for aging parents, the homosocial climate of the school possessed immeasurable appeal in retrospect.[17]

As Sarah Pierce's verses to Abigail Smith frankly demonstrate, and as Rowson's own written declarations of love for her many female friends suggest, same-sex attachments during this period were often passionate. Not only was an erotic element common to nineteenth-century homosocial friendships among both women and men, but it is also undeniable that, for some women, including Pierce, the "primary attachments were to women." Although Rowson's attachments cannot strictly be classified this way in light of her marriage, it is clear that, as she aged, other women—both students and peers—were increasingly important to her and came to form the basis for her happiness, productivity, sense of self, and willingness to continue.[18]

The name Susanna Rowson has long been synonymous with the ideology of genteel female domesticity—familiar to most through such concepts as republican motherhood and separate spheres—said to emerge in late-eighteenth-century Anglo-America. Given that the growing perceived significance of mothers paralleled burgeoning educational opportunities for girls, schools for the young were often figured as an extension of this all-important maternal influence. "Mothers" and "teachers" came to be spoken of in one breath, both to comfort those nervous about sending a daughter away from home and to justify her removal as preparing her to furnish her own ideological sanctum on her return.[19]

17. J. J. Clarke to "Dear sir" [Elias Nason], Aug. 10, 1859, Rowson Papers, MSS 7379–c, box 1, folder 74; Mary M. Batchelder to Nason, December 1859, ibid., folder 71; Batchelder to Nason, Sept. 11, 1861, ibid.; Isabella Child to Mrs. Batchelder, [1861], ibid., folder 73.

18. "Verses, Written in the Winter of 1792, and Addressed to Abigail Smith Jr.—by Sally Pierce," in Moore, "Swan of Litchfield," in Foster, ed., *Long before Stonewall;* see also 255, 270–273. The classic article on the subject of nineteenth-century female intimacy is Carroll Smith-Rosenberg's "Female World of Love and Ritual: Relationships between Women in Nineteenth Century America," *Signs,* I (1975), 1–29.

19. As Patricia Crain notes, Catherine Beecher was "echoing a common sentiment" when she wrote, "It is to mothers and to teachers that the world is to look for the character which is to be enstamped on each succeeding generation." Crain also cites William Alcott, who proportioned well-educated women into "mothers" and "teachers" at a ratio

According to Linda K. Kerber, a Miss P. W. Jackson, one of Rowson's students, exemplified how an early republican woman justified her new intellectual reach by placing it at "her family's service." (Like most of the material performed by students at the academy's yearly public expositions, Miss Jackson's address was probably written by her preceptress, especially as it was one of the pieces selected for publication in the *Boston Weekly Magazine,* to which Rowson was a frequent contributor.)

> A woman who is skilled in every useful art, who practices every domestic virtue . . . may, by her precept and example, inspire her brothers, her husband, or her sons, with such a love of virtue, such just ideas of the true value of civil liberty . . . that future heroes and statesmen, when arrived as the summit of military or political fame, shall exaltingly declare, *it is to my mother I owe this elevation.*

Miss Jackson does indeed depict educated maternity as the bedrock of future civic greatness, tracing her visions of "heroes and statesmen"—or war and state governance, two arenas of public endeavor largely closed off to women—back to the maternal source. When considered in this light, Miss Jackson's words lose intimations of hyperbole to speak aptly, and even modestly, to the importance of the female schoolroom to the American family and by extension the new Republic.[20]

---

of approximately three to one (Crain, *The Story of A: The Alphabetization of America from the New-England Primer to the Scarlet Letter* [Stanford, Calif., 2000], 129, 131). In a study of female education in England, Jane McDermid notes that conservative women writers "saw education . . . as a means of expanding the confines of the home to embrace society" (McDermid, "Conservative Feminism and Female Education in the Eighteenth Century," *History of Education,* XVIII [1989], 309–322, esp. 309). For a useful definition and critique of separate spheres ideology, see Cathy Davidson and Jessamyn Hatcher, eds., *No More Separate Spheres!* (Durham, N.C., 2002). For an updated assessment of republican motherhood, see Linda K. Kerber's preface to the 1986 edition of her *Women of the Republic: Intellect and Ideology in Revolutionary America.*

20. Kerber, *Women of the Republic: Intellect and Ideology in Revolutionary America,* 1st ed. (Chapel Hill, N.C., 1980), 228, 229. Rowson's mid-twentieth-century biographer, Elisabeth Anthony Dexter, claimed that she held an editorial position at the *Boston Weekly Magazine,* but Patricia L. Parker challenges that claim, pointing out among other things that the magazine published a lukewarm review of her novels during her supposed tenure there. The review suggested that "Rowson's works are not without dangerous tendency," a point of view Rowson dedicated most of her prefaces to disproving. See Dexter, *Career Women of America,* 98; Parker, *Susanna Rowson* (Boston, 1986), 120.

If female academies prospered by purportedly extending the realm of maternal influence, the question remains exactly how that influence functioned. In implicit tribute to Foucault's work on an early modern shift from punishment to surveillance, many Americanists have noted an "affection-based authority" associated with powerful mothering in the early-nineteenth-century United States. As the century progressed, so, it would seem, did the instrumentality of maternal love. As the nineteenth-century child worked to secure a love increasingly contingent upon correct behavior, he or she experienced the "introjection of authority" such that "secured consent" became no more than "inward colonization."[21]

Rowson's written record provides ample evidence that the kinds of love associated with the influence of adults over children tend to intensify order, unlike the romantic attachments of her earlier novels, which generally subverted it. But to think of any love associated with female authority as suspect or hypocritical may prevent us from considering how it provided new forms of knowledge to young women on their way from playing the role of child to that of parent—or to some other, cloudier fate. Moreover, although Rowson wedded correction to affection, she never seemed to consider one merely as a means to the other or to value affection only as much as it helped her maintain discipline. In fact, she displayed an ardent need for the exchanges of the schoolroom that only intensified as she grew older. By examining Rowson's own teaching methods, then, we can parse out the degree to which consent and colonization functioned interdependently in the production of self-knowledge on the part of her students and readers.[22]

21. Crain, *Story of A,* 128; Fliegelman, *Declaring Independence,* 36, 43, 45, 60, 200; Brodhead, *Cultures of Letters,* 21.

22. Describing "the creation, not to say the cult, of a personal memory of maternal influence," Crain writes that "the mother's task is to surround objects with the sound of her voice, so that everything in the world adverts to her authority." Two of the scholars to investigate this cultural sea change from a preoccupation with force to one with persuasion bear significant relationship to one another and, through their counterpoint, to this chapter. Taking a phrase from John Adams, Fliegelman concerns himself with "soft compulsion," whereas Richard Brodhead, describing a slightly later formation, discusses "disciplinary intimacy." There are important differences between these two concepts—the first describing the early Republic up to about 1830, the other taking up where it leaves off with the 1830s and 1840s; one comprehending all acts of "attention," the other the relationship between mother and child. Taken together, however, they provide a virtual continuum on which to chart the intensifying degree to which the display of maternal affection was recognized for its instrumentality. See Crain, *Story of A,* 125; Fliegelman, *Declaring Independence,* 40; Brodhead, *Cultures of Letters,* 21.

There is no doubt that Rowson's presence as a teacher made deft use of affection-based authority, thereby lending support to the idea of the female academy as an extension of the mothering home. In the words of her first biographer,

Mrs. Rowson was intended for a teacher. Loving ardently the pursuit of literature, she had the rare and happy faculty, without which no instructor can succeed, of inspiring others with her own emotions. Her own enthusiasm awoke enthusiasm.

Just about every former student who left written record of her experiences at Mrs. Rowson's Young Ladies' Academy corroborated this emphasis on affective attachment at the root of Rowson's theory and practice of education. Eliza Southgate, who had arrived at the academy from far dimmer scholastic accommodations nearby and whose initial impression of her new preceptress was that "no one can help loving her," continued to claim at the end of her schooling that Rowson "governs by the love with which she always inspires her scholars." Other scholars also remembered Rowson with affection.[23]

Despite their deep feeling for Rowson, her students also perceived her methods as intrusive: the governing was not fully obscured by the love. Indeed, Rowson's practice of requiring students to write their parents and friends on slate in the evening and then to submit their letters to her for "correction" annoyed many students enough to be documented in their later correspondence. (Mr. Matthews is also fond of correction: as he explains to Lucy's grandfather upon assuming responsibility for her, "The correction of those erring propensities which are the sad inheritance of all the sons and daughters of Adam . . . should be his own peculiar care.") Decades later, Mrs. Samuel Batchelder wrote Elias Nason that, although she now approved of the policy, it "was considered generally as hardships by the misses," who "all stood in much awe of her piercing eye." Batchelder explains why the surveillance rankled—"You may suppose we could not unlock the secrets and wishes of our hearts to such a presence"—and, indeed, keeping her students from speaking ill of their experiences at school might not have been the last thing on Rowson's mind in implementing such a policy. In a similar vein, Southgate, informed by Rowson that she had written on an "improper

23. Elias Nason, *A Memoir of Mrs. Susanna Rowson, with Elegant and Illustrative Extracts from Her Writings in Prose and Poetry* (Albany, N.Y., 1870), 99-100, quoting letters by Eliza Southgate, July 17, 1798, Sept. 31, 1800.

subject" in asking a friend about the romantic prospects of another, complained to her mother, "This is *refining* too much, and if I can't write as I feel, I can't write at all." Even more significant, Southgate showed the fruits of her education in treating her sister to the methods under which she had bridled: "You will think this is harsh; you will not always think so; remember those that wish it must know better what is proper than you possibly can." The degree to which Rowson invaded the recesses of her students' epistolary displays of self provides an unsettling endorsement of the culture of instrumental affection discussed above.[24]

That the students were capable of complaint suggests the limits of this endorsement. The strongest evidence that affect played more than a disciplinary role in the production of knowledge at Rowson's academy is that, despite her attempts at public relations damage control in censoring the information that reached parents, discontent remained articulable at the school. Even students' dismay at being hemmed in by epistolary surveillance suggests that they left school with a sharper capacity for critique than they entered it. As Laurel Thatcher Ulrich astutely argues, Eliza Southgate's indictments of her education minimize its true significance, evident in the transformation in her letters written before and after her time at Rowson's academy. Clearly, Eliza has learned more than obedience at Mrs. Rowson's, penning a series of arguments worthy of a Wollstonecraft or a Murray on female independence, mind, and education in letters to her cousin Moses Porter before her death in 1809 at the age of twenty-six.[25]

Thus, for every framing of early national female education as but an extension of and anticipated return to the embellished domestic—and, by extension, national—circle, and a training ground for its particular methods of linking power to truth, one should also note that such female academies provided one of the first "challenges to the traditional prerogatives of the family." Rowson's aforementioned valedictory student, Miss P. W. Jackson, herself finds the most apt image for the "reading and reflection [which] has stored her mind with knowledge," not in the home, but in the pioneering farm, which wrests "cultivated minds" out of "the wild sallies of un-

24. Batchelder to Nason, December 1859, Rowson Papers, MSS 7379-c, box 1, folder 71; Rowson, *Lucy Temple,* ed. Douglas, 139; Eliza Southgate to Mary Southgate, July 3, 1800, and Eliza Southgate to Octavia Southgate, Sept. 14, 1800, in Eliza Southgate Bowne, *A Girl's Life Eighty Years Ago: Selections from the Letters of Eliza Southgate Bowne* (Williamstown, Mass., 1980), 27, 30.

25. Laurel Thatcher Ulrich, "'From the Fair to the Brave': Spheres of Womanhood in Federal Maine," in Laura Fecych Sprague, ed., *Agreeable Situations: Society, Commerce, and Art in Southern Maine, 1780–1830* (Boston, 1987), 221.

cultivated nature." Such an establishment is more akin to the outmoded household economy than the modern domestic sanctuary in which women held new behavioral sway precisely because economic productivity was no longer their provenance. Throughout Miss Jackson's valedictory lecture, she is more concerned with diamond mines and extirpating insects than with raising the "sons" who receive but one brief mention. In fact, she seems far more intent upon celebrating her position as grateful daughter (grateful in part for being allowed to leave home to attend school) than in trying on the maternal role itself. Her exultations over having a mother take place in the first-person singular (tributes to "my mother"), whereas she reserves the more formal third-person singular and first-person plural to describe the duties associated with being one. In a sense that is embedded within the language itself, then, this unusual moment in an early American woman's life—in which she speaks to a public assembly, probably for the first and last time—represents a lingering within the exceptional space of the female academy as surely as it does an anticipated return to the much-vaunted family, either as offspring or wife.[26]

Miss Jackson's speech resists its own posited symbiosis between school and family, suggesting that the "dreams of personal and social progress" nurtured in female minds by a "republican-Protestant pedagogy" did not necessarily mesh with women's anticipated role as gatekeepers of national virtue through their newfound authority at home. In fact, Rowson, the likely author of this speech, nurtured dreams of an alternative to the family entered

26. Lee Soltow and Edward Stevens, *The Rise of Literacy and the Common School in the United States: A Socioeconomic Analysis to 1870* (Chicago, 1981), 48; *Boston Weekly Magazine,* Oct. 29, 1803. In a study of the era's most eminent school for girls, Philadelphia's Young Ladies' Academy (at which Rush delivered his lecture discussed above), Ann D. Gordon points out that, at school, "girls discovered a world different from family life." These differences included new forms of hierarchical relationship (such as that between students and teachers who "intervened between the child and her parents") and new commonalities (such as "the terms of friendship and esteem arising from the common experience of being students together in the academy"). Most important, school provided a utopian environment in which perceived inherent qualities such as "merit" or "competence" overshadowed external differences in "wealth, religion, social circle, or location" that had structured the family's social world. Nancy Cott provides the starkest assessment of such an environment: "Class-blind but sex-specific education for women more loudly affirmed that economic mobility existed in America, while it promised to deter chaos by enforcing a sexual order." See Gordon, "The Young Ladies Academy of Philadelphia," in Carol Ruth Berkin and Mary Beth Norton, eds., *Women of America: A History* (Boston, 1979), 77–81; Nancy F. Cott, *The Bonds of Womanhood: 'Woman's Sphere' in New England, 1780–1835* (New Haven, Conn., 1977), 123–124.

into through birth or marriage: a distinct unit of social and political order based in, and premised on, the female academy. In her pedagogical writings, she explores this alternative, and her posthumous publication, *Lucy Temple,* renders it in fictional form. These works encourage us to ask how seeing female education as a counterpoint to, as well as an elaboration of, domestic disciplinarity can influence the way we understand the interpenetration of power and love suggested by the feminization of domestic authority in the early nineteenth century.[27]

If the words Rowson puts in Miss Jackson's mouth forestall the future to which they allude, Rowson's discussions of pedagogical technique further challenge the equation of female academic education in the early Republic with a maternally inflected introjection of authority. Since Rowson taught girls from five to twenty, we can begin with her opinions on teaching literacy to the very young. Here one finds a startling concern with the role of individual agency. This concern stood in stark contrast to the prevailing method of instruction in the early Republic, "imitative learning," which did little to foster independent invention but rather "inculcated strong habits of conformity in belief." Drawing largely from the pedagogical texts of Noah Webster, the nation's leading author of reading instruction manuals (as well as the author of its first dictionary), teaching literacy "played an important role in preparing the child for life in a world of fixed forms and ideas."

> Potentially liberating uses of reading were largely ignored by rural New England reading instructors throughout the eighteenth and early nineteenth centuries. . . . The primary goal of early education was not to instill in the child information about the world or to provoke a challenge to society's basic institutions, but to inaugurate the assimilation of a universe of previous "wisdom."

The chief method by which such conformity was established through the mid-1820s was the "pronouncing-form method" taught by Webster, in which students gathered together to read the same text aloud. Such a method not only conflated oral and reading skills for a culture "rooted in oral modes of communication"; it also emphasized pronunciation over comprehension. In Webster's speller, words were organized according to sound rather than significance: "Each sound, syllable, and word served as a type, preparing the novice for other, similar-sounding words to be encountered eventually."

27. Soltow and Stevens, *Rise of Literacy,* 48, 49.

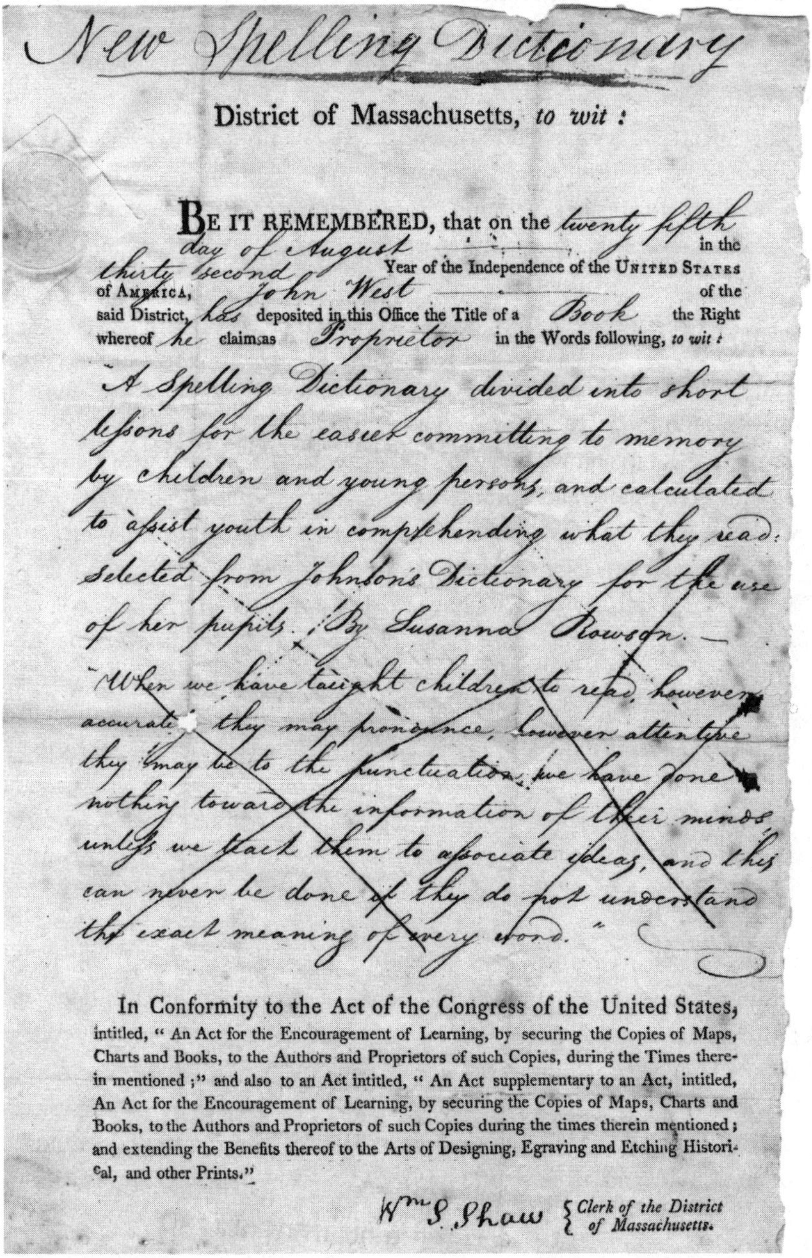

New Spelling Dictionary

District of Massachusetts, *to wit :*

BE IT REMEMBERED, that on the *twenty fifth* day of *August* in the *thirty second* Year of the Independence of the UNITED STATES of AMERICA, *John West* of the said District, *has* deposited in this Office the Title of a *Book* the Right whereof *he* claims as *Proprietor* in the Words following, *to wit :*

A Spelling Dictionary divided into short lessons for the easier committing to memory by children and young persons, and calculated to assist youth in comprehending what they read: Selected from Johnsons Dictionary for the use of her pupils. By Susanna Rowson.

"When we have taught children to read however accurate they may pronounce, however attentive they may be to the punctuation, we have done nothing toward the information of their minds unless we teach them to associate ideas, and this can never be done if they do not understand the exact meaning of every word. "

In Conformity to the Act of the Congress of the United States, intitled, " An Act for the Encouragement of Learning, by securing the Copies of Maps, Charts and Books, to the Authors and Proprietors of such Copies, during the Times therein mentioned ;" and also to an Act intitled, " An Act supplementary to an Act, intitled, An Act for the Encouragement of Learning, by securing the Copies of Maps, Charts and Books, to the Authors and Proprietors of such Copies during the times therein mentioned ; and extending the Benefits thereof to the Arts of Designing, Egraving and Etching Historical, and other Prints."

Wm S. Shaw { *Clerk of the District of Massachusetts.*

PLATE 22. *Copyright agreement for Rowson's* New Spelling Dictionary *(referring to* A Spelling Dictionary *[Boston, 1807]). Papers of Susanna Rowson, MSS 7379, Clifton Waller Barrett Library of American Literature, Special Collections, University of Virginia Library*

Students "would recite the letters of each syllable, pausing to pronounce the syllable, and then . . . proceed to the next syllable, until the whole word had been spelled and pronounced from memory. . . . The whole procedure could take on a rhythm not unlike a chant."[28]

Rowson strongly objected to this practice. The preface to *A Spelling Dictionary* (1807) describes the automatons that emerge from such "inculcation" and constitutes her own polemic against the mental passivity fostered by these methods. Distinguishing between a "store of ideas" and one of mere "words," she begins:

> Engaged as I have been, for some years past, in the important task of Education, it has ever appeared to me a most essential object, to store the young mind with ideas. Almost every child of a tolerably good capacity has its tender memory burthened with vast store of words; but as they are in general ignorant of the meaning of more than two thirds of these words, how is it possible any ideas can arise or associate themselves in their minds, from reading, study, or recitation? I have myself witnessed young people who have read with precision and even elegance; every stop was scrupulously observed, every mark, every pause, attended to, and the voice modulated to the sense of the subject; yet I have been convinced by subsequent questions, that they have attached no idea whatever to what they have read, but that any string of words with the same capitals, breaks and points, would have been read exactly in the same manner. To this mechanical kind of reading I was a perfect stranger, till repeated instances assured me it really did exist; it then appeared to me a very serious evil; but how was it to be remedied?

The remedy, naturally, is to be found in the pages she sets forth, which differ from most reading instruction manuals of the period by supplying the definitions for each word. If children "are early habituated to connect ideas with words," she concludes,

> as they advance in life this pleasing association continues, their minds become informed, their studies and readings are pleasures, for they afford some degree of amusement. I do not say all these good conse-

28. William J. Gilmore, *Reading Becomes a Necessity of Life: Material and Cultural Life in Rural New England, 1780–1835* (Knoxville, Tenn., 1989), 35, 37, 38, 40. Webster published his magnum opus, *An American Dictionary of the English Language,* in 1828 (New York), the same year *Lucy Temple* was published.

quences will arise from the study of my little book; but if it in the least contributes to the advancement of so desirable an end, I shall have attained my purpose; for it is my fixed opinion, that it is better to give the young pupil one rational idea, than fatigue them by obliging them to commit to memory a thousand *mere words*.

Although the "giving" of ideas, as opposed to "mere words," might be taken as precisely the refinement of authority suggested by disciplinary models of the self, it is clear at the very least that Rowson considered learning to read a matter of reflection, as opposed to repetition. If rote literacy methods could be linked to a "profoundly conservative end: the education of all white American women as 'Republican mothers,'" it follows that more independent methods might also foster more independent ideologies of adult womanhood. Rowson's program for teaching the young to read, then, helps to bring about the kinds of resistance evident in Jackson's valedictory speech.[29]

Rowson's second challenge to disciplinary models of female self-formation has to do with the signature substance of such models, namely, affect. It would be easy to read Rowson's fostering of an intense teacher-student bond as more evidence of her complicity in affection-based authority, akin to reading her students' letters home, only this time without needing them to write down their thoughts. The more students loved her, the more willing they would be not only to obey her but to adopt her expectations for them. But what I emphasize here is how, in myriad ways, these bonds resisted being put to instrumental ends. Rowson's students' affection for their head teacher was playful, irreverent, spontaneous, and sometimes even mocking; it did not subject them to her so much as liberate their capacities for humor and critique. Student Myra Montgomery, who noted that during the yearly valedictory exercises Rowson "sat on the stage and appeared as dignified and firm (and I had almost said as *large*) as Mount Atlas," also commented that she "was one of the *lightest* prettiest dancers she ever saw." Another indication of the Montgomery sisters' fondness for their precep-

29. Susanna Rowson, preface, *A Spelling Dictionary, Divided into Short Lessons, for the Easier Committing to Memory by Children and Young Persons* . . . (Boston, 1807); Gilmore, *Reading Becomes a Necessity of Life,* 37. An 1850 circular from the Clark Female Seminary claims the school seeks "rather to cultivate than to store the mind; to make it an active agent in educating itself, rather than a mere receptacle for the ideas of others" (Schools and Academies Collection, American Antiquarian Society, Worcester, Mass., quoted in Kelley, *Learning to Stand and Speak,* 92).

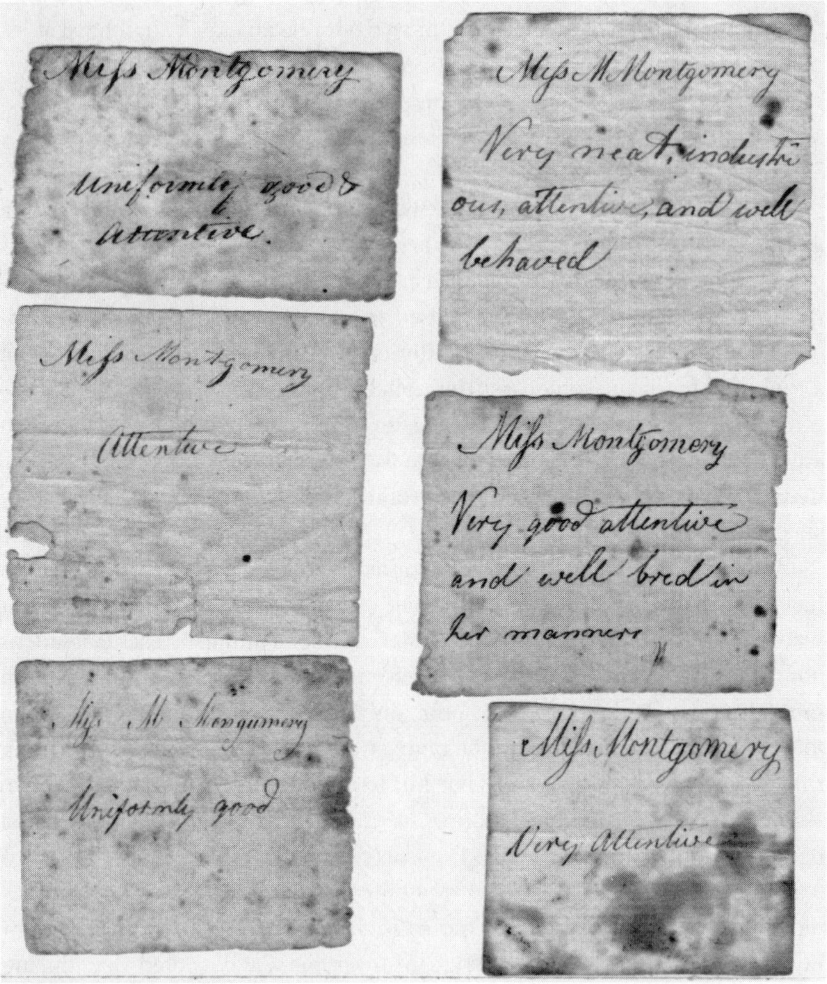

Miss Montgomery
Uniformly good & Attentive.

Miss M Montgomery
Very neat, industri ous, attentive, and well behaved

Miss Montgomery
Attentive

Miss Montgomery
Very good attentive and well bred in her manners

Miss M Mongumery
Uniformly good

Miss Montgomery
Very Attentive

PLATE 23. *Mary Montgomery's student report cards from Susanna Rowson's academy. Papers of Susanna Rowson, MSS 7379, Clifton Waller Barrett Library of American Literature, Special Collections, University of Virginia Library*

tress is that Mary saved her weekly "characters," or notes on deportment. The word most frequently employed on these slips is, not "good" (that is, obedient), which appears three times, but "attentive," which appears five. Isabella Child, an experienced teacher who enrolled in the academy specifically to study Rowson's educational "method" before establishing her own school in Boston, wrote of the enthusiastic reception that met these characteristically kind notes upon their distribution every Saturday and of the after-prayers surge of students eager to be kissed by their preceptress. As Southgate suggests by her defection to Mrs. Rowson's from a nearby school, life at the Young Ladies' Academy, for all its annoyances, also possessed much of the egalitarianism that marked such locations as a reprieve from the worlds from which these girls had emerged and to which they would likely return.[30]

Further evidence that discontent remained a legitimate category of experience at the school, despite an overall climate emphasizing order, compassion, and self-control, appears in the exposition performances. The dramatic dialogues that comprise most of these (for the very young, Rowson wrote short rhymes, such as the charming "Bee: A Fable") make room for discontentment by repeatedly and extensively detailing the situation of an outlier before summarily reclaiming her almost as an afterthought. Often, the recitations present two opposed positions sympathetically. When a character named Lucy chides her friends for gushing over a waxen doll, calling them vain and silly, they retort that she is self-important and faultfinding. When her companion Mary professes that gambling and dancing are her two chief aims as a married woman, Lucretia (another friend) induces a change of heart that has Mary "working for the poor"—but not before a loving rendition of the pleasures of "living at my ease." Those who loved play go to work, yes, but the work is never as clearly defined as the play. And when it comes to arguing politics, Napoleon is either a "Woglog" or "invincible, noble, intrepid, and bold," depending on which young lady is speaking. Rowson makes her anti-French, pro-British sympathies clear, but only gently; she gives the argument full sway, and it seems to be what she enjoys most, far more than its resolution. Even that is disarming: when the three girls decide to go shopping and "leave the more arduous cares of the

30. Myra Montgomery to Mary Ann Means, Nov. 22, 1808, Historical Society of Pennsylvania, Philadelphia; Batchelder to Nason, Sept. 11, 1861, Rowson Papers, MSS 7379-c, box 1, folder 71; Child to Batchelder, [1861], ibid., folder 73. On egalitarianism, see Gordon, "Young Ladies Academy of Philadelphia," in Berkin and Norton, eds., *Women of America,* 68–91.

nation / To the wise and magnanimous lords of creation," their tribute is decidedly tongue-in-cheek.[31]

But the most profound indication that the bond between student and teacher subverted its own potential instrumentality lay in the recorded feelings of the teacher herself. In contrast to descriptions of disciplinary relations in which the authoritative figure, as institutional perpetuator, finely calibrates her affectual performance to elicit a particular response from her charges while exhibiting no such malleability in return, Rowson not only influenced her students but was profoundly influenced by them; indeed, her feelings for them increasingly exceeded any reciprocity. Thus in 1811, near the middle of her tenure at the academy, Rowson claimed that her "chief pleasure arises from being loved, esteemed and applauded by a few; the children whom I have educated, and the friends who are satisfied with my endeavours to please, constitute those few." Thanking those who made such pleasures possible, she then stated, "The memory of your kindness will rest upon [my] heart, the warm sense of gratitude with which that heart glows can be chilled only by the hand of death." Again in the preface to the last book published during her lifetime, *Biblical Dialogues between a Father and His Family,* Rowson—now much nearer to the "hand of death" that once served merely as a pretty figure—returned to the theme of the debt owed her many students. Describing her response to "the momentous business of instructing females of the rising generation," she explained that "in many an hour of sickness and lassitude it has made me forget my pain, and often-times in the wish to succeed in my endeavour, care and sorrow have lost their power to annoy." These are not the words of a disciplinary figure that merely embodies the status quo and serves as a vehicle for its transfer through generations. Rowson clearly expresses longings of her own: she describes "care and sorrow" reflective of a profound, if generally contained, malaise.[32]

Yet if the preceptress's position does not render her impervious to despair, it does allow her to receive succor from her charges. They help her "forget" the pain, they provide intermittent relief from the care and sorrow, and their love provides her "chief pleasure." She even suggests that her schoolgirls are the last people she will contemplate on her deathbed; "the memory of your kindness" is sacrosanct, and she plans to take it with her. Among all her life experience, then, it is the image of her "young ladies"

31. Rowson, *Present for Young Ladies,* 18–19, 23, 25, 34–36.

32. Rowson, preface, ibid., 156; Rowson, preface, *Biblical Dialogues between a Father and His Family: Comprising Sacred History, from the Creation to the Death of Our Savior Christ . . . ,* 2 vols. (Boston, 1822), I, v.

that will accompany her to the grave. Rowson not only "governed by love" but also fostered and experienced it in her school in a manner that, far from reconciling daughters to their fate, alerted them to the possibility that canny self-management could help them negotiate the perils ahead—better than their esteemed and beloved, but at times openly disconsolate, guardian.

When Rowson considers the effect of reading methods on young minds, and when she looks to an affectual bond between students and teachers as the basis for the development of knowledge, she is not thinking of boys and girls interchangeably. This becomes particularly evident in the preface to the only novel written and published while she directed the academy, *Reuben and Rachel; or, Tales of Old Times*. Rowson makes numerous references to her current occupation, which she calls "an avocation of a more serious nature" than the authorship of novels, and spells out her plans to turn from novel-writing to the production of textbooks. Thus *Reuben and Rachel* forms an important link between her teaching and her novelistic personas, highlighting how both endeavors aim at the creation of a specifically female community of student-readers. "It is observable," Rowson notes, "that the generality of books intended for children are written for boys." She then repeats her damaging assessment of these books before making a startling claim for a book directed at the "instruction" of the "youthful mind." "For my own sex only I presume to write; and if hereafter one woman should think herself happier or wiser from the fruits of my endeavour, I shall be overpaid for the time or pains bestowed in writing and arranging them."[33]

Those familiar with Rowson's earlier novels may hear an echo here, one that portends a number of other important links between her novelistic and pedagogical endeavors. First, as suggested above, she extends the explicitly female narrative address of her novels to her teaching persona as well, invoking for female scholars nationwide ("my own sex") an implicit, if ephemeral, communion like that promised by her novels. Second, and countering this inclusive gesture, she pictures the act of learning as an intimate solidarity between teacher and student ("one woman"), not unlike that between a novel's narrator and its implied reader. Although in the case of *Reuben and Rachel* the solidarity inheres in the act of reading, the fact that Rowson emphasizes her role as a teacher in this preface links it closely to her own teaching style, which depended on a fantasy of intimacy between student and

33. Susanna Rowson, *Reuben and Rachel; or, Tales of Old Times* (Boston, 1798), University of Virginia, E-Text Center, Early American Fiction Collection (1789–1875), http://etext.lib.virginia.edu/eaf/authors/shr.htm.

teacher that seemed to defy the ratio of children to adults in the classroom in order to assume the mythic proportions of a caring love relationship.

Not only, then, does Rowson employ teaching methods that foster independent thinking and direct these methods explicitly to girls, but she also devises a pedagogy that mimics her novelistic authorial voice's most important aspect: using the mechanisms of presumed intimacy between a solitary reader/student and her loving narrator/teacher to reconstitute her female readership into a new, public entity. In *Reuben and Rachel,* "resistance . . . depends on women's ability to create and sustain communities capable of reading and interpreting, rather than simply internalizing, national(ist) fictions." When we extend this process to the classroom, we see that its constitutive paradox—managing the many by appealing to the solitary heart—remains intact.[34]

Together, Rowson's emphases on active learning, on affective bonds as the basis of female scholarly knowledge, and on female scholarly communities summoned through the pages of a textbook to be distributed among bodies who might never meet add up to a blueprint for increased female agency, fueled by a neoromantic attachment between student and teacher that at first seems merely a leftover from Rowson's earlier, melodramatic days. Her love for her female students and her wish to be loved by them in return served more than compensatory purposes for a woman whose own marriage admittedly provided little solace; they also helped form a newly emboldened, imagined community of elite female graduates. In her ardency, Rowson no doubt served personal ends, demanding reciprocity—which, she had demonstrated in novel after novel, was useless to expect in a heterosexual relationship—from women over whom she exercised considerable influence. In the process, however, she also invented a more stable (and, not coincidentally, exclusively feminine) alternative to a heteroerotic marital economy and the disordered families that resulted from it. To better understand this alternative, it is time to turn to the novel in which, despite having bid her adieus to her novelistic readership, she spelled out her utopian vision.

Lucy Temple is most readily comprehended as the book that brought Rowson, and with her the early American novel, out of a fixation on female sacrifice and into the new dawn of what Nina Baym has called the "woman's novel" and many term the "domestic novel." As opposed to the critics discussed in

---

34. Christopher Castiglia, *Bound and Determined: Captivity, Culture-Crossing, and White Womanhood from Mary Rowlandson to Patty Hearst* (Chicago, 1996), 142.

Chapter 3, who used the term "sentimental domestic novel," those referred to here see the domestic aspects of the text in tension with early sentimentalism's tendency to favor self-improvement over social critique. For Baym, a concern with domesticity does not equate with the assumption of its benevolence. Rather, the "woman's novel" "excoriate[s] an unhappy home as the basic source of human misery and imagines a happy home as the acme of human bliss." She also makes clear that domesticity itself contained multitudes; "the domestic ideal meant not that woman was to be sequestered from the world in her place at home but that everybody was to be placed in the home, and hence that home and the world would become one."[35]

Baym describes a self-conscious opposition between the two stages of the early American novel identified here. The authors of woman's fiction thought little of "the genre of seduction novel in which emotional, narcissistic heroines came to ruin in their first encounter with opportunistic men. Authors of woman's fictions detested such books and projected their work as alternative or antidote. . . . The spectacle of victimized innocence, though affecting, denied just what woman's fictions insisted on: that innocence was compatible with agency." That Rowson wrote at least one of each kind of book and that she instituted a filial bond between the two suggest that the scorn later authors felt for this earlier form was more complex than simple other-directed rejection: it also involved a degree of projection. At the very least, the relationship between these two types of works is more than strictly oppositional: each informs and in a sense derives from the other.[36]

Thus, using *Lucy Temple* as proof, Winfried Fluck takes what Baym, focusing primarily on authorial perspective, had seen as an opposition and posits a progression. Despite Fluck's tendency to exaggerate the seduction novel's obsessions with female vulnerability and sexual desire, he argues that the struggle for personal distinction lies at the center of both *Lucy Temple* and *Charlotte Temple*. Domestic fiction merely "opened up new possibilities for the project that also lay at the center of the sentimental novel, namely the struggle for individual recognition and self-esteem." In particular, *Lucy Temple* introduced a model in which "social learning replaces the exclusive focus on the cultivation of affect which is still typical of the sentimental novel." The heroine derives an alternative to dependence by learning to understand the cultural systems she occupies and to manipulate them to her

35. Nina Baym, *Woman's Fiction: A Guide to Novels by and about Women in America, 1820–1870* (1978; Chicago, 1993), xxvii, 27.
36. Ibid., xxix.

benefit. In this novel, Fluck concludes, "society becomes a potential source of self-esteem."[37]

Despite this lineage, there are two important differences between the early novel as typified by *Charlotte Temple* and the nineteenth-century domestic novel, of which *Lucy Temple* forms an early example. The first is a dawning emphasis on womanly resourcefulness, which is most starkly noted in the fact that a protagonist's lasting claim on her friends both within and without the text must no longer be purchased with her death. The second concerns an explicit acknowledgment of gender-based social oppression, such that female misfortune no longer correlates with individual errancy alone but also with recognized patterns of arbitrary institutional power. The domestic heroine survives by learning to face the particular difficulties of her lot as an unprotected woman, managing to "win her own way in the world."[38]

If *Lucy Temple* presaged the domestic novel, however, it also stepped beyond it. As Laura Morgan Green points out, domestic novels often made an important place for female education, containing a "profusion of representations of women as students, teachers, or frustrated scholars." What makes *Lucy Temple* so surprising within this context is that it seems to anticipate what Green identifies as the "alternative narrative . . . emerging from the women's higher education movement" that began in the 1840s: a narrative for which the domestic novel held "little room." Green cites three key developments in these later narratives: "a corporate, rather than an individual protagonist"; a location "partly in public and institutional settings that nevertheless stressed the private and internal occupations of study and contemplation"; and a narrative movement "not from maidenhood to marriage and the conventional closure of social reproduction but from the tragic position of downtrodden governess to the open-ended status of university scholar."[39]

Although it would be misleading to suggest that Lucy ends up in a woman's college of the sort that had yet to be founded, the novel does assert each of these agenda in some recognizable shape. It is "corporate" in that it departs from early American novelistic convention by structuring itself

---

37. Winfried Fluck, "Novels of Transition: From Sentimental Novel to Domestic Novel," in Udo J. Hebel, ed., *The Construction and Contestation of American Cultures and Identities in the Early National Period* (Heidelberg, 1999), 100, 111, 112.

38. Baym, *Woman's Fiction,* ix.

39. Laura Morgan Green, *Educating Women: Cultural Conflict and Victorian Literature* (Athens, Ohio, 2001), ix, xii, 4.

around three protagonists rather than a single benighted heroine. It occupies "public and institutional settings" primarily by placing Lucy at the helm of a school, rather than a family, at novel's end. Yet more important, it structures its supposed family so as to resemble a student body—and its supposed home to resemble a school—far more closely than it does any domestic entity of the period. Thus the so-called "private" family is rendered both public and institutional. Finally, in denying Lucy her long-anticipated husband only to provide her with a celibate existence in the service of her very own schoolhouse, the novel takes pains to emphasize her own sense of freedom and accomplishment. By comparison to her romantically led companions, Lucy perceives her life as "open-ended" and centered in an environment that represents one pinnacle of female education and influence at this point. She is, after all, the founder, director, and preceptress of an academy. In these respects, *Lucy Temple* is far more than a point of transition between novels ending in death (the seduction novel) and those ending in marriage (the domestic novel); it is an anomalous and radical moment of departure within this tradition, envisioning a female community in which romantic love and sexual reproduction play little or no part—in which neither heterosexuality nor motherhood is essential to finding one's voice or living a satisfying life.[40]

Lucy Temple provides an alternate source of intimacy, social harmony, and female self-esteem to the family—it is a "domestic novel" only in that it allows the affectual bonds and self-development associated with family structures to flourish in an environment devoid of the latter's fraternal ties or sexual legitimation. It's not just that both Lucy and Rowson find love and personal satisfaction at their school that are unavailable elsewhere. Rowson also makes this experience the template for a utopian alternative to the families she aims to enrich by educating their daughters in the protofamilial environment of her school. A few hours out of their day or a few months out of their lives lay the foundation for a different conception of family. In addition, the skills women developed in the academy prepared them for the

---

40. On American women's educational history, see Thomas Woody, *A History of Women's Education in the United States* (New York, 1929); Elizabeth Seymour Eschbach, *The Higher Education of Women in England and America, 1865–1920* (New York, 1993); Catherine Hobbs, ed., *Nineteenth-Century Women Learn to Write* (Charlottesville, Va., 1995); Louise Schutz Boas, *Woman's Education Begins: The Rise of the Women's Colleges* (New York, 1971); Joel Perlmann, Silvana R. Siddali, and Keith Whitescarver, "Literacy, Schooling, and Teaching among New England Women, 1730–1820," *History of Education Quarterly*, XXXVII (1997), 117–139.

three most viable professions for women: authorship, teaching, and editing. In fostering economic independence through paid employment, the female academy and the novel to which it gave rise not only improved women's material standing in early American society but also encouraged students and readers to develop the more intangible qualities of self-sufficiency and self-esteem.[41]

Rowson, I have stated, taught both toward and beyond the consolidation of authority by means of maternally inflected affect, ultimately fostering a climate in quiet defiance of domestic regulation. How did *Lucy Temple,* which takes up where *Charlotte Temple* left off, inscribe this defiance? The first thing to note is that the former did so "quietly" enough as not yet to have been observed. Karen Weyler, for one, pronounces the novel to submit fully to the disciplinary regime of the early Republic as one of several "conservative fictions of the early national era" that "showed readers the inevitable punishment of those who transgressed against their families and communities." Although Weyler notes the novel's attention, through its blending of female financial profligacy with unlicensed sexual activity, to the fact that "marriage, one of the most personal of human relationships, is nonetheless also an economic transaction," she views such attention as "pathologizing female desire outside the bounds of matrimony," as part of her wider emphasis on how fiction of the period inculcated the female "virtue of self-discipline." But if the novel pathologizes the excessive desire for financial gain or the company of one's female schoolmates, it also—as such cautionary tales necessarily must—inscribes such impulses so as to undermine the pathological mode.[42]

As a sequel, *Lucy Temple* may seem more antidote than complement to its precursor. Although each novel starts with a question, the answers lead in opposite directions. *Charlotte's* Lieutenant Belcour thinks it would be a fine thing to walk instead of drive with his fellow officer Montraville, and there begins the trouble, as they saunter by a schoolyard containing the young Charlotte. But Lucy, the same age as Charlotte at her seduction, doesn't even answer Mr. Matthews's caviling sister-in-law, who questions Lucy's decision to kneel and attend to an old soldier's injured leg. The question must be repeated, and even then, Lucy deliberately overlooks the "sharp

41. Rowson's was primarily a day school, but it also took in boarders. The school generally had a class roll of more than one hundred students and boarded anywhere from three to thirty. See Brandt, *Susanna Haswell Rowson,* 177.

42. Weyler, *Intricate Relations,* 8, 81.

tone" so as to complete her task. Throughout the novel, Lucy displays a "resolve" that we saw in Chapter 1 was only intermittently available to her mother, and the novel itself is similarly untroubled, managing to overcome its two romantic near-catastrophes to provide fulfilling lives for every one of its three female protagonists. Unlike the novels of female undoing upon which early republicans feasted, women in this novel get a second chance, whereas men tend to be blighted by one mistake. Despite their differences, however, there is one point on which both novels agree.[43]

Charlotte Temple, we saw, took the standard frame of the seduction novel and retrofitted it to avoid the matter of sexuality almost entirely, in favor of a meditation on female agency. And *Lucy Temple* reenacts this skittishness. If *Charlotte Temple* transposed the terminology of erotic play onto that of self-definition, here there seems almost nothing erotic to transpose. Even legitimate avowals of love are strangely bloodless, as marriages are generally based on affection rather than yearning. Lucy's guardian, Mr. Matthews, and his wife, whom he chooses in deference to her evident affection for him, have no children and exchange none of the embraces that inspired Mrs. Beauchamp's fond blushes. Mr. Matthews proposes to Philippa instead of her younger sister merely because he sees that she prefers him, and he wishes not to hurt her feelings. In a novelistic culture where children appear as physical evidence of almost every sexual act, this couple's childlessness suggests a dearth of sex.[44]

Just as significant, the novel refuses to consummate Lucy's promised union. Her love affair is cut short by the discovery late in the novel that her would-be swain, Lieutenant John Franklin, is her half-brother through her father: in other words, he is the birth child of Lieutenant Montraville and Julia Franklin from *Charlotte Temple.* Lucy remains celibate from then on, as if in direct atonement for her mother's sexual transgression, as does her former intended until his death in battle several years later. In forming itself around an erotic vacuum, this novel divests itself of any remaining trappings of the narrative of seduction—and indeed of the traditional heterosexual family itself, with its sexual unions and infant incarnations. In their stead, it constructs a utopian and gynocentric alternative: the young ladies' school of life, rendered first in Mr. Matthews's home and then by Lucy's plan for

---

43. Rowson, *Lucy Temple,* ed. Douglas, 135, 240. Of *Lucy Temple,* Susan C. Greenfield writes: "Female characters are linguistically empowered and male characters are erased" (Greenfield, *"Charlotte Temple* and *Charlotte's Daughter:* The Reproduction of Woman's Word," *Women's Studies,* XVIII [1990], 269–286, esp. 269).

44. Rowson, *Lucy Temple,* ed. Douglas, 140–141.

"founding a little seminary for the education of female children." In what follows, we will examine the currency of affective exchange in a universe devoid of the traditional markers of heterosexual union. As it turns out, the alternative world that Lucy occupies looks remarkably like the one from which Miss P. W. Jackson emerges to deliver her valedictory address, with one exception: its raging, obsessive concern with cash.[45]

Money is everywhere in this book—not in an abstract or general sense but in bills and promissory notes. When Lucy plans to throw a birthday party, she asks her guardian for "one hundred pounds, in guineas, half guineas, crowns and half crowns," to be distributed to the poor of the village who are her invited guests. When a village girl's faithless husband is arrested, it is not merely for "debt" but "for fifteen hundred pounds on his note which he had given for stock, and as we afterwards learnt, sold at under price." Acts of charity are broken down into crowns and half crowns, and when the novel's most wayward protagonist, the young Mary, insists on five guineas for a poor family, Mr. Matthews demonstrates to her how "a little tea, oatmeal, sugar, and materials for brown bread, half a cheese, half a side of bacon, some coals and candles, were all purchased for less than a guinea and a half."[46]

In the above examples, a fascination with money exists in only a loosely contiguous relationship with the avoidance of romantic intrigue. But as often, it plays a direct role in fostering erotic disaffection. Thus a secondary character, Alice, "thoughtless in her expenses," fosters her husband's dissipation rather than "weaning her unhappy partner from his pursuits." (This financial rewording of a standard adage of the time, that a man's conduct is deeply influenced by his wife's, appears two more times, when wives further irritate already dissipated husbands: a subject on which Rowson spoke with some authority.) When a young woman threatens to fall out of favor with her suitor, again, the matter of expense is to blame. When characters do fancy one another, as Edward Ainslie does Mr. Matthews's third ward, Aura Mel-

45. Ibid., 240. In another genealogical link between the mother and daughter texts, Sergeant Blandford, the old soldier at whose feet Lucy kneels at the start of her novel, is the man who rescued her mother after Mrs. Crayton, née La Rue, cast her out. Sharon M. Harris describes an actual post-Revolutionary mother-daughter relationship that recalls Lucy and her mother's in its blend of attachment and differentiation. Margaretta Bleecker Faugeres, daughter to poet Ann Eliza Bleecker, "honors her mother's ideals, but she also allows space for her own, differing artistic development." See Harris, *Executing Race: Early American Women's Narratives of Race, Society, and the Law* (Columbus, Ohio, 2005), 114.

46. Rowson, *Lucy Temple*, ed. Douglas, 158, 165, 211.

ville, unlikely inheritances must fall into explicitly depicted place before the relationship can proceed to marriage. Everywhere, money is intimately tied up with implicitly sexual relationships both legitimate and illegitimate.[47]

Even when sexual congress seems an inevitable feature of a subplot, the thematic weight falls on financial profligacy instead. The most direct substitution of financial for erotic obsession in the novel occurs with the quality orphan Mary, who replays Charlotte's story at low volume, except that Mary recovers. Yet in the account of her misadventures, unlike Charlotte's, not a single false step is unaccompanied by a reference to financial indiscretion. When Mary is seduced, it is not her virginity that she squanders but her "seven thousand pounds." Every aspect of the seduction is described in such terms. When Mr. Matthews warns her that her fiancé is "a bankrupt in both fortune and character," Mary retorts, "In a short period the law will consider me of an age to dispose of my own person, and take care of my own interest," and in fact it's the interest on her account to which she refers (elsewhere she calls herself a "free and independent agent"). At every opportunity, she equates person and property: "When I make him master of my person, I shall also give him possession of my property." Thus Mr. Matthews's claim that she has "ruined herself" speaks to her financial ruin first and foremost, and her lament to her presumed husband upon learning his true colors—"I have given you all"—is quite literal. (Mary does bear Sir Stephen's child, alone and friendless, but unlike Charlotte's eponymous progeny, Mary's infant dies nameless after a few days, easing her return to a life of sanctioned— and solitary—docility.) Instead of lamenting her sexual surrender, the novel obsessively recounts how a woman who had enough "to secure to her those comforts and conveniencies of life to which she had ever been accustomed" ends up penniless.[48]

We thus have two mysterious features in what otherwise seems a highly systematic novel: an erotic divestiture and a corollary fascination with filthy lucre, expressed in cautionary terms very much like those formerly reserved for sex. In these, it is possible to discover both why Rowson chose a school as her model for affective exchange and the overwhelming and ultimately unfulfilled need such a choice reveals. The substitution of an asset denied most women (money) for one with which they are universally allied (erotic attraction as the basis for either marriage or seduction) validates early American women's desire for self-support while critiquing most contemporary novels' emphasis on romantic entanglements as the stuff of female subjectivity. The

47. Ibid., 159, 165, 224, 229.
48. Ibid., 179, 180–181, 191, 199.

location of this substitution in an academy emphasizes that female education is crucial to women's ability to attain the economic independence they
crave.

At the turn of the nineteenth century, a financially independent woman,
although unusual, had more control over her destiny and more capacity to
remain an accepted member of her socius than did a sexually defiant one;
and it is this capacity for self-determination within the bounds of the social
contract that Rowson favored above all else for both her students and her
female readers. Sacrificing intimacy to general acceptance, intense pleasure
to measured well-being, and immediacy to longevity, Rowson traces in *Lucy
Temple* both the joys and the quieter lamentation that accompanied a successful female entrant into the earliest nineteenth-century public sphere.

We first meet Lucy, as mentioned above, kneeling "at the feet of an old
man." She spends the next three pages getting up. She "ris[es] on one knee"
before "rising" to walk home with her senior companion, Mrs. Cavendish,
and continues "rising" at home into an embrace with her fatherly guardian, Mr. Matthews. By emphasizing Lucy's upward motion, the narrative
lets us know which side it's on in the battle Lucy quietly wages with her
guardian's sister-in-law, who repeatedly accuses her of staying close to the
ground. According to Mrs. Cavendish and her sister, Mrs. Matthews, Lucy
tends to "demean" herself, to associate with "low people," and to possess
a "vast number of low ideas and habits." At issue here is how one defines
stature, or, in the lexicon of the novel, "consequence." The elderly sisters
think that spending one's time on the floor of dirty cottages is not in keeping with Lucy's status as both a "splendid heiress" and a young, unmarried
woman. Mrs. Matthews professes herself "astonished that Miss Blakeney
has not a higher sense of propriety and her own consequence." Lucy's retort, however, suggests an alternate understanding of this statement: "It
was to make myself of consequence that I did it; for . . . sergeant Blandford
calls me his guardian angel, his comforter; and I am sure those are titles of
consequence." Through its staging of Lucy's postures as she defends her
behavior, the narrative grants her victory in this struggle over the meaning
of a word, staking its claim in favor of behavior over lineage as the key factor
in determining individual worth. Indeed, even the older ladies are won over
to a degree, pronouncing that Lucy "can sometimes assume the *hauteur* and
air of a duchess."[49]

This passage establishes the novel, like the schools described above, as a

49. Ibid., 137, 139.

locale that values competence over wealth or social stature. But it simultaneously reveals that the novel is not immune to distinction; it praises Lucy's democratic behavior in terms of aristocratic rank. Another way of perceiving this conundrum is to note that the passage merely upends, rather than discards, the elderly ladies' posited ratio of posture to consequence. To them, important people stand tall, whereas to Lucy, they crouch. The notion that some people are more important than others, however, is never at issue.

Thus the most significant aspect of this introductory passage, as far as revealing the tenor of the novel, is not merely its attempt to determine a just standard of measurement but rather its concern with measurement itself. The following discussion disentangles *Lucy Temple's* disregard for arbitrary status indicators, such as economic class, from its obsession with the tools of measurement, or what Jean-Joseph Goux, explaining the Aristotelian ideal of the "general equivalent," describes as a "measuring object"—something that allows for "parallels between quantitative and qualitative logics of value" and that, "by making things commensurable, renders it possible to make them equal."[50]

Lucy Temple is a book in search of a general equivalent, and one of its main candidates is money. There is no denying that money sows misery and misinformation throughout the lives of the three main characters. Mary is betrayed by a suitor in pursuit of her supposed wealth, Aura finds herself the object of sycophantic attention from men who (also falsely) believe her to be the richest of the three, and even Lucy's late-discovered fraternal relationship to her love interest is the result of her father's abandoning her poor mother in favor of a wealthy heiress. Nevertheless, the novel uses money to represent the possibility of just and fulfilling human exchange. And it does so through a discussion of charity.

In an act of charity, as it is defined by Mr. Matthews, the connection between "quantity" (how much is given) and "quality" (what effect the money has on the behavior of the recipient) is exact. Thus, although he might smile upon Lucy as she lavishes her time and affection on her less fortunate neighbors, when it comes to providing them with material goods, thrift is key. Nothing is to be given unless in exchange for an expected alteration of behavior. "Had you given the sum you intended," Mr. Matthews warns Mary when she rushes home pleading for cash to help some destitute neighbors, "they would have squandered it away, and not made themselves half so comfortable. . . . I shall see that they are comfortably clothed, and, if I find that

50. Jean-Joseph Goux, *Symbolic Economies: After Marx and Freud,* trans. Jennifer Curtiss Gage (Ithaca, N.Y., 1990), 3.

the clothes are kept whole and clean, I will befriend the family farther. But if they are let run to rags, without washing or mending, I shall do no more." The key is to give only enough to stimulate further effort.[51]

The degree to which this model of measured generosity pervades the "qualitative" recesses of the novel becomes evident from another gem of Mr. Matthews's wisdom.

> It is not the bestowing large sums that constitutes real benevolence, nor do such donations ultimately benefit the persons on whom they are bestowed, they rather serve to paralyze the hand of industry, while they lead the individual to depend on adventitious circumstances for relief, instead of exerting his own energies to soften or surmount the difficulties with which he may be surrounded.

When one considers this passage in light of Lucy's fate, its significance is both poignant and ironic. Lucy began the novel in hopes of consummating a great romance. When her love interest turned out to be her brother, she fell apart briefly, then collected herself and began to reconstitute the basis of life's worth. From then on, Lucy, who once seemed destined to have had great love "bestowed" upon her, becomes known for her unflagging "industry" as the founder of a highly successful academy for young girls of all stations. The narrator writes, not entirely convincingly, "In these pursuits it is hardly necessary to say that she found a tranquility and satisfaction which the splendid awards of fortune and fame can never impart." But even the narrator must admit on the last page of the book that Lucy, like her author, bore "private griefs and recollections" to her grave. The humble poor, then, aren't the only ones who must learn to make do with just enough.[52]

If charity provides *Lucy Temple* with its general equivalent, the schoolhouse represents the world governed by such a law, wherein, because all "logics of value" are "commensurable," it is possible for them to be made "equal."

51. Rowson, *Lucy Temple,* ed. Douglas, 166. Mr. Matthews's program is typical of "the character reform strategy" that informed the emergence of charitable institutions in America. "Poverty, unemployment, and other social concerns were seen not as issues of economics or politics but of morality. . . . Charity had several moral functions," including "to help settled citizens (particularly the affluent) meet their own Christian duties" and "to shape and maintain the morals of others, particularly the poor" (David Wagner, *What's Love Got to Do with It? A Critical Look at American Charity* [New York, 2000], 50–51).

52. Rowson, *Lucy Temple,* ed. Douglas, 264–265.

Teaching, in this novel, exemplifies the potential for human interactions to exist within a closed system in which every gesture is both legible and reciprocal: what an instructor teaches, a student learns and is the better for it. In this utopia, human relationships are protected from both excess and deprivation, from wasted passion and arbitrary loss.

In an attempt to create such a world, Rowson describes in Mr. Matthews's home an almost exact simulacrum of the school she directed for most of her adult life and in which she wrote this novel. Lucy Temple does not grow up in a house so much as an expertly run academy, one in which mutual affection is necessary for learning. In the preface to the *Biblical Dialogues,* Rowson outlines the rudiments of her educational system in a manner that is fulfilled within the confines of Mr. Matthews's home. First she describes her student body: "young persons of my own sex of all ages, from five years old to twenty." Then she describes the tripartite formula of "ornamental" accomplishment, intellectual endowment ("understanding"), and practical virtue ("strict moral and religious principles") that characterizes the curriculum of the school. Mr. Matthews, too, has an all-female student body, which the novel follows from young childhood to about the age of twenty; and, as he explains to Lucy's grandfather upon assuming responsibility for her, he runs his home according to the same three categories: "Under his eye [she should] receive instruction in the accomplishments becoming the rank she would most probably fill in society from the best masters; whilst the cultivation of her mental powers, the formation of her religious character . . . he solemnly promised should be his own peculiar care."[53]

Mr. Matthews's task is depicted as the "education," rather than the parenting, of these three girls. Only Aura holds the rank of "daughter," and this claim she lays chiefly on her adoptive mother, from whom—in a poignant allusion to Rowson's own stepmother and two adopted daughters—"though she experienced not the most tender affection, yet Aura Melville found in her all the care and solicitude of a mother." Mr. Matthews's engagements with his charges take on the character of lessons on almost every occasion, as was only too clear from his studied response to Mary's impulsive request that he help a family down the way.[54]

53. Rowson, preface to *Biblical Dialogues,* iii; Rowson, *Lucy Temple,* ed. Douglas, 139.

54. Rowson, *Lucy Temple,* ed. Douglas, 146. McDermid notes that, in England during the eighteenth century, conservative women writers "warned women against the dangers of sensibility . . . indeed against any excess of feeling, even of charity, that great feminine virtue" (McDermid, "Conservative Feminism," *History of Education,* XVIII [1989], 309–322, esp. 309).

Not only Mr. Matthews but the girls themselves reveal the pedagogical subtext of the setting. Each one arrives either imperfectly or insufficiently educated. Mary's vanity, vague aspirations to royalty, and easily wounded pride are "the fruits of the imprudent system of her education" on the part of a now-deceased mother once given to class pretensions and "an indiscriminate perusal of every work of fiction that issued from the press." Aura is motherless almost from birth, still suffering from the death of her beloved father, and poor; since "her father had laid a good foundation in her innocent mind," Mr. Matthews need not correct, but merely "complete . . . the education he had begun." Lucy, we have already seen, arrives modest and rich (a happy combination); in her case, it is thus of special importance that Mr. Matthews befit her for "the rank she would most probably fill in society." These students are also carefully selected to represent the limited diversity of class, temperament, and educational background one might encounter in a girls' academy at the turn of the century. Further, Rowson is as careful to stress their interchangeability within the economy of the group—another key feature of the early American girls' academy, according to Gordon—as she is their distinction from one another outside it. In a tribute to the implicitly egalitarian setting of a school, in which, ideally, pupils of varying backgrounds come together on one plane before leaving the utopia of the classroom to resume their true rank and file, onlookers are forever taking Aura, as Lucy's "pursebearer," for the heiress. In another indication of the degree to which education has permeated the recesses of the family structure, Aura, the only student not rich enough to leave the house for further instruction in art and music, receives those lessons from the more privileged girls on their return.[55]

In this seemingly faithful reproduction of Rowson's own school, however, one substitution begs to be explained. Given the near-identity of Mr. Matthews's house with Mrs. Rowson's Young Ladies' Academy, why did she make her own stand-in a man? This act of surrogacy provides a clue, akin to Lucy's veiled melancholy, that the closed system represented by the ideal academy—in which every gesture is geared to engendering positive change and from which erotic entanglements, with their potential for wasted affect, are excluded—did not fully suit the novelist's experience. The substitution of male for female instructor provided her with an opportunity to explore the affectionate intensity—even erotics—of the teacher-student relationship in which she had come to place so much store. Mr. Matthews exchanges the greatest tendernesses with each of his charges that they are to experience in

55. Rowson, *Lucy Temple,* ed. Douglas, 139, 143, 146, 172.

the course of the novel, whether because their lovers are cruel or cruelly de-nied them by "a terrible fate." This is not coincidental. As a teacher, Rowson constructed an alternative affective model to the tragic seductions of many of her early works, one that approached the erotics of seduction in its intensity, its overwhelming effects on the body, and its role in organizing the subject's emotional understanding and sense of self. Mr. Matthews, then, both pro-vided a systematic antidote to irresolvable grief in his emphasis on measure and introduced the possibility of erotic affection by serving as the teacherly "crush" for his charges. In the preface to *The Inquisitor,* Rowson writes the following exchange between her and a friend: "But why do you make your Inquisitor a man?, said he. For a very obvious reason, I replied. A man may be with propriety brought forward in many scenes where it would be the height of improbability to introduce a woman."[56]

At the end of *Lucy Temple,* however, a woman is "brought forward." In the best possible end for a favored student from a teacher's point of view, Lucy herself becomes a preceptor, filling quite a different "rank" than that alluded to early in the book—but, in its own way, one just as "fitting." Out of the home-school chrysalis emerges a full-fledged school, as Lucy establishes her own girls' seminary as part of "her plans for ameliorating the condition of the poor." Lucy's act reveals her education to be complete, as she begins to create systems for the more efficient implementation of what had once been merely impulse. As she sits "planning in her own mind the internal ar-rangement and economy of the little establishment," Lucy demonstrates her ability, acquired over the course of the novel, to harness affection to correc-tion, kindness to measure. The "child of benevolence" has indeed matured and is now able to make "the true economy of benevolence her study." And an economy of benevolence, unlike a child thereof, does not bestow equal merit upon all but apportions its limited resources. Thus her school is to possess roughly identical rooms on the ground floor, in which the separate but equal disciplines of "needlework," "common branches of instruction," and "principles of morality," echoing Rowson's and Mr. Matthews's simi-lar divisions, are to be taught. But "over all these, there was a sort of High School, to which a few only were promoted who gave evidence of that degree of talent and probity which would fit them for extended usefulness. These, under the instruction of the preceptress of the whole establishment, were to receive a more finished education than the rest."[57]

56. Ibid., 240; Rowson, *The Inquisitor; or, Invisible Rambler,* 3 vols. (Philadelphia, 1793), I, 3.

57. Rowson, *Lucy Temple,* ed. Douglas, 135, 240, 259.

In short, Lucy has learned to discriminate. No longer a child, she now demonstrates her adult state not only through her expert skill at both charity and pedagogy but through her ability to link the two. When she gives, she teaches, serving as a "stimulus" to the recipient's "exerting his own energies." And when she teaches, she gives, both by welcoming poor students and by employing a technique, developed at Rowson's own academy, in which, by "learning the natural bent and disposition of the young pupils," she is able to "develop their affections." Lucy's school has become the ideal pedagogical unit, in which all energy expended, both intellectual and emotional, is reciprocal and has its desired effect.[58]

It is at this moment that the narrator shifts her allegiance, leaving Mr. Matthews behind and entering the body of her young protagonist. The transition is elongated, as the first skill Lucy demonstrates—the above-named ability to read her students' own "natural bent"—is one Mr. Matthews has also practiced and is, we know from Rowson's own teaching records, a quality on which she prides herself. But Lucy, it soon becomes clear, possesses one thing her male mentor lacks—she has suffered. One can almost hear Rowson taking stock of her own travails—her increasing physical infirmity, her persistent financial instability, her long unsatisfactory marriage—as she pens the following lines:

> But it was in developing their affections and moral capabilities that she chiefly delighted. There was a field of exertion in which the example of the patroness was of infinite value to the instructers [sic]. Her own education, her knowledge of human character and of nature, her cultivated and refined moral taste, and above all, the healing and religious light, which her admirable submission to the trying hand of Providence had shed over the world and all its concerns as they appeared to her view,— all these things served to fit her for this species of ministry to the minds and hearts of these young persons.

Mr. Matthews was a way for Rowson to get her female readers used to the intimacy between preceptor and student; but Lucy is her ultimate model, showing that not only female students but also female educators possess a capacity unavailable to their more privileged brothers: the capacity to harness, in the vocabulary of *Charlotte Temple's* preface, "friendship" to "understanding," the production of affect to that of knowledge.[59]

58. Ibid., 155, 241, 259.

59. Ibid., 241. The preface to *Charlotte Temple* states that the novel "may, I flatter

Given that Mr. Matthews makes a school of his home and a family of his students, what kind of education does the novel provide the reader? How does it suggest that learning involves more than introjected authority? In that the novel demands a restraint of its reader similar to that which Mr. Matthews is constantly harping upon in the arena of financial management, this possibility is by no means self-evident. Rowson's contribution to the schoolroom seemed to be that one can't learn without deep emotional investment, but beneath this premise lurks the possibility that one is perfectly capable of expending emotion without learning a thing. It is in order to achieve the former goal and ward off the latter that Rowson structures *Lucy Temple* as an answer to the best seller of her early days.

Thus the reader of *Charlotte Temple* and *Lucy Temple* proceeds along a similar trajectory to that of Lucy, as she develops from a child on her knees before a fallen soldier to a headmistress mentally placing her students within her schoolhouse. Where readerly emotion in the former novel was full, uninhibited, and lavished upon a single subject, here (as we have seen) the story apportions that energy along three trajectories simultaneously, weaving together the life courses of Mr. Matthews's three young female wards in such a manner that no single story can demand an overweening stock of sympathy. Having problematized largesse in the arenas of both charitable giving and heteroerotic relationships, the novel extends this emphasis on measure to the reading process itself. The result is equally prophylactic. Regularly required to weigh each protagonist's fate in relation to her companions', the reader cannot but diversify her affective portfolio and is correspondingly protected from sudden and overwhelming loss such as transported *Charlotte's* early readers. If a novel such as *Charlotte* failed to train its readers in the art of sympathy, according to Rush, because it wasted their store of compassion on useless fantasies, *Lucy Temple* can be accused of no such license; it leaves plenty for real life. And like Lucy, behind the sense of secure well-being such emotional thrift provides, one is left nursing a lingering sense of lost opportunity.[60]

But if Rowson's emphasis on measured giving correlates with her plan for an educational novel and an emotionally safe universe, it also overflows

---

myself, be of service to some who are so unfortunate as to have neither friends to advise, or understanding to direct them, through the various and unexpected evils that attend a young and unprotected woman in her first entrance into life" (Rowson, *Lucy Temple,* ed. Douglas, xlix). Parker notes that, near the end of Rowson's life, her husband incurred debts that her illness prevented her from repaying (Parker, *Susanna Rowson,* 23).

60. Rowson, *Lucy Temple,* ed. Douglas, 155.

its bounds at every opportunity, as financial signifiers crowd the page to proclaim their message of thrift. There exists a similar tension in the tripartite frame itself between our would-be love for Lucy and our kind regard for her near-sisters, already evident in the title originally chosen for the novel: *Charlotte's Daughter; or, The Three Orphans.* (A popular variation appearing on several subsequent editions was *Lucy Temple; or, The Three Sisters.*) Which will it be, the one or the three? In its juggling of protagonists and its final, wistful attention to Lucy, the novel ends up attesting to our readerly craving to attach to one figure above all others, our demand for imbalance in our narrative as in our extracurricular relationships. This need is rendered all the more intense by Lucy's own eternal celibacy, her explicit substitution of the moderate exchanges of the schoolroom for the passionate embrace. Despite the erotic parsimony of *Lucy Temple,* whereas we longed only to be Charlotte's comforter, we want to adore Lucy—if only to assuage a melancholy that no amount of good works seems to obliterate, narrative protestations to the contrary. This desire is, by definition, not returned, since Lucy, after all, is only words on paper and has no idea we exist. Wasted affect and lasting loss are to have their day after all. Reading is to be the ultimate unreciprocated relationship.[61]

Charlotte Temple, we saw at the outset of this study, undercut its call to vigilant self-articulation with subtle invitations to indulge in Charlotte's passivity. To a certain degree, its sequel resolves the imbalance between narrative lavishness and semantic calls to regulation. Tempering that play of indulgence and regulation, the "affective pulsation between identification with fictional characters and withdrawal from them, between emotional investment and divestment," *Lucy Temple* embeds methods for narrative withholding within its implied reading strategies. But its economy remains unable to encompass every impulse generated by the text, and this incompletion is signaled by the cash that lies scattered among its pages, tracks of the unfinished business in human exchange. These footprints save the novel, and the pedagogical utopia it depicts, from the total conflation of power and affect suggested by a critical emphasis on self-regulation as the early American novel's signature task. Cast out from the safety of the schoolroom novel, we leave longing to "bestow . . . large sums" upon one of its favored

61. Many of the titles chosen for various editions of Rowson's last novel replicate the original indecision whether to emphasize one or three protagonists. See, for instance, the editions of *Lucy Temple: One of the Three Orphans* published between 1842 and 1929; and see R. W. G. Vail, *Susanna Haswell Rowson, the Author of Charlotte Temple: A Bibliographical Study* (Worcester, Mass., 1932), 28, 87–90.

students—in defiance of all we have learned therein about economizing on benevolence—just as Rowson, it seemed, went to her death contemplating "the memory of [their] kindness."[62]

Nevertheless, if reading *Lucy Temple* fostered passions it did not requite, it also created a like-minded community of readers engaged in this pursuit. This community both paralleled and no doubt intersected with the sociability that took place within Rowson's academy and in the reading groups and exchanges of letters that followed upon students' departure from her motto-covered walls. Such acts of social engagement were a key feature of the female academy movement of which Rowson's own school was but one small part, just as *Lucy Temple* formed a small element in the exploding novelistic industry whose domination by women Nathaniel Hawthorne was famously soon to lament. Whether or not readers discussed *Lucy Temple,* then, the novel both fostered and described a moment in which female sociability was irrevocably altered by new practices of intellectual and imaginative exchange. Thus did Rowson and those she influenced imagine and act out ideals of self-fulfillment within and against prescriptive constraints that would shape women's activism, benevolence, and domesticity in the antebellum era.

In an acrostic found in Rowson's papers, she honored a favored student, Hannah Swan, who went on to teach in another academy. This brief poem crystallizes the aspects of Rowsonian pedagogy that formed the basis for a subversive new female public not bound to the disciplinary use of affection. The poem's first ten lines spell out the subject's name with the first letter of each line. In the last four lines, Rowson distinguishes between the young woman's fate and her own:

> Dear Hannah, may your morn as brightly shine
> And your meridian be
> From those dank vapors free
> Which overshadowed mine.

Not only does Rowson's life experience fail to serve as a template for Hannah's own, but the supposed mentor looks to her charge for relief. The older woman's life is already "overshadowed"; only Hannah's rosier future can make up for the poetic persona's losses and mistakes. At the same time,

62. Catherine Gallagher, *Nobody's Story: The Vanishing Acts of Women Writers in the Marketplace, 1670–1820* (Berkeley, Calif., 1994), xvii–xviii.

Rowson's unhappiness is a caution to Hannah and other young female readers of this poem, one that Lucy Temple seems to have heeded unwittingly by avoiding marriage and dedicating herself to community service. Indeed, the idea that Lucy's fate should in some way compensate for Charlotte's—not only in a religious or moral sense but in the satisfaction provided the reader of both tales—is uncannily echoed in this brief lament from a despairing mother figure to an untried younger woman.[63]

The last four lines of this poem seem to violate the titular claim that it is an acrostic. But it is quite possible that Rowson deferred to grammatical precedent by substituting "which" for an originally intended "that" in the last line. With "that," the last stanza would have spelled out "daft." And "daft" was an abbreviation for "daughter," based on its occasional spelling as "dafter." (It is thought that "daughter" was pronounced like "laughter" in some dialects.) In that case, Rowson would have adopted Hannah as her own, based on the claims of a female intimacy fostered in a nondomestic and intellectually centered environment.

Documented relationships such as these suggest that the Rowsonian academy environment neither reinstated nor abandoned contemporary familial bonds but rather transposed them so as to render them voluntaristic rather than genealogical. The presumed intimacy between mother and child was to be available to any teacher and student with the requisite temperament and determination. And it was not to consist of one-way instruction only; the "dafter" would often provide both wisdom and solace to the mother figure. Thus did Rowson take the behavioral expectations for post-Revolutionary daughters, which frequently culminated in an early marriage that removed the young woman from one patriarchal home to another, and redirect them to the formation of sisterly bonds outside the familial realm. Although this sorority involved instruction, its lessons were not coeval with indoctrination into a social world presumed just or satisfactory to its female inhabitants. Rather, as the acrostic to Hannah suggests, such instruction emphasized the perils ahead and the importance of anticipating arbitrary setbacks. Most important, the relationship nominally organized around the greater wisdom of the teacher also compensated for the times when her own fate became intolerable. "Dank vapors" serve no disciplinary purpose, but they are enormously educational as to what might lie ahead for a woman

63. Susanna Rowson, "Accrostic" and "On the Death of Miss Eliza Bradley," n.d., Rowson Papers, MSS 7379-a, box 1, folder 1 (see also Nason, *Memoir of Mrs. Susanna Rowson*, 149–150); Brandt, *Susanna Haswell Rowson*, 177.

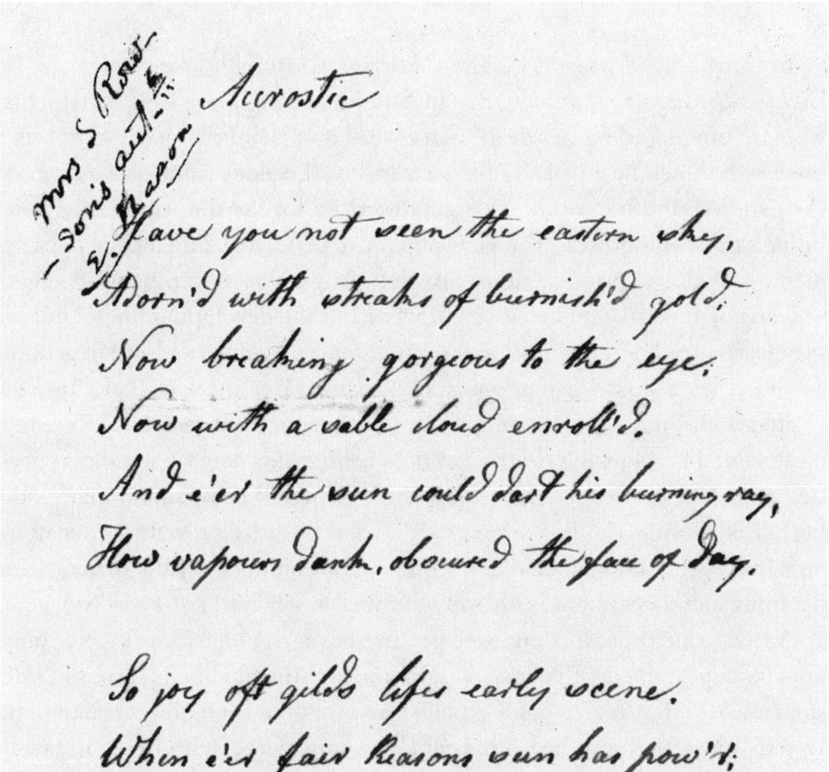
Mrs S Rowson's auth. E. Mason

Accrostic

Have you not seen the eastern sky,
Adorn'd with streaks of burnish'd gold;
Now breaking gorgeous to the eye;
Now with a sable cloud enroll'd.
And e'er the sun could dart his burning ray,
How vapours dank, obscured the face of day.

So joy oft gilds lifes early scene.
When e'er fair Reasons sun has pow'r;
A sombre cloud will intervene,
Nor pleasure gild the prospect more.

Dear Hannah may your morn as brightly shine,
And your meridian be,
From those dank vapours free.
Which overshaddowed mine.

PLATE 24. *Susanna Rowson, "Accrostic." N.d. Papers of Susanna Rowson, MSS 7379, Clifton Waller Barrett Library of American Literature, Special Collections, University of Virginia Library* whose perceived "rights" consisted of the opportunity to choose her servitude.

In *Memory's Daughters: The Material Culture of Remembrance in Eighteenth-Century America,* Susan Stabile documents a case in which a woman, upon reading her dead mother-in-law's claim that she did not like the way her own face looked in a portrait, cut the elder woman's face out of the painting and burned it. This act describes for me the American Revolution's greatest betrayal. Forced economic dependence, intellectual debasement, sexual and physical abuse, denial of rights just then being deemed universally human, and delegitimation within the developing liberal public sphere shaped the early national oppression of women and other groups excluded from post-Revolutionary citizenship. But the fact that those so treated took their rage out on one another remains oppression's crowning ornament. The shocking destructiveness behind this daughter-in-law's gesture suggests the deep identification and misplaced compassion that made her think she was doing her senior relative a favor by preventing her ugliness from being known. And any woman who commits so fully to another's damning self-assessment is unlikely to think much better of herself.[64]

At the same time, this punitive gesture has a righteous aspect. Not only does it suggest the depth of one daughter's resentment at being brought into such a world, but it also holds an elder accountable for failing to change it. In retrospect, perhaps the vandal came to commiserate with her mother-in-law at a deeper level and to wish for the portrait back. With such wisdom might have developed the ability to empathize with those who had formerly shared the bulk of her misplaced resentment: other women. In such perceived sameness would have begun a strike against pervasive sex-based injustice.

It has been my contention that Rowson experienced the same transmutation of rage and resentment into sororal fellowship, intellectual and imaginative ambition, and resolute, if strained, optimism that I have ascribed to this woman. Rowson made faces instead of destroying them. Moreover, her creations both register and inform the cultural moment in which post-Revolutionary female intellectual development, imagined community, and same-sex sociability became widespread. With almost manic intensity, she continually fashioned her world into an embodiment of her utopia. Her

64. Susan M. Stabile, *Memory's Daughters: The Material Culture of Remembrance in Eighteenth-Century America* (Ithaca, N.Y., 2004). In 1934, Maria Dickinson Logan destroyed a portrait of Deborah Logan by Charles Willson Peale, completed in 1825 (129–131, 177).

schoolroom took on the very shape of a mind at work with every new motto inscribed upon its walls. Her behavior, whether dressing an awkward body in tasteful clothes or crossing the Atlantic to revisit a nation from which she had recently been expelled, attested to the power of stubborn will to modify circumstance. And her writings infiltrated scattered homes, libraries, and schools to insist that isolated young women conceive of themselves as part of a common project: the attainment of social influence through unremitting self-regard. Judith Sargent Murray, Rowson's closest sister in this capacity, brilliantly articulated the transforming power of female "self-complacency." And Rowson herself attested to it: not only on her own behalf, but on behalf of the many she helped fashion into early America's first female public.

index

Blandford (character, *Lucy Temple*), 286

Bliss, Louisa, 1–2

Body, female: and determination of identity, 29, 203–207; and pregnancy, 51–55, 56n. 10, 60, 64–65, 167, 204; references to, by Cobbett, 128, 150, 203–205; cultural authority obtained through, 146. *See also* Sexuality, female

Boyer, J. (character, *The Coquette*), 84–85, 177

Brown, Charles Brockden, 90–92, 112, 187, 209

Brown, William Hill, 13n. 12, 63, 177

Burney, Frances, 170

"Candid" (anon.), 107, 142

Capitalism, 211. *See also* Market economy

Carey, Mathew: as publisher and publicist, 24n. 24, 77, 86, 114, 121, 124, 130–133; relationship of, with SHR, 107, 123, 125, 132–136; and support for women's equality, 124, 130–131, 133; and Mary Wollstonecraft, 124, 133; relationship of, with Cobbett, 128, 134–136; background of, 131–132, 161; and respect for women authors, 132–133, 150; "Wages of Female Labour," 133–134; *Porcupiniad*, 134–135; *Plumb Pudding for Peter Porcupine*, 134–136

Cavendish, Mrs. (character, *Lucy Temple*), 286

Cavendish, Georgiana, duchess of Devonshire, 25, 146

Cervantes Saavedra, Miguel de, 228

Charlotte: A Tale of Truth (Rowson). See *Charlotte Temple*

Charlotte's Daughter; or, The Three Orphans (Rowson). See *Lucy Temple*

Charlotte Temple (Rowson), 27, 34, 58–59, 62, 64, 72, 97; popularity of, 14n. 14, 22, 24n. 24, 64, 77, 80, 97; tension in, 32, 69, 71–76; masculine structures in, 32n. 32; as seduction novel, 34, 57, 64, 279; sex and sexuality in, 60, 65, 283; eroticism in, 60–61, 74; reviews of, 61, 120–122, 129, 132; and mother-daughter continuity, 67; agency in, 71–76; narrative persona in, 75–76; advertising of other works in, 86, 133; comparison of, to *Story of Margaretta* (Murray), 98; distribution networks for, 113–114; payment for, 113–114; preface of, 138–139; comparison of, to *Slaves in Algiers*, 201–202; heroine's transformation in, 223; comparison of, to *Lucy Temple*, 252, 260, 279–280, 282–283, 293–294. *See also* Temple, Charlotte

—readers of: and education through pleasures of text, 34; marginalia of, 48–50, 80; responses of, 49–51, 67; themes important to, 65; and entanglement with the novel, 75–77; typical, 77, 80–82; and visits to Charlotte's gravestone, 77; diversity in, 80–81, 217; and identification with single protagonist, 254, 293

—themes in: return, 45, 69; retribution for lost chastity, 49–50, 82; virtue fallen, 57, 60–61; virtue reclaimed, 65; making choices, 71, 102–103; lack of self-estimation, 98; effects of male privilege, 98–99

Chestnut Street Theatre (Philadelphia), 25, 210, *211–212*, 216

Child, Isabella, 275

Citizen Snub. *See* Swanwick, John

Clara (character, *Trials of the Human Heart*), 173

Clarissa (Richardson), 80–81

Cobbett, William: and Mary Wollstonecraft, 87, 127–130; criticism of SHR by, 87–88, 108, 123, 125, 127–130, 134–139, 160, 163, 219; *Grammar of the English Language*, 126; "Kick for a Bite," 126; SHR compared to, 126;

background of, 126–127; political allegiance of, 126, 208; on women's participation in politics, 128, 197, 201–204, 228; Carey's attack on, 134–136; description of, by SHR, 149

Common Sense (Paine), 24n. 24

Conduct literature, 34n. 35

Constant (character, *Slaves in Algiers*), 216, 225

Constantia. *See* Murray, Judith Sargent

Conversion narratives, 68–69

Coquette (Foster), 7n. 8, 61, 63, 77, 177

Courtland, Sinisterius (character, *The Story of Margaretta*), 98

Crayton, Mrs. *See* La Rue

Declaration of Independence, 251

Deborah (character, *Trials of the Human Heart*), 173

Devonshire, duchess of. See Cavendish, Georgiana, duchess of Devonshire

Dexter, Elisabeth Anthony, 257

"Dialogue for Three Young Ladies" (Rowson), 4n. 4, 14n. 13

Dictionary of the English Language (Johnson), 69–70

Domesticity: in post-Revolutionary America, 35–36, 191–193; sentimental, 165–168, 191–193; SHR and, 264

Don Quijote (Cervantes), 228

Downing, Miss (character, *Hope Leslie*), 193–194

Drinker, Elizabeth Sandwith, 88–91, 93, 102

Dunham, Josiah, 240

Dustan, Hannah, 162

Eaton, John, 4n. 44

Eaton, Margaret, 40

Education of women: and novels, 34, 139–141; and female anti-intellectualism, 88–94, 97; and virtue, 93; ambivalence toward, 102; early supporters of, 107, 124–125, 130–131;

growth in, 110, 258; Federalists' support for, 207–208; national benefit from, 249, 265; function of, 259–260; and maternal influence, 260, 264–269; promotion of, in domestic novel, 280

Edwards, Jonathan, 34

Eldridge, Lucy (Mrs. Temple). *See* Temple, Mrs.

Embargo Act, 1, 4

"Eulogy to the Memory of *George Washington*, Esquire" (Rowson), 243–244

Eumea (character, *Reuben and Rachel*), 233–234

Everyone Has His Fault (Inchbald), 210

Fatherless and Widows' Society, 22, 254

Federalism: traditions of civic humanism and, 29; sexual politics and, 203–209; theater funding and, 210–211; expansionist ideology and, 211, 213; Reign of Terror and, 239–240

Federal Street Theatre (Boston), 25, 210, 238

Female Biography (Knapp), 124, 141

Female Quixotism (Tenney), 106, 178–179

Female Spectator (Rowson), 161

Fentum, Mrs. (character, *Mary; or, The Test of Honour*), 225

Fetnah (character, *Slaves in Algiers*), 216, 224, 226–231, 246

Foster, Hannah Webster, 7n. 8, 13n. 12, 61, 63, 77, 177

Franklin, Benjamin, 51–53, 54n. 8, 146, 214, 214n. 26

Franklin, John (character, *Lucy Temple*), 69, 283

Frederic (character, *Slaves in Algiers*), 225, 230

Gannett, Deborah Sampson, 24

Gender equality: and sexless soul model, 100–102, 118; polarizing frames for, 125; Federalists' support for, 207–208; in theatrical works, 209–210

Lucy Temple (Rowson): autobiographical elements in, 45–46, 256, 289–291; return as theme in, 46–47; *Charlotte Temple* compared to, 252, 260, 279–280, 282–283, 293–294; money as theme in, 252, 254–256, 260, 284–289, 294; readers of, 254, 281–282, 293–295; significance of home in, 260, 280–281; as domestic novel, 278–279, 281; sexuality in, 283–284; charity in, 287–288, 293; teacher-student relationship in, 289–293; and women's entrance into public life, 294. *See also* Temple, Lucy

McCauley, Catharine, 119–120
Maria (character, "The Prostitute"), 186–188
Market economy: and the new gentility, 6, 105–106; women's role in, 108; publishing in, 112–114; and Federalist economic agenda, 211, 213
Marriage: academies' role in training for, 1; SHR on, 1–2; brutality of, 24; in SHR's works, 60, 283; women's rights after, 82, 249–250; and increases in voluntarism, 83; dependence enforced by, 83–84; and men's choices, 83–84; in *Coquette* (Foster), 83–86; and self-determination, 85–86; jokes about obedience in, 206–207
Mary (character, *Lucy Temple*), 284–285, 287, 290
Mary (character, *Mary; or, The Test of Honour*), 218–220
Mary; or, The Test of Honour (Rowson), 218–220, 225
Matthews, Mr. (character, *Lucy Temple*), 260, 267, 283–285, 287–293
Matthews, Mrs. (character, *Lucy Temple*), 286
Melville, Aura (character, *Lucy Temple*), 284, 289–290
"Memoir" (Knapp), 123, 138–141, 254
Memoirs (Godwin), 90–91, 93, 108

Memoirs of Abigail Abbot Bailey (Bailey), 24
Memory's Daughters (Stabile), 298
Men: in post-Revolutionary America, 51–56, 83–85; as womanly, 127. *See also individual men*
Mentoria; or, The Young Lady's Friend: autobiographical elements in, 41, 146, 160–161; and mocking of genteelly educated, 41; distribution networks of, 113–114; reviews of, 129; popularity of, 132; and claim to non-novelhood, 181–182; epigraph to, 184
Merchant class, 5, 105
Minerva Press, 86, 113–115, 125, 163
Mirvan, Mrs. (character, *Trials of the Human Heart*), 172
Miscellaneous Poems (Rowson), 90, 118, 198, 237, 243
"Model of Christian Charity" (Winthrop), 29n. 30
Monroe, James, 239
Montgomery, John, 1
Montgomery, Mary, 1, 274–275
Montgomery, Myra, 1, 273
Montraville, Lieutenant (character, *Charlotte Temple*), 57, 60–62, 72–73, 282
Morse, Jedidiah, 14
Mossop, Mrs. (character, *Trials of the Human Heart*), 172
Mossop, Hester (character, *Trials of the Human Heart*), 172, 189
Mossop, Susan (character, *Trials of the Human Heart*), 172, 189
Motherhood, 1, 8, 67, 260, 264–269
Motherless daughters, 45–46
Mrs. Rowson's Young Ladies' Academy, 37; and training for the new gentility, 1, 265; and preparation for marriage, 1–2; and defiance of domestic regulation, 2–3, 261, 281–283; curriculum of, 41–42, 261–262; deportment standards of, 41–42; exposition performances in, 261, 275–276; and prepara-

tion for public life, 261, 263, 285–286; and fostering of female intimacy, 263–264, 278, 295–296; mother-daughter intimacy in, 266–267; and economic independence, 281–282, 285–286; and development of self-determination, 286; replication of, in *Lucy Temple*, 289–291. *See also* Rowson, Susanna Haswell: as teacher

Murray, Judith Sargent, 22, 66, 86, 95–102, 118, 146. *See also specific works*

Nason, Elias, 6, 264, 267

Netterville, Charlotte, 48–51

New Pleasing Instructor (Tenney), 263

Newtrams family (characters, *Trials of the Human Heart*), 173

Novels: role of, in print culture, 8, 295; function of, 34, 61, 117–118, 139–141, 148–149; seduction, 34, 52–53, 55–57, 187; singlehood reassessed in, 82; in *Story of Margaretta* (Murray), 98–99; political efficacy of, 116n. 12; women as suitable writers of, 138, 140–141; legitimization of, as genre, 139–141; role of, in civic discourse, 140; corrupting influence of, 180–181; censure of, 250–251; domestic, 279–282

Obedience, female, 206–207, 210

"Observations on Female Abilities" (Murray), 100–101

"Ode on the Birthday of *John Adams*, Esquire" (Rowson), 243

"Ode to Sensibility" (Rowson), 163

Oliver, Jessy (character, *Reuben and Rachel*), 234

Olivia (character, *Slaves in Algiers*), 25, 213, 216, 226, 228–230

Omeeah (character, *The Volunteers*), 233–234, 236

"On the Equality of the Sexes" (Murray), 95, 100

Ormond (Brown), 209

Paine, Thomas, 24n. 24, 127–128

"Parody on the Marseilles Hymn, Adapted for the Sons of Columbia" (Rowson), 240–241

Performance culture, 208–211. *See also specific theatrical works*

Pers, Ann, 80

Personality, representative, 145–157

Peter Porcupine. *See* Cobbett, William

Philadelphia, sexual tolerance in, 8, 27n. 28, 185–186

Philippa (character, *Lucy Temple*), 283

Pierce, Sarah, 258, 261, 263–264

Pinckney, Charles Cotesworth, 239

Pinckney, Maria, 214

Plumb Pudding for Peter Porcupine (Carey), 134–136

Poems on Several Occasions (Swanwick), 136

Poems on Various Subjects (Wheatley), 106

Politics: women's exclusion from, 8, 23, 27n. 28, 66–67, 123, 128–129, 201–207, 228; influence of women on, 24–25, 40, 196, 199, 201–203, 227–228. *See also* Power

Polwhele, Richard, 88, 93

Poor Richard's *Almanack* (Franklin), 53

Porcupiniad (Carey), 134–135

Porter, Moses, 87, 268

Power, 25, 37, 40, 82, 90–91, 191–193. *See also* Politics

Power of Sympathy (Brown), 61, 63, 98, 177

Pregnancy, 51–55, 56n. 10, 60, 64–65, 167, 204

Priestley, Joseph, 127

Pringle, Master (character, *Trials of the Human Heart*), 172, 179–181, 189

Pringle, Dolly (character, *Trials of the Human Heart*), 172

Print culture: beginnings of, 8, 104, 115, 137; battle of the sexes in, 53, 206–207, 246; growth in, 56, 80–81, 104, 108, 111–112, 157, 295; female sexuality

Welldon, Mr. (character, *Trials of the Human Heart*), 172–173, 175–176

Wharton, Eliza (character, *The Coquette*), 62–63, 77, 80–87

What Is Gentility? (Smith), 40–41

Wheatley, Phillis, 106

Whiskey Rebellion (1794), 232–236

Whitman, Elizabeth, 55, 63

Wieland (Brown), 187

Winthrop, John, 29n. 30

Wollstonecraft, Mary: influence of, 86; critics of, 87–91, 119, 127, 170; "Letters Written during a Short Residence in Sweden, Norway and Denmark," 89; defenders of, 100, 123–124; SHR compared to, 108, 146; Carey and, 124, 133; *Vindication of the Rights of Woman*, 124, 133, 210

Women, 7, 80n. 40, 85, 92, 189; and attainment of power, 40, 82, 191–193; self-determination in, 51–56; and culture of female subservience, 67, 230–231; national identity and, 67, 119–120, 204–205, 227–228, 231; changing attitudes on, 82–83; economic independence and, 82–83, 188–191, 285–286; unmarried, 82–83; as manly, 87, 93, 108, 118, 127–130; and dawning of self-expression, 87–91; American, compared to European, 88–89; intellectual existence and, 100; exclusion of, from bourgeois liberalism, 104, 129, 142; as book buyers, 133; Federalist allegiance and, 207–208. *See also* America, post-Revolutionary

—as authors: and growth of print culture, 104, 111–112, 157, 295; portrayal of, by men, 108–109; status of, social and economic, 111–113, 117; criticism of, 119–120, 123; supporters of, male, 132–133, 135–136, 138–141; Swanwick's model for, 137; and equation of publication to prostitution, 169–170, 191; on seduction narratives, 279. *See also specific authors*

—rights of: after marriage, 82, 249–250; SHR's duty-bound notion of, 90, 198–199; animosity toward, 93; supporters of, male, 124, 130–131, 133, 150; Carey as supporter of, 133–136

"Word of Comfort to Mrs. Rowson" (Swanwick), 136

Wright, Susanna, 95

Yankoo (character, *Reuben and Rachel*), 234

Young Ladies' Academy of Philadelphia, 124, 258

Zaire (Voltaire), 216

Zara (Hill), 216

Zoraida (character, *Don Quijote*), 228–231

Zoriana (character, *Slaves in Algiers*), 216, 226, 228–231